THE WARRIOR'S CAMERA

The Warrior's Camera

Revised and Expanded Edition

STEPHEN PRINCE

PRINCETON UNIVERSITY PRESS

PRINCETON, NEW JERSEY

Library of Congress Cataloging-in-Publication Data

Prince, Stephen, 1955–
The warrior's camera : the cinema of Akira Kurosawa / Stephen
Prince. —Rev. and expanded ed.
p.   cm.
Filmography: p.
Includes bibliographical references and index.
ISBN 0-691-01046-3 (pbk. : alk. paper)
1. Kurosawa, Akira, 1910–   —Criticism and interpretation.
I. Title.
PN1998.3.K87P75   1999
791.43'0233'092—dc21   99–24982

This book has been composed in Linotron Melior & Optima

First printing of the expanded paperback edition, 1999

The paper used in this publication meets the minimum requirements
of ANSI/NISO Z39.48-1992
(R1997) (*Permanence of Paper*)

http://pup.princeton.edu

Printed in the United States of America

10 9 8 7

FOR TAMI AND
MY PARENTS

Contents

Illustrations

Acknowledgments

A book of this kind cannot be written without the generous support of friends and colleagues, and I am indebted to the following people and organizations whose help made this book possible.

Thanks go to Films, Inc., New Yorker Films, Audie Bock of East-West Classics, and Michael Jeck of R5/S8 Presents for making prints available for study. One of the challenges in the age of video is in being able to see anamorphic wide-screen films in their proper format. Since many of Kurosawa's films use an anamorphic wide-screen format, it was essential to study them as they were meant to be seen.

Audie Bock generously shared her extensive knowledge of Kurosawa in several lengthy conversations. Kyōko Hirano spoke with me about Kurosawa's relationship with the American Occupation authorities and with the younger generations of Japanese directors. She also graciously furnished an unpublished paper for me to study. Leonard Schrader spoke with me about Kurosawa's career and work. A very special thank you goes to Michael Jeck, who read an early version of the manuscript, shared his boundless passion for Kurosawa with me in many conversations, and furnished some of the photographs that appear in the book. Other photographic materials are used courtesy of the Museum of Modern Art/Film Stills Archive.

Quotations from Kurosawa's *Something Like an Autobiography* are used with permission of Alfred A. Knopf, Inc., publisher.

Patricia Ratsimanohatra and Betsy Keller assisted with translations from French, and Yōko Kobayashi and Hiromi Tacheda assisted with the formatting of Japanese names, most of which have been Westernized here. The Westernized format has been bracketed in the notes to indicate those authors who have published under the Japanese form of their names.

Robert Kolker's influence upon my thinking about film has been strong and enduring. Paul Messaris helped clarify for me the links between the study of film and the broader area of visual communication. Heartfelt thanks are extended to both of them.

Donald Richie's ground-breaking work on Japanese cinema and on Kurosawa has helped establish many of the paradigms through which that country's cinema is viewed. The importance of his contributions to the field and to the study of Kurosawa cannot be overstated. Indeed, when one thinks of Kurosawa in this country, one also thinks of Richie.

Joanna Hitchcock, my editor, liked the idea for the book from the beginning. She carefully and patiently saw the project through to completion. Thanks also to Cathie Brettschneider for an exceptionally careful editing of the manuscript.

My colleagues in the Department of Communication Studies at Virginia Polytechnic Institute and State University helped by making that an exciting and rewarding place to work and study.

A special thank you goes to Carole Cavanaugh and Dennis Washburn, who organized and hosted "Wording the Image," a 1997 symposium on Japanese literature and film. My participation in that conference gave me the first opportunity to think systematically about the issues explored in Chapter Eight.

I'd also like to acknowledge Kristen Thompson and David Bordwell's use of the term "axial cutting" in relation to Kurosawa's work. I have employed this term as the label for an important feature of Kurosawa's cinematography and editing.

Introduction

Akira Kurosawa has been called Japan's greatest living film director. In the West, he is the best-known Japanese filmmaker, and works like *Seven Samurai* and *Yōjimbō* have retained a consistent popularity both in Japan and abroad. They have, moreover, greatly influenced Western filmmaking, from genres such as the Western to directors like Sergio Leone and Sam Peckinpah. Kurosawa's career has been a long and prolific one, and it stretches from the chaos of war-torn Japan to the present day and has ranged from contemporary films (*Drunken Angel, The Bad Sleep Well*) to period works (*Sanjurō, Kagemusha, Ran*), from works based on Japanese literature (*Sanshirō Sugata, Rashōmon*) as well as foreign sources (*The Idiot, Throne of Blood, High and Low*), from exercises in established genres (*Stray Dog, The Hidden Fortress*) to inventions of new genres (*Rashōmon*). But Kurosawa's eclectic tastes are unified by his consistent concern that his works be popular, that they move and excite a large audience. This they have done, uniting a seriousness of purpose with an ability to command the affection of a mass audience.

That audience is now a global one. After a series of films seen only by the Japanese, Kurosawa made *Rashōmon*, the film that was largely responsible for igniting Western interest in the Japanese cinema. His extraordinary reception by the West enlarged his stature as a major filmmaker but, ironically, has perhaps helped limit discussion of his work. Many of Kurosawa's films, such as *Seven Samurai* and *Yōjimbō*, have been repeatedly screened, and his handling of action, his fast cutting, his affection for detectives, doctors, and samurai as characters—all have endeared him to Western audiences and have helped make his work comprehensible in relation to Hollywood movies, especially if gunfighters are imaginatively substituted for samurai. The popularity of Kurosawa's work, and the length of his career, has helped make his films seem perhaps too familiar, especially if one feels that he has been largely influenced by Hollywood productions. So popular a filmmaker, one whose work is so frequently revived, can become established as a fixed icon of popular culture. Such continual exposure can, paradoxically, prevent a closer look. Certainly it is paradoxical that a director of Kurosawa's stature has been infrequently studied. First published more than twenty-five years ago, Donald Richie's *The Films of Akira Kurosawa* has remained the only full-length English-language study of Kurosawa's entire body of work.

There may be another reason for this comparative neglect besides Kurosawa's popularity. In his book on the director's samurai films, David Desser points out that the interests of film scholars studying the Japanese cinema have shifted away from Kurosawa to favor directors whose narrative and visual codes challenge and depart from the model of filmmaking established by Hollywood. "Since the middle 1970s Kurosawa's cinema has been devalued in the sparse critical literature produced on the Japanese cinema. Kurosawa has been displaced, to all intents and purposes, by the so-called 'modernists' of the Japanese cinema, Ozu, Mizoguchi, and Ōshima."[1] The latter three filmmakers have been venerated by this shift of attention, and the study of their films has emphasized the extreme formalism, the visual experimentation and eccentricities of their style, while attempting to link that style with currents of popular and political culture.[2] This emphasis is related to a major accomplishment of film studies in this period. Film scholars had long been fascinated with the Hollywood cinema, with its ability to efface its forms and to manufacture tightly stitched entertainments in which none of the seams showed. The patient studies of these scholars at last yielded a detailed and specific understanding of how Hollywood film operated.[3] This accomplishment helped generate a renewed appreciation of, as well as a specific methodological context in which to situate, filmmakers like Ozu and Ōshima who departed from Hollywood norms. The corollary has been the displacement of Kurosawa. Understanding the Hollywood cinema seemed to imply that Kurosawa, too, was a known quantity. Ozu, Mizoguchi, Ōshima, now regarded as modernists and exemplars of an alternate filmic tradition, triumphed over Kurosawa, whose style never constituted the kind of rejection of narrative or genre that their work exemplified.

We have, therefore, few extended, detailed considerations of Kurosawa's visual and narrative structures that draw from the contemporary insights of film studies. Noël Burch's analysis is an exception, notable for its close attention to the forms of the films, but the attention tends to be selective.[4] Burch attempts to recoup Kurosawa within the modernist ground occupied by Ōshima and others, and this leads him to emphasize such films as *Throne of Blood* and *Ikiru* at the expense of others. In addition, Burch develops a strictly formal explication of Kurosawa's work at the expense of thematic issues.

In his study of Kurosawa's samurai films, Desser begins to rectify this neglect. He remarks that much yet remains to be explored in Kurosawa's cinema, and he offers his study "in the spirit of inspiration, as a place to begin."[5] Desser perceptively recognizes Kurosawa as a "dialectical" filmmaker operating "to create works of narrative brilliance which reveal their own tensions,"[6] and he points to the need for an expansive and comprehensive treatment of Kurosawa's work that will explicate the significance of the extraordinary tensions within the films. "In-depth studies of his oeuvre must reveal the significance of his patterns, not just their appearance. . . . Further studies must show how certain narrative patterns, character traits and formal means can be used most appropriately in certain kinds of films."[7] Desser recognizes, as have other writers, that Kurosawa's cinema is a turbulent one, beset by tensions between premodern and modern values, between Eastern and Western traditions, and, stylistically, between flashes of extreme violence and moments of quiet and contemplation. Kurosawa's continual alternation of period with modern-dress films has also been remarked on by commentators.[8] But an appreciation of the organic nature of these tensions throughout the entire body of work has not yet been attempted. How are the competing Eastern and Western values within his films linked to visual and narrative structures? How may we reconcile the apparently disparate aesthetic traditions represented by montage and the long take in Kurosawa's work? Of what are the oscillations between period and modern-dress films a symptom? And what are the relations among the issues that these questions address? Above all, it is necessary to emphasize Kurosawa's work as a project, as a specific undertaking influenced by an immediate social challenge (i.e., the cataclysm of the second world war and the general cultural upheavals that it precipitated). These events are of central importance to Kurosawa's cinema, where they are revealed, transformed, in and by visual form and narrative style.

What has not been extensively studied as yet are Kurosawa's most distinctive features of visual style and the specific kind of cinematic space they help create. His understanding of cinematic space is unique in film history, and it is a direct function of his method of choreographing on-screen movement, of his reliance upon the telephoto lens and techniques of multicamera filming, and, in the later films, of his use of the anamorphic frame. These choices of movement, lenses, and framing not only give the films their distinctive look but also have a direct, if subtle, bearing upon the cultural project they announce. The mediations and connections between Kurosawa's visual form and the cultural circumstances that contextualize the work are fascinating to trace. The forms of his films are charged with ideological value—indeed, are set in motion by a specific ideological commitment—and the visual and narrative codes must be grasped as the material transformation of urgent social questions.

The forms of Kurosawa's films will be studied closely, then, because they represent, in Rudolf Arnheim's terms, a kind of visual thinking. Kurosawa's reluctance to verbalize about the meaning of his films is well known. He has always insisted that his meanings are there, in the films themselves, and that people should watch them. We will take him at his word. Our primary evidence will lie in the material of the films, yet throughout the following chapters I shall also draw upon Kurosawa's autobiography as a parallel text to the films themselves. This is not intended as a rhetorical maneuver to seal my arguments by resort to a theory of origins. Indeed, as I will discuss later, the most fascinating thing about Kurosawa's autobiography is the extent to which it, too, can be viewed as one of his film narratives. Its chronicle presents Kurosawa as a Kurosawa character and the story of his life as the kind of spiritual odyssey witnessed so often in his films. The autobiography will be placed alongside the films, as one text among others. Yet it is distinct in possessing much valuable evidence on Kurosawa's attitudes, values, and sensibility. These are important to understand, not so that the films may be reduced to a biography, but so that the structures which inform them may be grasped. With Kurosawa and his work, we must employ a multiplex perspective because we are dealing with manifold levels of transformation: cultural, individual, cinematic. Even though his curious autobiography serves to establish him as yet another text, it is essential to understand the terms of his self-portrait so that we may establish a pathway from Meiji, Taishō, and Shōwa-era Japan into the material of the films.

Kurosawa has directed thirty films (including his last, *Madadayo*), a large number for a study of this kind. Rather than approaching the films chronologically and considering each in turn, I have chosen to group them topically, arranging them according to particular formal or cultural issues that they address. This method will emphasize both the diversity of Kurosawa's work and the logic of its internal development, the social and aesthetic problems around which it is organized, to which it continually returns, and for which it seeks resolutions. Each chapter has its own focus, yet they are all organized with reference to the central problematic of Kurosawa's work, which is to find a method for constructing a viable political cinema that is, at the same time, popular. The chapters trace Kurosawa's effort to use film politically, the genesis of this attempt and the context in which it developed, its maturation and evolution, and its eventual defeat. Thus, though each chapter is concerned with a single general issue, taken together they attempt to reveal the structuring dynamics of Kurosawa's cinema.

Chapter 1 begins with the general context of Kurosawa criticism, considered through a review of some of its features, specifically, Kurosawa's reputation as a humanist and as a director influenced by the American cinema. I then outline the approach of this study by considering Kurosawa's work as part of a generational response to the tensions and strains of cultural modernization and democratization.

In Chapter 2, I discuss the development of Kurosawa's visual and narrative style in the early films. *Sanshirō Sugata* Parts I and II, *The Most Beautiful,* and *They Who Tread on the Tiger's Tail* are examined for what they tell us of Kurosawa's understanding of framing, editing, and the choreography of camera and object movement. The hallmarks of his style emerge very early and are organized in ways that frustrate attempts to establish dominant lines of influence from other filmmakers.

Whereas Chapter 2 deals with issues of form and Kurosawa's understanding of the visual image, Chapter 3 focuses on the collision of those forms with the urgent problems arising in the aftermath of World War II. Kurosawa's films of the postwar years—*No Regrets for Our Youth, One Wonderful Sunday, Drunken Angel, The Quiet Duel, Stray Dog, Scandal,* and *Ikiru*—attempt to participate in the tasks of postwar reconstruction. It is within this context that his conception of a political cinema is forged. These films directly engage the milieu of social and economic collapse and attempt to specify the terms of the new individual required by a new world. These works initiate what I call the heroic mode of Kurosawa's cinema, those films that hinge their political analysis on the exploits of an extraordinary individual.

Chapter 4, in many ways, represents the transition to Chapters 5, 6, and 7. It considers the appearance in Kurosawa's work of a tone and outlook that are counter to the heroic mode. This outlook first surfaces in the films he adapted from literature, and this chapter accordingly seeks to understand how the literary adaptation has functioned for Kurosawa. These adaptations are exercises in aesthetic experimentation as well as attempts to expand the boundaries of his cinema by considering the relationships between verbal and visual signifiers. Kurosawa comes to demonstrate a profound understanding of the differences between the literary and the cinematic modes, and the early acts of translation— *Rashōmon, The Idiot*—are superseded by acts of transposition—*Throne of Blood, The Lower Depths*—in which the literary and the cinematic modes are no longer assumed to be equivalent. Three of these films are adapted from foreign literary sources, so the issue of cross-cultural borrowing may be explicitly posed with reference to Kurosawa. In addition, *The Idiot* will permit us to discuss one of the great unexamined topics in Kurosawa criticism, the relationship of Kurosawa's work to that of Dostoevsky. Kurosawa's fondness for Dostoevsky is well known, and an influence from the Russian master is often suggested by many writers, but it has never been closely explored. We will want to consider points of correspondence and divergence between these two artists.

In Chapter 5, I discuss Kurosawa's attempt in *Record of a Living Being, The Bad Sleep Well,* and *High and Low* to apply the visual and narrative structures developed in the immediate postwar years—structures that dramatized forms of heroic individualism—to systemic, transindividual social problems: the atomic bomb and the nuclear state, corporate corruption, class division and exploitation. Kurosawa attempted to use the old forms to deal with political issues of a new scale and scope. This examination re-poses the question of form, and the discussion will reconsider the nature of Kurosawa's style, especially in terms of its mature features: the use of telephoto lenses, multicamera filming, and the anamorphic frame.

In Chapter 6, I examine Kurosawa's use of the past in his period films, works whose aims and design are dialectically related to those of the modern-dress films. Desser notes that samurai films, like Westerns, work by transforming history into myth,[9] and while we will have occasion to discuss this process in Kurosawa's work, it will be contextualized as a symptom of the strain and contradiction developing in his cinematic project. Moreover, his period films are not just examples of mythic storytelling. *Seven Samurai, Yōjimbō,* and *Red Beard* announce a critical investigation of the past, of the relation between the individual and the social and cultural landscape. (*The Hidden Fortress* is briefly considered.) This investigation is conducted via a detour through the past, but it is immensely relevant to Kurosawa's efforts to come to terms with contemporary Japan. His cinematic forms have always been marked by an extraordinary degree of internal tension, and these films reveal the profound source of that tension to lie in the threat posed by time and history to his cinematic project.

Dodeskaden, released in 1970, was something of a shock for those who had closely followed Kurosawa's career. It looked like no other Kurosawa work, and the three films that followed—*Dersu Uzala*, *Kagemusha*, and *Ran*—announced a radically new aesthetic. In narrative structure, emotional tone, and visual style, these works initiate a break with the films that preceded them. But the apparent abruptness of the break is deceiving. What appears to be a stylistic cleavage is, instead, a culmination of the logic by which Kurosawa's formal structures had been developing in previous decades. In Chapter 7, I explore the complex relationship of these late works to the earlier films and their implications for the kind of cinema Kurosawa had attempted to construct.

I explore Kurosawa's final works in Chapter 8 and discuss the altered terms through which his filmmaking now operated. The final films mark a distinctively different phase of his filmmaking, one that is virtually without precedent in cinema, i.e., a fully elaborated artistic late period. By living so long and remaining active as a filmmaker until nearly the end of his life, Kurosawa brought his cinema to a point of closure and conclusion, one rarely encountered in the world of cinema, where careers tend to be brief and filmmaking remains a young person's game.

More than any other Japanese filmmaker, Kurosawa exerted a tremendous influence on world cinema, particularly on American films. In Chapter 9, I explain why his films have been so influential and why, in some ways, the terms of this influence have distorted the work and minimized the complexity of his film style. This chapter assesses his place in cinema history, with particular reference to the generation of filmmakers who adopted his work as a template for their own.

Kurosawa's works are extraordinarily important, not just for their singularly rich and complex formal structures, but for what they show us of the interrelations between form and culture, the artist and history. His attempt to fashion a cinema engaged with the contradictory demands of his time tells us much about the ideological nature of artistic form and about the place and the possibility of a committed aesthetic, its aspirations and its limitations. In the intersection of the imaginary vision with the material world, Kurosawa has taken his stand and has sought to change that world. The trajectory of this project forms one of the most compelling chapters in cinema history.

I should end this introduction on a more personal note. This study has been very much a labor of love. When I was younger and just learning about the cinema, it was the films of Kurosawa that taught me the most about what movies were capable of. They had a visual energy, a passion and sheer love for moviemaking, that I had seen in few other filmmakers' work. Of course, when we are first encountering and falling in love with a medium, everything can be exciting. But Kurosawa's films have retained these qualities for me over the years, and I have tried to convey something of that in this study. Inevitably, there were some aspects of his work that I could not cover. I do not consider at length, for example, the extraordinary repertory company of actors that dominates the films. Toshirō Mifune and Takashi Shimura are well known, and they do figure in the analysis that follows. But those who care for Kurosawa's work also know of the incomparable presence of Minoru Chiaki, Eijirō Tono, Daisuke Katō, Bokuzen Hidari, Kō Kimura, Seiji Miyaguchi, Eiko Miyoshi, Nobuo Nakamura, and, of course, the actor who embodied the first great heroes, Susumu Fujita. What I have closely studied, instead, are Kurosawa's images, his methods of constructing them, their organization and relation to his narrative structures. He has worked, and thought, through his forms. Through them, he has sought to engage his culture and his country, to map out the course of development he thought Japan needed. To understand Kurosawa, it is above all necessary to understand the nature of his images. Toward that end, this study is directed.

· · ·

When I initially wrote *The Warrior's Camera*, Kurosawa's career seemed essentially closed, with *Ran* his last grand statement as a filmmaker. But he kept working and went on into territory that virtually no other filmmaker has defined or explored. I am, therefore, especially grateful to now complete this study by examining the remarkable direction of Kurosawa's filmmaking after *Ran*. Now that his career has ended, it is clear that his work occupied four creative stages: the early films, the heroic works of postwar reconstruction, the transitional and pessimistic films of 1970-85, and the psychobiography of the last films. The new chapters thus complete and bring closure to this study of Kurosawa's entire career. Writing them, though, had a special sadness. He lived while the bulk of the book was composed. This was no longer true for the new material, and the single hardest thing was writing about Kurosawa in the past tense.

THE WARRIOR'S CAMERA

1   Viewing Kurosawa

In the late 1960s, following a spectacularly successful career, Kurosawa faced the threat of its imminent disintegration. Plagued by ill health and no film work, in 1971 he slashed his wrists with a razor, aligning his personal despair with a recognized cultural practice of self-immolation. Yet this was a man who had never included a scene of ritual suicide in his films, a man whose regard for the worth and integrity of the self had always compelled his film characters to reject the codes of self-destruction. Watanabe, the dying clerk of *Ikiru*, refuses suicide as the answer to his problems, reasoning that he cannot die yet because he does not know if his life has had meaning. Witnessing the horrible massacre of his retainers in *Ran*, the warrior Hidetora reaches for his sword to commit seppuku, but the scabbard is empty. Hidetora, too, is compelled to live. In a culture that emphasizes *giri*, or obligation, and ties of joint responsibility linking members of a group, Kurosawa has repeatedly broken with tradition to challenge the social determinants structuring the individual. Yet, during his most painful travail, he sought a solution he had never permitted his heroes. It was not quite the warrior's chosen end, opted for as a sign of fealty when the clan leaders were defeated in battle. But the attempt did resonate with a tradition possessing a certain cultural legitimacy. In this small contradiction lies an important clue to the nature of the films. To explore this contradiction is to define the shape and focus of this study.

A convenient place to begin is with the dilemma Kurosawa faced in the 1970s, since in some ways it grew from the nature of his work. Since 1943, when he began directing, he had averaged at least a film a year, sometimes several annually. Occasionally, a year would lapse between releases, but in general he worked steadily and consistently. Following *Red Beard* in 1965, however, the work

1. Akira Kurosawa. (Museum of Modern Art/Film Stills Archive)

dried up. Since then he has completed only five films, as compared to twenty-three in the first two decades of his career (excluding *Those Who Make Tomorrow*, a studio-compelled production co-directed with Kajirō Yamamoto and Hideo Sekigawa, for which Kurosawa has denied responsibility[2]). (Kurosawa's latest film, *Dreams*, consists of eight episodes based on memorable dreams extending back to his childhood. Steven Spielberg and George Lucas were instrumental in helping the project get started. With George Lucas's help, Kurosawa tries modern special effects for the first time.[3])

The reasons for this sudden loss of work are generally, but insufficiently, understood as economic and sociological: the Japanese film industry was changing and had shut out directors like Kurosawa whose work it could not accommodate. Television arrived in the early 1950s, and, as in other countries, the audience and the motion picture industry changed forever. In 1953, according to Richie and Anderson, only 866 television sets operated in Japan, but by the late 1950s that number had greatly increased, nearing two million.[4] By the mid-1960s, 60 percent of Japanese homes had television sets, and by the end of the decade, 95 percent of all households were tuned to the new medium.[5] As in the

United States, popular acceptance of television was swift and unswerving. The audience stayed at home, and annual movie attendance sharply dropped from a high in 1958 of 1,127 million to under 200 million after 1975.[6]

Television also affected film content as the Japanese audience came to be divided into distinct groups of television viewers and cinema viewers.[7] Kurosawa was recognized as a master of the period film, or *jidai-geki*, yet these films became a mainstay of television, where, as Anderson points out, their formulaic nature was easily accommodated to the demands of a weekly series: in 1982, more than a quarter of televised dramatic series were *jidai-geki*.[8] Theatrical film responded by heavily promoting soft-core pornography, and the production firms themselves, like their counterparts in the United States, diversified into related leisure-time markets.

Kurosawa, long established as one of the most expensively budgeted Japanese directors, found himself unemployable in the new cost-conscious climate of the late 1960s. Sweeping historical epics of the kind he often specialized in had become too expensive to produce for an industry that was scaling itself down both economically and artistically. The result, for Kurosawa, was a long, deep freeze, and his reputation suffered following an abortive involvement with 20th Century Fox's production of *Tora! Tora! Tora!*. Kurosawa claims to have quit the production, but other accounts suggest that he was fired because of a perfectionism some thought bordered on insanity.[9] *Dodeskaden* (1970) was his response to the collapse of the Japanese industry and of his own reputation. "I made this film partly to prove I wasn't insane; I further tested myself with a budget of less than $1 million and a shooting schedule of only 28 days."[10] But the film also signals the beginning of a progressive, steadily deepening pessimism that has characterized all his subsequent works and that marks them as radically different from the earlier films. This change is not entirely explainable by the collapse of the Japanese film industry.

Dodeskaden was not well received, and again Kurosawa's career languished. Unable to obtain funding for further projects in Japan, he accepted an offer from Mosfilm to work in Russia and used the opportunity to realize a project he had long cherished, a film of the diaries of the Russian explorer Vladimir Arseniev. *Dersu Uzala* (1975), however, was not the remedy for the long hiatuses plaguing Kurosawa's recent career. His next film, *Kagemusha*, would not appear until 1980, and *Ran* not until 1985, and both only as a result of financing obtained through international co-production.

Kurosawa has not been silent through these vicissitudes. He accuses the industry of greed and timidity and argues that filmmakers must fight to regain artistic control of their projects:

> I feel that what's wrong with the Japanese film industry today is that the marketing side has taken over the decision-making power on what film is going to be made. There's no way that marketing-type people—at the level their brains are at—can understand what's going to be a good film and what isn't, and it's really a mistake to give them hegemony over all this. The film companies have become defensive. The only way to compete with television is to make *real* films. Until this situation is corrected, it's really going to be difficult for filmmakers in Japan.[11]

Compounding the economic problems Kurosawa began to face in the late 1960s was a shift in ideological film practice among newer Japanese directors. The questioning and politicizing of film form and of the role of the audience, which was so common at this time in the European cinema, also typified the work of such directors as Nagisa Ōshima, Masahiro Shinoda, and the Japanese "new wave."[12] The Art Theater Guild, a small circuit of theaters, provided an outlet for their independent productions, and for a time radical filmmakers explored, expanded, and evaluated the codes and values of the traditional Japanese cinema, of Kurosawa's cinema.[13] With Ozu and Mizoguchi gone, Kurosawa was condemned to be a symbol of reified tradition. In his commitment to linear narrative, his apparent lack of interest in Brechtian distancing devices, his refusal to develop a rigorous mode of political filmmaking, and his seeming inability to move beyond a method of social analysis centered on the individual, Kurosawa stood for the newer directors as the representative of all that was moribund and reactionary about the Japanese cinema.

The denunciations of Kurosawa were often extreme and painful. Shinoda, for example, cast his criticisms of Kurosawa in terms of an explicit generational revolt: "My generation has reacted against the simplistic humanism of Kurosawa in, for example, *Rashōmon*, *The Bad Sleep Well*, and *Red Beard*. Kurosawa has also been resented by the younger people not only because they were looking for a new metaphysic, but also because he had the advantage of large sums of money to spend on his films and they did not. . . . Kurosawa has exhausted himself pursuing the traveling camera."[14]

Shūji Terayama described his relations to Kurosawa's work with greater equanimity but indicated that Kurosawa's kind of cinema was no longer compelling: "At twenty-four I liked the work of Kurosawa very much. Now I don't hate it, but I felt pity when I saw *Dodeskaden*. Ōshima and Shinoda say they hate Kurosawa, but I don't hate Akira Kurosawa."[15]

Eventually, the newer filmmakers would be caught in the same economic contradictions that Kurosawa faced, though for different reasons. With the collapse of a lively audience for motion pictures as well as the general formal and political retreat of the industry, it became harder for directors like Ōshima to maintain the stylistic and political aggressiveness that typified their earlier work. Ōshima has more recently described the contemporary industry with a disillusionment very close to Kurosawa's: "Filmmaking here has become very hard since the 60s. In the 60s, there were students and other young people who were interested in seeing serious films. In the 70s, the film industry lost that audience, and the general public looked for entertainment in films rather than seriousness. In the 70s, the public stopped pursuing any idea of revolution. That has altered the industry significantly."[16]

As with Kurosawa, Ōshima's political outlook has darkened at the same time the industry changed: "In 1960, when I made *Night and Fog in Japan*, my hope was that the movements on the left would grow and strengthen. Now, as you can read in the newspapers today, only the worst has remained. The rest has vanished. Nothing has improved since the 1960s."[17]

It is ironic that Ōshima, representative of the countercurrent to Kurosawa, should have found himself with similar problems (even to the necessity of seeking out international financing for his projects). But what both filmmakers were facing is the same: the decline of the auteur and the ascendancy of teams of producers and market researchers. Kurosawa, in particular, is the exemplar of an earlier mode of filmmaking that surfaced in the industrial countries following World War II. That mode has been termed the "art" film, and its practitioners—Kurosawa, Bergman, Fellini, Ray—caused a great deal of excitement in the film world of the 1950s. They helped make film an acceptable object of culture and study at a time when it was regarded much as television is today. In the halcyon days of *Rashōmon*, *Bicycle Thieves*, *La Strada*, and *The Seventh Seal*, filmmaking became firmly established as an expression of national culture capable of international reception, and at the core of this new recognition stood a handful of directors. They were thrown forward by their era: authors functioning as codes legitimizing the seriousness of film and its identity, not as a machine or an industry, but as sensuous human expression, like the other arts. They were romantic times but exciting ones, and Kurosawa's contemporary plight symbolizes the final eclipse of this cinema, of the director as superstar. When he speaks, a nostalgia for those days is expressed. Describing earlier decades of the Japanese cinema, he says:

> It was the springtime of Japanese film-making. There was growth and optimism. The top management of the film companies were also film directors and they didn't try to restrict you for commercial reasons. But in the late 1950s and 1960s the climate changed: it was tragic when people like Mizoguchi, Ozu and Naruse all died—we began to lose our stand as directors and the companies took over the power. After that came the Dark Ages.[18]

Referring to the decline of the kind of director who made the art cinema possible—the "auteur"—Kurosawa has observed: "In today's Japanese films, it would be possible to interchange titles, names of directors, without anyone noticing it. Anyone would be able to sign today's films. None is marked by the personality of the creator."[19]

When Kurosawa's moment of despair came in 1971, his desperation was triggered by loss of position in the industry and by the eclipse of the international art film (as well as by an undiagnosed illness). Yet there was another reason. The economic and sociological changes in the industry were external factors, impinging from without. But an internal crisis had developed within Kurosawa's work, a crisis of form in response to culture. It was not a new problem, but instead it had run through all the films as a kind of fault line, threatening always to rupture and split the work. Finally, it did.

From his first film, Kurosawa had employed a particular mode of address for his Japanese audiences that preserved suspended in dialectical tension a mix of Eastern and Western values. As his career progressed, the particular mix of values would shift and alter, but always for Kurosawa the overriding importance was to use film to make history, to address the Japan shattered by World War II, and to help reshape its society. In the films of the late 1940s and early 1950s, from *No Regrets for Our Youth* to *Ikiru*, an extraordinary involvement with the contemporary social moment is manifest. This participation by the films in the specifics of postwar reconstruction dimmed in the later 1950s, when Japan had regained its economic and social bearings. But the urgency of Kurosawa's address in his role of moral leader continued unabated, particularly in his belief that social values, borrowed from the West, could be therapeutic additions to Japanese culture. This general project of addressing Japan by way of selective Western values reached its culminating expression in 1965's *Red Beard*, a film whose making exhausted Kurosawa both physically and philosophically. If a work as ambitious as *Red Beard* could have no effect on a society whose economic expansion, he believed, masked deeper social misery,[20] then a life's work devoted to a belief that film could help make history would have to be revised, or else some other model of filmmaking would have to be found. In either case, a profound crisis in his art faced Kurosawa after *Red Beard*, and the long periods of inactivity and the very different form and tone of the later films testify that he has not yet solved this problem and never may.

Thus, to lay the burden of Kurosawa's artistic problems exclusively on the greed or crassness of the contemporary industry is to miss seeing the very painful dead end, internal to the works, in which Kurosawa the filmmaker was stranded after 1965. I will clarify this crisis and trace its development, but first a foundation for the analysis must be established. This may be done by considering some general features of our critical understanding of Kurosawa to see in what ways they might be extended.

Because Kurosawa belonged to the tradition of the art cinema, the initial reception of his films was shaped by the influence of that tradition.[21] *Rashōmon*'s exhibition at the Venice Film Festival in 1951 dramatically announced the talents of Kurosawa to an international community, and each film after that received a great deal of critical attention. The reception and discussion of these films during the rise of the international cinema in the 1960s was connected with the effort of film scholars to define the legitimacy of film criticism at a time when film studies was only just emerging as a field in the universities and was still regarded with suspicion and hostility. A close relationship exists, then, between the terms by which Kurosawa's films were understood and the needs of the discipline at that time.

Consistency and harmony were stressed as the measures of artistic stature. It was, of course, the age of the auteur, when the greatest distinction a film could claim was its revelation of the "signature" of the author, the director. The films that were regarded as being most accomplished were those that revealed a creator's recognizable, coherent imprint. This standard of authorship was vitally important because it helped make film like the other arts, not brute technology or a commodity, but an expression of culture fashioned by human design. The great filmmakers could be studied, as were the great painters and writers. A human presence could be disclosed within the machine.

The critical work of revealing the auteur's presence implied a corollary: that the films themselves contain and communicate values of demonstrable social importance. Moreover, by revealing the latent meanings of a work, film criticism itself could help communicate these values and thereby establish its worth as an enterprise. Toward this end, a major code discerned within the films was the ideal of "humanism." The films of Kurosawa and his peers—Rossellini, De Sica, Ray, Bergman—were praised for revealing the dignity of human life and a concern with human welfare. Anderson and Richie, in their history of Japanese film, wrote, "This then is the famed 'humanism' of Kurosawa. He is concerned with the human lot above all else and he particularly insists upon the equality of human emotion. All of his films share this basic assumption."[22]

Charles Higham noted that Kurosawa believes in "man's fundamental decency" and that the director's is the "tradition of humanism and optimism, of the courage of people who fight for goodness in the midst of a cynical world."[23] Writing shortly after *Rashōmon* had electrified the international film culture, Jay Leyda discerned that "a high point is that element of Kurosawa's films that will keep them alive—their pity and humanity."[24] Similarly, Vernon Young felt that, in his films, Kurosawa "restores to man the quality which individualizes him."[25] Norman Silverstein observed Kurosawa's "Dostoevskian faith in man."[26] David Robinson wrote of "the essential human quality and human optimism" of *Dodeskaden*.[27] For Akira Iwasaki, Kurosawa is "a humanist at heart."[28] Audie Bock noted that Kurosawa may "be counted among the postwar humanists."[29] Keiko McDonald referred to *Red Beard* as "the most humanistic" of Kurosawa's films.[30] Donald Richie observed that in *Red Beard* Kurosawa "had vindicated his humanism and his compassion."[31]

While, as these scholars point out, Kurosawa's films are frequently marked by an extraordinary compassion for the suffering that they depict, what is curious and should also be noted are ways in which Kurosawa's cinema is not congruent with all the ideals that have been subsumed under the label "humanism." Humanism is an elusive term, as it has been understood in a variety of contexts and applications. While it may sometimes be other than, or more than, the following attributes, it has sometimes been construed to include the values of restraint, decorum, balance, and proper proportion. Irving Babbitt, the American proponent of humanism, wrote that a decorous manner, behavior that eschewed the excessive, was "the central maxim" of all genuine humanists.[32] For Babbitt, humanists "aim at proportionateness through a cultivation of the law of measure."[33] Similarly, Norman Foerster considered restraint and self-control central to a humanist outlook.[34]

In contrast to a stress on correct balance, propriety, and good measure, Kurosawa does *not* emphasize these elements, either in terms of the portrayal of his characters or stylistically, at the level of visual form. As Noël Burch has pointed out, the keynote of the characters' behavior is the strange persistence and the wildness of their dedication to their goals, the single-mindedness and the consuming energy with which they pursue their ends.[35] Richie has made a similar point, noting that "the Kurosawa hero is distinguished by his perseverance, by his refusal to be defeated."[36] The actor most closely identified with Kurosawa's films, Toshirō Mifune, exhibits very little in his screen excesses in the way of restraint and balance, and this is precisely why Kurosawa liked him. But these are trivial points. More important, Kurosawa's film style stresses the excessive, the transgressive, the flamboyant. As Akira Iwasaki has noted, in these films the "very air is denser, the air pressure greater than in the atmosphere we normally breathe, sounds fall on the ear an octave higher than their usual pitch, and physical movements are speeded up or slowed down abnormally."[37] The films "are dramas of violent emotions, their traumatic effect heightened still further by exaggeration, emphasis, and extremes."[38] Kurosawa himself has observed: "I am the kind of person who works violently, throwing myself into it. I also like hot summers, cold winters, heavy rains and snows, and I think my pictures show this. I like extremes because I find them most alive."[39] In their celebration of the extremities of human behavior, the staccato, jagged rhythms of their cutting, and the undermining of a stable visual world through decentered compositions and the foregrounding of character and camera movement, Kurosawa's films have more of the Dionysian about them than is perhaps consistent with a thoroughgoing humanism.

Furthermore, as subsequent chapters show, Kurosawa's cinematic embrace of humanity is somewhat compromised by his affection for the codes of the samurai class and by the aesthetic form to which his affiliation with warrior culture has helped lead him: a continuing reliance on heroes, on the few for whom moral growth is portrayed as a possibility, as distinguished from the masses of people who are portrayed in film after film as afflicted by a kind of moral entropy, unable to live like a Watanabe, Kambei, or Niide.[40] It is, therefore, perhaps better to speak of

2. Kurosawa on location during the filming of *Seven Samurai*. Kō Kimura, as Katsushirō, is on the left. (Museum of Modern Art/Film Stills Archive)

a humanist impulse within the films, but one that is constrained by the ambiguities of a commitment to heroic narratives. (In his latest films, Kurosawa has moved away from a reliance on heroes, but he has become deeply pessimistic about any notion of human perfectibility.) In any event, as Desser has pointed out, the time has come to move beyond notions of humanism in explaining Kurosawa's work and to rely instead on close scrutiny of cinematic codes.[41]

In addition to exploring the commitment to human welfare in Kurosawa's films, another recurring focus of Kurosawa criticism has been upon the question of influence. Who influenced whom the most, Kurosawa or Hollywood? Kurosawa has frequently been described as the "most Western" of Japanese filmmakers, and many scholars have discerned stylistic similarities between his work and a range of Hollywood directors. While these have included George Stevens and Howard Hawks,[42] very often comparisons are made with the work of John Ford. Both men were attracted to stories of masculine adventure (though, perhaps, Kurosawa more consistently than Ford); both men continued to rely on a stock company of trusted performers; and both men, of course, had a certain regard for Westerns. Kurosawa himself has been most gracious in acknowledging his affection for Ford's films and his respect for Ford the man. In his autobiography, he humbly says that, compared to Ford, he is no more than "a little chick."[43]

Charles Higham suggested that Kurosawa learned "his handling of mass action, of the complexities of location shooting, from Ford."[44] Tom Milne found the redeeming values of *Dersu Uzala* to be its Fordian qualities: "*Dersu Uzala* is rescued from the reefs of sentimentality by direction as calmly matter-of-fact in its elegiacs as the best of John Ford."[45] John Pym found the images of *Kagemusha* to be "painterly . . . derivative of Kurosawa's revered Ford."[46] John Gillett suggested that a composition from *Kagemusha* of warriors crossing the plains "was not only exciting and beautiful but seemed to forge yet another link between the landscape painting of Kurosawa and Ford."[47] Richie and Anderson found Takashi Shimura to be to Kurosawa "what Ward Bond was to John Ford,"[48] and Richie finds Toshirō Mifune to be to Kurosawa "what John Wayne was to John Ford."[49] The town in *Yōjimbō*, Richie also suggests, "is very much like one of those god-forsaken places in the middle of nowhere remembered from the films of Ford."[50]

Of course, it is difficult to establish definitive lines of influence, and Kurosawa himself, while acknowledging his admiration for Ford, has indicated that he has avoided any conscious imitation of the American filmmaker. "I'm sure that my films do show some influence from John Ford, whose work I like very much, but I'm certainly not conscious of doing anything to imitate him."[51] Moreover, as I suggest in a later chapter, Kurosawa works from a rather different orientation to the past, to tradition, and to marriage and family than does Ford.

One of the most productive lines of inquiry for understanding Kurosawa's cinema and its potential debt to, or influence upon, Hollywood has been the consideration of his relationship to the American Western. Many scholars have contributed to this debate by drawing comparisons between images or weaponry from Kurosawa's films and Westerns, by affirming that Kurosawa has been influenced by Westerns, or by using the Western as a kind of metaphorical category for describing Kurosawa's own films or patterns of imagery. In the latter case, an influence is not alleged so much as is the presence of strong, general similarities of narrative, image, or characterizaton. Kenneth Nolley reports that Kurosawa has been "deeply influenced" by American Westerns.[52] Ralph Croizier suggests that in "structure, mood, and basic values the similarities might well appear more important than the differences between a six-gun and a samurai sword."[53] Alain Silver compares the gunfighter's display of weaponry to that of the samurai.[54] Nigel Andrews compares *Sanjurō* with *True Grit* and calls it "the most autumnal of Kurosawa's Japanese Westerns."[55] By contrast, David Desser finds that *Sanjurō* reveals the influence of *Shane*.[56] Tom Milne compares *Dersu Uzala* to Sidney Pollack's *Jeremiah Johnson*.[57] Richard Combs found an evolution in Kurosawa's use of the genre. Writing of *Kagemusha*, he suggested that "The modern weaponry of the enemy clans, and some scenes of slow motion death agony, might nevertheless suggest an updating of Kurosawa's Western imagery, from Ford to Peckinpah."[58] (This suggestion, however, tends to reverse the direction of influence, since Kurosawa's use of slow motion for the depiction of violence in films as early as 1943 clearly predates its appearance in the American cinema in the late 1960s in such films as *Bonnie and Clyde* and *The Wild Bunch*.) Donald Richie cites *Bad Day at Black Rock*, *Shane*, and *High Noon* as models for *Yōjimbō*.[59] (In this case, it seems likely that Kurosawa has borrowed a small bit of business from *High Noon*—the sound of coffins being hammered.) Writing on the American film *The Magnificent Seven*, Joseph Anderson observed that "Kurosawa's self-acknowledged debt to the American Western, particularly John Ford's, helped to determine the shape of *The Seven Samurai*. This foreign influence has nourished him."[60] Anderson then adds that "Without the American cinema, there would be no Kurosawa."[61]

In considering the relationship between Kurosawa's samurai films (and the samurai film in general) and American Westerns, David Desser points out that the "obvious similarities of being set in the past, of having armed heroes who protect the weak or who seek bloody revenge, and the subscription to a codified set of behavioral norms like 'The Code of the West' or the code of 'Bushidō,' give the two forms an obvious affinity," but he also cautions that the extent to which the samurai film is indebted to the Western "is questionable."[62] The differences between the two categories of film are as important as the apparent similarities. Desser, for example, discusses differing conceptions of the frontier and of nature in the two genres.[63] Also stressing the differences, Stuart Kaminsky has observed that the samurai film "deals with myth in a way which the American Westerns cannot attempt because of different national needs, conventions, and historical film traditions."[64]

Both types of film are about men of violence who are defined in terms of their weapons, yet the characters and stories are embedded in networks of different social structural values, which firmly separate the two classes of film. Each articulates a different response to history and culture. Class identity, relations, and conflict are all central to the samurai film while being quite peripheral to the Western, which is why Kurosawa's *Seven Samurai* does not really translate to an American context. Historically and socially, the gunfighter–peasant relationship is not the same as the samurai–farmer relationship. As Tadao Satō notes, unlike the samurai film, "there is no distinction in the rank of characters who appear in Westerns. The sheriff, outlaw, cowboy, farmer, etc., are more or less on an equal social footing."[65] The samurai belonged to a distinct space in the social hierarchy that marked him off from such other classes as the farmers or the aristocracy. During historical eras preceding the Tokugawa period, the class lines between samurai and farmer were far more fluid than they were after the seventeenth century, but in both eras the samurai as a class depended for their identity on the codes of obligation that bound them with their lord: the obligation to serve their lord in time of conflict, and the lord's obligation to reward their service with land or rice, which they depended upon for their existence. Many samurai films deal with samurai who are in the employ of their lords, and many others deal with the rōnin, or unemployed, samurai; but in either case samurai behavior is clearly prescribed by custom and constrained by the class hierarchy. Even when a samurai had fallen from his respected position in society, an implicit comparison with the prescribed codes of the class might be made: much of the humor of *Yōjimbō* and *Sanjurō* depends on the distance between Mifune's shaggy, dirty, self-interested rōnin and the warrior ideal.[66]

By contrast, the mythological appeal of the American West was precisely its supposed classlessness: it was the region where failed Easterners or oppressed Europeans could find the space and the opportunity to build a new society free of the political and economic corruptions of the old world. Drawing on this mythology, Westerns are implicit celebrations of the building of civilization, dramatizing a future full of promise and optimism (*My Darling Clementine, Red River, Shane, Once Upon a Time in the West*). Either that, or they dramatize the collapse of the myth, the closing of the land and of the opportunities that it promised (*The Wild Bunch, McCabe and Mrs. Miller*). Westerns portray society as embodying the progressive unfolding of history, or they bitterly attack it for failing to do better. The logic of these portrayals depends on the gunfighter as a catalyst, a character free of ties to the past, obligated to no one, and thereby able to help usher in the golden future or, because of his "pure" isolation, able to bring down violently the old order. In either case, his actions are purifying and have an explicit social function. The gunfighter, because of his isolation, is able to exercise *choice*. He may have to ride off into the mountains at the end, as in *Shane*, but his decision to intervene in the action has historically progressive consequences. It may, for example, permit the safe growth of a town in a formerly violent region. Nihilism is rarely the Western's reply to history and society.

By contrast, a nihilist response is a possibility for samurai films (or else the films will uncritically celebrate the glories of fulfilling samurai duty, as in the cycle of films about the loyal forty-seven rōnin who stoically endured all sorts of indignities in order to avenge the honor of their lord) because the samurai's actions are ferociously constrained by giri, the social codes of obligation. In his discussion of subgenres of the samurai film, Desser points out that nihilism or fatalism suffuses several of these subgenres.[67] Films like Kobayashi's *Hara-Kiri* and *Samurai Rebellion* rely "heavily upon the juxtaposition of a trapped individual existing within a rigid social structure."[68] These films by Kobayashi ruthlessly reduce the range of the samurai hero's choices until the only one left him is a lonely death, after which, in *Hara-Kiri*, his very existence is obliterated from the historical records. Peckinpah did something similar in *The Wild Bunch*, foreclosing the options his outlaws faced, except that he allowed them to die fighting together, affirming the bonds of friendship, and, in the final images, he permitted them to live on in folklore and song.[69] Only in Sergio Leone's Westerns, and in those he inspired, has a nihilist response been evident, but Leone derived his cycle of films from Japanese samurai films, specifically Kurosawa's *Yōjimbō*. While Westerns celebrate in the gunfighter the isolationist and individualist components of American culture, the space for such an individual in medieval Japanese culture was far more problematic. The nihilism of a film like *Hara-Kiri* is the response to unyielding historical and cultural patterns. The gunfighter rides away at the end of Westerns because, to American culture, this is the essence of freedom: the ability to shed social ties and move on. The samurai hero has a harder time doing this. The codes of giri are everywhere and have constituted his identity. Thus, violence in samurai films (e.g., in *Yōjimbō* or in *Hara-Kiri*) may be portrayed as impotent and futile. By contrast, Westerns define violence as necessary for social progress.

Westerns and samurai films are structural expressions of differing cultural perceptions of what constitutes the social self. The gunfighter is skilled and pure in his isolation from society, while the samurai may be diminished or destroyed when attempting to escape the constraints of social obligation.[70] Thus, Kurosawa cannot simply make Westerns, since the social perceptions and the national tradition that they express are quite foreign. He cannot simply translate them into a Japanese context, no more than John Sturges and his crew could translate Kurosawa's seven samurai into gunfighters. The generic codes of Westerns and samurai films do not freely circulate from one genre to the other. Instead, what Kurosawa has said about Westerns is quite different and instructive: "Westerns have been done over and over again and in the process a kind of grammar has evolved. I have learned from this grammar of the Western."[71]

This statement is provocative. It indicates that what Kurosawa found useful in Westerns was not their content but certain syntactic features. Rather than borrowing at the level of content, rather than telling stories about gunfighters with swords, Kurosawa may have found the Western's syntax of movement and framing to be of value. The Western's ability to integrate figure and landscape in a long shot in ways that describe relations between humans and their environment, and its tendency to treat the landscape as a morally symbolic terrain such that the land itself becomes a character in the films, would certainly resonate in a culture like Japan's, where traditions of nature veneration are very old. Kurosawa's films partake of these traditions and treat the physical environment in a highly active way: rain and wind are passionate indices of human character in his work. The symbolic structure of such films as *Rashōmon* and *Red Beard* is built around the weather and the seasons. This is quite consistent with Japanese aesthetic tradition, where each of the seasons had its own affective properties, where the performance of particular Noh plays was correlated with appropriate seasons, and where one of the rules of good haiku composition was that it contain a seasonal reference.[72]

In addition to the almost animistic treatment of landscape in the Western, the genre has another characteristic of relevance to Kurosawa. It takes as one of its subjects cinematic properties of movement. The narratives frequently assume the form of journeys, where travel by horse across the frame accentuates the boundaries of the screen, and in 'scope films the flatness of the image. By panning to follow a moving horseman, strongly lateral patterns of movement may be established. As we will see, Kurosawa displays in his work a profound affection for this type of movement: lateral motion across the frame is one of the visual signatures of his cinema. But, in addition, Kurosawa is deeply interested in studying the variables of movement on screen, and much of his film style is comprehensible as an effort to emphasize the experience of kinesis. His favored choice of lenses of long focal length is particularly governed by this interest in emphasizing the dynamics of motion on screen. Kurosawa brings an almost analytic interest to bear on his organization of lenses, camera, and object movement, an interest in exploring the motion-enhancing capabilities of differing combinations of these elements. As a genre that exploits cinematic properties of motion and relates them to the coordinates of the frame, the Western is a compelling genre for Kurosawa to study. But this study has occurred primarily at the level of form, of "grammar," and not of content.

Kurosawa studied the Western as a visual form, much as he studied the prints of Hokusai and the paintings of Van Gogh, and he found sympathy with those elements that fit his own cultural experience and cinematic interests. In this he remained a thoroughly Japanese filmmaker. Kurosawa himself has made this point. "I don't think I'm Western at all. I don't understand how I could have that reputation. I feel that among Japanese directors today I must be the most Japanese."[73]

In addition, there is ample evidence that Kurosawa has been at least as influential upon American Westerns (and American films) as they have been upon him. Obvious examples are John Sturges (*The Magnificent Seven*), Sam Peckinpah, and George Lucas.[74] Though Sergio Leone is Italian, his visual style is strikingly indebted to Kurosawa (from the sinuously tracking camera to the use of wind and dust as visual signs of dramatic tension), and Kurosawa's influence found its way back to the American cinema by way of Leone. *A Fistful of Dollars* initiated a cycle of American Westerns modeled on their Italian cousins.[75] (It is worth pointing out, however, that Leone would go on to transcend the Kurosawa influence. *Once Upon a Time in the West* is a magnificent creation and one of the best of all Westerns.)

In summing up, then, an important point to make when considering the vexed and probably unanswerable question of which way the influences go between Kurosawa and the American cinema is that Kurosawa's cinematic references, the heritage that he has drawn from and enjoyed, are extraordinarily diverse. They include John Ford and Westerns but go considerably beyond these. For example, he has repeatedly cited the silent cinema as a source of inspiration:

3. The influence of Kurosawa: direct remakes as in *The Magnificent Seven* (1960), freely adapted from *Seven Samurai*. (Museum of Modern Art/Film Stills Archive)

> frequently, in conversation, people have pointed out to me that a particular scene in one of my films reminds them of something as far back as the silent film era. When I'm told this, I suddenly realize that it may be true, because I've seen many films that I admired very much—and the ones I like stay with me in my subconscious and perhaps I have some kind of impulse to recreate the same impression when I make my own films.[76]

> I like silent pictures and always have. They are often so much more beautiful than sound pictures are. Perhaps they have to be.[77]

Moreover, Kurosawa indicates that his cinematic tastes (and debts) range globally. In the autobiography, he lists close to 100 films that impressed him during his youth and adolescence, and it is a very eclectic list, ranging from works by Griffith, Chaplin, and Stroheim to works by

4. and 5. The influence of Kurosawa: lessons in wide-screen composition and the stylization of violence. (Top) Peckinpah's warriors stoically meet their end in *The Wild Bunch*. (Bottom) Frank (Henry Fonda) confronts Harmonica (Charles Bronson) in Sergio Leone's *Once Upon a Time in the West*. (Museum of Modern Art/Film Stills Archive)

Victor Sjöström, Lupu Pick, and Daisuke Itō. Given Kurosawa's fondness for the moving camera, Murnau, not surprisingly, figures in the references. More important, so does Sergei Eisenstein. Not only would Kurosawa include an homage to *The Battleship Potemkin* in *The Hidden Fortress* (the spectacular massing of the crowd on the castle stairs), but much of his work may be regarded as an attempt to work out and extend the implications of Eisenstein's theory and practice of montage. Noël Burch has noticed this and written that Kurosawa "may be regarded as the direct heir of Eisenstein in so far as he returned the shot-change to its true function as a visible, avowed parameter of filmic discourse."[78] A quick glance at these references clearly indicates the richness of the cinematic culture from which Kurosawa has been nourished.[79] Kurosawa has never exhibited any of the "anxiety of influence" that one would expect from a filmmaker conscious of working from the forms and traditions of another. Instead, he very quickly found his own voice in film and displayed his own stylistic synthesis of fluid camera movement and montage cutting.

With these considerations in mind, then, how might Kurosawa's work be contextualized? What are the issues that it addresses? How may his style be accounted for in all its contradictions, its tempestuousness and passion, as a response to Japan and the Japanese, for whom Kurosawa has said he really makes his movies?

Kurosawa himself has provided clues. He has spoken of the peculiarities of the era that was formative for him and his generation:

> In the Edo period Japan was a very closed society; then in the Meiji era everything came rushing in from abroad at an incredible rate. We all tried to absorb this as quickly as possible—western literature, painting, music, art. So it's all part of my make-up and comes to the surface very naturally.[80]

> as I was growing up, my education—as that of most people of my generation—compared to younger people today, covered a broader span: Shakespeare, Balzac, Russian literature. It's quite natural that my education would manifest itself later in my work.[81]

Kurosawa was born in 1910, and his life spans the tail end of the Meiji period, the era of interwar social protest, the war years of intense nationalism and anti-Westernism, and Japan's postwar period of rapid economic growth. His life, therefore, is virtually consonant with twentieth-century Japanese history. Moreover, these were periods that posed questions about Japanese identity in especially acute terms. Born at the very end of the Meiji period, Kurosawa would, in his art, grapple with the fundamental challenge posed by this period: the relation between Japan and the West, specifically the tensions between Japanese cultural identity and economic and political modernization. For the Meiji period (1868–1912) saw Japan embarking on an ambitious program of social, economic, and political development. This was presaged by a challenge from the West in the form of Admiral Perry's gunboats. Japan's answer was a program of rapid modernization coupled with explicit study and borrowing from the West. From a parliamentary government replete with a constitution, to telephone and train lines, a postal service, and developing industrial capacities, the accoutrements of the modern Western world were swiftly adopted. But such a program could not be separated from a sometimes powerful anxiety about whether Japan would cease to be Japan. In an account of the travels of the Iwakura embassy, Eugene Soviak remarks that the problem confronting the Meiji modernizers was the dilemma of whether it was possible "to transplant Western industry and technology without adopting the whole socio-political structure and value system of the West."[82]

John Whitney Hall has pointed out that among the challenges posed by modernism for those Japanese living through the changes was a dilemma of meaning. Because of a historical congruence between modernization and Westernization, sensitive Japanese were led to a project of studying the West in an effort to fathom its "meaning" and the secrets of its development and apparent civilization (though to other Japanese, the Westerners were simply barbarians). "The assumption that modernization in Japan was equivalent to Westernization has tended to direct the search for [the] definition of modernization among Japanese toward the task of finding 'meaning' in Western civilization."[83] Modernism posed a "problem of meaning" for many Japanese passing through its swiftly moving currents.[84] There were fears that Japan would lose its identity in a "flood of Westernization," and in some quarters there was a backlash against Western culture by the 1880s.[85] Carol Gluck quotes an editorial by Katsunan Kuga in the late Meiji period that is indicative of these fears: "not only is our national autonomy impaired but foreign influence threatens to rush in and buffet our island country about until our manners and customs, our institutions and civilization, our historical spirit, even our national spirit are swept away."[86]

Several scholars have suggested that generational differences prevailed among the responses of Japanese to the force of the new and the novelty of the West.[87] In his account of Japan's early student radicals, Henry DeWitt Smith suggests that, after 1868, young Japanese displayed shifting commitments to issues of national integrity and strength, to a fascination with self-centered introspection or, by the 1920s, to a concern for social problems that led many to Marxism.[88] In a discussion of the historian Saburō Ienaga, Robert Bellah points to Ienaga's perception of generational differences in the responses to the new changes in Japan. "[T]he generation of the great enlighteners grew up in Tokugawa times. Those men all came to know who they were when the traditional order was intact." For the next generation, however, "modernization implied the 'spiritual breakdown' which [the novelist] Natsume Sōseki spoke of as following the impact of Western culture."[89] Whether, and to what extent, historical vicissitudes are realized in recognizably distinct personality types is probably an unresolvable issue. The salient point, however, is that for some Japanese the changes that beset the nation during and after the Meiji period could be experienced in intensely personal, existential terms.

This period did not have to be, in actuality, historically discontinuous with preceding eras to be experienced as such. In a discussion of Japan's apparently radical political and social realignment during the Allied Occupation following World War II, Robert Ward points to the Meiji era as a time that appears similarly discontinuous with what preceded it. "These seem to be years when enormous and highly discontinuous changes of an institutional and behavioral sort are compressed into very short periods of historical time."[90] But, contra Foucault, he cautions against overvaluing the discontinuous in history, maintaining that in both cases—Meiji Japan and the Occupation years—what seems so novel was in many cases prepared for by the developments of earlier eras. "In the light of recent scholarship the Restoration has not turned out to represent so abrupt a break with the institutions, values, and behavior of the past . . . history affords few, if any, examples of real watersheds of that sort."[91] Marius Jansen and other scholars have pointed out that the Meiji leaders were enacting a dynamic of change that had its roots in the Tokugawa era and earlier.[92]

The diachronic view available to the historian, however, may not be the same as the necessarily limited synchronic perspective of the individual subject to, and living out, a specific history. Jansen points out that the problem of cultural reintegration, which followed in the wake of modernity, "was seen less as one of modern vs. tradition, as it was in the West, than of modern vs. Japan; a generation that asked itself whether it was Japanese or modern, Japanese or Christian, experienced a special kind of loneliness and uncertainty."[93] Kurosawa's remarks quoted earlier, about how natural a part of his character is the coexistence of East and West, would seem to belie what has just been suggested about the individual's experience of apparently sudden historical change. If one looks at the films and reconstructs their signs, however, rather than focusing on Kurosawa's claims about his own personality, then abundant evidence emerges of an aesthetic sensibility that prizes discontinuity, shock, and the apocalyptic. Kurosawa's generation was one for which the West contained special meaning, and if he has negotiated in his personal life a harmony between East and West, the films tell a different story. There, narratives abound of social collapse, of psychic crisis, of worlds shaken to bits by social, cultural, and economic conflicts. As Keiko McDonald has noted, Kurosawa's films "begin with an acute awareness of a fragmented world."[94] Throughout it all—in the form of jazz, neon lights, nightclubs, striptease shows, and, in the period films, the deadly firearms—the shadow of the West and the signs of its impact are everywhere and are viewed with an ambivalence that is profound and constitutes the motor of the narratives.

John Whitney Hall has remarked that, in searching for the meaning of the West, each generation of Japanese laboring under its impact has had differing sensitivities about the significance of Western culture.[95] As Japan itself changed and developed, "Western culture" acted as a multidimensional category, a dynamic, multivalent signifier. Herbert Passin pointed out that it never signified only one range of meaning but was shifting through the varying perceptions of differing observers and generations, constructed and reconstructed as a social category to suit "felt needs":

> If it is never the same "Japan" in contact with the West, neither is it the same West. "The West" is not and has never been univocal. It has always offered a range. Sometimes the West has meant liberalism and individualism, sometimes German conservative philosophy; . . . What ultimately comes to be selected depends upon an intricate dialectic between felt needs at particular times, what was available in the West, and the particular West to which people were responding.[96]

Engaged in a generational search for meaning, carried out through his aesthetic forms, Kurosawa would come to construct the West in his own manner: visually, by defining a particular stylistic relationship with the Hollywood cinema; narratively, by shaping plot so that social crises are portrayed as opening up a range of choice to, and thereby defining, the autonomous individual; and socially, by borrowing ideals of individualism and economic democracy from Western social thought and the reforms of the Occupation. In responding to the challenge of meaning posed by the West, and in constructing a version of the West as well as of "Japaneseness," Kurosawa was certainly not alone. Shūichi Katō has described such Japanese novelists as Mori Ōgai and Natsume Sōseki as "creators from cultural confrontation,"[97] transforming the impact of East and West into a creative force, while, in his essays on Sōseki and Kafū Nagai, Donald Keene has pointed to the importance of their ambivalence in choosing between East and West, and to occasional revisions of choice, as a tension fueling aesthetic form.[98] More recently, David Bordwell has suggested that Ozu's films can be viewed as reflections of and meditations upon "the broken promises of Meiji," that is, the notion "that Japan could modernize without suffering a dislocation of what were defined as its central traditions."[99]

Like the work of these other artists, Kurosawa's cinema addresses the themes of modernity in the Japanese experience. His films convert them into felt challenges of individual conscience by telling stories of strong protagonists grappling with the social ills of a developing nation and the modern order: poverty, disease, industrial and political corruption, fear of the bomb. As Jansen has pointed out, these dilemmas "combine to make more complex the search for autonomy of personality and freedom of choice."[100] Kurosawa's cinema is powerfully resonant because it clarifies the stakes of this search and so directly, and poignantly, exhibits the probability of its failure.

Considering possible relationships between an artist's chosen style and a given historical moment, Shūichi Katō has remarked that style ought to be understood as an emblem of the artist's times.[101] Also concerned with the social grounding of aesthetic forms, the film scholar Tadao Satō has noted that the cinema is especially sensitive to the crosscurrents of an era: "Japan had cast off feudalism to embrace modernism with such haste and vigor that repercussions of the battle between old and new were being felt at all levels of society. However, as the movements in the film world have been the most active and lively, it is through film that we will witness the clearest tremors of that battle."[102]

Indeed, in Kurosawa's films we witness tremors of great magnitude that have one of their roots in anxieties about the dynamics of social change, anxieties left as a legacy of Meiji and which continued to be felt throughout the succeeding Taishō era.[103] Would a program of development necessarily unleash an uncontrollable cultural process that would forever transform the tiny island nation? Gluck maintains that "the late Meiji rendition of modernity" as a potentially negative and divisive condition, threatening to established traditions and social orders (e.g., breeding labor unrest, threatening the peasantry's ties to the land) "was, until 1945, the authoritative one."[104] George Wilson, discussing the crisis atmosphere that prevailed among political circles in the 1930s, points to a fear that, as was perceived to have happened during the Meiji Restoration, social conflict and change, once let loose, could potentially sweep the state away and realign the course of Japan's development.[105]

A caveat is in order. Development has a dark side, yet Japan has been remarkably successful in charting and realizing a course of rapid social and economic development, and many scholars have pointed with pride to the nation's accomplishments in creating a reasonably democratic state capable of responding to redress social injustice and the grievances of its citizens.[106] Nevertheless, while recognition of Japan's very real social and economic successes is in order, when studying the films of Kurosawa, it is necessary to point to the ambiguous legacy of modernization. Jansen suggests that along with an abundance of material goods and an improvement in living standards come other developments that are not strictly directed toward "progress in the sense of better and happier lives. . . . Violence, uneasiness, and unhappiness have everywhere been the companions of modernization processes. Everywhere there is a consciousness of a loss of values, a search for reintegration with new groups."[107] Kurosawa's cinema is extraordinarily responsive to these ambiguities of development and to the contradictions between social recovery from the war and official policies of rapid economic growth on the one hand, and on the other, continued inequities of wealth, low living standards for some, and a system of big business that has not traditionally been responsive to citizens' grievances.[108] His cinema is profoundly contradictory in its formal design and discourse and, to this extent, Kurosawa himself should not be regarded as a transcendent author. He may, in fact, be viewed as yet another text, formed like his films by the strains of an unfolding social process. This conclusion is bolstered by a reading of his autobiography, a text in which Kurosawa creates himself as text by constructing his life as a story and the films as a part of that story. What most impresses one from a reading of this account is the degree to which Kurosawa emerges as one of his own characters and the story of his life as a film he might have made. I discuss this later in more detail, but the point here is that the structural design of Kurosawa's cinema, more than that of many other directors, is one that is highly charged by formal, thematic, and narrational ambiguities and tensions. This is what David Desser alluded to when he referred to Kurosawa as a "dialectical filmmaker."[109]

The design of Kurosawa's cinema, and its response to felt problems of cultural identity, needs to be regarded as a dynamic one: as a process marked by tensions, by achievements and setbacks, rather than as a consistent, and therefore static, system of themes and forms. Organized by a social conception that accords great value to the autonomous individual, these forms are charged with ideological value. The narrative design of the films and the unfolding of their visual codes are shaped by a central, organizing problematic. Kurosawa's films form a series of inquiries on the place and the possibilities of the autonomous self within a culture whose social relations stress group ties and obligations.

Differing views prevail about the significance and the strength of these group ties. Some go so far as to suggest that because Japanese social institutions seem so hierarchical and group-oriented, the social space resting on the family as foundation and the emperor and state as "capstone," conformity to social dictates is an ever-present tendency, even a threat to democractic life.[110] In this view, group-derived norms centered about the family, clan, village, and emperor seem to swallow up the individual. Pointing to the antecedents of such a condition, Takeo Yazaki has remarked that "In Edo society one could not observe any emerging freedom of the individual based on the rising power of the people from the bottom. There was lacking among the people any strong critical spirit or thought pattern based on respect for individual worth."[111]

By contrast, in his discussion of the construction of the Japanese self, Robert Smith strongly disagrees with such conclusions. He points out that "it is frequently taken by foreign and Japanese observers alike that the ultimate goal of the individual is the complete suppression of the self or, more drastically, that the Japanese have no sense of the self at all. The conclusion does not follow."[112] Other observers, even if seeming to subscribe to the view of Japanese society as rigidly hierarchical, have pointed to the existence of a tradition of rebellion throughout Japanese history, a tradition that celebrates nonconformity and the rejection of authority.

> [W]hile the formal organization of Japanese society and the official norms of social behavior have been rigidly hierarchical and authoritarian, there has paradoxically always been a tacit acceptance, or sometimes even an open idealization, of certain trends which were in apparent opposition to the official norm. Thus, in Japanese social history there has been a tradition of glorifying such trends as the defense of their own rights by dissident groups, defiance of authority, individual action, and open personal achievement.[113]

Kurosawa's films, with their strong, rebellious protagonists and their visual style that celebrates excesses and transgressions, clearly belong to this latter tradition. They caution against resignation in the face of social oppression and offer heroes whose rebelliousness is meant as a role model for the audience. In developing the terms of these portrayals, Kurosawa clearly drew upon his own cultural heritage of agrarian uprisings, rebellious armed monks, and the strong samurai personalities of legend and folklore. Moreover, an ethic of individualism had begun to take root in late Meiji Japan. By the Taishō era, H. D. Harootunian writes, Meiji ideals of public dedication and self-sacrificing service had to accommodate a new ethic of success that honored the individual, that valorized "the pursuit of the self alone in the private interest, a self no longer limited by concerns for family name or honoring one's native place."[114] As is well known, the arts reflected these shifts. Sōseki and other novelists, for example, began to explore the coordinates of this inner, individualized experience.

Is the individualism of Kurosawa's characters primarily Japanese or Western? It is difficult to say in any definitive way. As noted, clear cultural precedents existed for the kind of rebellious heroes who would populate Kurosawa's cinema. It is also important to note, however, that when he began to work, it was under the constraints of war, when Imperial ideology was officially dominant, and subsequently under the Allied Occupation, when ideals of democracy and individualism gained renewed currency, this time by way of the West. It seems certain that, in this context, Western individualism furnished an ideological example. As I suggest in a later chapter, Kurosawa also drew from this influence, from the Western tradition where the autonomous individual is ac-

6. Kurosawa directs Toshirō Mifune (seated) on the set of *High and Low*. (Museum of Modern Art/Film Stills Archive)

corded a discrete place in the social arena, a positioning that is less problematic than in Japanese culture. The wave of political repression and assassinations in the 1930s, when a virulent form of militarism cowed intellectuals and the Left with violent dreams of expanding empire and service unto death in honor of emperor and nation, demonstrated for Kurosawa the need for such an experiment at cross-cultural fertilization.[115] "The Japanese see self-assertion as immoral and self-sacrifice as the sensible course to take in life," Kurosawa has said.[116] Referring to the chaotic condition of Japan's culture and economy immediately following the second world war, Kurosawa remarked, "I believed at that time that for Japan to recover it was necessary to place a high value on the self. I still believe this."[117] In his autobiography, he repeated his commitment, reiterating the terms of his own distinctive construction of the West for Japan: "I felt that without the establishment of the self as a positive value there could be no freedom and no democracy."[118]

Through his cinema, Kurosawa has attempted to establish the autonomous self as a positive value, but to do this he had to construct a model that was counter to dominant cultural practices. As Smith has pointed out, Japanese culture has constructed an awareness of self that is quite clearly marked and that might be termed an "interactionist" one, whereby self and social groupings exist only in relation to each other. "A person is invariably identified as acting in some kind of human relationship, never autonomously. . . . [B]oth self and other can be expressed only in relational terms."[119] Smith quotes Christie Kiefer's observation that the Japanese regard outward role demands as "the really important center of the self" and include within the boundaries of the concept of self "much of the quality of the intimate social groups [e.g., the family or work associates with whom one is expected to spend a great deal of social time] of which the individual is a member."[120] By contrast, Kiefer remarks, Americans' sense of self seems to "stop at the skin." Kurosawa's radical gesture is to substitute a variant ideological conception of the self as an independent consciousness, bounded by its own imperatives, heedless, even defiant, of outward role demands.[121] Kurosawa's heroes are severed from these intimate social groupings. Even if they have a family, they often struggle alone. By necessity, given a cultural context of interactionist, relational identities, the temerity of Kurosawa's gesture must couple the supremacy of the heroes' quest with a concomitant loneliness and anguish.[122]

The films that have resulted from this experiment form an extraordinarily rich cultural dialogue addressing their immediate moment: recovery from the second world war and the projection of a future course of cultural development. As such, these are implicitly, and very often quite explicitly, political films. Kurosawa himself, however, denies that politics figures in his films in any direct or conscious manner. In an interview in 1965, he was asked if he considered himself a committed filmmaker, and he replied: "Absolutely not. People may think I am from watching my works, but that is the opinion of critics who judge a film right afterwards. My commitment is not deliberate or conscious. It's never the result of a decision. Politics is very important for me, but more as a private man . . . and not as a director."[123] Politics for the private man, not the director.[124] Kurosawa would have us believe this, yet his films speak another voice. They have addressed such topics as black-market criminality, government and corporate corruption, the partnership between political officials and gangsters, the inequities of wealth in contemporary Japan, the problem of nuclear weapons, and so on. These are not the subjects of a filmmaker indifferent to politics. Kurosawa himself has observed that if films lack topicality, they are also without meaning.[125] In fact, if we read his words closely, it becomes clear that what he is rejecting is not a committed cinema but the ciné-tract, the film that exists only to advance an ideological position and that is ultimately reducible to it. Suspicious of ideology, Kurosawa stresses that the responsibility toward the world that he feels as a filmmaker enters his films unobtrusively: "Of course, I'm concerned with the moral responsibility of a creator, but without expressing it in such an obvious way. This feeling of responsibility developed in me through being a Japanese and a man. Without my being aware of it, it penetrates my films."[126]

As these remarks might indicate, Kurosawa's cinema is deeply ambivalent in its social role, unsure how far that responsibility should carry it. This ambivalence will create innumerable problems for the films in their attempts to visualize the social challenges of the postwar era and will generate the formal contradictions and dialectical tensions studied in the chapters to come. What happens to a political cinema that is not always explicit about its intentions and roles and that refuses to look closely at its own ideological nature? In many ways, this is the central question of the book. Kurosawa would never interrogate form in the self-conscious manner of Ōshima, Brecht, or Godard, but he clearly demonstrated the same commitment to his own time and culture as they did. We can, therefore, learn a lot about the efficacy of political art from his cinema and especially from the fate of his experiment. For by the late 1960s, he was engulfed by an internal crisis that had been developing in his work for many years. What lends the films their richness and constitutes their historical value is that Kurosawa's attempt at a cultural synthesis did not succeed, and that failure is significant because, in addition to being full of pathos, it clarifies the limitations of a particular kind of political filmmaking and, more generally, the dilemma of the artist who seeks to use art to make history.

2 The Dialectics of Style

Kurosawa trained as a painter, but fortune did not permit him to work at that vocation. He and his family were too poor, paint was too expensive, and he began to have doubts about his ability to support himself in that calling. Besides, he reports a reluctance to submit himself to the academic training required by art school, preferring instead the freer style of the Impressionists and Postimpressionists. Kurosawa relinquished his plans to become a painter and, instead, "set out on a winding path beset by wind and snow."[2] It would not, however, entail a complete abandoning of his love for painting. The interest would persist to infuse his filmmaking, which, while not "painterly" in an overt manner, as are some films by Carl Dreyer and Jean Renoir, would nevertheless exhibit a love for the "rich and expansive visual image."[3] This, perhaps, is one of the reasons for Kurosawa's fondness for the silent cinema: its exclusive reliance on imagery. *Rashōmon* was planned as an experiment in recovering the aesthetics of the silent cinema, the loss of which during the sound era Kurosawa had regretted. As a filmmaker, he had found a dynamic medium for exercising and developing his gifts for creating the potent image. And, as it turned out, he was able to keep on painting. He visualized both *Kagemusha* and *Ran* as paintings at a time when he did not believe he would ever get to make the films.

Unable to devote himself completely to painting, Kurosawa was led to explorations of literature, music, and theater, and eventually toward prospects for real employment. He answered an advertisement from the P.C.L. (Photo Chemical Laboratory) in 1935, through which P.C.L. hoped to acquire a roster of new assistant directors. Each candidate had to submit a written essay, and, in light of subsequent developments, the topic was ironic. The candidates were to write on the fundamental deficiencies of the Japanese film industry and suggest ways to remedy them. In later years,

Kurosawa was to become intimately familiar with a host of these fundamental deficiencies, but with the exuberance of youth, he approached
the assignment with humor and verve. Reflecting that fundamental problems could not be cured, he nonetheless submitted an essay that earned
him an interview at the studio. The interview resulted in an additional
essay, more interviews, and a job offer.

Once at P.C.L., he was assigned to a production unit headed by the
director Kajirō Yamamoto, who would become his mentor during the
years of training. Kurosawa quickly made himself indispensable to Yamamoto and gained experience with virtually all facets of filmmaking,
from screenwriting and editing to carpentry on the sets. In part this was
P.C.L. policy, but Kurosawa found the thorough training invaluable.
"Unless you know every aspect and phase of the film-production process, you can't be a movie director. A movie director is like a front-line
commanding officer. He needs a thorough knowledge of every branch of
the service, and if he doesn't command each division, he cannot command the whole."[4]

In the years before his tenure at P.C.L., Kurosawa had been vocation-
ally unfocused, and in his autobiography he reports having suffered from
anxiety about a future that seemed uncertain and without direction. But
from the time he joined the Yamamoto unit, the doubts lifted and the
direction appeared. Kurosawa gives this account of his realization that
the cinema was to be his future. It is framed in terms that tell us a great
deal about the nature of his films:

> The work in the Yamamoto "group" was fun. I didn't want to
> work for anyone else after that. It was like the wind in a moun-
> tain pass blowing across my face. By this I mean that wonder-
> fully refreshing wind you feel after a painfully hard climb. The
> breath of that wind tells you you are reaching the pass. Then you
> stand in the pass and look down over the panorama it opens up.
> When I stood behind Yama-san in his director's chair next to the
> camera, I felt my heart swell with that same feeling—"I've made
> it at last." The work he was doing was the kind that I really
> wanted to do. I was standing in the mountain pass, and the view
> that opened up before me on the other side revealed a single
> straight road.[5]

This is one of many passages in the autobiography where one feels
Kurosawa is a character from one of his films. Watanabe, Kambei, Na-

kajima, all Kurosawa's heroes live life as if it were stretching before them as a sharply defined road. In order to get to that road, they are all subjected to a "hard climb," to many ordeals, but once the way is glimpsed, they do not deviate. It is instructive that Kurosawa has framed his moment of enlightenment in these terms. He has found his calling, and it is expressed as a Way. In Japanese culture, the Way is an orientation found within both religion and art. It signifies, in general terms, persistent devotion and hard work dedicated to mastering the secrets of a discipline. Ninth-century Buddhist monks of the Tendai sect, for example, were to remain secluded in Mt. Hiei for twelve years, meditating and mastering their discipline before becoming qualified as moral leaders.[6] Working from the influence of Zen Buddhism, Zeami—the medieval theorist of Noh drama, for which Kurosawa professes a great admiration[7]— conceived of Noh as a profoundly demanding discipline whose aspirants should "show a total dedication to the path of nō."[8]

> Morning and night alike, and in all the activities of daily life, an actor must never abandon his concentration, and he must retain his resolve. Thus, if without ever slackening, he manages to increase his skills, his art of the nō will grow ever greater.[9]

> If an actor really wishes to master the nō, he must set aside all other pursuits and truly give his whole soul to our art; then, as his learning increases and his experience grows, he will gradually of himself reach a level of awareness and so come to understand the nō.[10]

In his analysis of Japanese society, Robert Smith points out that strict dedication and training to achieve disciplined ends in, for example, art or the professions is strongly emphasized throughout the social order. It is a quality of the general social ethos. "At all levels of Japanese society, one finds marked interest in the development of what is called seishin, 'spirit.' "[11] The harder the training one endures, the more developed one's character becomes. Endurance and physical or emotional trials become essential to self-mastery. "The stricter and more arduous the training, the more it is thought to serve the aim of constantly polishing one's character. Through discipline and adversity a person achieves self-development and, crucially, self-mastery."[12]

Kurosawa's characters exhibit these ideals, as does his own intense dedication to the perfection of his craft and art. Standing at the pass on his imaginary mountain, he experienced a flash of insight with the realization that cinema was to be his calling. From this moment on, he would be deeply committed to mastering the medium and learning its secrets. But this path had its rites: those secrets were not ones that could be verbalized. They had to be grasped sensuously. Realization of cinematic structure and of visual patterning had to be learned through experience and, once learned, could not be communicated in words. Kurosawa's reluctance to talk about his films is well known. He once told Donald Richie that if he could have expressed the meaning of a scene in words, he would not have had to film it.[13] Elsewhere he has remarked, "I believe that you should say everything you have to say in a movie and keep quiet afterward."[14] Responding to modern currents of film criticism, such as structuralism, he has objected to an ververbalization and overintellectualization of the medium: "They use extremely pedantic terminology. I do not believe in such rationalization or jargon. Film should be more related to human feelings, more candidly."[15]

This distrust of verbal language is not unique to Kurosawa. It is typical of many creators who prefer not to analyze what they have done. Given, however, the models of instruction and education that prevail in the films, it might also be seen as analogous to doctrines of enlightenment that are centuries old and which typify practices found not only in Japan. The Chinese Taoist master Lao-Tzu, for example, is said to have remarked, "Those who know do not speak, those who speak do not know."[16] Heinrich Dumoulin observes that the doctrine of enlightenment in Mahayana Buddhism seems to deny the connections between words and their referents in favor of a policy whereby "meditation must avoid language."[17] Zen Buddhism, for example, distrusts verbal language and abstract conceptualization, preferring instead the realities of concrete experience. The master Dōgen's instructions for sitting meditation involved banishing all desires, concepts, and judgments from the mind.[18] D. T. Suzuki relates the story of a novice monk seeking to learn about Zen, impatient at his teacher's silence. " 'It is some time since I came here, but not a word has been given me regarding the essence of the Zen teaching,' " the student objected. The teacher replied, " 'When you bring me a cup of tea in the morning, I take it; when you serve me a meal, I accept it; when you bow to me, I return it with a nod. How else do you expect to be taught in the mental discipline of Zen?' "[19]

Kurosawa's film style, then, is not an intellectualized one; it has not been shaped through fidelity to a previously constructed political or theoretical position, as are films by Eisenstein, Godard, or Straub. His approach to style has consequences for the kind of political cinema he has attempted to construct, and it has certainly affected the kind of audience he has sought to reach. Rather than aiming for a narrow community of viewers already committed to the theory underlying a particular film practice, Kurosawa has always directed his films at the broadest possible audience, and this constitutes a kind of ethic for him. "A film should appeal to sophisticated, profound-thinking people, while at the same time entertaining simplistic people. Even if a small circle of people enjoy a film, it will not do. A film should satisfy a wide range of people, all the people."[20] As Kurosawa describes his work, technique is never to be used for its own sake. He has said he cares far more for content than for form.[21] "[T]echniques are there only to support a director's intentions. If he relies on techniques his original thought cannot help but be cramped. Techniques do not enlarge a director, they limit him and they tend to undermine the basic idea which should prevail."[22] Yet, as we shall see, his is a deeply formalistic cinema that lacks entirely the kind of recessive visual style typical of Hollywood productions.

Moreover, Kurosawa's stress upon the content of a film should be seen as a primarily ethical emphasis, concerned with the social reception and impact of his art, and not as evidence that his formal design is simply a means of visualizing a predetermined content. Unlike many Hollywood directors, Kurosawa does not use the camera merely to illustrate a screenplay. His conception of content as socially efficacious form links him with another twentieth-century artist, whose association with Kurosawa may seem, at first, surprising.[23] Yet, the work of Bertolt Brecht also developed and was shaped by the crisis of war. Like Kurosawa, Brecht, too, was disturbed by the fanatical militarism of World War II. The work of both men can be seen as an attempt to use art to intervene progressively in a dark historical moment.

Though he has eschewed the kind of radicalizing of form that Brecht's approach exemplifies, like the German playwright, Kurosawa was committed to using his chosen medium to intervene in the world. He has also insisted that pleasure was the means through which he might attract and keep his audience. The side of Brecht that stressed the role of pleasure and play in theater has often been underappreciated, especially by oppositional critical approaches that place an importance on making the audience *work* toward critical understanding of a play or film.[24] Brecht urged an attempt to find appropriate forms of entertainment for communicating a materialist view of the world. Though lacking the explicitly Marxist politics of Brecht's theater, Kurosawa's is a cinema of profound sensual pleasure, through which a consistently critical portrait of the social order is communicated. Brecht, however, inquired into the social construction of different emotional responses and sought to find new theatrical forms to embody a new social order with its correspondingly novel emotional demands. Above all, Brecht rejected a theater in which spectators responded to the drama in an unreflective manner. "The spectator was no longer in any way allowed to submit to an experience uncritically (and without practical consequences) by means of simple empathy with the characters in a play."[25] By contrast, Kurosawa's relation to the role of empathy is considerably more problematical. While never entirely abandoning an empathic cinema (hence, perhaps, a basis for his reputation as a "humanist"), Kurosawa demonstrates in many of his films—No Regrets for Our Youth, Ikiru, Red Beard—an awareness of the limitations of empathy for a socially committed cinema and a desire to explore modest formal mechanisms for limiting the extent to which his films might elicit uncritical emotional responses from their viewers. A useful way of understanding Kurosawa's cinema is as an exploration and demonstration of how far film might go in the attempt to alter society without, at the same time, politically radicalizing its own forms. All this, however, was not apparent at the onset of his career. The early films, in particular, demonstrate amazing formal abilities, but a validating social perspective had not yet been found.

Though Kurosawa's creative approach stresses visual thought and communication, it is important to point out that these do not negate a characteristic emphasis upon scholarly research and a finely tuned script as the foundations of a successful film. "Reading and writing should become habitual," he has said,[26] and he routinely advises aspiring filmmakers to develop a habit of writing so that they might become proficient at producing screenplays. Before he was allowed to direct, Kurosawa used to write screenplays for money. "On location, a chief assistant director's work was extremely hard and busy, so I used to write at midnight, in bed. I could easily sell such screenplays, and make more than my assistant director's salary."[27] He typically writes with at least one other screenwriter, sometimes with a group of people, so that each contributor might function as a kind of foil, checking the dominance of any one person's point of view. His small repertory group of screenwriters has included Shinobu Hashimoto, Hideo Oguni, Ryuzō Kikushima, and Eijirō Hisaita. The characters in the script are allowed to grow and develop on their own. "It's less a matter of working within a defined structure than of letting myself be moved by the characters I've chosen to work with."[28] He says he writes not from his own will but from the will of the characters.[29] Most important, these screenplays are typically informed by historical research on Kurosawa's part. He has thoroughly studied the samurai world, which figures in many of his films. *Kagemusha*, for example, grew from his historical research on the civil wars of the late sixteenth century and from his fascination with the Battle of Nagashino and the generals Takeda Shingen and Oda Nobunaga.[30] He is critical of most samurai films for not being more faithful to the historical identity of the warrior, for creating instead "the impression that the samurai is somebody who wears a top knot and flails his sword around."[31] Japan's past is, for Kurosawa, very much alive, and he is seriously interested in visualizing that past in what he regards as authentic detail. Richie points out that Kurosawa resents the "slipshod reconstructions" of the past found in ordinary period films and that he admires Mizoguchi because of the apparent realism of his period films.[32]

With these considerations in mind regarding the general nature and shape of Kurosawa's cinematic design, a close exploration of its emergence in the early films may begin. I am concerned with isolating and describing those features of visual form that are central to Kurosawa's style and that will be elaborated and extended in the films to come. In order to understand these features, some comparison with the norms of Hollywood filmmaking will be useful. This mode of film practice is often referred to as the "classical" period of the American cinema, and it has been demarcated as extending from the late teens through the early 1960s.[33] It will be important to indicate the central features of Kurosawa's style as they may be observed in the early films and how they differ from standard American practice.[34]

Kurosawa's early work as an assistant director is evidenced by *Horse* (1941), which deals with the struggles of a poor family and the horse raised and beloved by the daughter, Ine (Hideko Takamine). Although the film is a handsomely mounted and often amusing and poignant production, little of the style Kurosawa would come to develop is apparent. Kurosawa edited the film, and one particular sequence—the montage showing the frenzied horse searching the countryside for her missing foal—does exhibit the kinetic qualities associated with his style.[35] Especially interesting is the way its repetitive imagery of the horse moving in and out of the mist over a rough landscape foreshadows the similar, and more famous, montage of Washizu and Miki galloping through the fog in *Throne of Blood*.

Kurosawa's extensive training at P.C.L. in a wide variety of production roles apparently prepared him well for the move from assistant director

7. Kajirō Yamamoto's *Horse*, on which Kurosawa served as assistant director. (R5/S8 Presents)

to director. His first film as director, *Sanshirō Sugata* (1943), demonstrates an astonishing mastery of the medium. There is none of the stylistic hesitation or derivativeness one sometimes finds in a first work. Kurosawa was employing his camera in a manner that clearly marked the direction he would follow in later years. As Richie has noted, Kurosawa here "showed fully the profile which the entire world would come to know."[36] In many respects, the stylistic fireworks of *Sanshirō Sugata* are the result of a powerful and profound visual form searching for an appropriate content. I would like to discuss the film primarily in terms of its formal design and of what that design reveals about Kurosawa's approach to image construction. But, in doing that, I also want to consider how this construction relates to Kurosawa's handling of character and narrative.

The film is set in 1882, during the Meiji period, when Western influences were altering the sense of what it meant to be Japanese, even to the extent of provoking an anti-Western backlash. As Joan Mellen has noted, many of Kurosawa's films will be set in such transitional times.[37] As indicated in the previous chapter, such times were formative for Kurosawa himself. A new school of combat, judo, is in competition with jujitsu, and as the film begins young Sanshirō Sugata (Susumu Fujita) has come to train with the jujitsu master Saburō Momma. Like many of Kurosawa's other films, this one will deal with Sanshirō's spiritual education, with the narrative cast in the form of a chronicle studying the stages of the hero's growing mastery and maturity.[38] The film opens, under a printed title giving the era in which the story is set, with what appears to be an extremely conventional establishing shot showing us a Meiji street. Structurally, the shot (and the use of an optical title "setting" the film) looks as though it could have come from any Hollywood production of the 1940s (except, of course, for the details of clothing and architecture). The camera begins high up and then cranes down, presenting a street scene in which various pedestrians hurry by, looking busy and pretending not to notice the camera tracking down the middle of their town. As usual during such establishing shots, these pedestrians are signifiers of setting and atmosphere and tell us that the narrative, though not yet commencing, is about to do so. At this point, a Hollywood production would cut to another long or medium shot, giving us additional preliminary information necessary to establish the time and place of the story.

Kurosawa, however, does not do this. Instead of cutting in additional establishing material, he tracks the camera down the middle of the street, passing gentlemen dressed in Western suits and other Japanese in traditional garb, and turns the camera left, down an alley, continuing the track. As the camera approaches a group of singing women, an off-screen male voice begins to say that he has business here. Before he has finished, a reverse-field cut has disclosed the speaker, Sanshirō. The cut has also disclosed the film's play with our expectations. An establishing shot has turned into a subjective shot or, rather, has been one all along, presenting Meiji Japan to us as it is to Sanshirō. Our point of view as spectators has been developed within the same cinematic and narrative space occupied by Sanshirō, who steps out, as it were, from our place in the narrative. In many of the films to come, Kurosawa will employ his heroes as explicit role models for the audience, so it is worth noting the alignment of spectator–character viewpoint in the first shot of the first film. More important, however, as a structural gambit, the elision of point of view achieved in this shot works because, by convention, the first shot of a narrative film is almost never a subjective one. As David Bordwell points out about Hollywood narration, the opening of an American fiction film typically features narration that is highly dense and prominent.[39] Credits, dialogue, and inserts of billboards or calendars provide an abundance of information about time and place, and narrative point of view in the opening sequences is, as a general rule, at its most knowledgeable, if not omniscient. By contrast, Kurosawa has deformed the establishing shot according to the perceptual selectivity of a single consciousness. What appears to be the usual omniscience of the early narrative voice is, instead, a highly restricted and restrictive point of view and one that is, as subsequent scenes make clear, as yet unformed and immature.

Sanshirō has come to the quarters of the jujitsu master Saburō Momma, but he is not to become a jujitsu pupil. He accompanies Momma and his men to a midnight ambush of the judo instructor Shogōrō Yano (Denjiro Ōkochi). Momma intends to teach Yano a lesson about the primacy of jujitsu, and this is also Sanshirō's first lesson, for instead of being ignominiously defeated, Yano succeeds in tossing all Momma's men in the river and in subduing Momma himself. As Momma's men converge on Yano, Sanshirō watches with rapt fascination, but Kurosawa does not merely observe the confrontation. He formalizes Sanshirō's relation to the combat in explicitly visual terms, and this formalization discloses a fascination with a particular kind of movement that will continue to be foregrounded in his work.

Yano takes his position at the edge of an embankment overlooking a river. Momma's men face him and declare they are with the Shinmei school. As one of the men walks to the right, Kurosawa begins a lateral track to follow him, and the camera passes in turn the other six men. The camera continues past them and comes to rest on Sanshirō, framed alone, some distance from the others. Kurosawa then cuts to Yano, similarly framed alone, who asks the men who they are. A cut then returns us to the medium shot of Sanshirō watching Yano, and this time the camera begins a reverse lateral track back in the direction it has come, following again the first man, who has now begun walking to the left. The film then cuts to Yano, who is attacked by several men, whom he throws in the river. Then Kurosawa begins another tracking shot, in a manner identical to the first one of the sequence, across the remaining antagonists, coming to rest on Sanshirō, alone in the frame. A cut returns us to Yano, then back to Sanshirō and a track in the reverse direction back across the antagonists. A lateral tracking shot has been introduced and then repeated three times.

As in the Hollywood cinema, camera movement is initially motivated because it is introduced by, and serves to follow, character action. Kurosawa, however, then leaves the character whose motion triggered the initial track and extends the moving frame until it encloses Sanshirō. The subsequent repetitions and reversals of this shot serve to foreground the tracking camera to a degree beyond anything one would find in an American film of the 1940s. The camera moves in an almost ritualistic manner, duplicating and reduplicating its initial pattern. In addition, this visual structure serves to bind Sanshirō and Yano, since each track ends with a pattern of intercutting between the two characters, each framed in isolation, in contrast to Momma's group. Here we can see clearly Kurosawa's injunction to use form in a meaningful manner: Yano is to be Sanshirō's teacher and spiritual guide, and the bonds between them are set out in visual terms during this early sequence, in which Sanshirō functions as an observer, learning a first lesson by watching a master. Throughout his cinema, Kurosawa will be interested in exploring and extending the capacity of camera movement to situate characters according to important psychological and social relations prevailing among them (an interest that reaches something of a climax in *Seven Samurai*).

In this, we can observe another departure from the standards of Hollywood practice. The eyeline match—in which two characters engaged in conversation, each framed separately, gazed in opposite directions so that their eyelines would cross at an imaginary point just beyond the camera—was a basic code in the Hollywood cinema. It was used to unify space across the cut and establish a physical relationship between characters within a screen geography whose coordinates were consistent from shot to shot.[40] Kurosawa does not often structure space in this manner. Instead, camera movement often substitutes for the eyeline match. For example, during a later sequence, Yano announces to his students that they will participate in a police tournament against a rival jujitsu school. Were the film an American product, the sequence would have been constructed by cutting back and forth from Yano and the students and linking the shots through matching eyelines. By contrast, Kurosawa pans and tracks between Yano and the students, situating them within a fluid, shifting space. As a general rule, in Kurosawa's films we cannot expect to observe stable spatial fields and the orderly visual flow that continuity cutting makes possible.[41]

To complete this discussion of camera movement, let us return briefly to the sequence treating the assault on Yano. As the camera tracks across Momma's fierce men, they are arranged side-by-side across the frame in a linear fashion parallel to the direction of the camera's motion. The result is a strongly frontal composition, in which lateral movement takes precedence over depth of field, a privileging that will assume much greater dominance in later films when Kurosawa begins to use lenses of long focal length. Again, the repetition of the track serves to emphasize the frontality of the composition and to highlight the structural device. It is as if the film was studying its own construction. The signifier, the structural device (in this case camera movement), becomes its own signified. Such an aesthetic practice, in which relations of pure form begin to generate their own content, has always been quite rare in the Hollywood cinema. Very few American films demonstrate the kind of visual self-consciousness and intense contemplation of form that Kurosawa brings to *Sanshirō Sugata*. The closest example one might find to this lies in Welles's *Citizen Kane* (also a first film), a work of baroque structure in which several tracking shots—through the grounds of Xanadu, across the roof, and through the neon sign of Susan Alexander's nightclub—are repeated with the kind of ritualistic emphasis we have observed in *Sanshirō Sugata*.

There may, in fact, be a cultural precedent for Kurosawa's portrayal of lateral movement, and it might be briefly mentioned here. It lies in the compositional style of the Heian and Kamakura-era scroll paintings, which were expansive pictorial narratives dealing with episodes from fiction or history (e.g., *The Tale of the Heike* or Murasaki Shikibu's *The Tale of Genji*). Because the scrolls were designed to be "read" as they were unrolled, the compositional design often stressed horizontal patterns of movement, so that the narrative might be visualized in a manner that "flowed" with the physical unrolling of the scroll itself. At least one writer has suggested that the pictorial style of these scrolls has influenced Kurosawa.[42] Whether that may be or not, in subsequent films we will see a far more radical visual form, far more emphatic articulations of lateral movement. In *Sanshirō Sugata* we are seeing Kurosawa's pictorial style in its period of earliest formation.

The features of visual design observed in the scene dealing with the assault on Yano—repetition, linearity, and frontality—are also strikingly displayed in the film's next major sequence. After Yano defeats Momma's men and refuses Momma's request to be killed (a refusal typical of Kurosawa's characters, who disdain suicide or ritual executions), Sanshirō offers himself as Yano's driver and begins to train with him. But initially, Sanshirō's emotions do not become as disciplined as his martial skills. Instead, he becomes a bully and a show-off, given to rampaging through the streets, grabbing people and tossing them to the ground. It is during one of these displays of prowess that Kurosawa engages in some visual bravado of his own. But in order to describe that, one should really start with the short sequence that precedes it and that serves as a bridge from the scene dealing with the assault on Yano. The reason for this has to do with the film's formal intricacy. Kurosawa has connected these scenes with exceptional cinematic grace in a manner that extends the narrative in terms of a continuous flow of camera and object movement.

Sanshirō, acting as Yano's driver, throws away his wooden clogs and begins to pull the carriage. The camera tracks laterally to the right to follow Yano and the carriage but then tilts down past the spinning wheel to the discarded clog. In a series of brief shots connected by dissolves, we see the clog lying abandoned in the street as people pass by and as rain falls, being tugged at by a puppy, hanging atop a fence beneath wafting snow, and drifting downsteam. As the water carries the clog, the camera pans left to follow it but then tilts up to the street above. A group of excited people run across the frame from left to right. In the midst of this movement, Kurosawa cuts to a high-angle framing of a narrow alley, as the camera violently cranes down to street level. Sanshirō is showing off his newly learned judo by throwing the townspeople about. The framing is a strongly linear one: the camera's axis of view is aligned with and extends down the center of the street. Shops with hanging lanterns sharply bound each side of the passageway. As Sanshirō chases the townspeople, he runs toward and away from the camera in perfect alignment with its axis of view. When, dashing toward the camera, he passes it by and vanishes from the frame, Kurosawa cuts to a reverse-field composition just like the previous shot, high angle, with sharply booming downward movement. Because of the reverse-field, Sanshirō is now running away from the camera. He turns and then, again, runs toward and past the camera, and Kurosawa repeats the reverse-field and crane-down a third time and then, with perfect symmetry, a fourth time.

After the fourth setup, however, the dominant frontality of motion—toward or away from the camera in alignment with its axis of view (thus, a frontality that does not negate spatial depth)—is broken as the frame "opens up" at last. The camera is positioned outside the alleyway and the crowd, chased by Sanshirō, spills out, engulfing the camera and spilling over the edges of the frame. The frontality of the previous compositions is now succeeded by a series of obliquely angled setups that record Sanshirō flipping more opponents and that are match-cut on action.

In this sequence, and in the montage that preceded it, Kurosawa is, of course, describing his central character and making clear the vanity and self-interest that Sanshirō will have to discard in his growth and pursuit of enlightenment. The transitional montage showing the fate of the clogs marks the passage of time during Sanshirō's early training with Yano and comments on Sanshirō as well. Like the clogs, whose compositional shifts define them in terms of process and change, Sanshirō is also in a state of flux. He is an unformed character, whose gradual defining and polishing the film studies. But, more important, the construction of the sequence typically stresses motion: the track with the carriage, the dissolve from image to image, the pan along the river, the tilt up to the street. These are connecting movements that link one thing to another, motions that not only propel the narrative but that begin to elaborate a basically metaphorical understanding of kinesis as that which both reveals and defines character while situating it in moral terms within a sensual world. For Kurosawa, character *is* movement, and this conception will dominate the work until a major realignment of style occurs in the most recent films, where an aesthetic of stasis prevails.

The sequence just described constructs patterns of camera and object movement in sharply contrasting terms. Frequently, camera and object movements are at odds with each other, as when Kurosawa vertically tilts up from the river to reveal a lateral motion across the frame and then cuts to a rapid crane-down that reverses the direction of movement inscribed by the tilt. Like Eisenstein, Kurosawa conceives of cinematic structure in terms of explosion and strife, and he orders his visual materials to produce a maximum of dialectical shock. Relations of camera and object placement and movement and of image and soundtrack are conceived not in terms of smooth continuity, as in the American model developed by the Hollywood cinema, but in terms of clash, contradiction, reversal.

This may be seen best during one of the film's many judo contests. When Sanshirō learns humility and has submitted himself to Yano's teaching so that he becomes the school's outstanding pupil, Yano permits him to face Momma in a match that tests not only the two men but also the opposing disciplines of judo and jujitsu. Sanshirō, with the calmness of one who has attained enlightenment, faces a loud, blustering Momma and defeats him easily by throwing him into a wall. Kurosawa choreographs this triumph as a montage of internally contesting formal elements. Movement, film speed, and sound are all manipulated so as to produce a state of maximum tension among and within these elements.

As Sanshirō lifts Momma in the air to throw him, Kurosawa elides part of this action by cutting to a fragmentary close-up showing Momma already flying in midair. The shot works because it is a flash, no more than an impression. Kurosawa then elides an additional amount of movement by jump cutting, from a slightly different angle and closer position, another flash of Momma helplessly flying along. The effect of the jump cut is as a tiny explosion, a momentary visual and perceptual dislocation. Kurosawa then cuts from these extremely close and unstable shots to a prolonged long shot of the room's spectators as, a moment later, a loud crash sounds from off-screen. Momma has landed. In a very slow and lengthy pan to the right, the camera scans the room. All the spectators are frozen in place and are glancing in the direction of the camera's pan. Compared to the quickness of the shots dealing with the throw, the pan is frustratingly long and thereby builds considerable suspense. After passing across most of the room, the camera finally discloses Momma lying against a wooden wall that has been partially smashed by his impact. Kurosawa cuts to a medium close-up of Momma as, a moment later, a screen, dislodged by the fall, drifts down in silence and slow motion and falls across Momma's head. Kurosawa cuts back to a long shot that frames Sanshirō on the right in the midground and Momma center-screen in the background. This image is held for a long time, and then a loud scream is heard off-frame. As Sanshirō begins to turn in response, a match-cut on action takes us into a close-up that shows him looking off-screen right. Then, in what is to become one of Kurosawa's visual signatures, a rhythmical series of three shots shows us the woman who screamed, first in long shot as part of a crowd, then in medium close-up, finally in extreme close-up. The camera's angle of view remains the same, but its distance changes to produce a series of perceptual shocks as the image is repeatedly enlarged.

I hope this lengthy description makes clear the intricate structure and extreme formalization of the design of this sequence. It is visualized in terms of Eisensteinian principles of film form. Eisenstein's position, revealed in his film practice and clarified in his writings, that conflict—visual, temporal, acoustical—was the basis of cinematic communication is well known. Kurosawa is working from a quite similar aesthetic, though his montage structures are not informed by the Marxian politics that generated those of Eisenstein and his grasp of visual pattern has not been intellectualized at a theoretical level as was Eisenstein's. In the sequence described above, Kurosawa has developed a montage whose internal contradictions, as in Eisenstein's famous metaphor, indeed constitute a series of explosions propelling the narrative forward. The sequence explores contrasts of scale, as it moves violently from extreme long shot to extreme close-up, and of duration, alternating flash cuts with a long take and normal film speed with slow motion. Contradictions in the direction of movement are explored: Momma is hurled through the air toward the left, whereupon Kurosawa cuts to a panning movement toward the right. Image and soundtrack are placed in relations of counterpoint as well. During the long pan to Momma lying unconscious against the wall, no sound is heard, but this seems to be motivated by what we see in the frame: everyone is staring in shock at Momma's lifeless body. As the screen falls to the ground in slow motion, however, we realize that the sound has been shut off entirely, and when Kurosawa returns to the long shot of Sanshirō looking at Momma, the silence continues, and again we assume that the soundtrack is being manipulated. Again we are wrong and receive a perceptual shock because of our error: the loud shriek of Momma's daughter shatters the silence and our composure. The sequence is formally as explosive as the event it depicts. It is riddled by discontinuities of scale, movement, duration, and sound, and these demonstrate as clearly as anything in Eisenstein's *The Battleship Potemkin* the power of a cinema fashioned according to principles of montage construction. Kurosawa's is to be a cinema of perceptual shocks, and this is announced quite clearly from his first film.

It would be incorrect to assert, however, that Kurosawa is necessarily following within the cinematic tradition established by Eisenstein. Both filmmakers prize visual shock, and both regard editing as the seminal stage in filmmaking. The valuing of contrast, however, that we have observed in Kurosawa has ample cultural precedent. Throughout Japanese aesthetics, one finds a delight in the juxtaposition of contrary values, and it was this, in fact, that attracted Eisenstein to Kabuki theater in the first place. Haiku composition, for example, frequently incorporated a "cutting-word" that divided the poem into sections by omitting a crucial verb, thereby interrupting the flow of meaning by opening a perceptual and linguistic space that the reader was required to fill.[43] The silence surrounding the cutting-word contrasted with the delicate sensual qualities of the rest of the poem. The "empty" space of a sumi-e painting was not empty but generated its own plenitude.

The Noh theater, patronized by the ruling military class during its mature period beginning in the late fourteenth century, displayed an abundant dialectics of style, which may be a reason for Kurosawa's affection for Noh. Its aesthetics were structured about dance, music, and chant. Zeami, its most important aesthetician, decried the "monotony of any single means of expression"[44] and urged an acting style that deliberately mixed contrary signifiers. Discussing the appropriate style of an actor's movement, Zeami wrote that when "he moves himself about in a powerful way, he must stamp his foot in a gentle way. And when he stamps his feet strongly, he must hold the upper part of his body quiet."[45] He added:

> When an actor opens his hands quickly, he should finish the gesture by closing them in a slow and heavy fashion; when he extends his hands gravely, however, he should then finish by withdrawing them quickly. If an actor moves his body more quickly than usual, then he must complete his movement in a solemn manner. If, on the other hand, he is moving more slowly than usual, in a quiet fashion, then he must cease his movements in a quick and nimble fashion.[46]

Zeami noted that frequently the most compelling moments of the Noh were those in which a performer stood quietly, doing nothing. But the apparent stasis was deceiving, for it contained a dynamic "inner tension."[47] Kurosawa's affinity for the clash of autonomous signifiers is comprehensible within this more general aesthetic context. That a filmmaker like Eisenstein, however, working from a different cultural and political situation, would employ a similar aesthetic structure does not argue for his influence on Kurosawa so much as it indicates that style, while being shaped and constrained by culture, is not finally reducible to it.

The perceptual shocks that inform Kurosawa's cinema are not merely exercises in formal extravagance. They have a relevance to the content, the characters, and the narratives of his films. The heroes are beset by a series of moral, and often physical, traumas, and the narratives study the progress of the protagonists toward enlightenment and socially committed action. Like Kurosawa who characterized his own path in life as one of "wind and snow," the film characters are subjected to tests and trials, and if they do not prevail they are often likely to be killed. In the case of Sanshirō, his failure to attain enlightenment, that is, to lose his arrogance and learn humility, would subject him to the fate of Higaki, the film's villain, a character without goal or direction, consumed by hate, whose skills have become an elaborate means of destroying the self. Higaki, in fact, is Sanshirō's double, which Kurosawa makes clear through similar actions that he has each character repeat. The narrative of the film, then, pivots on Sanshirō's ability to transcend his physical skills and on the arrogance that their incomplete development has generated. Thus, his discovery of spiritual direction is the centerpiece of the film, and it is

8. Surrounded by howling winds, Sanshirō (Susumu Fujita, right) confronts Higaki for their climactic duel. *Sanshirō Sugata.* (R5/S8 Presents)

constructed as a physical and psychological trauma. Kurosawa's use of an oppositional, strife-ridden cinematic form, then, finds its justification and validation in his conception of character: growth is possible only through shock.

Following Sanshirō's bullying display in the town street, Yano chastizes him and says that teaching judo to such an unformed person lacking in self-discipline is like giving a knife to a madman. Yano tells Sanshirō that loyalty and fidelity underlie the truths of life and that Sanshirō does not know what they mean. Sanshirō objects that Yano is wrong, that he would die for him at any time. To prove his words, he races to the shōji screen, slides it open, and leaps out—a fantastic moment—into the lotus pond below. He grasps a wooden post in the middle of the pond and hangs on. Yano looks at him a moment and shouts for him, then, to die and shuts the shōji. Sanshirō spends the night in the pond, quizzed by a Buddhist priest about the nature of truth and advised to contemplate the moon, which, Donald Keene points out, is a frequent Buddhist symbol of enlightenment in Noh plays.[48] In the morning, Sanshirō sees a lotus flower in bloom, another Buddhist image. Overcome with emotion, he shouts for his teacher, and Yano, the priest, and two of Yano's students hurriedly open their screens. Affecting unconcern, they had really been keeping watch all night. Sanshirō rushes from the pond, calling "Sensei" (teacher) and performs a deep, prolonged bow to Yano.

Sanshirō's leap into the pond in defiance of Yano's demands that he be silent isolates him as an individual. He spends a lonely night, ignored by Yano who refuses the entreaties of other students that he allow Sanshirō to come out of the cold water. The pond and the post to which Sanshirō clings—the post of life, as the priest calls it—are, as symbols, not very subtle, but they do constitute a concrete visualization of the dilemma confronting Kurosawa's heroes: that the discovery of self is a lonely process which no one else can assist, yet a life without devotion to an ideal, and frequently to a teacher, is a life of selfishness and vanity. Sanshirō's leap is a radical gesture that rejects Yano's words while binding him ever more closely to his teacher. Sanshirō's discovery of self, the moment of satori, is predicated upon attaining greater absence of self, the devotion and humility that Yano says are the truth of life. There is an ambiguity here that structures the film: Sanshirō attains self-distinction through greater submission to his teacher. The long, low bow that he gives Yano when he leaves the pond is in acknowledgment of the wisdom that Yano represents. Earlier, when Sanshirō and Yano see a young woman (Sayo, whom Sanshirō will later love) praying before a Shintō shrine, Yano, deeply moved, asks from where such beauty comes. He says that to pray is to throw one's self away and become one with a god. "Nothing is stronger than that beauty." The ideal that Yano holds out for Sanshirō is a similar kind of devotion, a merging of the self with a greater spiritual ideal, and this is why Sayo becomes the appropriate woman for Sanshirō. Knelt in prayer before a shrine of Japan's native cult, Shintō, she represents the purity, selflessness, and devotion that Sanshirō seeks and which Yano wishes him to find.[49] "A pure heart and deep sincerity characterize what Shintō refers to as 'truth' (makoto). 'Truth,' here, is distinctly not some right or wrong view about the nature of things; it is a state of the mind/heart. Truth is as truth is lived in purity and emotional sensitivity."[50] This is Sayo's example in the film.

In order to discover this, Sanshirō must learn yet another lesson, and that concerns the empty and illusory nature of glory. His next opponent turns out to be the aging jujitsu master Hansuke Murai (Takashi Shimura), Sayo's father. When Sanshirō discovers this, he hurries away from Sayo, pausing to tell her that he wishes her father luck. But he cannot concentrate on the upcoming match, and in a series of shots, linked associatively on the basis of purely graphic properties that recall an editing style of avant-garde films, Sanshirō "sees" Sayo praying for her father to win the match. Overwhelmed by the vision, Sanshirō wonders how he can beat such beauty, and the priest tells him that he must become pure again, as he did before. The priest points to the pond and says that Sanshirō was born there. Reminded of the satori he once attained and of the obligations he owes his teacher, Sanshirō confronts and defeats Murai in the tournament, but it is a painful victory. Murai is old and smiles at him with compassion and without rancor. "You were magnificent," he tells Sanshirō. "You are not my enemy." The victor, yet visibly upset, Sanshirō realizes that the defeat of Murai has brought no pleasure and no glory. Afterward, he seeks reconciliation with Murai and Sayo.

Sanshirō's enlightened allegiance to his teacher, Yano, and to the model of conduct exemplified by Sayo, is symptomatic of a deep ambivalence within Kurosawa's work. He will consistently champion the cause of individualist values, yet he will never completely abandon an allegiance to a hierarchical conception of human relationships. Such a conception is sometimes described as "feudalistic." It was perhaps in recognition of this ambivalence that Richard Tucker wrote that "there are other film-makers [than Kurosawa] who have a clearer regard for the individual in Japanese society, the individual free from the constraints of a feudal relationship."[51] By contrast, David Desser questions Tucker's assessment by asking whether master–pupil relationships are, in essence, feudal, since a similar structure may be found in American Westerns.[52] Desser, however, writes that "much of the feudal ethos remains in contemporary Japan."[53] Whether, and to what extent, medieval or contemporary Japan was, or still is, feudalistic in its social and economic features has been a vexed question. In a discussion of the Tokugawa period and Japanese feudalism, Joseph Strayer observes that a feudalistic component may inhere in family or personal relationships where avenues of potential resistance are not explicitly coded and where acts of rebellion are regarded as breaches of the respect and piety normally owed elders or superiors.[54] But he points out that behind an "apparently unchanging façade" of Tokugawa social and political relations, the development of a bureaucratic class of administrators was helping undermine "feudal" relations: "The bureaucratic tendencies which were strong even in sixteenth-century feudalism had developed to a point where they made the official feudal hierarchy almost meaningless."[55]

Similarly, John Whitney Hall points out that in Tokugawa society, authority was increasingly being exercised through institutional and legal channels and "less as a personal right," as might be the case in a feudal regime.[56] He cautions against the indiscriminant use of the term "feudalism," observing that a single category cannot be representative of a total society, and points out that a semantic shift has occurred in the use of the term whereby it tends to be applied to describe any custom or feature of contemporary life that seems old-fashioned or backward.[57]

Thus, as Desser points out, it is difficult to establish that Kurosawa's attention to master–pupil relationships necessarily embodies a feudalistic core of values. On the other hand, it does seem clear that Kurosawa frequently codes human relationships in terms of a hierarchy of status and ability: master and pupil, hero and masses. Implicit within this coding are social relations and obligations prevailing among its constituents. Like the ties that bound the warrior to his lord, the pupil demonstrates allegiance to the master, and the hero discovers it is incumbent upon him or her to protect the welfare of the masses. The tension within this coding is between the impulse toward individual autonomy and a countervailing recognition of the obligations of the interactionist self.

Such a tension will generate truly magnificent formal structures in later films, but in *Sanshirō Sugata* it is relatively relaxed because Kurosawa's work has not yet come to grapple with the problems of individual autonomy. Like most of his films, this one is cast in the form of a spiritual journey during which the hero eventually attains self-insight and self-mastery. But unlike later heroes, Sanshirō is permitted to retain his intimate connections to traditional normative sources: teacher, family, religion. Sanshirō remains firmly bound to Yano as his master, and this arrangement is never abandoned. Yano, at the end, observes that Sanshirō will always be like a little baby. In addition, Murai and Sayo become a surrogate family for Sanshirō, whose life, therefore, is not typified by the isolated and lonely conditions afflicting such other Kurosawa heroes as Watanabe, Kambei, Sanjurō, and Dersu Uzala. These are characters shorn of the support of families and loved ones or of the defining identities offered by the corporation or the state. The price of their enlightenment is far more severe than that exacted of Sanshirō. The defining characteristic of these heroes is that they must reject the normative codes offered by established society in order to live in a politically and socially just manner.

By contrast, *Sanshirō Sugata* demonstrates a far less troubled relationship between the hero and the social order. Sanshirō is a strong individ-

9. Still a boy at heart, Sanshirō gently tends to Sayo. *Sanshirō Sugata.*
(R5/S8 Presents)

ual who has internal sources of strength and dignity, yet the film does
not commit him to the path of lonely rebellion that the other heroes take.
The image of Sayo praying before the shrine, which so moves Yano, is in
this sense the structuring principle of the film's discourse on the relation
between the individual and society. Other Kurosawa heroes confront a
corrupt and predatory social order, yet Sanshirō inhabits a benignly un-
troubled world where the ethic of submissiveness does not, at the same
time, entail a posture appropriate for being economically or politically
exploited. The ethical examples offered by Yano and Sayo are uncondi-
tionally affirmed. *Sanshirō Sugata* lacks the socially critical dimension
so important in the later films. Those heroes, too, learn discipline and
dedication, but unlike them Sanshirō does not place these values in the
service of socially progressive action.

It is in this sense that the earlier statement that *Sanshirō Sugata* is a
form looking for a content should be grasped. In this film, Kurosawa
understood and demonstrated the analytical and explosive capabilities

10. The individual alone and determined: a young factory worker prays before beginning the search for a missing lens. *The Most Beautiful*. (R5/S8 Presents)

of a dialectical film style, yet that analysis and those detonations have not yet been applied to the arena of social values. At this point, the dialectic exists in terms of style only and has not been extended to the culture that informs that style.

None of Kurosawa's other films of this period demonstrates the consummate and passionate command of form so evident in *Sanshirō Sugata*. These other works were made under conditions of official compulsion or were thematically and formally constrained by the exigencies of wartime. *The Most Beautiful* (1944) was produced as a piece of wartime propaganda and celebrates the tenacity and determination of women working in an optical factory, an important war industry. We see them laboring at their workbenches, marching in a fife-and-drum band, and playing volleyball, always as a team, buoyed by a passionate group spirit. Kurosawa has said that he wanted to achieve a documentary quality in this film, and he required the actresses to live and work under difficult factory conditions so that the usual theatrical gloss and polish would be rubbed from their performances.[58] The ensemble acting that results does give the film a naturalistic quality unique in his oeuvre, but the documentary texture for which he aimed is as much a matter of the severely restrictive camerawork as of the acting styles. The camera is largely stationary and avoids extreme angles, and the editing lacks the shocking shifts of perspective and abrupt shot transitions that typified *Sanshirō Sugata*. Nevertheless, several sequences do clearly exhibit the marks of Kurosawa's style, in particular a quick flashback to a moment of crisis when one of the girls realizes she has produced a defective lens that could endanger the lives of Japanese soldiers. In a brief shot that is no more than a flash, she explains her error to her comrades, but Kurosawa expressionistically employs a harsh sound effect to obliterate her words and accentuate the drama of the moment. This is only one of many instances in his work of the "multiplier effect of sound and visual image," the counterpointing of image and sound to enhance each.[59] This stylistic transgression against the generally naturalistic surface of the film has the effect of a small detonation, produced by the impact of two very different stylistic orientations, the documentary and the expressionistic.

Most important, the film clearly demonstrates the ethical ambiguity of Kurosawa's cinema. The head of production at the factory (Takashi Shimura) asks for an enormous increase of production and calls on all workers to become extraordinary individuals in terms of their discipline, attitude, and sense of responsibility to the war effort. Good production is dependent on good character, he says, and the film demonstrates in anecdotal fashion what this good character is. The women fall ill, sustain physical injury, even lose family members, but never waiver in their commitment to the factory and their quotas. Like all Kurosawa's films, this one is centered around a scenario of service and austere self-discipline, but it shows how these codes may produce individuals in submission to nation and emperor as easily as, in other films, they produce characters in postures of heroic social rebellion. It should not surprise us that Kurosawa, normally so socially critical an artist, should have produced so effective a wartime propaganda film.

Sanshirō Sugata, Part II (1945) was completed at the studio's behest because of the popularity of the original and did not interest Kurosawa at all.[60] The film's flat visual qualities are evidence of his indifferent participation. *Sanshirō Sugata, Part II* exhibits a close conformity to Hollywood codes of continuity cutting and none of the radical violations of spatial perspective that typified the first film. The fight scenes are especially good illustrations of what is missing. When Sanshirō confronts a sleazy American boxer in the ring and defeats him, Kurosawa cuts the fight so that the action flows smoothly and lacks the spatial and aural distortions that distinguished the combat scenes in the earlier film. Similarly, when Sanshirō converses with his teacher Yano, Kurosawa scrupulously follows the Hollywood codes, presenting the scene with correct eyeline matches, an observance of the 180-degree rule, and a use of the shot-reverse-shot technique to visualize the conversation. That which is missing gives us an important insight into Kurosawa's style. As we shall see, the fragmentation of screen space is the essential component of his cinema, the mark of his creative involvement and, in later films, the vehicle of his social analysis.

The propaganda element is especially strong in the film, which opens with a scene in which a brutal American sailor beats a rickshaw boy, who is rescued by Sanshirō. Richie points out that, with his stern, solemn, somewhat pompous demeanor, Sugata is displayed as the perfect wartime hero.[61] His boyish charm and childish spontaneity, so affecting in the original film, have disappeared. He has become a stick figure, scowling at Western corruption and giving a sinister American boxer a sound and symbolic thrashing.

Despite the routine nature of the production, several sequences stand out as intimations of things to come. When Sanshirō rescues the rickshaw boy, Kurosawa frames Sanshirō and the sailor as they stand parallel to a brick wall that is directly behind them. The camera is placed at a right angle to the scene, resulting in a composition of marked frontality and depth compression. This flattened image points toward the more extreme foreshortening of space Kurosawa would achieve in the 1950s. In addition, when Higaki's sulking, brutish brothers threaten Sanshirō, Kurosawa intercuts a series of medium shots in which the three characters are arranged in triangular designs, each new cut altering the occupants of the base and apex. This design anticipates the cutting of certain sections of *Rashōmon*, where angular compositions visualize the three-corner relationships among the bandit, samurai, and noblewoman.[62] Except, however, for these small occasions when Kurosawa's style may be glimpsed, the film remains an otherwise routine production.

Kurosawa's other work of this period, *They Who Tread on the Tiger's Tail* (1945), is considerably more interesting. It was shot very quickly and cheaply to satisfy a studio strapped for products. It has its immediate source material in *Kanjinchō*, a highly regarded Kabuki play, and, more distantly, in the Noh play *Ataka*. Both works dramatize an incident[63] from medieval Japan, when rival warrior clans were struggling for power and a military government was replacing the authority of the Heian Court. At the close of the twelfth century, Minamoto Yoritomo had suc-

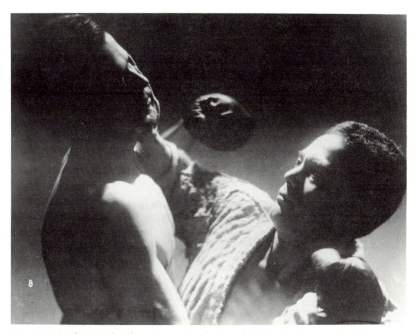

11. Serving the needs of wartime, Sanshirō symbolically thrashes the American boxer in *Sanshirō Sugata, Part II.* (R5/S8 Presents)

ceeded in consolidating power among the warrior class, and with the defeat of the rival Taira clan, the way was clear for him to assume the title of Shōgun or military ruler of Japan. His brother, Yoshitsune, had fought for him, but Yoritomo became jealous of Yoshitsune's fame and suspicious of his ties to the aristocracy. Eventually, Yoritomo came to believe that Yoshitsune was plotting to move against him and issued orders that he be captured and executed. Accompanied by a warrior-priest named Benkei, a mistress, and a few retainers, the once-proud Yoshitsune, hunted like a fugitive, fled in search of safe territory. *Kanjinchō* deals with Yoshitsune's attempt to cross a barrier manned by guards under Yoritomo's orders. In the play, he gets safely through, though in reality he was eventually cornered by Yoritomo's men. His head was taken as a present to his brother. As Sansom points out, this ugly affair has passed into legend because of its powerful symbolic value.[64] The fall of the mighty and the evanescence of glory have been favorite themes of Japanese literature and drama, and the fate of Yoshitsune—like that of the

Taira clan whom he helped defeat—has become a mythic embodiment of these themes.

Kurosawa, like other Japanese, has demonstrated a deep attraction to what Ivan Morris has termed the nobility of failure. *Seven Samurai* is the paramount exploration of the elusiveness and paradoxical nature of glory. But Kurosawa's version of the Yoritomo–Yoshitsune story does not deal at all with this cultural subtext. Indeed, he seems quite uninterested in offering a traditional reading of the fratricidal conflict. Instead, he undermines the lofty and noble tone of *Kanjinchō* by adding a comical porter (played by the popular comic Kenichi Enomoto) who accompanies Yoshitsune's party and who provides a prickly, subversive point of view on the samurai and their codes of honor.

The invasion of the sanctity of *Kanjinchō* by this alien perspective is announced immediately at the opening of the film. As in *Sanshirō Sugata*, Kurosawa uses the repetition of a formal device to heighten its effect, in this case, to establish the clash of class perspectives that structures the film. After a series of low-angle shots of trees in the imperial forest, the camera pans left to reveal a party of samurai hiking with packs on their backs. They hold themselves with dignity and travel in silence, except for a diminutive but animated porter who trots excitedly along and fires questions at them. Who are you and where are you going? he asks, and his childish laugh undermines the stately chorus that has introduced the film. The samurai do not deign to answer, and a wipe moving in their direction prepares the frame for the next shot. In it, again, the samurai are hiking silently and the porter is laughing impishly. He says they are fortunate to have such good weather for traveling. Again, no response. Another wipe, another cackle by the porter, and once more he tries to solicit a response from the men he is guiding. He taps the pack on the back of one warrior and asks what it contains. Getting no answer, he proceeds to sing, and the warrior turns and shouts at him to follow them quietly. Crestfallen, his spontaneity briefly curbed, the porter is silent. A wipe, and this time, instead of a laugh, the porter yawns very loudly with a child's aggressive boredom and bumps into the warrior in front of him.

Using the wipe as a recurrent linking device, Kurosawa has opened the film with four symmetrical vignettes describing the terms of the film's world. As an adaptation of *Kanjinchō*, this film will present the samurai with their customary dignity, but it will not be a straightforward celebration of that dignity. As he does later in *The Hidden Fortress*, Kurosawa views the world of the mighty through the eyes of the meek. After the four opening vignettes, the samurai stop to rest, and the porter climbs up on a little hillock in the middle of camp to watch them. He hops around

12. The antics of a timid, bumbling porter (Kenichi Enomoto) undercut the
historical drama of Yoshitsune's flight in *They Who Tread on the Tiger's Tail*.
(R5/S8 Presents)

on his perch, flitting a fan restlessly, and the camera pans from the porter
to the group of warriors, passing each one in turn. They sit with a rigid
composure, neither speaking nor looking at each other. The film then
cuts back to the porter perched mischievously on his hill, fidgeting and
fanning himself. We view the samurai from his point of view, mysterious
and provocative in their disciplined silence, remote and awesome in
their majesty. Movement has been used to express character. The static,
frontal groupings of the samurai, who sit facing the camera, locked into
rigid behavior patterns, are explicitly contrasted with the expansiveness
and spontaneous gestures of the porter, for whom the codes of *giri* and
bushidō are not determinative, and who is simply an observer of this
medieval drama.

The principle organizing the film's structure is made explicitly clear
when the porter spies a peculiar-looking member of the party. The porter
tells them they are traveling quickly and expresses his admiration at
their lack of fatigue, but then he sees one dressed in finery sitting apart

from the others and remarks that this one seems tired and looks different, like a girl. This last remark elicits an explosive command from the warriors to be silent. The strange member is, of course, Yoshitsune, and Kurosawa films him from the rear so that his face is mostly obscured. This compositional strategy is extended throughout the film. Yoshitsune is filmed from behind or in long shot, while the porter is frequently presented in close-up. After the porter realizes who these men are, he hides his face behind the fan in an extreme close-up, afraid to look upon their greatness. Off-screen, Yoshitsune calls Benkei (Denjirō Ōkochi), and the porter peers out from his fan but then covers his face again. Then the film cuts to a medium long shot of Yoshitsune, again filmed from behind, as he tells Benkei that the barrier will be hard to cross if the guards know they are coming.

This sequence discloses the duophonic structure of the film. Several textual voices will compete for our attention. As in the opening vignettes, a discourse on the integrity of class identity—on the dignity and nobility of the samurai—is placed in tension with a discourse celebrating the absence of class constraint, spontaneity of behavior, and the extension of emotional connection across class lines. The two voices vie with each other for control of the film, each one displacing and being displaced by the other. The filming of Yoshitsune is tentative and respecting of his stature. The lord is too great to be looked upon directly, especially by a commoner, and the framing enforces a distanced perspective by inhibiting direct access to the character. Moreover, as one voice speaks, the other discourse is effaced. Yoshitsune calls Benkei, and the porter hides his face behind the fan, withdrawing his point of view from the film, permitting the distanced framings of Yoshitsune and Benkei to communicate the values of their class uncorrupted by noise from the porter.

Later, at the barrier camp, when a guard guesses their identities, Benkei transgresses samurai codes and beats his lord, Yoshitsune (who is disguised as a commoner), in order to fool Togashi (Susumu Fujita), the commander of the guards. This event is filmed in a way that affirms established class values. The dramatic power of the play hinges on this ultimate act of fealty, in which Benkei demonstrates service to his lord in a supreme manner by doing the unthinkable, striking his commander. To really strike the lord would be too great a violation of taboo, so the horror is communicated by suggestion. Kurosawa cuts away from the event to show the porter's dismayed reaction, and by doing this he reinforces a sense of the validity of the established class norms. Ironically, it is the porter, the outsider, who tries to stop Benkei and enforce the normal coding of relationships.

The porter, however, is not generally so self-effacing. It is he who insists that a feud between two brothers is easily repaired and who, by doing so, implicitly questions the necessity for all the bloodshed that the legend accepts as fated. Once in the barrier camp, he pantomimes reactions of fear before the spears of the guards. Seeing this, Togashi laughs and remarks, "What a funny fellow." Togashi's reaction is a signifier of the compassionate nature that will lead him to permit Benkei and Yoshitsune to pass safely. This is the pivotal action of the story, and Kurosawa chooses to make the porter the vehicle for its revelation. In responding to the antics of the commoner with a similar spontaneity, Togashi's own ethical distance from the imperative to obey his lord's, Yoritomo's, commands is revealed.

But, more important, the porter's exaggerated mugging and pratfalls gradually undermine the stately pace and tone of the action. Before they reach the barrier, the samurai boast with bravado of their ability to fight their way through, and they laugh with masculine pride. The porter joins in, and his peculiar cackle defuses the martial spirit of the moment. The warriors leave him behind as they approach the barrier, and in a series of vignettes linked by wipes as in the opening, he attempts to join them, offering to help guide them to the enemy camp. One of the samurai rejects the offer, pointing out that they can't ask a commoner for favors. The porter replies that, to the samurai, he doesn't seem good enough, again adding a critical dimension to the class perspective of the film. Later, after they have all passed through the camp, Togashi sends them a gift of sake, a moment of deep solemnity in the Kabuki, which is sacralized in the film by a chorus that sings with inflated sentiment of the cup of friendship, the taste of kindness, the grail of humanity. Rather than endorse the sanctity of this moment, Kurosawa unleashes the other textual voice. The porter watches all this with an outlandish panic, gazing greedily at the sake and frantically licking his lips, afraid he will receive none, and desiring nothing so much as a good sousing.

At last, under the influence of drink, the two voices are momentarily reconciled. Benkei is thoroughly drunk, and the porter has had his share. He does an impromptu dance and collapses coyly in the lap of a beefy warrior. Everyone joins together in a hearty laugh. The porter at last is accepted, and the samurai have shown a flicker of spontaneous emotion. But this moment of relaxed class tension is as fleeting as Yoshitsune's glory, for in the next second the warrior has disdainfully dumped the porter out of his lap. Not especially upset, the porter falls asleep and wakes the next morning covered by Yoshitsune's brocade robe, a last gift from the samurai. The porter looks around: the world is empty, the warriors have departed. Their codes were felt to be oppressive by the commoner, but the world will now be a duller place without them. He does a final Kabuki dance, exiting off-screen, and the film closes, the ambiguities of class and point of view quite unresolved.[65] The two voices of the text have contested one another, but neither finally emerges as dominant. If the porter's impulsive indifference to the class hierarchy has been intended as a corrective to the constraints of the medieval class codes, it is clear that, for Kurosawa, the samurai world also represents a source of deeply compelling values. As Richie remarks, "One would not expect Kurosawa to uphold the feudal thesis of *Kanjinchō* and he does not. But neither does he denigrate it."[66] The film's own history points to this confusion: it has the odd distinction of having been attacked, first by the Japanese, for not taking the dignity of the Kabuki source seriously enough, and then later by the American occupation authorities because of its alleged glorification of feudal ideals.[67]

Despite its textual ambivalence, *They Who Tread on the Tiger's Tail* is not, finally, an especially rich film, and this may be due to the haste in which it was conceived. In contrast to *Sanshirō Sugata*, the film has a very restrained and quite static visual structure. Much of it, especially the scenes in the barrier camp, are excessively given over to what Hitchcock derisively termed pictures of people talking, and these are cut without the analytic formalism displayed in *Sanshirō Sugata*. Later, in *The Lower Depths*, Kurosawa would confine himself to one set, but there he would demonstrate that physical space in no way corresponds to cinematic space. Here, however, it very largely does. Nonetheless, a few sequences demonstrate Kurosawa's sensitivity to the coordinates of visual motion. Two have already been mentioned: the opening vignettes and the variation played upon them when the porter tries to rejoin the samurai before the barrier camp. An additional scene might be mentioned because, although it is composed merely of transitional material, it illustrates how Kurosawa translates narrative shifts into spatial dynamics. When the porter guesses the identities of Yoshitsune's party, he flees in terror to a safe distance where he can watch without fear of being speared. He dashes screen-right, and a rapid wipe follows his figure. The next frame is a medium shot of forest undergrowth with the porter's head peeking above it. The camera tracks in through the foliage to a close-up, and then a reverse-field cut presents a long shot of the samurai sitting in camp.

In this brief transition, lateral motion has been succeeded by frontal movement and by an explicit compositional conflict of scale between shots. Judged solely on its ability to furnish us with narrative information, the structure of this transition must seem excessive and unnecessary. But this is to miss the point. Narrative exists for Kurosawa as a field of spatial energy, and the act of narration is synonymous with the charging of this field. The unfolding of a narrative in Kurosawa's cinema entails the translation of time into space. Narrative time becomes spatialized, and temporal dislocations, as from scene to scene, exponentially increase the visual energy on-screen. This approach is to be distinguished from that of a filmmaker like Ozu, in whose cinema space is realized in terms of time and is fundamentally experienced as duration. For this reason, the transitions in Kurosawa's films are often moments of extraordinary visual excess, when the pictorial energy on-screen far exceeds what is strictly necessary at the narrative level.

Here lies a profound difference between Kurosawa's cinema and the model of Hollywood filmmaking to which his films are often compared.[68] A great deal of attention has been devoted in recent film scholarship to studying the cinematic codes of Hollywood filmmaking, so that what for a long time appeared as a natural or invisible style, or better as the absence of style, is now understood as a highly constructed mode of cinema.[69] The goal of this construction is to deny its own presence. The continuity system of editing worked very hard to construct films that, to a viewer, would not seem to be edited. As the name "continuity editing" indicates, the images would appear to flow continuously, without interruption or cut. A cinema that sought to hide its own forms, based on assumptions of realism or verisimilitude, necessarily implied a certain orientation to narrative and a certain relation between narrative and space. In discussing the approach of Hollywood cinema to the construction of narrative, David Bordwell points out that the clear communication of narrative information is the dominant, organizing consideration of visual design: "In making narrative causality the dominant system in the film's total form, the classical Hollywood cinema chooses to subordinate space."[70] This occurs in a variety of ways. Editing rhythms follow the flow of dialogue, and the potentially disruptive cut is stabilized through the use of eyeline matches and observance of the 180-degree rule, which works to maintain a consistent geographic orientation on-screen. Camera movement follows and is motivated by character movement. Panning is used to reframe compositional imbalances caused by a character's sudden departure from the scene, or it is employed to open a space in preparation for a character's entrance. In either case, the dynamics of Hollywood screen space are actualized by the actions of the characters and are placed in the service of communicating information about what those people are doing and why. In all, as Bordwell points out, space becomes a "container" for the characters' personalities and actions.[71]

By contrast, an extreme visual formalism prevails in Kurosawa's cinema. Editing carves up and dissects space in a perceptually disturbing manner because, for one thing, camera setups are often not repeated. In Hollywood practice, it was standard to film a scene from a minimal number of setups and to keep returning to these vantage points as the action unfolded. Kurosawa, however, does not confine the action in this manner. Many of his camera positions are unique and are not duplicated within the scene. In addition, Kurosawa rarely employs the eyeline match to unify spatial coordinates, using, instead, camera movement, which introduces a fluid, unstable perspective. Frequently, the 180-degree rule is flouted. In *Sanshirō Sugata*, for example, a cut from a long shot to a medium close-up of Shōgorō Yano crosses the axis of action with the result that Yano is shifted from screen-right to -left. In addition, the camera's angle of view is shifted from front to back. In the first shot the camera is in front of him, in the second, behind. The resulting images are discontinuous and dislocated from each other.

It is in this context that Kurosawa's frequent use of reverse-field cutting should be understood. These reverse fields are not to be confused with the shot-reverse-shot technique conventionally used by Hollywood to film conversation scenes, in which first one speaker is presented and then the other. Each camera position in the shot-reverse-shot technique remains on the same side of the axis of action, thereby maintaining consistent screen direction. But with reverse-field editing, as Kurosawa practices it, the axis of action is crossed, thereby disrupting coherent screen geography. Moreover, each field is the mirrored image of the other, as the cut shifts the field of view by precisely 180 degrees. When this type of cutting occurred in Hollywood cinema, it was strictly coded: it signified subjectivity. The reverse-field shift was meant to be read as a subjective shot, presenting a view understood as what a character was literally seeing, and it was generally introduced by a shot showing the character looking at something significant off-screen.

By contrast, reverse-field cutting in Kurosawa's cinema has no relation to subjectivity. Only once in *Sanshirō Sugata* (excepting the establishing shot that turns into a subjective shot) does he explore subjectivity in the conventional way by including a blurry reverse-field cut signifying Murai's dazed perceptions, just after Sanshirō has thrown him to the mat. But Kurosawa then goes on a moment later to discover a much better representation of subjectivity. Sanshirō throws Murai again, and as the old man struggles to get up we hear his daughter's voice saying, over and over again, that her father surely will win, as Murai, responding to the voice, tries to rise. But the source of the voice is never established. No shot informs us of her presence at the tournament, or her absence, so we do not know if the voice we hear is Murai's hallucination or if his daughter is really there among the spectators. The principle of dislocation is applied not only to the construction of the images but to the soundtrack as well.

The viewer, then, in Kurosawa's cinema, is continually being reoriented by a succession of noncontinuous spatial fields, complicating the perceptual process.[72] In addition, we have seen that his cinema foregrounds a geometry of space, with great attention given to features of linear design and a fascination for pure geometric form.[73] A sequence from *Sanshirō Sugata*, which describes a series of meetings between Sanshirō and Sayo on the steps leading up to the Shintō shrine, is an elaborate exercise in exploring the dialectics of form. A series of brief shots, linked by wipes, constitute an almost arithmetical meditation on the permutations of screen direction and angle of movement, as Kurosawa visualizes every combination of character and camera placement on the stairs and every possible arrangement of ascending and descending motion. The attraction to geometric design is especially evident toward the beginning of the sequence when Kurosawa pauses to offer a series of Ozu-like still images, which include close-ups of the umbrellas Sanshirō and Sayo carry. Sayo's fills the lower half of the screen as an abstract visual form, with upwardly curving artwork offset by the downwardly sloping arcs of its webbing. The sequence on the steps climaxes with a long shot of the stairs viewed from above, with a gate and fence in the foreground displayed as vertical elements, beyond which are the sloping diagonals of the handrails and the stable horizontals of the steps themselves.

In addition to this Eisensteinian fascination with the geometry of the image, the frequent repetition of a formal device in Kurosawa's work underscores the nature of the film as a construction. With the later additions of lenses of long focal length and multicamera filming to the technical repertoire, the formal distance between Kurosawa and Hollywood cinema would be irrevocable. This distance has also been noted by Noël Burch.[74] In his work on Japanese cinema Burch studies its general structural differences from the Hollywood product, but he feels these differences typify Japanese films of the 1920s and 1930s. He suggests that by the 1940s, after the war, Japanese film was becoming Westernized and was basing its construction on the principles of the Hollywood system. Working from this hypothesis, he states that all Kurosawa's films up to *Rashōmon* are made in accordance with the Hollywood model and show an increasing mastery of the codes of continuity cutting. Only after *Rashōmon* does a decisively non-Western cinematic aesthetic appear. We have seen abundant evidence, however, that *Sanshirō Sugata* already inaugurates a break for Kurosawa from the codes of Western cinema. Space for him is not subordinated to the narrative and does not exist as a "container" for the characters. Rather, narrative is a means toward the charging and energizing of space.

By 1945, in a very short time, then, the essential features of Kurosawa's visual patterning had begun to emerge, and they pointed to a unique and singular cinematic exploration of space. What remained unformed at this time was its application, the content that would justify this form as an exercise in filmmaking conceived as an ethical act. But the conditions that would validate Kurosawa's form were soon forthcoming. The end of the war and the devastation of the Japanese mainland gave him the meaning and the challenge his cinema needed.

3 Willpower Can Cure All Human Ailments

Japan emerged from the war with its cities burnt and uninhabitable, its industry destroyed, and its people near starvation. Massive incendiary bombings of the major cities had completely destroyed the fragile wood and paper houses and displaced the urban population. Nearly 50 percent of the housing facilities were wiped out in the 66 cities subject to attack by air.[1] "By the end of July [1945], 188,310 people had died in air raids, a quarter of a million had been wounded, and about nine million were homeless."[2]

With the destruction of the cities, much of the urban population looked to the countryside for shelter and food, but it was scarce, and by early November 1945, Japan faced a drastic shortage of rice. "Had the war continued, there would have been starvation in the urban centers of Japan during the winter of 1945–46."[3] The demand for food, and its insufficient supply, fed a voracious black market that, in turn, depleted available supplies. "The chief concern of most Japanese in the postwar period was how to avoid starvation."[4] But hunger was not the only privation. Clothing was in short supply because the country had dismantled its textile industry so that the equipment could be converted to war manufactures.[5] In addition, much of Japan's industry and nearly all its merchant shipping had been destroyed by bombing. Deprived of adequate shelter, clothing, and food, those who survived the firebombings faced a grim future.

Looking back on the disastrous military path Japan had followed, a Foreign Ministry official observed:

> For a poor country like Japan, the construction of costly warships meant a crushing burden upon the national treasury. And yet we built a good number of them. We also maintained a vast Army and an ever ex-

panding Air Force. In the end we became like the mammoth whose tusks, growing ever bigger, finally unbalanced its bodily structure. As everything went to support the huge tusks, very little was left to sustain the rest of the body. The mammoth finally became extinct.[6]

It is in this general context of physical trauma, economic collapse, and psychological defeat that Kurosawa's films of the late 1940s and early 1950s should be viewed. As we have seen, in later years Kurosawa remarked that he believed after the war that spiritual and cultural recovery was incumbent upon the adoption of social values that emphasized the individual. During the war years, the avenues for public expression or social criticism had certainly narrowed. The Peace Preservation Law, for example, passed in 1925 and revised in 1928, became an important tool in repressing the Left. The law banned any words, deeds, or writing that urged the abolition of private property or the imperial regime.[7] It provided the legal mechanism for the mass arrest of radicals by the police during the 1930s.[8]

The official state ideology during the war was formulated in terms of service to the imperial heritage, a "national polity" ("kokutai") whose origins Carol Gluck suggests should be seen as a response to the strains of modernism. Tracing policies of imperial orthodoxy, in which the Emperor was regarded as the "axis" of the nation, Gluck points to their roots in the Meiji era as an ideological effort to seal fissures in the modernizing state, where "labor disputes, like socialism, were an unmistakable sign that modern economic life engendered conflict on a large and unacceptably divisive scale."[9] "It was as if the unique glory—and the reassuring immutability—of kokutai became that much more important as the world fell away around it."[10] This official ideology during the war years became enmeshed with a resurgent anti-Westernism and antimodernism.[11] "Fundamentals of Our National Polity," published by the Ministry of Education in 1937, was designed to describe the contours of Imperial service.[12] It decried the influence of Western values centered on the worth of the individual, and it argued that socialism, communism, and social unrest were due to the influence of the misguided individualism of the West. "When people determinedly count themselves as masters and assert their egos, there is nothing but contradictions and the setting of one against the other," and this was in contrast to the Japanese Way of harmony with family and state.[13] A reawakening of devotion to the emperor was necessary to counter these harmful influences. The country was a great family, and the 'Imperial Household is the head family of the subjects and the nucleus of national life."[14] Serving the nation can be done only by overcoming individualism, by "dying to self and returning to [the] One," a process that "can never be understood from an individualistic way of thinking."[15] War is a means of bringing about, not destruction, but great harmony.[16]

The degree to which Imperial ideology penetrated the culture, and the extent of cultural and state authoritarianism during the war, are debated by scholars. Daikichi Irokawa describes allegiance to the emperor system as a kind of mass cultural blindness, "an enormous black box into which the whole nation . . . unknowingly walked."[17] Kazuo Kawai suggests that the rise of the militarists was tied to an alleged lack of a cultural tradition of individualism and social equality. "There was as yet no widespread conception either of the essential equality of all men or of the supreme worth of the individual."[18] Ben-Ami Shillony suggests, however, that there were spaces in the society where individuals and groups could remain relatively free of wartime ideological imperatives. He argues that the Japanese state during the war was not a fascist one like Nazi Germany because there was no party ideology or dictatorial leader and because the state was much less repressive and the society not totally politicized. "[S]ocial, communal, and occupational loyalties continued to exist independently of the state, and no mass party could abolish them."[19]

However authoritarian the state may have been during the war, however large the gap between "kokutai," official ideology, and actual practice, upon the nation's surrender the codes of individual behavior and the relation between the state and its citizens were subject to intense changes. The Allied Occupation of Japan resulted in a new constitution that assured basic human rights and popular, rather than Imperial, sovereignty.[20] Moreover, because of Allied suspicions of zaibatsu (big business) complicity with the militarists,[21] a program of economic reform was implemented that aimed to decentralize economic power and institute labor and land reforms as a basis for establishing the foundations of a democratic political order.[22] As economic, political, and educational reforms were implemented by American Occupation authorities, building on existing democratic traditions in Japanese politics,[23] Western social and political ideals gained a renewed pervasiveness and popularity compared with the war years. Robert Bellah notes that "The loss of the war and the beginning of the American occupation . . . precipitated a rush to the standard of 'democracy' in the Japanese intellectual world."[24] Western ideals of democracy, freedom, and individualism were the new slogans replacing those of state nationalism.[25] Shūichi Katō has suggested that this shift of attention brought with it a renewed focus upon the initial Meiji project, that is, upon the meaning of modernization and the American influences conjoined with it: "it was not until the end of the Second World War that the modernization of the country as a whole became once again one of the major concerns of Japanese intellectuals and writers. As in the Meiji period, modernization is again identified with Westernization, or more recently . . . with Americanization."[26]

Kurosawa's work is tied to these cultural shifts and to the renewed currency that Western ideals received in the immediate postwar era. In his films, he attempted to work through the crisis that the militarized nation had suffered and to point a way out of the darkness such that it could not happen again. Indeed, Tadao Satō finds the theme of suffering to be central to Kurosawa's work and to the kind of redemptive model it offered the culture during this chaotic time.

> With defeat in World War II, many Japanese, who had made the objectives of the nation their objectives in life, were dumbfounded to find that the government had lied to them and was neither just nor dependable. During this uncertain time Akira Kurosawa, in a series of first-rate films, sustained the people by his consistent assertion that the meaning of life is not dictated by the nation but something each individual should discover for himself through suffering.[27]

Kurosawa has remarked, "During the war, there was no freedom of expression. At the end of the war, I had so much to say, I was overfilled with things to say about Japan."[28] In this effort to internalize and portray a new set of values, he felt he had to work much harder than one who had known such values for a lifetime. He points out that, like most others,[29] he did not resist Japan's descent into militarism. "Unfortunately, I have to admit that I did not have the courage to resist in any positive way, and I only got by, ingratiating myself when necessary and otherwise evading censure. . . . In wartime we were all like deaf-mutes."[30]

This political passivity, however, changed after the war. Occupation reforms extended to the cinema, where, as Kyōko Hirano has pointed out in her study of the Japanese cinema under the Allied Occupation, mass media (including films) were used as part of the reform effort:

As early as September 22, 1945, the Civil Information and Education Section (CIE) of SCAP summoned representatives from each
Japanese film company, and told them that SCAP would like the
Japanese film industry to pursue the principles of the Potsdam
Declaration and help reconstruct Japan positively. At the same
time, CIE established the three principal aims of the Occupation:
complete disarmament and demilitarization of the nation; en-
couragement of individual liberties and fundamental human
rights; and directing Japan to contribute to world peace and
safety. To pursue these principles, desirable subjects and directions for films were suggested by CIE.[31]

Allied control over the Japanese cinema was exercised by way of both
censorship (prohibiting material contrary to Occupation goals) and propaganda (promoting American values).[32] Filmmakers were subject to
firm guidelines specifying what kinds of subjects would be tolerated.
Generally, films were to extoll individual freedoms and be critical of
militarism and feudalism.[33] Hirano points out that many filmmakers
and studio officials, who yesterday diligently promoted the war effort,
now performed a rapid ideological flip-flop to turn out films promoting
Occupation-style democracy.[34] The cost of this flip-flop, Hirano suggests, was a lack of genuine commitment to the new values, an ideological vagueness "about what democratic values actually are."[35] She finds
many of the postwar films made by Japanese directors under the aegis of
CIE to be curiously apolitical.

Like other filmmakers, Kurosawa rode out these changing tides, working successfully within the industry to produce several mild wartime
propaganda films (e.g., *Sanshirō Sugata, Part II* and *The Most Beautiful*),
then swiftly adjusting his cinematic vision to the changed postwar political context. Nevertheless, we need not read this move as opportunistic.
Kurosawa chafed under the constraints of wartime censorship and recalls his struggles with the Japanese censors with intense bitterness.[36]
Furthermore, the emergence of his mature cinematic talent occurred during the Occupation period. Beginning in the postwar years, Kurosawa's
cinema acquired a depth and power that are simply not present in the
works produced under wartime constraint. A happy congruence of circumstance linked his artistic temper with the turbulence of Occupied
Japan and an atmosphere in which he felt free, at last, to speak. Ironically, CIE's guidelines and the energy for social reform that lay behind
them helped establish a context in which Kurosawa's postwar cinema

could thrive and in which he could express his visions of the new Japan. The shock of the war and defeat seemed to create a cultural opening in which new alternatives could be considered. "The Japan of August 1945 appeared to some extent to be a tabula rasa both physically and ideologically; and for a time the country was undoubtedly in an extremely receptive state so far as outside influences were concerned."[37] Although one must doubt the extent to which native cultural traditions could simply be erased, as the metaphor of a tabula rasa would seem to require, the imagery is nevertheless suggestive for Kurosawa's cinema because the evidence of the work indicates an attempt to inscribe a new set of values and messages upon the culture. Desser suggests that Kurosawa was faced with "the task of making films whose themes and subjects could be seen to be appropriate propaganda for the United States' desire to demilitarize and defeudalize Japanese attitudes" and that Kurosawa's strategy was "to adapt Western modes in a deliberate manner so as to explore the nature of Western ideals as they impact upon Japan."[38] Kurosawa has clearly scrutinized his own culture by way of the West. But rather than viewing his films of this period as simply carrying out the reformist policies of SCAP, we would do well to recall that Kurosawa's pre-Occupation films—*Sanshirō Sugata* and *They Who Tread on the Tiger's Tail*— exhibit the strong, quirky individual characters and the ambivalent, even critical view of established normative patterns that MacArthur's reforms later incarnated. Keeping that in mind, then, it should be noted that Kurosawa welcomed the changed political climate and sought to fashion films that would be responsive to it, but in doing so, he was able to find his own mature cinematic voice: "The freedom and democracy of the post-war era were not things I had fought for and won, they were granted to me by powers beyond my own. As a result, I felt it was all the more essential for me to approach them with an earnest and humble desire to learn, and to make them my own."[39]

Kurosawa's films of this period are explicit attempts to dramatize the spiritual and the psychological dilemmas that the country faced in the aftermath of militarism. As Tadao Satō has pointed out, Kurosawa's films suggested that "Japan's recovery from defeat did not have to be only an economic one."[40] Kurosawa tried to visualize the moral and social contours of national recovery in the very moment of its unfolding. In the films of this period, history would be understood in moral terms, as a structure of events presenting his protagonists with a range of choices. This range of choice signified the space of their freedom and, in the type of response chosen, symbolized the future course of national development. In short, Kurosawa's was an unabashedly didactic cinema that, in its union of ethics and aesthetics, attempted to use art as a mode of instruction. Zeami had proclaimed that his Noh theater would "serve to praise the Buddha and provide the means to spread his teachings, will chase away evil affinities, and will call forth happiness, so that the country will remain in tranquillity, bringing gentleness and long life to the people."[41] Kurosawa's cinema belongs to such a practice, wherein art is treated as the vehicle of enlightenment. He relates an incident during the filming of *Rashōmon* when, at the completion of location shooting at the Kōmyōji temple forest, the abbot of the temple gave him a folding fan as a gift in tribute to the crew's hard work. On the fan were inscribed the words "Benefit All Mankind." Kurosawa says, "I was left speechless."[42]

In carrying out such a task, the works of the immediate postwar era belong to the heroic mode of Kurosawa's cinema. This chapter is concerned with the structure of that mode and its gradual articulation, the contradictions that articulation entailed, and its culmination in Kurosawa's first masterpiece, *Ikiru*. All these works are attempts to construct a cinema connected to its topical moment. Even the weakest films of this period—*One Wonderful Sunday* (1947), *The Quiet Duel* (1949), and *Scandal (1950)*—are all interpenetrated by the exigencies of wartime collapse and the emergence of a new Japan. By contrast with the other, tumultuous works of this era, these three films have a placid surface that is marked by a general absence of radical formal experimentation. *One Wonderful Sunday* chronicles the alternately whimsical and despairing adventures of two lovers as they wander through the city, pitting their fantasies against the disturbing presence of war orphans and ruined buildings. Buffeted by misfortune, the young woman cries out that she would die without her dreams. The couple becomes depressed by their poverty and the ruined surroundings, but their spirits are rescued by an imaginary symphony (Schubert's Unfinished) that the young man conjures in an empty outdoor auditorium. As he pantomimes the motions of a conductor, the imaginary music appears on the soundtrack, heard by the characters in the film and the audience watching it. Its affirmation of the power of dreams to counter dispiriting realities points toward the obsessions of *Dodeskaden* (1970) and contrasts greatly with the other works of this period, which caution against policies of escape.[43]

The Quiet Duel visualizes the war as a corrosive, invasive agent, the effects of which are felt long after hostilities cease. Toshirō Mifune plays a surgeon who contracts syphilis while operating on an infected patient at the front, and the remainder of the film studies his efforts to isolate

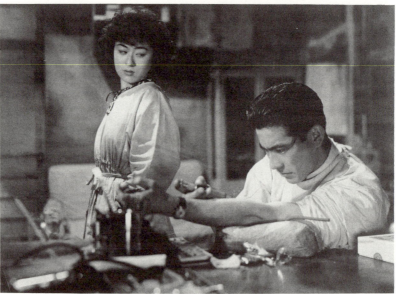

13. and 14. (Top) Dreams of their own coffee shop cheer an impoverished couple, amid the postwar rubble. *One Wonderful Sunday*. (Bottom) Disease as a social metaphor: a young doctor (Toshirō Mifune) battles syphilis in postwar Japan. *The Quiet Duel*. (Museum of Modern Art/Film Stills Archive)

himself from those who love him and to eradicate the infection. Although the presentation of the hospital clinic includes many incidents and characters that would receive their consummate expression in *Red Beard*, the situation is essentially melodramatic in that it depends on Mifune *not* telling others of his condition. This melodrama displaces the implicit metaphor of the war as disease, and the metaphor does not receive the kind of elaborate treatment that distinguishes *Drunken Angel* and *Stray Dog*.

Scandal attempts to criticize the sensationalistic reporting of lurid newspapers, one of which falsely reports a sexual liaison between a well-known artist and a singer. Kurosawa felt that such abuse of power by the press was symptomatic of the postwar obsession with freedom of speech.[44] These issues, however, are never really explored. Most of the film concentrates on the corrupt lawyer Hiruta (Takashi Shimura), his tubercular daughter, and his last-minute act of moral redemption. As Richie observes, "When the lawyer enters he takes over the picture."[45] The psychological focus on Hiruta tends to undermine Kurosawa's desire to expose the injustices of yellow journalism, and he has acknowledged that the film developed in a direction he had not intended.[46] The imagery of *Scandal* is, for Kurosawa, amazingly pedestrian, but this may be in reaction to the formal energy of *Stray Dog* (1949), the film that preceded it and which Kurosawa felt was too full of "technique."[47]

These three films are perhaps best viewed as necessary mediocrities, productions that enabled Kurosawa to relax between the rigors of the major works, *No Regrets for Our Youth* (1946), *Drunken Angel* (1948), *Stray Dog* (1949), and *Ikiru* (1952).

No Regrets for Our Youth, Kurosawa's first film of the postwar period, is directly concerned with the process of cultural transformation. It "takes the problem of the self as its theme."[48] It launches the works of this period by offering a heroine who, in a dogged search for meaning in her life, breaks with the class and gender roles assigned to her. Yukie (Setsuko Hara) is the daughter of a university professor, schooled, as a marriageable bourgeois woman, in the arts of the piano and flower-arranging. But she chafes at the inert and passive life that awaits her and seeks a principled outlet for her passions and strengths. She initially finds this in one of her father's students, Noge (Susumu Fujita), who is active in left-wing movements fighting Japan's drift toward war. The film charts two transformations, the nation's plunge into militarism and Yukie's ascent to the strength of self that enables her to endure privation and to sustain a principled commitment to a community. Noge is impris-

15. The corrupt lawyer Hiruta (Takashi Shimura) and his victim (Toshirō Mifune). *Scandal.* (Museum of Modern Art/Film Stills Archive)

oned for his leftist activities and dies mysteriously in his jail cell. Yukie, now on her own, determines to join Noge's parents in their poor village, where she works and lives as a peasant, dedicating herself to improving the farmers' living conditions. Her desertion of family and class background to assist a poor village, her perseverance in the face of enormous obstacles, her assumption of responsibility for her own life and for the well-being of others, and her existential loneliness once she is severed from her family, friends, husband, and class—all these qualities are essential to Kurosawan heroism and make of Yukie the first coherent expression of that example.

The film was inspired by a well-known incident in which Yukitoki Takigawa, a university professor, was dismissed from his post for allegedly leftist thought. The character of Noge is modeled on Hotsumi Ozaki, who was arrested and executed as a spy during the war. Intensifying the political background of the film, it was shot during a series of strikes at Tōhō studios in the immediate postwar period, at a time when left-wing movements were resurgent, buoyed by prestige accruing from their opposition to militarism before the war and by the Occupation's initially lenient labor policies.[49] As a symptom of this background, the film offers an acute and pointed evocation of the nation's embrace of militarism. As Kyōko Hirano has discussed, however, the film's politics are ambiguous and muted.[50] Noge's precise antiwar activities are not specified, and he keeps them a secret from Yukie, who does not carry on his work after his death. Despite the charismatic leftist Noge, who is a central character, *No Regrets for Our Youth* can hardly be said to be a politically acute, or even a Marxist, work. Instead, its passionate drama reflects the heated atmosphere of its time, and following Noge's death, the narrative substitutes Yukie's apolitical participation in peasant life for his antiimperialist struggle. Indeed, rather than a politically focused work, Hirano finds the film to be an embodiment of general CIE film policies. Its plot is constructed so as to emphasize a number of the Occupation's reform programs: highlighting characters who stood for political freedom, the emancipation of women, and agrarian reform.[51] Indeed, so emblematic of SCAP reforms does Hirano find the film to be, and so well received was it by the Occupation authorities, that she suggests the idea for its production may even have come from CIE, though Kurosawa disagrees.[52]

No Regrets for Our Youth is the only Kurosawa film with a woman at its center, the only work in which he offers heroism with a female face (excepting *The Most Beautiful*, in which the characters exist as little more than sketches).[53] Yukie's responses to her stifling middle-class environment are handled with great compassion, and her transformation from bourgeois woman to peasant is rendered with reference to cultural codes of physical beauty.[54] Yukie exchanges her soft blouses and makeup for coarse farm clothing and assumes a ruddy complexion. Kurosawa dissolves a shot of her gentle, delicate hands playing the piano into a shot of those same hands, coarsened and roughened by rice planting, making explicit the class component that constructs the codes of beauty and physical deportment. Discussing this imagery and these contrasts, Joan Mellen has noted that Yukie as a peasant is a far more vibrant and compellingly beautiful woman than as the soft and rather pampered professor's daughter.[55] Kurosawa, however, would never again extend such attention to a female character in his cinema. In all future works, the protagonists would be men, and the kind of philosophical and dramatic issues that would attract Kurosawa would be unrelated to issues of male–female relations. Indeed, one is struck by how asexual Kurosawa's films are. Their almost complete lack of interest in erotic matters aligns them somewhat with adolescent masculine fantasies, in which adventure always takes precedence over eros. Kurosawa's is a world of men, and his interests are not piqued by the sexuality or the psychology of men and women in relation to each other. In this respect, *No Regrets for Our Youth* does not explore differences of gender identity so much as it merely extends the social roles and narrative functions usually assumed by men in his cinema to a woman. Unlike a male-oriented director like Sam Peckinpah, Kurosawa is not hostile to women, but his general lack of interest in them should be regarded as a major limitation of his work.

No Regrets for Our Youth offers the initial definition of Kurosawan heroism, but this is worked out almost entirely as a matter of content and is expressed through the actors' performances. In general (excepting a notably "jump-cut" sequence), the film lacks the clashing images Kurosawa brought to *Sanshirō Sugata* and would extend in later films. Despite its dramatic excellence and the heartfelt quality of the performances, the film is without the formal energy of his best work, and this may be due to his disappointment at having to film from a script that was revised against his wishes.[56] The contest between the individual and the culture driving his work entailed a confrontation of structures, of medieval and modern, of East and West, and the aesthetic transformation of these structures. The language of Kurosawa's films had to learn to speak this transformation. In doing so, future films would search in greater detail for the shape and nature of the self that would help the cause of national recovery and for the cinematic forms that would be appropriate imaginative groundings for this new individual.

With *Drunken Angel* (1948), one of his most celebrated works, Kurosawa felt, at last, that he had come into his own as a director.[57] In this film, he is explicitly engaged in the tasks of postwar reconstruction and the corresponding search for appropriate cinematic forms. He has set his characters and narrative in the midst of a desolate and ruined Japan, where the buildings are blasted shells and the black market thrives.[58] As a film that chronicles the realities of wartime collapse, *Drunken Angel* has often been compared with the work of the Italian neorealists, yet this comparison is misleading since the neorealists stressed the importance of a recessive style, the imperative for the filmmaker to interfere with the materials of the film as little as possible. The essential truths of a film's subject were to emerge by way of unmediated observation.[59] The sequence in *Open City* where Rossellini cuts from Anna Magnani's remark about the proximity of the Allied forces to a shot of a bombed building is a rare instance of stylistic intervention and the use of editing to make an editorial point. This kind of manipulation, infrequent in neorealist

16. Yukie (Setsuko Hara) before her transformation, as a privileged professor's daughter. *No Regrets for Our Youth*. (Museum of Modern Art/Film Stills Archive)

films, is very common in *Drunken Angel*. The film is filled with objects treated as explicit symbols, a character who functions in a purely theatrical manner to signal narrative shifts, and the familiar use of repetition to heighten the presence of a structural device. In short, though it responds to the same general circumstances, *Drunken Angel* should not be regarded as a film in the neorealist manner. Style is simply too important to Kurosawa for him to attempt to hide it. Moreover, he is not concerned with explicitly working-class realities, as were De Sica and Rossellini. The problems his characters grapple with are larger than life in the manner of Dostoevsky—spiritual and symbolic crises rather than such deliberately mundane issues as the theft of a bicycle.

In the film Kurosawa studies the relationship between a diseased gangster and a doctor working in the slums of a destroyed city. Through the dynamics of this relationship Kurosawa attempts to describe a new ethic for Japan and the shape of a new social order. The narrative—and the film itself—is dominated by a huge sump, a filthy cesspool into which the urban residents dump their garbage and which becomes "the center of the film, its core."[60] It bubbles viciously, and in its mire are stuck pieces of wood, a bicycle, an umbrella, a child's toy. The imagery of the sump provides the structuring principle of the film. The narrative and the characters keep returning to it, and the efforts of the doctor to cure the gangster of tuberculosis are as much an attempt to free him of the destructive codes of a corrupt and ruined world. "Your lung's like this place," Sanada (Takashi Shimura), the doctor, tells Matsunaga (Toshirō Mifune), and the image cuts to a close-up of the festering pool. The wartime destruction of society provides both the hope for regeneration as well as the near impossibility of accomplishing it. The remarkable quality of *Drunken Angel* is its ability to sustain this tension, its suspension of the hope for recovery within an encompassing and tragic vision of its foredoomed nature.

In the first sequence Kurosawa lays bare his narrative geometry, the causal laws that will form and shape his story. As the credits end, a close-up shows the sump with the lights of the city reflected on its fetid surface. A medium shot of three women follows, and as they leave the frame, a guitar player is revealed in the background. The camera then tilts down from the guitarist to the pool and begins to track along its surface as the city is once more mirrored in its waters. The track is interrupted by a cut to a shot of two members of Matsunaga's gang, as one complains about all the mosquitoes that swarm near the water. A cut then takes us inside Sanada's office, where Matsunaga has come to have a bullet removed from his hand.

This opening sequence, as often happens in Kurosawa's films, has illustrated in purely visual terms the essential narrative structure. The coordinates of the film have been defined: the sump, mosquitoes, and criminality. Mosquitoes breed in the cesspool and linger about, as do the hookers we have seen, and "they come out when he plays," as Sanada observes about the guitarist. The musician is a formal device, a character who serves to signify transitional moments in the narrative. The camera returns to him in a long shot or tracks across the sump to reveal his presence. He plays when Matsunaga comes to Sanada in a drunken plea for help, and his playing signals the return from prison of Okada, Matsunaga's boss, a character who, like Sanada, lays claim to Matsunaga's soul, but with the intent of destroying it.

The action and the characters are circumscribed by the proximity of the sump, to which the camera repeatedly connects them. These linking shots demonstrate Kurosawa's affection for the repetition of a formal device, but they also describe the terms of the moral equation that the film lays out. An elaborate linkage is established, first for Miyo, Sanada's nurse, and then later for Matsunaga, and the connection is appropriate because both are characters Sanada is trying to reform. He has taken Miyo, who is Okada's wife, as his nurse and has cared for the woman and helped heal her emotional scars while Okada was in prison. Miyo worries, however, about Okada's return and often suggests that she should go to him. This precipitates a fight with Sanada one evening at dinner, and Kurosawa ends the scene with a slow track away from Miyo, past the shōji screen, out to and across the sump. The track is interrupted by a dissolve back to Miyo, but then another dissolve returns us to the sump, and the track resumes, ending with a tilt up to the guitar player. The images have suspended, and defined, Miyo in terms of an iconography of decay. The same visualization is repeated with Matsunaga. When he finally submits to Sanada for treatment and collapses on the floor in a drunken stupor, the camera tracks past him to the pool outside and tilts up to the guitar player (and to Okada who appears a moment later). Both Matsunaga and Miyo, the victims of Okada and of the postwar world, are bound by linking movements to the film's central symbol of postwar collapse. The camera constrains their freedom of action by patterns of movement that confine them in a narrow and malignant space. Later, when he meets Okada, just back from prison, Matsunaga is standing by the sump, and Okada's shadow, announcing his entrance, appears first on the surface of the pool and then falls across Matsunaga.

The film, then, traces a series of movements and describes a pattern of imagery that has the pool as its center. Richie sees these tracking shots as describing cause-and-effect—the sump and sickness—but the imagery is more multitextured, and the social realities to which it points more intricate than a metaphor of linear causation can express.[61] We should consider more precisely the symbology of the sump and how this structures the relationship between Sanada and Matsunaga, for the pool is a contradictory signifier, and this ambivalence drives the film. The film takes its rhythm from a series of meetings between Sanada and Matsunaga, which are heralded, and then closed, by shots of the sump. The doctor wants to cure the gangster of his tuberculosis, but this is to be more than a physical cure. As in Ikiru and Red Beard, the illness of an individual functions as a metaphor for a more general social and spiritual sickness.[62] The doctor tells the young gangster that men living as he does get tuberculosis easily, and Sanada is referring to more than the condition of his lungs. He examines Matsunaga yet continually offers a gloomy diagnosis, saying that he cannot last much longer and is beyond hope. These remarks enrage Matsunaga, and the narrative dynamics are sparked by the sustained

17. Matsunaga (Toshirō Mifune) struggles with Sanada (Takashi Shimura), the doctor who wishes to cure his diseased body and spirit in Kurosawa's allegorical *Drunken Angel*. (Museum of Modern Art/Film Stills Archive)

tensions, the clashes and brawls of these characters as they meet, argue, fight, separate, and obsessively seek each other out once more.

Sanada's apparently gratuitous and insulting remarks are actually a kind of instruction. In Sanada's relationship to Matsunaga, Kurosawa is defining the first really important master–pupil relationship in his cinema that incorporates a social critique. The doctor's ethical instruction proceeds by way of moral and emotional shock, by confronting Matsunaga with his own mortality and insisting that he face it. In this, his instruction is like that of the Zen masters who would bang their pupils on the head with a log if they gave the wrong answer. Sanada repeatedly taunts Matsunaga with his imminent death because the gangster denies his fear with a front of bravado and swagger (which Kurosawa portrays satirically—he does not take gangsters seriously).

A clue to the importance of the imperative for Matsunaga to confront his illness comes when Sanada extracts the bullet from his hand. Sanada brutally clamps the wound open without anaesthetic while he probes and cleans the damaged tissue. Matsunaga cries out that he needs an anaesthetic, but Sanada refuses to give him one. This is Kurosawa's prescription for postwar Japan: a direct confrontation with social illness and the courage to take the remedy straight, without anaesthetic. It is, as well, the general moral stance of his cinema and a command Kurosawa personally experienced in his own life. After the great Kantō earthquake in 1923, he and his brother, Heigo, went to view the destruction. Confronted with mountains of grotesque, decaying corpses, his brother told him, "If you shut your eyes to a frightening sight, you end up being frightened. If you look at everything straight on, there is nothing to be afraid of."[63] But what, exactly, is it that Sanada wants Matsunaga to face?

The gangster defiantly tells the doctor that he doesn't want to be saved, that everyone has to die. Matsunaga's resignation to fate and death is precisely what Sanada struggles to overcome. He tells Matsunaga that he wants to cure him but can't when he's dead and cremated. Sanada's challenge to Matsunaga is to discard this passivity, to have the courage to change, to get well, and this is a message intended for all Japanese in the postwar period. But in order to recover, Matsunaga will have to leave the yakuza (gangster) world because that world incarnates a stock of behavior inappropriate to modern life. The codes of the yakuza enforce a hierarchical model of human relationships, founded on notions of obligation and sacrifice, that is consistent with a contractual, perhaps even feudal, conception of human relationships. The Occupation authorities apparently thought so. The Supreme Commander for Allied Powers considered the black market social organization, which involved a system of reciprocal obligations and rights between superior and subordinate gang members, a threat to the democratic program of the Occupation since these relations were thought to be "feudalistic."[64] Through its caustic portrayal of such relationships, embodied in the Matsunaga–Okada pairing, *Drunken Angel* sets out a thoroughgoing social critique that earlier films like *Sanshirō Sugata* and *They Who Tread on the Tiger's Tail* could not bring off. As Kurosawa said, he wanted to "take a scalpel and dissect the yakuza."[65]

Matsunaga, obligated to his boss Okada, has been managing the gang's territory while Okada was in prison. When he walks through town, shopkeepers bow to him and offer him free goods. When Matsunaga enters a bar to converse with Sanada, everyone else leaves, and the crowd watches Matsunaga with awe from outside the window. Matsunaga loves his place atop the local hierarchy, but his obligations to the yakuza world will kill him as surely as his tuberculosis. The bullet in the hand was just a warning. Okada's command to drink in celebration of his return is contrary to Sanada's warning to avoid liquor, and the drunken night of revelry that follows precipitates a hemorrhage that nearly finishes Matsunaga.

While under Sanada's care, Matsunaga is visited by Okada, who demands to know why he is there. Matsunaga answers that he is indebted to Sanada for the health care, which precipitates an angry outburst from the doctor, who tells him to forget about debts and act like a patient. Sanada rages not only against the sump and the tuberculosis it breeds, but also against the retrograde codes of duty, debt, and obligation that strangle characters like Matsunaga and Miyo. After Okada's visit, Miyo is restless and is about to return to him, but Sanada warns her not to, saying bitterly that the Japanese like to punish themselves with petty sacrifices. In place of her traditional, submissive response, Sanada insists on Miyo's right to determine her own life and to decide whether *she* wants to live with Okada.

Sanada told Matsunaga earlier that he had come to him out of kindness. Stop being proud, come and see me, Sanada had said. The antidote for tuberculosis is not simply a matter of medicine but requires finding a new way of acting that is not structured by formal hierarchies and forgetting about pride, indebtedness, and all the rest of the traditional baggage. "Willpower can cure all human ailments," Sanada proclaims to his patients. This willpower refers to a new set of social codes, and the film urges their necessity by dramatizing how destructive the old ways are. For Matsunaga's fate is not cure but death, and he goes to his extinction out of concern over his reputation. He loses his honor when Okada finally seizes his territory, and against Sanada's wishes he leaves the clinic and provokes a showdown with Okada. During the fight, he is knifed and dies alone, leaving Sanada, in the film's coda, to rage with frustration over the senselessness of his death.

The film's critique of outmoded behavioral codes is strikingly visualized in this fight. It is filmed with baroque angles as the grappling men pant with exhaustion and grimace wildly with fear. The fight is awkward and ugly, especially so when they upset a can of paint and slide grotesquely on the slippery floor, trying to inflict death while escaping their own. Kurosawa carefully avoids creating images or music that would glorify the fight or add a falsely noble drama, as he does in the final encounter between Sanshirō Sugata and Higaki. Instead, he films it as a tragic and repellent affair, as Matsunaga, splattered with white paint like a clown, dies a pitiful and lonely death.

Earlier, Sanada's housekeeper asked if Matsunaga had any parents, and the gangster snarled in reply that he had no such things. Bereft of parents and the ties to the past that they signify, dislocated by the upheavals of the war, enjoying American jazz and Western-style night-clubs, Matsunaga represents the emergent generation of Japanese youth, cut off from the past yet bound by the terms of its behavior and the compulsion of its social rituals. In this sense, the imagery of the sump to which Matsunaga is continually linked describes the ambivalence of the film. For, on the one hand, the sump is associated with the self-sacrificial, and suicidal, codes of the yakuza. Matsunaga's relation to Okada is bound by the same terms of fealty as that between a samurai and his lord. When, at the end, Matsunaga comes to kill Okada, both men are linked by a long, slow dissolve to the sump. Yet, on the other hand, the sump also represents a historically novel form of corruption, a newly emergent cultural degradation. Early in the film, Kurosawa cuts from a close-up of the pool to a shot of a loudspeaker blaring Western jazz. The social chaos and confusion that the film documents are due not only to the recent bombings and the widespread disease but also to the gaudy, neon-lit night-clubs that blight the landscape and fill the air with raucous music. When Okada first appears in the film, he is framed so that the bright sign of the "No. 1" dance hall is visible just beyond his shoulder.

This is the club Matsunaga will visit with Okada during the night that ends in hemorrhage. As Matsunaga, drunk, slumps half-dead in his seat, a jazz band starts to play, and Kurosawa, emulating Busby Berkeley, uses an elaborate crane shot to move into a close-up of the band's singer (Shizuko Kasagi, a popular singer of the period whose exaggerated bodily swaying was emblematic of the more liberal postwar atmosphere). He then cuts back to Matsunaga, semi-conscious, as the music blares. Borrowing syntax from the American cinema, Kurosawa stages a self-consciously "musical" sequence to comment on the Americanization of Japan. More interestingly, by cutting back and forth from Matsunaga, half-dead, to the band, he suggests that this disturbance of the indigenous culture is killing Matsunaga as much as the tuberculosis. The very codes of the Western cinema become signifiers of corruption and of Matsunaga's fall from power (and life). If the sump is the source of the disease, it is linked to another disease, pernicious foreign influences and the loss of Japanese culture during and after the American Occupation. Although American music was popular before the war, Kurosawa uses American boogie-woogie to portray the yakuza and to evoke a con-

fused and frenetic cultural atmosphere. As viewed in the film, these influences have disturbed the landscape nearly as much as the bombings
have, and although Kurosawa seeks to soften the brutal yakuza network
of honor and obligation by creating a safe space for the individual (visualized in terms of Sanada's clinic, which shelters the wounded psyches
of Miyo and Matsunaga), he does not do so by embracing the culture of
the West. Its presence in this film, as in many of the later works, is felt as
poisonous.

Drunken Angel is a film about a double loss of identity. One loss the
film urges as progressive. This is Sanada's effort to cure Matsunaga of his
resignation and passivity before death and the yakuza culture. This loss
implies the necessity of forging a new sense of self, of separating from
social customs and institutions in which the individual is a subordinate
appendage of family, clan, or nation. But the price of this necessary separation is isolation and loneliness. Sanada is a poor doctor working in the
slums, and, when he meets his old classmate Takahama, who drives a car
and carries a gilt cigarette case, he sees the doctor he might have become
had he used the profession for its profit-making potential. Matsunaga
says he doesn't like doctors. They are always lying to make money. But
Sanada speaks wistfully of being too old to change and thinks of the
money he might have made. He is an isolated member of his profession,
but his anonymous work in the slums is endorsed by the film as the
honorable course. The codes of established society clearly will not do
because they harm and oppress the individual, yet an alternate set of
codes has not yet emerged. In the meantime, Kurosawa insists that his
heroes take their stand, alone, against tradition and battle for a better
world, even if the path there is not clear. Separation from a corrupt social
system in order to alleviate human suffering, as Sanada does, is the only
honorable course.

Yet this course is complicated by a larger, national schizophrenia constituting a second erosion of self. This schizophrenia is the result of the
Americanization of Japan. *Drunken Angel* describes a world out of kilter
and control, suffering the devastation of bombs and cultural imports.
"The period immediately following the end of war was marked by social,
cultural, economic, political, and religious confusion. . . . [People] were
bewildered at the loss of direction and meaning in life, for they sensed
that the Japan they had known was crumbling before their eyes."[66] During a later sequence when Matsunaga, dying and abandoned by his yakuza friends, huddles by the sump, Kurosawa films him with a series of
extremely fragmentary and destabilized compositions that recall Eisen-

18. Matsunaga falls under the influence of the gang boss, Okada. *Drunken Angel.* (Museum of Modern Art/Film Stills Archive)

stein's montages of graphic design within the frame. Matsunaga leans against a collapsed post to form a harsh diagonal in the frame, and Kurosawa then reverses the orientation of this diagonal by a series of reverse-field cuts and alternating, oblique camera angles. These compositions describe a world that is skewed and wildly off-center, and the camera's perspective reels in a drunken fashion.

The film cries out angrily, in the person of Sanada, against a defeatest mentality and a tolerance for the black market and the criminality rife in postwar Japan, and it urges that Japanese have the courage to change, as Sanada tries to get Matsunaga to do. But change to what? The film offers no effective alternative. Sanada is effectively vanquished by Okada, whose world reclaims Matsunaga and executes him, and the postwar landscape itself confuses and undermines a sense of direction. Matsunaga has internalized these contradictions, embodying the fragmentation of the new and its culture. During the fight with Okada, Kurosawa frames Matsunaga in a three-paneled mirror, splitting and reduplicating his image. Matsunaga can only die, poisoned by the sump and postwar Japan, yet bound to the old ways and unable to free himself of them. He is doubly trapped and murdered, by the future as well as the past. That past is clearly foreclosed. The war has wiped it out. Yet the future is dark, too, for the raucous nightclubs can offer no solace. There is only the limited hope that, through willpower and the moral courage to face social contradictions, one may prevail and a direction for the future be found.

The film has been powerfully involved in its social moment, its critique far more passionate than the serene, earlier works. Nevertheless, Kurosawa has come to an impasse. His hero, Sanada, has been defeated, and Matsunaga, now ashes in an urn, has been linked to the sump for a last time when a bar-girl who loved him pauses with his ashes by the pool before leaving the city. Unable to find a way out of this dilemma, Kurosawa wishes his way through. One of Sanada's patients, now cured, visits him, and the doctor, cheered by this success, walks off with her into the crowds of postwar Japan, proclaiming once more that willpower can cure all human ailments. As they disappear into the crowd, the camera cranes up and back, and Fumio Hayasaka's music swells triumphantly. Yet one feels it is the sump that has had the last word.

Despite Sanada's rage for personal and social reform and his brute determination to mollify the condition of a world controlled by the yakuza, all the doctor can do at the end is to comment bitterly, and without real conviction, that Matsunaga was not worth saving. He mutters that hoodlums end that way, as a harsh wind stirs the murky waters of the sump. Kurosawa's is an essentially tragic vision of life, and this sensibility upsets the moral equilibrium of the film and impedes his efforts to realize a socially committed mode of filmmaking. Kurosawa has indicated an awareness of the structural weaknesses of the film, although he attributes these weaknesses to the intense presence of Toshirō Mifune (in his first work for the director). He feels Mifune's performance as the gangster overshadowed Takashi Shimura's work as the doctor, who was to have been the central character.[67] This account of Mifune overpowering the director, however, is not fully supported by the finished film because Shimura's doctor is an equally memorable character and just as powerful. More important, Kurosawa would continue to pair the two actors together in subsequent films, often with Shimura in the role of the master and teacher. Throughout the first half of Kurosawa's career, Shimura's performances very often provide the moral center of the films (*Drunken Angel, Stray Dog, Scandal, Rashōmon, Ikiru, Seven Samurai*) until he is eclipsed by Mifune in the mid-1950s, beginning with *Record of a Living Being*. The gentleness and compassion that Shimura projects are central to the moral dialogue of these films, and this was never fully recovered after the displacement by Mifune. Mifune's presence in many of the later films is superhuman, unlike Shimura's, and the aggrandizing of this presence is a symptom that the stakes in the battles are higher and the attendant anxieties over the fate of Kurosawa's project are greater.

The structural imbalances and thematic vagueness of *Drunken Angel*, then, may be due to other factors than Kurosawa's inability to control Mifune on their first outing. They are due, I would suggest, to an essential darkness within Kurosawa's outlook, a darkness held in delicate suspension throughout this early portion of his career but which emerges with great power later on. *Drunken Angel* is a film of spatial and narrative confinement in which the images and events obsessively center on the symbol of the sump. The lotus pond of *Sanshirō Sugata*, place of enlightenment, has in the postwar world become this source of malignancy. The action occurs in only a few locations—Sanada's clinic and the surrounding bars—that are proximal to the sump. This rigorous visual and narrative restriction generates the central thematic question posed by the film: how may good people and a humane ethic, that is, a path toward recovery, emerge within such terrible postwar conditions?

The film is simply not able to answer this question. It is a film of anger and blind optimism. "Willpower" must prevail. *Drunken Angel* poses the question basic to the director's postwar project, yet it cannot find the answer and thereby imperils the effort. In a film made the following year, Kurosawa confronts this impasse again, but this time he is able to suggest a way through. *Stray Dog* portrays the struggle to create a viable postwar social ethic and shows explicitly what is the personal cost of implementing such an ethic. Kurosawa communicates, and locates, these issues within the familiar formulas of a genre picture. The film's focus on social crime was shaped by Kurosawa's affection for the detective novels of Georges Simenon, which, like this film, transform familiar genre formulas into intense psychological dramas.[68] *Stray Dog* is a police thriller about the search by dedicated cops for the "stray dog" of the title, a robber and murderer who is leaving a trail of suffering in his path. Kurosawa would return again in *High and Low* to this formula because he finds that in this genre he can draw a composite portrait of society. As the detectives search for the criminal, a cross-sectional view of Japan emerges. In contrast to the formal confinement of *Drunken Angel*, *Stray Dog* is an expansive film, which takes as its subject postwar Japan and becomes a kind of epic of national reconstruction. The action is set amid grimy bars, tenements, nightclubs, flophouses, amusement parks, train stations, restaurants, and hotels during a blazingly hot summer when

19. Competing visual tensions in *Stray Dog*. While Satō (Takashi Shimura) questions a witness, two geisha set off a sparkler in the corner of the frame. (Museum of Modern Art/Film Stills Archive)

dirt, poverty, and unemployment mix with sweat and anger to ignite acts of murder.

Stray Dog is a visually restless film. Kurosawa fills the frames during the scenes in the nightclubs and dance halls with a kind of von Sternberg-like clutter, as nets, hanging plants, gauze, and stairways obscure the view and characters have to negotiate their way through these obstacles. Frequently, he will place in the frame subtle visual distractions that draw our eye away from the thread of the narrative. As Richie notes, "The screen is continually fluttering with the motion of fans, folded newspapers."[69] The flutter of these fans, mechanical and hand-held, creates an undercurrent of visual energy that is omnipresent. During one scene where a policeman interrogates the madam of a geisha house, two women set off a sparkler in the lower right corner of the frame, and the detective's words must compete with its shower of light.

This visual restlessness is also manifest in the alternation of rapidly cut montage sequences with scenes shot in a single long take. This results in a dynamic push-and-pull quality that characterizes the entire film.[70] This may be clearly seen by analyzing the opening two sequences, the first of which is a montage showing how a cop, Murakami (Toshirō Mifune), loses his pistol and the second a single scene in which he converses with a department official specializing in pickpockets and looks through the records on file of currently operating thieves. The opening sequence, dealing with the loss of the gun, consists of 23 shots, which last two minutes and 45 seconds on screen and have an average length of just seven seconds, in contrast to the single scene that follows, which lasts four minutes and five seconds and consists of just six shots, having an average length of 31 seconds. Two of these shots, however, are merely informational inserts held on screen for only a few seconds. If these two inserts are eliminated, the average length of the remaining four shots (four minutes of screen time) is 40 seconds. By structuring the film in this manner, Kurosawa is able to create a rhythm of explosion and recoil, during which tension builds until another explosive montage occurs.

Kurosawa's tendency to handle narrative transitions as moments of formal excess reaches something of a climax in this film,[71] where a single montage showing Murakami's search through the districts of Asakusa and Ueno lasts an amazing eight minutes and 35 seconds. During this sequence, the narrative completely halts while Kurosawa explores the purely visual properties of wipes, dissolves, superimpositions, and shots articulating movement from the right, left, diagonally, and horizontally. Much of the sequence is filmed silently, except for environmental sources of music that compete with each other and are cut as an acoustical montage.[72] As the cop hangs out, trying to look like someone displaced by the war, as he is caught in the rain, eats meals, sleeps in a flophouse, is interrogated by an unsuspecting policeman, and does a lot of walking, narrative time is experienced in a new mode, as duration. The montage structure, conventionally used in films to supply brief narrative transitions, becomes a sequence in itself and instead of collapsing time, as such transitions usually do, expands it to an astounding degree. This is as purely formalistic a sequence as Kurosawa has ever created.

The energy and impatience of the film's structure are grounded in the urgency of the tasks of social reconstruction. A pickpocket steals Murakami's pistol on a crowded bus, and the film chronicles the cop's anxious efforts to find his gun and the killer who is using it. Kurosawa begins in the midst of the action. In the first shot, police chief Nakajima looks up from his desk and cries, "Your pistol's been stolen?" as the camera quickly tracks back from him and around to the right to reveal Murakami stooped slightly with humiliation. Screen space is articulated in terms of rapid movement violently enlarging perspective, as the track shifts the composition from a narrow close-up to a medium shot framing both characters. This movement, with its jarring perspectival shift, typical of Kurosawa, becomes a synedoche for the larger moral and narrative structure of the film. Murakami will learn in his search to see his own life and actions in relationship to all other members of society, while the killer, Yusa (Kō Kimura), inversely will come to see only one thing, his own need for survival and escape. By beginning the narrative in medias res, Kurosawa is also able to define Murakami by his loss, the pistol, and by a larger insufficiency, his own sense of disconnection from others. This disconnection is clarified, and remedied, through his relationship with Satō (Takashi Shimura), the officer investigating the crimes committed with Murakami's stolen pistol.

When he discovers the gun missing, Murakami tells Nakajima that he's ready for his punishment, but he is told not to talk like that. Nakajima says that this isn't the army. Instead of an institutionalized punishment, the film submits Murakami to an emotional and psychological ordeal. A girl is robbed and shot, and when the bullet from her arm proves to have come from his gun, Murakami cannot escape a feeling of being responsible for her suffering. He submits his resignation, but Nakajima tears it up, telling him that even though he feels responsible, he can't afford to be sensitive in homicide. This is the first of many times Murakami's superiors, especially Satō, will criticize his emotional involvement with the case. Kurosawa is interested in studying Murakami's responses to the case, to the crimes, and to the bleakness and criminality of the postwar environment because in these responses a means to a better future may be found.

The nature of this future is clarified through the relationship with Satō, as the narrative, characteristically for Kurosawa, centers on the ethical example he offers to Murakami and on Murakami's own initial distance from it. Like Nakajima, Satō warns Murakami not to let his feelings be involved in the case. An officer who is all nerves is no good, Satō tells him and reminds him of the consequences for others of his actions. When a blackmarketeer who knows the identity of the thief with Murakami's gun is spotted at a baseball game, Murakami rushes to arrest him but is stopped by Satō, who tells him that an arrest in the stands may injure others.

Satō's is a harshly dichotomous view of society, in which people are divided into the good and the evil. As he learns more about Yusa's tortured life, Murakami tells Satō he feels sorry for Yusa, but Satō snaps back that they can't afford to think that way, that many lambs are killed by one wolf. Satō says that writers can analyze the criminal mind, but he hates it because it is evil. Murakami, however, cannot think like this yet. The war has taught him otherwise, has taught him about the power of circumstance to affect behavior. He tells Satō that he saw men turn bad very easily during the war. Satō wonders reflectively whether their differences are due to their ages or to the changing times.

This is the central passage, describing the moral dilemma the film addresses. How may people be expected to behave well in such bad times? If they cannot so behave, as Murakami sometimes seems to suggest, how may one avoid the necessity of concluding that crime and social oppression are inevitable? The answer to this question will define the shape of Kurosawa's attempt to formulate an engaged cinema. In order to explore the response of the film to this problem, we need to consider not only Murakami but also the peculiar portrayal of Yusa and, especially, the relationship between these characters. Murakami not only feels sorry for Yusa but accountable for him, just as he cannot escape a similar sense in connection with the suffering of Yusa's victims. In part, this is because he helped create Yusa's need to steal. Murakami's arrest of a girl working for the pistol thief resulted in the confiscation of Yusa's rice ration card. Times are so bad that food is the currency of exchange on the black market. Guns are obtained in exchange for rice cards, and the loss of his card impelled Yusa to robbery for survival. Murakami points out that Yusa didn't steal the night he borrowed the gun, which means he didn't really want to use it. He stole only following the loss of his card.

But Murakami also feels a kinship to the criminal. Both Yusa and Murakami had their fortunes destroyed by the war. Yusa turned to crime, yet Murakami, feeling his life was at a dangerous point when he could begin to steal, decided to become a cop. Similar past misfortune produces the bond Murakami feels with the thief. Nevertheless, they responded differently, and it is on this difference that Kurosawa makes his film pivot.

For most of the narrative, Yusa is not seen directly. The conditions of his life are powerfully communicated through his personal effects and through people's memories of him. His sister tells the police that Yusa changed completely after the war. She says that his knapsack was stolen, and this made him go bad. She shows the cops the pathetic little room where he stayed. It is a small, pitiful hovel (like the shack where the kidnapper of *High and Low* lives). The sister recalls that he would sit here in the dark, hold his head, and cry. The police find a diary in which Yusa records his misery. He writes that he can't sleep and keeps hearing a cat that followed him home in the rain. He reflects that it would die anyway, so he decided to kill it and recalls how it felt to step on it, concluding that it was as worthless as he. In his alienation and abject misery, Yusa recalls characters from the work of Kurosawa's favorite author, Dostoevsky's Raskolnikov, or the underground man. The film's multivoiced perspective on the thief is very like the novelist's mode of presentation. An intensely compassionate presentation of Yusa's spiritual anguish is coupled with a horrified awareness of the injustices of his acts.

These acts are carefully rooted in the conditions of social and economic collapse and are symptoms of that disorder. Yusa had been a soldier doing his duty in the emperor's war. When he returned home, no jobs could be found, and all his possessions were stolen. The times are very bad. (The pickpocket who initially steals the gun was famous for working in a kimono but has since switched to a dress, perfume, and a permanent because she is down on her luck.) Yusa responds to the disorder with criminality, as Mastsunaga did in Drunken Angel. Yet Kurosawa suggests here that this is an insufficient response by arguing that individuals are still free to choose good or evil. Murakami tells Yusa's girlfriend that times are bad but that is no excuse for doing wrong. Satō says that Yusa and Murakami are different, that Murakami is "genuine," and this difference is indeed the point of the film. In this respect, the ending of Stray Dog is ambiguous. Murakami finally locates Yusa at a train station and, after a fight, apprehends him. During the fight, however, their similar clothing and the long-shot framing create a blending of their forms so that it is sometimes hard to tell who is whom. After the fight, they both lie exhausted in a field of flowers, positioned similarly and framed symmetrically. This has been interpreted to mean that Kurosawa is saying both men are the same, that cop and killer are, after all, brothers. "[S]ince both are human the fact that each assumes the identity of dog or cat, cop or robber, is accidental. . . . Man's fight against evil is artificial, man himself is both hero and villain, in himself."[73] But Kurosawa is not saying that both cop and robber are the same. Only on their necessary difference can Kurosawa fashion a standard of behavior appropriate for a new world. By insisting on the inescapability of choice, on that which differentiates the men, he is able to locate a space for the development of self. Murakami and Yusa must be different. Otherwise, the ethical model the film constructs will collapse.

Yusa is après-guerre, Satō says. The thief and killer whose crimes are symptomatic of the current social debris represents a national self, crushed and deformed by the war and its aftermath, and recovery entails suppressing and abandoning this self. In this sense, Yusa is Murakami's evil double, a doppelgänger who must be symbolically apprehended. The ethical component advanced by this portrayal is the insistence that people are not determined by their social conditions but retain a power of will and action independently of their circumstances, as Murakami demonstrated when he decided to become a cop. To this degree, then, *Stray Dog* is a film about the danger of feeling and about the need to renounce compassion. All Satō's warnings to Murakami are admonitions about the essential evil of criminals. They are evil because they lack the will to do differently and must be condemned and exorcised from the social fabric. Satō says that the police guard society, and Kurosawa cuts to shots of Satō's children sleeping peacefully, showing the prize and the tranquillity that Satō protects. From the sleeping children Kurosawa then cuts to an abandoned child's toy at the home of a woman Yusa has just murdered, clearly demonstrating that Yusa's essential sin is the breach of social sanctity, symbolized in the death of the mother and the child absent from its toy. Children figure as a recurrent motif throughout the film. Kurosawa lingers on a close-up of a toy horse at Satō's house, and in the tenement where Yusa's girlfriend lives, Satō pauses to play with a small toy doll. Children for Kurosawa, as for Dostoevsky, are emblems of the vulnerability of human life and, in their suffering, of the basic evil of the world (in contrast to a filmmaker like Sam Peckinpah, for whom kids embody the violence of life). Yusa's violation is unforgivable because it threatens the sleeping children of the next generation, those who will emerge from the ashes of the war and inhabit a new Japan.

Moreover, like Mitya Karamazov in Dostoevsky's novel, Murakami discovers his fundamental responsibility to all other members of the social order, discovers the interconnectedness of their lives. His lost gun results in two robberies, one murder, and an attempted murder, all with his bullets. "[M]ake yourself responsible for everything and for all men, you will see at once that it is really so, and that you are to blame for every one and for all things," Dostoevsky had written in *The Brothers Karamazov*. These are the terms informing Satō's and Murakami's guardianship of society, and they are terms that no Kurosawa hero after this will ever be allowed to escape. The problem, however, with this harsh lesson in the renunciation of feeling is that compassion may not be reconcilable with the kind of spiritual austerity that Satō exemplifies. He tells Murakami that, in time, he will forget his feelings for Yusa and for criminals like that. This prediction, however, is contradicted by the terms of Yusa's portrayal in the film. When he is finally apprehended, Yusa col-

20. Murakami (Toshirō Mifune) and Satō hunt for the killer. *Stray Dog.*
(Museum of Modern Art/Film Stills Archive)

lapses in a field, exhausted by the chase. He is handcuffed and looks up, seeing flowers against the sky and hearing the songs of a passing band of children. Remorse and misery overwhelm him, and he emits a long, hear-trending wail that does not stop. Kurosawa fades out on the cry, but it lingers and comes to inform the film as a destabilizing force. Despite Satō's confident words to Murakami, we remember far too well this awful cry and, probably, so does Murakami. He hears Satō's words but remains unconvinced, and Kurosawa ends the film here, with Murakami suspended between Yusa's scream and Satō's reassuring prediction. The dynamic between the older and the younger detective is the struggle for an emergent and coherent social program that takes as a central problem the place and role of the compassionate response in an oppressive world. The differences in the models offered by Satō and Murakami are left in tension, their irresolution haunting the film.

This lack of resolution is informed by what the film represses and by the energy of repressing it. In Yusa, Kurosawa investigates the genesis of criminality and the disintegration of what once was, perhaps, a good and gentle man. Despite the richly textured portrait of postwar Japan that emerges through the detectives' search, the focus of the film is an un-relentingly individualist one. Criminality is defined as a matter of indi-vidual choice. No matter how bad conditions are, Kurosawa is saying, people still have the power to determine how they will respond. With regard to this issue, he has observed:

> [P]eople are subject to what is called destiny. This destiny lies not so much in their environment or their position in life as within their individual personality as it adapts to that environ-ment and that position.[74]

> Granting that there is some truth to the theory that defects in society give rise to the emergence of criminals, I still maintain that those who use this theory as a defense of criminality are overlooking the fact that there are many people in this defective society who survive without resorting to crime. The argument to the contrary is pure sophistry.[75]

In arguing for the autonomous self as a positive value in postwar Ja-pan, Kurosawa overturns, and in a sense reverses, centuries of tradition in which an individual's range of choice *was* constrained, and largely determined, by the ties of family, class, and clan. But in taking the enormous step of locating destiny within the personality, of regarding the environment as a kind of psychical superstructure, Kurosawa's filmmaking loses touch with something essential to its committed na-ture: the social world. The restless visual and narrative energy of *Stray Dog* is comprehensible as a stratagem to contain and deny an arena of meaning that could prove fatal to the moral project the film announces, and this is a recognition of the social construction of criminality. Throughout much of the film, despite the centrality of the black market to the narrative, this recognition is absent. In two sequences, however, a novel and, for the film, a structurally disturbing perspective emerges. When Murakami confronts Yusa at the end, he is shot, and they grapple in the mud, their white clothing soiled by sweat, blood, and dirt—a primal scene. The power of this elemental encounter is heightened by the music of Mozart suddenly and eerily drifting through the woods from a distant piano. In contrast to this scene of primitive violence, the seren-ity of the Mozart is, literally, other-worldly.[76] It comes from the neat, well-ordered home of a bourgeois girl practicing her music by the open window. *No Regrets for Our Youth* has provided a context for evaluating this image: this girl is like a version of Yukie before her transformation, the Yukie whose pampered passivity Noge had gently chided. Here, in *Stray Dog*, two class perspectives briefly intersect as the girl stops playing, looks out her window, sees the men in the distance, and stifling an indolent yawn, returns to her music. Yusa is hungry, dirty, and jobless, but this girl is well fed and well dressed, ensconced in a comfortable, clean home. If Yusa is a legacy of the war years, she is a vision of a Japan untouched by war, poverty, and violence and, as she languidly turns away from the window, of the remoteness of the bourgeoisie from the sufferings of the people. She is the image of class difference and indifference.

The film is constructed as a general denial of class. The girl is but a brief intrusion into the narrative, and the important distinctions between people, the film suggests, are the moral ones, those that separate Murakami and Yusa. Such an assertion, however, can be founded only on repression, and what is repressed generally returns, as it does here with a vengeance. When Murakami questions Harumi Namiki, Yusa's girlfriend, he learns that Yusa committed the robberies to buy her an expensive dress she had seen in a store window. Kurosawa places them on opposite sides of the frame, with the dress spread on the floor between them, in a stable, balanced composition that he holds for a long time. Murakami tells her that bad times are no excuse for doing wrong, but like the young couple in *One Wonderful Sunday*, she points out that today bad people are living the best. They eat good food and dress well. They're the winners, she says, referring to the profiteers from the national misery, and adds that to display this dress in a store window in such times is a crime. We'd all have to do worse things to get it, she adds. Harumi's brief glimpse of the larger social forces at work, deforming her life and the lives of those about her, upsets the film's parable about individual choice. Capitalism, affluence, and murder are all linked in the dress, displayed in a store window where people too poor to buy it would be compelled to see it. As Harumi puts on the dress, an extraordinary, destabilizing visual energy is released. A violent squall suddenly breaks, and on a clap of thunder, Kurosawa cuts to a series of obliquely framed close-ups of Harumi dancing madly in the dress. She hypnotically chants that she's happy, so happy, it's all like a dream, as the frenzy of her dance is mirrored in the rapid cutting. Space is fragmented as a new political recognition suddenly erupts, deforming the imagery of the film. As Harumi spins faster and faster, her wild shadow flitting over the walls, the thunder rolling outside, Murakami watches in horror. But the out-

burst is quickly contained. Her mother tears off the dress, throws it outside, and Harumi collapses in tears at her mother's knees. Kurosawa cuts
to a shot outside the apartment, showing the rain falling on the dress.
The water dampens the emotional fires the dress has unleashed (as rain
does again in *Seven Samurai*, after the confrontation between Manzō,
Shino and Katsushirō). As the rain purifies the scene, the film purges
itself of its brief recognition of the social structural, transindividual
causes of criminality, in this case an economy that, by dangling expensive commodities before a poor people, encourages rage and selfishness
and corrodes society with an ideal of life as acquisition. But it is too late
to sweep this vision away; the damage is done. Murakami can make as
many existential choices as he wants, but it will not affect one bit the
power of those who put such dresses in store windows where they torture people like Yusa with their unattainable visions.

Both *Stray Dog* and *Drunken Angel* clearly demonstrate the difficulties Kurosawa's aesthetic project faced in response to postwar Japan. The
structure of each film is defined by contradictions between the imperatives of characters like Sanada and Murakami and the demands of the
social context in which they are located. Their struggles against this context are ambivalent, for they are as much a part of it as Matsunaga and
Yusa, their darker selves. Herein lies the power of the films: the characters and narratives are charged with ambivalent cultural values that are
sustained without resolution. Sanada vanishes into the crowd, defeated,
yet stubbornly proclaiming his credo. Murakami remains under the tutelage of Satō yet cannot shed his haunting feelings for Yusa. Contemporaneous with the age and the problems they depict, the films demand to be
read in a synchronic manner, which regards their search for, and refusal
of, closure as the structural embodiment of their engagement with history. The problem of how to foreclose on the political and moral dilemmas of the era is one of the fundamental questions informing the work
and, as we have seen, is responsible for films of great textual richness.
The temptation to foreclose, however, was great and can be clearly felt in
each film. When the films unequivocally yield to this temptation, their
multivalent structure collapses into a monologic perspective, in which
all the voices of the text speak as one and the film becomes program-
matic.[77] Such is the fate of a work like *Scandal*. But Kurosawa rarely lets
this happen. His sensitivity to cultural contradiction is too fine. Instead,
we observe a variety of textual strategies for refusing closure. The most
complex and elaborate of these is found in the climactic work of this
period, the film that represents the maturing of Kurosawa's ethical vi-

sion, *Ikiru*. Its textual structure builds on and magnifies the ambivalences of the earlier films, such that it might be regarded as a reply to their irresolution and to the cultural challenges informing them. But, in doing this, *Ikiru* goes beyond these films in discovering the coordinates of a morally complete vision and sustains this vision within a formal structure that serves to define it, analyze it, and question it. *Ikiru* remains among Kurosawa's most radical experiments with form and among his most searching inquiries into the nature and morality of human feeling, particularly in relation to its structuring by the cinematic image.

Stray Dog was a parable about the need for the guardians of society to renounce their human feelings and about the impossibility, and the danger, of doing so. Like Dostoevsky, Kurosawa is interested in the nature, and the essential duplicity, of compassion in a wicked world. The young doctor in *Red Beard* is nearly killed when he responds sympathetically to a mad patient, and the industrialist at the end of *High and Low* will never understand why the kidnapper refuses his attempt to establish a common, human solidarity. This interest in the deforming of feeling by worldly corruption and in the manner by which the world manufactures victims in its own image was also common to Brecht.[78] The affinity between the works of Kurosawa and Brecht was noted earlier. (Parenthetically, Kurosawa has remarked that he wanted to use the music from Brecht's *Three Penny Opera* for *Drunken Angel*.[79]) Their films and plays are structured as responses to the problems of war and militarism. It is now appropriate, however, to discuss this relation more fully because Kurosawa's concerns in *Ikiru* are very close to the terms of the Brechtian project.

As is well known, Brecht distrusted artworks that aroused an uncritical response in their audience. In place of this, he emphasized the blending of pleasure and reason. Brecht's imperative to use theater to alter and to better the conditions of the world compelled him to reject aesthetic strategies that reinforced the dominant images of society so that he might mobilize an audience's critical faculties. The characters in his plays, he suggested, are not a matter for empathy but for understanding. "Feelings are private and limited. Against that the reason is fairly comprehensive and to be relied on."[80] He called for a kind of "complex seeing"[81] in which the viewpoint of a play would emerge from a multivoiced montage of theatrical elements—characters, gesture, dialogue, set design, projected films and titles—rather than be easily localized within any one of these elements. Above all, Brecht emphasized the position of the spectator as observer, rather than as one implicated in the stage action through processes of identification, and the play as a nonlinear structure marked by jumps, curves, and montage that would emphasize human life as a process open to change.

Kurosawa, too, is committed in *Ikiru*, as in much of his other work, to the "unformed" characters, to those just starting out in life whose moral transformations the films study and place in relation to a detailed social context.[82] The heroes of Kurosawa's films—Kambei, Niide, Watanabe— are intended as explicit role models for the audience, but the values incarnated by their behavior are communicated through a "complex seeing" in which these lessons in responsible living are filtered through, altered, and sometimes deformed by the social order, whose competing values generate other voices in the texts that contest the example provided by the hero. In *Stray Dog* and *Drunken Angel*, this competition generates an extraordinary aesthetic power but also threatens to deflect the moral example of the hero from its intended course. By contrast, in *Ikiru* a more elaborate and carefully designed structure prevents this deflection. An uncommon clarity of vision prevails in *Ikiru*, yet this clarity entails no sacrifice of "complex seeing." The narrative is a nonlinear one, and its form is marked by the jumps, curves, and montages of which Brecht spoke. The formal experimentation of *Ikiru* has one central purpose: to sharpen the film's focus by controlling and limiting the audience's emotional response. A film about the last months of a man who knows he is dying is inherently threatened by a descent into bathos, as ample television movies have demonstrated. Yet the form of the film prevents this from happening and aids in its didactic task. This task and purpose may best be clarified by a remark of Brecht's that is strikingly relevant to Kurosawa's cinema:

> Empathy alone may stimulate a wish to imitate the hero, but it can hardly create the capacity. If a feeling is to be an effective one, it must be acquired not merely impulsively but through the understanding. Before a correct attitude can be imitated it must first have been understood that the principle is applicable to situations that are not exactly like those portrayed. It is the theatre's job to present the hero in such a way that he stimulates conscious rather than blind imitation.[83]

Using the hero to communicate with, rather than to blind, the audience: this is Kurosawa's deeply felt intention. In *Ikiru*, he is concerned to contain and to limit the viewer's empathic response so that it may yield enlightenment rather than catharsis. If *Stray Dog* dealt with the need for the characters to discipline their emotional responses, if this problematic existed in terms of that film's content, Kurosawa has taken it over at the level of structure and form in *Ikiru*.

The film is divided into two parts. The first deals with the reactions of Kanji Watanabe (Takashi Shimura), a bureaucrat in charge of the municipal department's Citizen's Section, to the knowledge that he is dying of stomach cancer. The second, more confined temporally and spatially, studies the behavior of family and co-workers at Watanabe's funeral. The clerk is largely absent from this second section, appearing only during brief flashbacks, but this absence is central to the film's formal design. It is not simply a matter that the second section shifts the focus from Watanabe to the other people in his life. Watanabe has been disappearing repeatedly throughout the film, as Kurosawa establishes a perspectival montage, a series of fluid, shifting points of view that prevents the spectator from occupying any single, reified vantage point. Instead, point of view, as incarnated by characters and camera, is deceptive and manifests a continual slippage between what we think we know, or where we think we are in the narrative, and the actual condition. The narrative proceeds by a series of jumps or gaps, during which Watanabe vanishes while other characters attempt to account for his absence, and temporal relations become unclear as events occlude, duplicate, or fold back around one another. The consciousness of Watanabe, like the meaning of "Rosebud" in *Citizen Kane*, becomes the central narrative enigma, as characters attempt to reconstruct this consciousness in ways that are compatible with the social order. The film oscillates between their attempts, the information provided by a narrator, and direct observation of Watanabe. From these shifting perspectives emerges a "complex seeing," a synthetic, inclusive understanding of this Brechtian hero.

As Richie notes,[84] Watanabe is defined by his disease (like Matsunaga in *Drunken Angel*). The first image of the film is a close-up of an x-ray showing the cancer, as the narrator tells us that it belongs to the main character of the story, who does not yet understand the full import of his symptoms. The x-ray dissolves to a medium close-up, frontal framing of Watanabe shuffling papers at his desk. (The formal perspective is symmetrical: this is also the framing of Watanabe's replacement at the end of the film.) Kurosawa holds the frame for a long time as the narrator gives us more information about the clerk: that he has been deadened by office routine so that he is now more like a corpse than a living being, that he has lost all initiative and merely drifts through life. Then, rhetorically, the narrator asks whether this is all right and then repeats the question. The x-ray, the narrator, the frontal framing: this is a purely formal presentation of character that eliminates suspense and distances (or, for Brecht, alienates) perspective. The viewer will never be permitted a direct, unmediated rapport with the hero.

A group of slum residents comes to the Citizen's Section to request that a foul drainage pond (another mosquito-laden sump), in their neighborhood be cleaned away and the land converted to a playground. Watanabe instructs an aide to send them to the Public Works section, precipitating one of Kurosawa's most trenchant sequences, a montage of mad bureaucratic logic, in which an endless series of clerks shuffles the slum dwellers off to other departments. At the end of the montage, when they have been sent back to the Citizen's Section, one of them exclaims that there's no democracy here (referring to the Occupation reforms), and they start to leave. Watanabe's aide, shamed by their response and the injustice of their treatment, rushes after them to say that there is nothing he can do, Watanabe is absent today.

This information establishes a first ellipsis, which appears so only in retrospect. Because of the way the sequence has been edited, with straight cuts from Watanabe's instructions to send the group to the Public Works Section to the logically contiguous onset of the montage, we assume that the group has made the rounds of the municipal building in the course of one day. It is shocking, therefore, to learn that a large amount of narrative time has passed unaccounted for, during which Watanabe has vanished. Before it becomes apparent that he is at the hospital, where we meet him again, several scenes follow, further delaying contact with the central character. A shot of his empty desk leads to three scenes in which the office clerks talk about his attendance record and the unusual quality of the absence. As this happens, the basic structure of the film is established: Watanabe will be manifest as a textual gap that the narrative tries to fill in and reclaim by inventing hypotheses for his behavior. This effort at reclamation is motivated by the same urgency as the defusing of a bomb, for Watanabe will come to represent a powerfully subversive example to established society.

Another perceptual dislocation follows close on the conclusion of this sequence. As the clerks gaze at their chief's empty desk, a cut takes us to the hospital corridor as Watanabe comes out of an x-ray room. As he crosses to the stairs, a very strange dissolve interrupts his movement and relocates him to a new position part of the way up the stairs.[85] By the logic of continuity cutting, this is an impermissible use of the dissolve

21. Watanabe's (Takashi Shimura) intensely personal confrontation with death alienates those around him and challenges the social order. *Ikiru*. (Museum of Modern Art/Film Stills Archive)

since there is not enough of a change in narrative time or space. Yet this is one of many perspectival deformities in the film (and may be the source for a similar use of the dissolve by Scorsese in *Taxi Driver*).

The second major narrative cavity occurs following Watanabe's meeting with the doctor, who, significantly, *withholds* the information about his cancer, telling him instead that he simply has a slight case of ulcer. Watanabe leaves in despair because he knows that "ulcer" is a code word for cancer, and the scene ends with a close-up of the x-ray. Kurosawa then cuts to a street scene showing Watanabe walking along, with the sound expressionistically absent as a signifier of Watanabe's obsessed state of mind. But this absent sound also enforces a formal cleavage between the character and his surrounding environment. Watanabe pauses at the curb, but the camera tracks away from him, across the street and through traffic, which suddenly begins to roar as the aural track reappears. The camera's track threatens to leave Watanabe behind and to remove us from his proximity, encapsulating the basic textual strategy. Once again, Kurosawa has demonstrated his essentially metaphoric understanding of movement—the track visualizes the film's structuring principle. From this track, Kurosawa then cuts to an "empty" point-of-view shot, another track, this time toward an object, a house, framed frontally in the darkness of twilight. On the soundtrack, we hear an American pop song, but it is not clear whether this is nondiegetic sound, part of Fumio Hayasaka's score. It turns out not to be. It is being hummed by Watanabe's son, Mitsuo, and Kazue, his wife, who are revealed in a reverse-field cut. But the long, mysterious track has opened up another perceptual void in the film, one we expect to be filled by Watanabe since it is he who is returning home from the hospital. Instead, characters we have not yet met prove to be the owners of the camera's gaze. They begin talking about money, acquisitions, and how they can get hold of Watanabe's retirement pay.

The perceptual tricks that the film has begun to play undermine a smooth, linear dissemination of narrative information. Instead, a series of perspectival blockages and misunderstandings occurs. These, in turn, are absorbed by the film and become its overriding theme. They are set out with particular pathos during a long montage as Watanabe recalls raising Mitsuo following the death of his wife. The memories follow a fight with Mitsuo and Kazue, after they find him waiting in their room upon their return. They lecture him about the impropriety of his behavior. He says nothing, but we know he wished to tell them of his cancer. He silently goes downstairs where he sleeps. Watanabe, in fact, will never tell his son of his condition, and the young man will end bitter and confused, unable to understand the reasons for his father's silence and the part his own selfish behavior played in that silence.

From downstairs, Watanabe hears the giggling and laughter of Mitsuo and Kazue, which intensifies his despair. The montage that follows is among Kurosawa's supreme creations, structured by a series of subtle visual and aural counterpoints. Kurosawa moves in and out of the past, juxtaposing shots of Watanabe kneeling in front of his wife's shrine with the images of earlier years, and counterposing the strains of the romantic pop song from Kazue's record player upstairs with a metronomic dirge accompanying the memory imagery. From a close-up of the wife's portrait, the film dissolves to a shot of the departing hearse carrying her body. Little Mitsuo, framed exactly as Watanabe had been framed as he gazed at the portrait, cries that Mother is leaving them behind, and his father embraces him. The hearse turns a corner and disappears.

From this first memory of separation, the montage traces a life full of other separations and emotional failures. Watanabe's brother tells him he is wrong not to remarry, that Mitsuo won't be so grateful as he thinks, that the father will simply be in the way as he ages. Within this flash-back, as if in answer to the uncle's words, Mitsuo's voice is heard calling "Father," and it continues as the sequence switches back to the present. Mitsuo is calling from upstairs for Watanabe to lock up for the evening. As Watanabe bars the door with a bat, an associative sound image cues the next flashback. The sound of a ball being hit precedes a cut to a ball game in which Watanabe watches Mitsuo round the bases and boasts to a man next to him, "That's my son." But Mitsuo is thrown out trying to steal second, and Watanabe slowly sits down in the bleachers with dis-appointment and shame. An extraordinary choreography of movement occurs. The camera tilts down with him, creating a displacement be-tween Watanabe, moving down in the frame, and the background, mov-ing upward in the frame. These conflicting planes of movement are ex-tended into the next two shots. In the middle of the tilt-down, the film cuts to a shot of Watanabe in the present, framed frontally, looking at the camera, as it simultaneously tracks up and tilts down, so that Watanabe again appears to move down before a background that slides upward. He cries "Mitsuo," but it is nonsynchronous: his lips remain closed. The cry, and the movement, continue over the next cut. Watanabe is standing beside Mitsuo in a hospital elevator, which is descending, displacing the background shaft upward. In these three shots, Kurosawa has used a tilt-down, a track-up, and a descending elevator to obtain the same perspec-tival dislocations between Watanabe and his environments. He calls his son by name and tells him that an appendectomy is nothing to fear, but he can't stay. He must return to the office. As Mitsuo is wheeled away, a cut returns us to the present. Watanabe crosses to the stairs leading to his son's room, as the nonsynchronous cry "Mitsuo" sounds again. Then a cut introduces another scene of separation, this time as Mitsuo goes off to war. Just before the train takes him away, he grabs Watanabe and cries "Father" and is answered by the nonsynchronous, ethereal "Mitsuo," which continues to echo as the train departs and a dissolve returns us to the present.

Throughout this sequence, scenes of trauma, failure, disappointment, and estrangement between father and son have petrified the past into a hardened fossil of what might have been. This past hangs like a heavy weight between them, sundering their current relations, yet the formal structure of the montage insists on the interpenetration of the temporal frames. Associative cutting and aural and visual links establish a con-tinuum between past and present, even if it is a continuum of unre-lieved failure and despair. This, then, is the stark legacy that Watanabe

overcomes during his transformation into a hero. The visual dislocations between the hero and his environment, repeated during the heart
of the montage, characterize the terms of this spiritual journey. For
Watanabe grows—and becomes an enigma for Mitsuo, Kazue, and his
officemates—by separating from, rebelling against, and rejecting the institutional frameworks of modern Japanese society, that is, the family
and the company.

As if in recognition of this incipient potential, the end of the montage
cues the third major absence of Watanabe from the narrative. The montage sequence ends with a devastating juxtaposition of close-ups of
Watanabe's office plaques, commemorating thirty years of service, with
the sound of his bitter weeping. After this, we learn that he has once
again disappeared. In a series of scenes, various characters hypothesize
about where he may be. A clerk from the office visits his home and
speaks with the housekeeper, from whom he learns that the old man has
been leaving for the office as usual every day. He replies that Watanabe
hasn't been coming to work. In the next scene, Kazue calls Mitsuo to
report the news. 'I wonder what he's been doing,'' Mitsuo says. In the
following scene, the clerks sit and gossip. "His family was astonished,''
one says. In the last scene of this sequence, Mitsuo visits his uncle and
tells him that Watanabe has drawn out 50,000 yen, and the uncle speculates that Watanabe has probably found a mistress.

The sequence then shifts to a roadside cafe, where a romantic novelist
is trying to get some sleeping pills from the proprietor. Only at the end of
this conversation does Watanabe reappear inside the narrative when his
presence is disclosed in the shadows of the cafe. As a protest against his
life up to now, the clerk embarks on a wild night of dissipation with the
novelist, reveling in modern, Westernized Japan: pinball machines, beer
halls, brass bands, jazz bands, dance halls, strip shows. The frames are
crowded and cluttered, and this whole night sequence has a hallucinatory, phantasmagorical quality to it, as Watanabe journeys through the
belly of a Japan he may never have known existed. But, as in *Drunken
Angel*, this proximity to the chaos and abandon of the modern culture
brings on a hemorrhage. Watanabe staggers down the darkness of an alley
to vomit beside open trash cans, as the novelist stares, his romanticism
about this man he thought of as a Christ carrying the cross of cancer
shattered by the physical brutality of the spasm. Watanabe's hemorrhage
closes the night of debauchery and seals the falseness of his attempt to
lose himself in the sea of humanity crowding the dance halls and the
streets.

22. Watanabe tries to reach out to Toyo but discovers that he remains alone. *Ikiru*. (Museum of Modern Art/Film Stills Archive)

Before the clerk may begin to live fully and responsibly (the title of the film refers to this condition), he must confront the emptiness of two conventional modes of being. One he has just encountered, the world of the pinball machine, the automatic vendor of dreams. The other is based in the effort to live through another person, and it is the fraudulence of this attempt that he next realizes. Watanabe "must be shown that it, too, is no refuge."[86] The day following his evening with the novelist is spent with Toyo, a young girl from the office who has come to see him because she needs an official validation for her resignation. She is bored by the work, and Watanabe, fascinated by her energy and youthful exuberance, takes her to an ice-skating rink, an amusement park, and the movies. But when he tries to continue the association over the next few days, she refuses, saying it is unnatural. They quarrel at a restaurant where a group of young people has gathered to celebrate a birthday. This conflict is the pivotal moment of the film for Watanabe, the point where he suddenly attains enlightenment, dissolves himself of past relationships, and sets out on a new path, triggering a final, major ellipsis in the narrative.

He tells Toyo that her energy is amazing and makes him envious, that he wants to live like her for just one day before he dies, that he must do something before the end. Only she, he says, can show him what it is. He urges her to teach him how to be like her. But she is horrified at his overtures and replies that all she does is work and sleep, referring to her proletarianization. A member of the working class, she will live through a succession of factory jobs, so different from the well-dressed youngsters across the restaurant, celebrating a birthday. As in *Stray Dog*, an incipient class perspective appears, describing the gulf between the haves and the have-nots, portrayed in terms of spatial distance: a stairwell separates the shabbily dressed Toyo from the celebratory crowd. But she finds satisfaction in her work. She shows Watanabe one of the toy rabbits churned out by her company, saying that though she only makes toys like this, she feels all the children in Japan are her friends. As, in an extraordinary image, the silly white rabbit hops in front of Watanabe's face, he collapses in despair, crying that it is too late to do anything. But suddenly his eyes lift, and he exclaims that it isn't too late, it isn't impossible. He says he can do something at the office if he's really determined, and he rushes out, clutching the rabbit, as the crowd sings "Happy Birthday."

In the next scene, Watanabe has returned to his office and announces his intention to honor the slum residents' petition to construct a playground at the drainage site. He will redeem his life by building a park for slum children. As he explains what must be done, he sits at his desk in the background of the shot while two co-workers stand in the foreground on each side of the frame so that their bodies visually entrap the dying clerk. As he tells them that all the sections of the bureaucracy must cooperate, the camera slowly dollies forward, between the co-workers who disappear off the edges of the frame, toward Watanabe who now dominates the frame by himself. The camera movement has altered the composition so that Watanabe shifts from being a submissive to a dominant visual element. 'Happy Birthday" again plays on the soundtrack. His newly found moral strength liberates him from the deadening bureaucratic world, and the camera celebrates this change in one of the most joyous movements in Kurosawa's cinema.

The transformation that this reorientation of the composition describes, however, is followed by another of Watanabe's disappearances from the narrative. He leaves for the park site, accompanied by two clerks who object that the project will be difficult. No, not if we're determined, he replies, echoing Sanada's words, describing once more the terms of the commitment to self that Kurosawa's films of this period manifest. As he walks out the door, a siren wails, rising and falling as the door swings shut, providing an aural marker to close this section of the film. The narrator dispassionately tells us that five months later, the hero of the story died. The film then cuts to a close-up of Watanabe's portrait at his funeral, followed by a medium shot and then a long shot, showing the room containing the portrait and its occupants. This will be the strategy of the second section of the film, moving from Watanabe to the social context containing him, describing the efforts of his family and co-workers to understand his final, strange behavior, when he seemed obsessed with the idea of the park and challenged the decisions of his superiors that the project would not be feasible.

The hero's death, then, opens another major gap in the narrative,[87] and the concluding funeral sequence, lasting a third of the film's length, deals with the meaning of Watanabe's actions and the question of who built the park. Family and friends remember significant moments from Watanabe's last days. Various theories are offered for his behavior. Mitsuo believes that his father's eccentric actions stemmed from his offense at overhearing a conversation with Kazue about how they could get his retirement pay and use it for their own benefit. Watanabe's brother continues to believe in the mistress. The newspaper reporters advance the theory that Watanabe's death in the park was politically motivated, was a deliberate suicide in protest of municipal corruption. The Deputy Mayor credits Watanabe with the idea for the park but points out that parks come under the Parks Section and implies that Watanabe was selfishly trying to claim credit for himself. After this character leaves, the other clerks begin to recall extraordinary moments: Watanabe standing in the rain at the drainage site without an umbrella, staggering weakly down the hallways, kept alive only by his work, asking the Deputy Mayor to reconsider a decision, facing down a group of gangsters who wanted the property for their own use. As the film cuts between the memory imagery and the funeral scene, the clerks struggle to understand why Watanabe attempted to build the park and if it was because he knew he had cancer. But significantly, as Noël Burch notes, none of the scenes recalled shows any of the decisive administrative decisions that resulted in the park,[88] yet another of the many informational ellipses strewn through the narrative. Our awareness of Watanabe's responsibility for the park emerges as a dialectical understanding, taking shape through the movement between the past images of his determined behavior and the present scene of bureaucratic callowness and through the contrast between the genuine grief of the slum residents and the cold complacency of the bureaucrats. The truth of Watanabe's action is never portrayed directly but is suspended between, and is established by, these opposites.

In order to live, finally, Watanabe has had to become dead to his son and his co-workers. He tells Toyo he has no son, that he is all alone. His pursuit of his own objectives is upsetting to municipal routine. His tactics—bowing repeatedly, patiently waiting while astonished officials react to his requests that they reconsider their decision—undermine the prevailing passivity of the office, which has been coded as an ethic of social harmony. As always, the Kurosawa hero must reject the established coding of human relationships, especially to the extent that the imperative of sociability works to nullify the pursuit of individual goals. "The unrestrained pursuit of one's own interest at the expense of another's goes against the norm of sociability. Concerned with his own interest, the individual will find the imperative of sociability and harmony oppressive."[89] Thus, Watanabe must continually violate bureaucratic etiquette for the sake of his park.

These office scenes are filmed with a wonderful expressionism, in which human beings are contained and confined by an overwhelming and alienating environment, as they are in the later films of Michelangelo Antonioni. Huge stacks of paper, beams supporting the ceiling, chairs and tables split the frame into a myriad of tiny spaces, inhabited by even smaller people, dominated by a world of paperwork and drudgery, separated from each other, and constrained by the objects in their environments. This is the Lukácsian meaning of reification: humanly made objects returning to dominate their makers. In a stratagem of great insight, these are the terms by which Watanabe is presented during the flashbacks at the funeral. He dominates the frame and splits and separates clerks from one another, as the stacks of paper, fans, and beams had done in earlier sequences. To the world of the bureaucracy, Watanabe's present actions are a source of discomfort and disruption, threatening their regimented identities as the reified environment has threatened their human identities. To their sensibilities, Watanabe's is a kind of reified behavior: it looms only as threat, and its critique of the erosion of freedom and the loss of responsibility for human society in the modern world must be defused, for it could dynamite the established order. Thus, explanations are offered for the clerk's actions: eccentricity, glory-seeking, the influence of a mistress.

The peculiar structure of the film may now become clear. The incessant slippage of point of view, the perspective tricks, the momentary losses of coherence regarding the temporal location of individual scenes, all work to describe the terms of a very special kind of "complex seeing," which grasps and analyzes simultaneously two antagonistic, competing cultural spaces. The conflict generating the film's structure is the dissension between the imperatives of the enlightened individual behaving according to the dictates of private conscience and of the social group seeking to constrain the consciousness and action of its members. The film oscillates between four modes of presentation: a direct apprehension of Watanabe, an apprehension of Watanabe mediated by the dispassionate narrator whose words enforce the artifice of the film, an apprehension of Watanabe mediated by the memories of misunderstanding bureaucrats, and an apprehension of purely group-oriented spaces from which Watanabe is absent. These are four separate epistemological terrains, and this manner of presentation serves several functions. First, and most immediately, it allows Kurosawa to adopt an analytic tone that regulates the flow of narrative information by blocking and repressing it at several points. This permits the film, very effectively, to constrain the inherent pathos of the subject. *Ikiru* is an extremely controlled work, and the emotions of the material are never permitted to get out of hand. Kurosawa is not interested in speaking about the sadness of Watanabe's death or, in a more traditionally Japanese manner, in adopting an attitude of *mono no aware*, a restrained melancholy over the transience of all things. Compassion is the enemy here, as it was in *Stray Dog*. The spectator is not allowed to identify emotionally with the hero, to live through him, just as Watanabe was not permitted to do this with Toyo. For Kurosawa, the terms of responsible living are far more demanding than what a merely compassionate response will enable. His hero must be disabused of this response, as the film must disabuse its audience of the expectation that an unmediated rapport with the character will unfold. As Brecht said, empathy can create the wish but not the capability to emulate a hero. Thus, empathy, as an interpersonal ethic and as an aesthetic form, must be abandoned. This discovery will play a major role in the films to come.

But the kaleidoscopic structure of the film also permits Kurosawa to fashion—if not closure, then—at least a new and more extensive bounding of the social challenges with which the forms of the earlier films grappled. The problem was to find a space where the individual could stand that would not entail a blindness to the social world and a collapse into selfishness or solipsism. *No Regrets for Our Youth, Scandal, The Quiet Duel, Drunken Angel,* and *Stray Dog* all address this issue with differing emphases, and the strife that marks their forms is evidence of the difficulty of the search. The hero of *Ikiru* learns the same lesson that

Sanada and Murakami, Yukie and Hiruta, have all realized: that they are responsible for everything and for all people and are to blame "for every one and for all things." This harsh ethic, couched in terms of individual responsibility, was difficult to square with the facts of transindividual, political and economic, sources of oppression. Murakami is advised by Satō to forget about Yusa, that is, to forget about the power of the environment to shape and structure human action. He must forget in order for this ethic to prevail, but the film is not sure that it will let him. Facing this intransigent contradiction—seeking to fashion a socially responsive cinema by locating a political ethic within the individual conscience—Kurosawa in films of this period struggles to resolve it. The difficulty of working this through, the ambivalent cultural energies that it unleashed, reaches a climax in *Ikiru* in its multivoiced, kaleidoscopic structure, where focus and point of view are never stable, never occupy the same ground for long. The multiple modes of presentation enable Kurosawa to realize successfully, temporarily, the contradictory project his cinema assumed, but at a cost. The shifting perspectives of the film describe the two irreconcilable cultural spaces of individual and group, but rather than leaving them suspended in tension as the earlier films had done, they are sundered and permitted to follow different trajectories. Watanabe confronts the spiritual and moral emptiness of the public spaces of the family and the company, even as these groups try to reinscribe him within their power. To the eyes of the public world, Watanabe's behavior is a mystery. To a world of group allegiances, his eccentric final action can appear only as a kind of negative image, a gap, a void. Thus, the ellipses, the gaps, the blockages, the misunderstandings, the emotional failures that characterize the structure and drama of the film may be regarded as a climactic tearing and rending of the force-fields that structure the works of this period. *Ikiru* proclaims the essential loneliness of its hero yet insists that he build a park for children, those archsymbols registering the violence and evil of the world. Never has the possibility of an accord between hero and society seemed so remote. Never has the imperative to reform a corrupt world been so urgent. Never has the task required so mighty an effort and left so small a legacy. Watanabe's example is a tiny ray of enlightenment in an otherwise forbidding world. *Ikiru* is one of the supreme statements of Kurosawa's heroic cinema. Yet, it seemed, the forces of darkness were getting ever more powerful.

4 Experiments and Adaptations

"Reading

and writing

should become

habitual."

— Akira Kurosawa[1]

We are now in a position to consider the general contours of the heroic mode of Kurosawa's cinema. The films examined in the previous chapter advance a particular model of the world that tries to engage aspects of the postwar cultural landscape. It is important to consider the terms of this model because they show Kurosawa's highly selective use of cultural materials. But this model must also be understood so that its disintegration in later films may be grasped. In Kurosawa's cinema, we are dealing with twin impulses. The postwar imperative to engage history and remake society will be offset in later films by a contrary inclination to conceive the temporal process as fate and human life as an insubstantial shadow in a world of tears. This latter impulse is in marked contrast to the social optimism of the early films like *No Regrets for Our Youth* and *Stray Dog*. The chapters that follow explore different facets of these contrary qualities, while in the present discussion I attempt to clarify some cultural bases for Kurosawa's conception of heroism.

Kurosawa's films valorize qualities of strength, discipline, courage, and determination in their portrait of the hero's engagement with the social world. Kurosawa deeply admires spartan attributes and the strength of character they disclose. He says the home in which he grew up possessed "a samurai atmosphere."[2] His father was a military instructor whose "educational principles were terribly spartan."[3] He reports that under his father's influence, he approached such sports as judo and kendō swordfighting with single-minded devotion. Kurosawa portrays not only his father but also his mother in these terms. He relates a remarkable incident that displayed her strength of spirit, and in its use of crisis to reveal character, the anecdote could have come from any of his films:

> My mother's strength lay particularly in her endurance. I remember an amazing ex-

23. Kurosawa, "the last of the samurai." (Toshirō Mifune is at the extreme left.) (Museum of Modern Art/Film Stills Archive)

ample. It happened when she was deep-frying tempura in the kitchen one day. The oil in the pot caught fire. Before it could ignite anything else, she proceeded to pick up the pot with both hands—while her eyebrows and eyelashes were singed to crinkled crisps—walk calmly across the tatami-mat room, properly put on her clogs at the garden door and carry the flaming pot out to the center of the garden to set it down.[4]

Afterwards, the doctor arrived and peeled away the scorched skin from her hands. Kurosawa says he was unable to watch this, but that his "mother's facial expression never betrayed the slightest tremor. Nearly a month passed before she was able to grasp something in her bandaged hands. Holding them in front of her chest, she never uttered a word about pain; she just sat quietly."[5] He adds, with deep respect, "No matter how I might try, I could never do the same."[6]

In foregrounding such qualities, Kurosawa's films display a warrior ideal, regardless of the historical era in which they are set. For one of the duties of a warrior was the injunction to maintain severe discipline. "[T]he true master of the way of the warrior is one who maintains his martial discipline even in time of peace," Tokugawa Ieyasu, one of the unifiers of Japan, is reported to have proclaimed.[7] In a world perceived as a place of violence and strife, a person of honor is obligated to choose a side and enter the battle. Kurosawa's world is an arena where his characters must be tested, where they must be victorious in their goals or must be broken and defeated. Passivity, acquiescence, and conformity to social norms are eschewed. The true life is one of conflict and even violence. The world through which the heroes move is often a frightful and terrible place and against which they must struggle. The environment—the deadening bureaucratic world that nearly claims Watanabe in *Ikiru* or the elements of rain and wind against which the seven samurai battle in their final fight—is at odds with the actions of the heroes. The world in these films admits of no kindnesses. The hero must fight to create humane perspectives.

It is through the terms of this fight that Kurosawa's ethical manifesto is presented. The strength of self he emphasizes is realized in the films through the capability of the heroes to face a society dominated by predators, where exploitation and oppression are the rule. Both Sanada and Watanabe confront gangsters, whose black market activities thrive in the postwar environment "like bamboo shoots after a rain."[8] Similarly, the corrupt corporations in *The Bad Sleep Well* are ravaging society, murdering and blackmailing those who oppose them, and the hero Nishi dedicates himself to overthrowing them, as he says, for all the people too weak to fight back. Here may be located a major distinction between Kurosawa and the American director with whom he is often compared, John Ford. The Fordian heroes in films like *My Darling Clementine* or *How Green Was My Valley* are strong supporters of conservative values. The latter film is a ringing affirmation of the family, with Donald Crisp the ideal patriarch. Ford creates a warm portrait of family life without admitting the ways that the patriarchal family can be a repressive extension of the state. In the early optimistic films, as well as in his later, darker works, Ford insists that his hero serve the institutions of the family, nation, or military. Films like *The Searchers* and *The Man Who Shot Liberty Valance* display a greater recognition of the cost these institutions exact, but their full meanings are not analyzed. That which Ford affirms, or cannot deny, of course, are those groups that the Kurosawa hero must reject: the state, corporation, and family.

In his films, Kurosawa views the larger context of established society as corrupted by the pursuit of position, wealth, or property. Keiko Mc-

Donald sees the basic question of the narrative of *Red Beard* as "How can one act in the face of a hostile social environment?"[9] In fact, this is a basic question of Kurosawa's narratives in general. The heroes struggle against their society: in *Ikiru*, against governmental bureaucracy whose stratified and hierarchical organization encourages submission and passivity; in *Red Beard*, against a culture that encourages doctors to get rich by treating a constipated aristocracy; in *Seven Samurai*, against a class heritage that demands that samurai refuse to help farmers and allow them to perish at the hands of bandits. And in *Record of a Living Being*, *Ikiru*, *The Bad Sleep Well*, *Yōjimbō*, and *Red Beard*, the central institution of the family is frequently viewed as cold, malignant, or repressive. Kurosawa's characters must break from these social groups to discover a regard for human dignity. But his work does not lapse into nihilism because the characters never reject the basic reality of human interconnectedness. The interactionist self is not abandoned, but in the films its field is reduced so that a space for autonomy can be opened. In acknowledging the interactionist self (i.e., insisting that the hero serve humanity), Kurosawa's films illustrate a cultural attitude described by Hajime Nakamura as dedication to the "human nexus": "The people to whom a human nexus is important place great moral emphasis upon complete and willing dedication of the self to others in a specific human collective. This attitude, though it may be a basic moral requirement in all peoples, occupies a dominant position in Japanese social life. Self-dedication to a specific human nexus has been one of the most powerful factors in Japanese history."[10]

Thus, although they pay great attention to the individualized self, Kurosawa's films also draw from this cultural basis in constructing their narratives and ethic. The characters embark upon a solitary path. Yukie, Sanada, Watanabe must climb their own mountains, and the price of this determined individualism is a profound loneliness that is the "other side" of individualism.[11] They are, however, rescued from nihilism or despair by their dedication to a human community. They reenter the social world to build parks, to defend farmers, to mitigate the general oppressiveness of things. It may be in this regard that Kurosawa's fondness for adventure stories should be understood. They permit him to construct a cinema of ideas in which human capabilities are defined as open-ended and developing, rather than closed, sealed by sets of institutional and social roles. Human life is portrayed as potential, as powerful energy flowing in new and sometimes frightening directions. Mikhail Bakhtin has pointed out that the adventure story "does not rely on already available and stable positions—family, social, biographical; it develops in spite of them."[12] The story is merely "clothing draped over the hero" that can change as often as he does. "It places a person in extraordinary positions that expose and provoke him, it connects him and makes him collide with other people under unusual and unexpected conditions precisely for the purpose of testing the idea and the man of the idea."[13] For Kurosawa, the adventure story becomes a metaphorical form probing the boundaries of the social world, the construction of the self, and the horizons of human development.

In this cinema of ideas, however, Kurosawa's valuation of the self should not be regarded as strictly the result of Western influences. As noted, his heroes are generated and informed by the ideals of the samurai warrior. Richie has described Kurosawa himself as "the last of the samurai."[14] The codes of *bushidō* defined the proper conduct of the warrior, and the director's protagonists manifest many of its principles. *Bushidō* emphasized courage, integrity, fortitude, and fealty.[15] The warrior ideal focused on the development of the individual's capabilities for strength: physical, moral, and spiritual. The ideal samurai combined athletic prowess with moral courage and unswerving allegiance to his lord. His martial skills received continual test in battle, and his moral development was expected to be no less rigorous. *Bushidō* achieved an imaginative and cultural dominance in Japanese life, and Kurosawa draws from this mythic significance in creating his heroes. All the best qualities of the warrior have been spiritualized by Kurosawa in his art. The hero is always as strong as the ideal samurai. This strength may be physical, as in the samurai heroes of *Seven Samurai*, *Yōjimbō*, and *Sanjurō*. But the protagonist may also be a person of ordinary or inferior physical capabilities, as in *Drunken Angel*, *No Regrets for Our Youth*, and *Ikiru*. As Tadao Satō remarks, their great strength is spiritual rather than physical.[16] Their will to create good is overwhelming, and this obsessive dedication, rather than any use of physical force, enables them to triumph. To the emphasis on individual willpower and physical might, Kurosawa adds an abiding commitment to securing the basic needs of other human beings. He thus translates the samurai's obligation to serve his lord into the hero's obligation to serve humanity. Both figures are bound by a duty of fealty, and the endurance of both is severely tested: the samurai in battle and in the bonds that link his fortunes to those of his lord, the Kurosawa hero in the conflict and struggle to humanize a corrupted world.

The samurai as a class were attracted to Zen,[17] and the director's sympathies for samurai culture may account for some features of the films that are analogous to certain Zen ideals. As Donald Keene remarked in a

24. The Kurosawa hero. Kambei (Takashi Shimura) in *Seven Samurai*. (Museum of Modern Art/Film Stills Archive)

different context, however, direct influence is difficult to prove, and it may be more accurate to say that these features "coincide" with Zen.[18] A comparison of Kurosawa's narratives and characters with the model of enlightenment posited by Zen Buddhism can be instructive and can help us to understand some of the ways that Kurosawa's work resonates with a Japanese cultural heritage.

Introduced to Japan from China, Zen was one of a number of Buddhist schools that gained in popularity during the Kamakura and Ashikaga eras. In contrast to the older Tendai and Shingon sects, The Pure Land, Nichiren, and Zen sects emphasized the certainty of salvation and its potential availability to all.[19] Furthermore, Neil McMullin points out that each of these salvationist sects had a pragmatic, empirical emphasis upon *this* world, as opposed to the next.[20] For example, "Zen Buddhism so identifies the transcendent with the immanent, the 'other shore' with 'this shore,' that there is no reason for people to raise their vision above the level of this empirical world."[21]

Whether seeking wisdom via zazen (sitting meditation) or via kōan exercises, the Zen initiate seeks to discover a potential for enlightenment that is inherent in all beings. "The Zen disciple . . . does not seek the Absolute outside himself; . . . he finds in himself the Buddha-nature as the foundation of his own being."[22] Since Buddha-nature is inherent in all things, enlightenment is truly the natural way of things, and it may be achieved by penetrating beyond the veils of illusion that attach to corporeal bodies and the material world. Worldly desires must be transcended to achieve enlightenment, but paradoxically, real-world consequences flow from this wisdom as it is applied to ameliorate human life. "To Zen, the enlightened mind is the truly natural mind, the mind allowed to be itself apart from all delusion or desire. It is awakened in meditation but is ultimately demonstrated in all arenas of life: work, caring for others, artistic creativity."[23]

In Zen there is a distrust of conceptualization because language is thought to foster artificial distinctions within a world that is whole in spirit. The "inner relationship between word and reality" is denied.[24] For this reason, action is favored over words, and the discipline is distinguished by its directness. The kōan, riddles, and word puzzles are meant to test the depth of a pupil's insight. The questions or answers may sound semantically absurd, but this indicates the limitations of conceptualizing and, by rupturing the boundaries of language, can stimulate in the pupil enlightenment or *satori*, which in the Rinzai school can occur instantaneously.

Suzuki describes Zen as a religion of "self-reliance." Instruction about the experience of enlightenment is futile. "Satori must be the outgrowth of one's inner life and not a verbal implantation brought from the outside."[25] There is an emphasis on the individual's unique and private search for wisdom, which can be realized only through experience. Accordingly, the Zen instructor does little explicit teaching and will even disclaim his own role as a teacher. For the Zen master Dōgen, "purposelessness" was essential to achieving enlightenment.[26] Thoughts, attachments, and the desire for enlightenment were to be discarded. The pupil must discover for himself or herself, but without intention or conscious goal.

Kurosawa's films demonstrate a fascination with a similar mode of instruction, appearing as a recurrent feature of narrative structure. In *Sanshirō Sugata*, *Drunken Angel*, *Stray Dog*, *Seven Samurai*, *Red Beard*, and *Dersu Uzala*, a master allows a pupil to observe and learn through experience, and the shocks that Matsunaga and Murakami undergo, shocks that are central to the experience of all Kurosawa heroes, are the necessary means toward enlightenment and are conceived as phases of moral transformation.[27] These shocks, in the words of a Zen priest, are "a trial to the soul, and can shatter the conventional lies with which it surrounds itself."[28] Kurosawa views enlightenment and spiritual development as necessarily predicated upon shock, and the narrative of his autobiography, like those of his films, is cast in this form. The events he recalls from his youth are often quite traumatic: nearly drowning several times as a boy, confronting mountains of corpses after the great Kantō earthquake of 1923 (an experience he describes as like "standing at the gates of hell"[29]), observing a young girl bound and tortured by a stepmother who, on the street, was the model of politeness. Of his memories, Kurosawa remarks, "The clarity of my memory seems to improve in direct proportion to the intensity of shock I underwent."[30]

The other component to this model of enlightenment is the unimportance of verbal instruction. Experience, often of a baffling, bewildering sort, is the guide. Kurosawa recalls his brother treating him with what seemed senseless cruelty—insulting him on the way to school, pushing him into a river when he could not swim—only to realize afterward that these harsh treatments were meant to contain a lesson and that, during moments of real crisis, his brother was always there to intervene on his behalf.[31] Throughout the autobiography, this brother assumes the role of a spiritual guide and a master. Indeed, for Kurosawa it is clear that this brother, Heigo, seems to live in a way that bursts the bounds of normal social life and may be a source for all the Kurosawa characters who do likewise.[32] As Kurosawa apparently did in life, his characters learn through similar examples.[33] In *Seven Samurai*, Kambei teaches the young samurai Katsushiro by allowing the young man to travel in his company, but it is a silent, wordless instruction, forged through experience and example. Similarly, Dersu Uzala rarely gives explicit moral lessons to Arseniev, yet the Russian explorer is a wiser man for his friendship with Dersu and reaches a new understanding of the spiritual power of nature. Though no master–pupil relationship exists in *Ikiru*, Watanabe's sudden realization of the path he must follow is precisely the kind of instantaneous awakening extolled in Zen, and it transforms his life, as it does the lives of the other heroes. (A similar literal rendition of satori occurs in *Sanshirō Sugata*.) "Satori is emancipation, moral, spiritual, as well as intellectual."[34]

Just as Zen emphasizes inner enlightenment, Kurosawa insists that spiritual awakening is a personal affair, that it cannot be imposed from without, and the pattern whereby his heroes must separate themselves from established social groupings is a structural embodiment of this inner wisdom. Enlightenment will not be found within an oppressive society but only through the individual's separation from it, although Kurosawa will also insist that his heroes, having attained enlightenment, return to the social order and attempt to reform it. That is, the enlightened mind demonstrates itself "in all arenas of life." For such a philosophical director, few scenes occur in the films in which a character speaks about what he or she has learned. Instead, knowledge is revealed through action. When Watanabe attains satori in *Ikiru*, he does not speak but returns to work to push the park project through to completion. His new behavior and its concrete symbolization in the slum playground he helps erect are the correlatives of this wisdom.

Kurosawa's model of devotion to the "human nexus" acknowledges the parameters of the interactionist self, while limiting that acknowledgment through characters who are obsessive in their lonely individualism. Kurosawa seems to accept the maxim found in Zen that truth is a private matter, but Zen posits enlightenment upon a renunciation of the ego and desire.[35] The goal of enlightenment may be attained, but the caveat is that it be achieved through a deliberate nonseeking. Zen's model of self-liberation is based on a posture of humility and reverence. "There is here no Promethean struggle for the liberation and elevation of human nature."[36] By contrast, epic, Promethean struggles abound in Kurosawa's films and are, in fact, the model of heroic, human relations that his work constructs. Watanabe's rebellion against the stultifying bureaucracy is an act of stealing fire, as is Yukie's forfeiture of a conventional class identity. Kurosawa's postwar films are cries that people do not have to submit meekly to injustice and to poverty of the spirit. Zen acknowledges that letting go of one's hold upon the world is necessary to allow the spirit behind all things to be felt. In this context, one is taught not to strive (while, paradoxically, striving), nor to seek (while, enigmatically, seeking), for these are intentions that will interfere with the goal of *satori*. By contrast, this paradoxical relation between striving-while-not-striving is absent from Kurosawa's films. His heroes fight to transform the world into more just terms.

A major paradox must now be acknowledged, which lies within the more general Buddhist orientation to the world, of which Zen is merely one variant. (And Buddhism, in turn, is but one component of the Japanese religious tradition, which, because of its diversity, has been described as a "syncretic" one, an admixture of Shintō, Buddhist, Taoist, and Confucian elements.[37]) Buddhist doctrine seems to point to a quietistic outlook, an extinction of desire, withdrawal from the world, and contemplation of spiritual matters. The implications of such a stance might seem to "support an uncritical acceptance of social and political institutions."[38] As a character remarks in The Tale of Genji, "Our life is far too short and uncertain for anything in this world to have much importance."[39] A character in the Noh play Obasute observes, "Ah, well, this world is all a dream—best I speak not, think not."[40] The apparent fatalism of such a perspective partly involves the doctrine of karma, which regards the events of one's life as being predetermined by the deeds of previous lives. If misfortune befalls one, it must be because of some sin one committed in an earlier life or the transgression of a family member. "All relations with other people spring from some past act, however trivial. To drink from the same stream as another, to touch with your sleeve the sleeve of another, even these acts are determined by some relationship in another life."[41] The destruction of the Taira clan by the Minamoto is attributed, in Japan's warrior epic The Tale of the Heike, to the effects of karma: "Their suffering was in retribution for the evil deeds of Kiyomori, the leader of their clan. He had held in his palms both heaven and earth; but to the throne above he paid no respect, and to the people below he paid no heed. He had put many men to death and had exiled many others at his whim, ignoring the mood of the people. None of his descendants could escape retribution for his crimes."[42]

Nirvana, the state of enlightenment and deliverance from worldly woes, from the cycle of rebirths, avidly sought by Buddhists, has been described as signifying a state of "motionless rest, where no wind blows, the fire is quenched, the light is extinguished, the stars have set, and the saint has died. . . . Such words and images evoke the concept of complete annihilation."[43] Yet such negativism, Dumoulin points out, should not be understood as a kind of nihilism because it furnishes the basis for supreme wisdom and for a commitment to the world. "Though aware of the nothingness of all things and of the ultimate irrelevance of all exertions of the spirit, he [the Bodhisattva, who has achieved enlightenment yet forgoes entrance into nirvana] never ceases to work for the benefit of all sentient beings."[44] Thus, to the extent that enlightenment leads to a dedication to benefiting others, the apparent negativism of the doctrine is not to be understood negatively.[45]

Moreover, from a historical standpoint, Buddhism was not disengaged from social and political realities. In fact, Buddhist monasteries had become such centers of economic, political, and military power that their subjugation was perceived by Oda Nobunaga in the sixteenth century as a prerequisite for the emergence of national unification, and he accordingly undertook such a campaign.[46] Thus, to separate Buddhist doctrine from the political, military, or economic power of the estates, or to regard the latter as of subordinate importance, is to risk losing sight of the this-worldly emphasis of Japanese Buddhism, especially of the salvationist sects such as Zen. Hajime Nakamura points out that Japanese Buddhism is "strongly imbued with an activistic behaviorism and practical tendency, which is tied up with its this-worldliness."[47] Religion and worldly affairs, religion and politics, were not separated in premodern Japan during the great periods of Buddhist power.[48]

> To separate the doctrinal and institutional dimensions of Buddhism, or to consider the former dimension to be more purely Buddhist than the latter, is to impose a false distinction on both the Buddhist and the Japanese traditions. The Buddhist tradition was never, least of all in Japan, simply a set of doctrines and religious practices. Rather, it was a complex economic, ethical, philosophical, political, and social phenomenon that wielded immense influence for over a millennium."[49]

With this important qualification in mind—that Japanese Buddhism played a powerful institutional, pragmatic role in worldly affairs—it may now be suggested that Kurosawa's films often seem drawn to formulations akin to the doctrinal negativism of the Buddhist outlook. His films insist that human beings grasp events tightly and make the conditions of their lives conform to their will, that intervention against oppression is a moral necessity. Counterposed to this insistence, however, is an affinity to a perception of life as an insubstantial shadow. We are not yet in a position to see this, but several of the films treated in this chapter—*Rashōmon, The Lower Depths,* and *Throne of Blood*—describe a vision diametrically opposed to that found in *No Regrets for Our Youth, Drunken Angel, The Quiet Duel, Stray Dog,* and *Ikiru.* In short, it will become apparent that one of the dialectics informing Kurosawa's works is a struggle between a belief in the materialist process—that human beings make their world and can change it—and an emphasis on dissolution, decay, and impermanence as fundamental truths of human life. To the first side of this dialectic belong the films of the heroic mode. To the other lie some of the works examined in this chapter, in a region of piercing autumn winds and circling crows.

Since it is in the literary adaptations that this perception first surfaces in his work, they should now be considered. The importance that Kurosawa places on literature, on reading and writing, has been discussed briefly at an earlier point, but it would be useful to consider this once again since these adaptations engage the differences between visual and verbal mediums. Kurosawa recalls, as a youth of eighteen, reading "classics and contemporary, foreign and Japanese literature without discrimination."[50] He has recommended that persons aspiring to become directors read the world's classic literature as a form of training and reread the works of favorite authors "again and again."[51] Reading and writing must become habitual.[52]

> In order to write scripts, you must first study the great novels and dramas of the world. You must consider why they are great. Where does the emotion come from that you feel as you read them? What degree of passion did the author have to have, what level of meticulousness did he have to command, in order to portray the characters and events as he did? You must read thoroughly, to the point where you can grasp all these things.[53]

This analytic passion is revealed in the films that we will now consider: *Rashōmon* (1950), *The Idiot* (1951), *Throne of Blood* (1957), and *The Lower Depths* (1957). These works represent a range of approaches and methods for coming to terms with the relationship between literature and film. Audie Bock points out that Kurosawa "believes that every adaptation must be an interpretation."[54] Between *Rashōmon* in 1950 and *The Lower Depths* in 1957, Kurosawa's grasp of the process of adaptation became quite profound. Whereas *Rashōmon* and *The Idiot* represent fairly uncomplicated adaptations, *Throne of Blood* and *The Lower Depths* are true cinematic transformations of a written source. With Shakespeare and Gorky, Kurosawa worked the hardest to find the appropriate cinematic equivalents for the structures of prose and poetry. It is with these authors that he specifically explored the expressive capabilities of the written word versus those of the image. These films should be regarded as investigations of the boundaries of different communicative modes and as a series of meditations on the possibilities of cross-cultural aesthetic creation. Kurosawa has referred to himself as a kind of global citizen, and of the cinema as a truly international medium:

> No matter where I go in the world, although I can't speak any foreign language, I don't feel out of place. I think of the earth as my home.[55]

> I make my films from the viewpoint of an individual who happens to live in Japan. But I don't believe that society is structured all that differently from country to country. So what I see from my experiences in Japan should be understandable to people of other countries. On top of that, the film medium is truly international.[56]

> I think it's important to establish a kind of global film culture.[57]

Given such an outlook, Kurosawa has not hesitated to use the art forms of other cultures as a basis for his own creation. He has discerned in the plays of Shakespeare or Gorky issues of relevance to Japan, but this has led to a process of active transformation, not slavish adherence to the original work. "I've read Shakespeare, and Russian writers like Dostoevsky and Gorky, many times but I would never let them lead me into making a film until I have thoroughly assimilated them. Only then can I let it come out naturally, as if it's part of my own writing."[58] The works examined in this chapter should be regarded as essentially experimental, as attempts to manipulate image and sound in what are, for Kurosawa, new directions. *Rashomon*, which will be discussed first and which, unlike the others, was taken from a Japanese source, is an attempt to place the fragmentation and angularity of Kurosawa's imagery within the structure of the narrative, an attempt that is incompletely realized but which made possible later success in *Ikiru*. *The Idiot* attempts to visualize and make concrete the interiority of the Dostoevskian world and confronts the same aesthetic challenge posed by the work of Shakespeare, that is, to find visual equivalents for an author who defines his world essentially in terms of dialogue. *Throne of Blood*, as many critics have pointed out,[59] transposes the verbal poetics of *Macbeth* into visual form. *The Lower Depths*, with one source in Gorky, with another perhaps in the set design and costumes of the Shingeki theater, which had mounted productions of the play, may be understood as an exercise in specifying the differing coordinates of physical and cinematic space. Much of the action is restricted to one set, but Kurosawa explores how the cinematic construction of this restricted area may yield an enlarged, dynamic space configured by the emotional and psychological conflicts of its inhabitants. The attempts at cross-cultural translation, then, are also opportunities for aesthetic experimentation. The discussion of these films will seek to clarify the kind of experimentation undertaken by Kurosawa and the extent of its success.

Rashōmon, based on two stories by Ryūnosuke Akutagawa, was the great breakthrough film for both Kurosawa and the Japanese cinema. His reputation had been hurt by the commercial and critical failure of The Idiot, but the success of Rashōmon at the Venice Film Festival in 1951, where it won first prize, helped renew his career. "Had I not won the prize, I would have been forced to remain silent for a considerable time. Thanks to Rashōmon, I was able to go on to make Ikiru."[60] The film was also responsible for the Western world's belated recognition of the Japanese cinema. The story of how Daiei, the studio for which Kurosawa made the film, was reluctant to submit it to international competition is well known.[61] What is harder to recall today, and more important to remember, is the wave of excitement the film caused among film scholars and enthusiasts. Jay Leyda remarked that "The surprise of the entire film world at the appearance of Rashōmon at the 1951 Venice Festival will surely be a dramatic paragraph in all future international film histories."[62] And, indeed, it is. Rashōmon was the most profoundly pictorial and cinematic work anyone had seen in years. Its visual flamboyance was quite unexpected and all the more startling. Not since the silent cinema of Eisenstein and Murnau, it seemed, had narrative been conceived as such a flow of pure imagery. Again and again, critics cited the film's unrelentingly aggressive images, as if rediscovering what the cinema was all about. In his review in the New York Times, Bosley Crowther remarked that "Everyone seeing the picture will immediately be struck by the beauty and grace of the photography, by the deft use of forest light and shade to achieve a variety of powerful and delicate pictorial effects."[63] Other critics called it "a symphony of sight, sound, light, and shadow"[64] and praised its "boldly simple, essentially visual technique."[65]

It was not, however, simply the unabashedly extravagant imagery of the film that was startling. It was also what the film seemed to be saying and how it said it. Rashōmon employs what has now become a well-worn and endlessly repeated convention. A group of characters recall the same set of events, a rape and an apparent murder, in strikingly different terms. Are these differences due to the effects of subjectivity? To the unreliability of memory? Whose story is correct? More has been written about *Rashōmon* than about perhaps any of Kurosawa's other work, and it has become one of those few films whose cultural importance has transcended their own status as films. *Rashōmon* has come to embody a general cultural notion of the relativity of truth. Certainly its success at Venice was partly due to its apparent congruence with then-contemporary currents of European thought, particularly a kind of fashionable existential despair over the instability of truth and value. But the film was also perceived as a useful ally by those waging a struggle to establish the value of the cinema as an art. As Bergman's films would do later in the decade, *Rashōmon* stimulated a great deal of commentary about what were regarded as its basic symbols—the ruined gate, the rain, the forest, the rescued infant, the patterns of light and shadow throughout the imagery. These essays now fill several volumes.[66] In the tradition of the "art cinema," the film seemed to reflect upon important philosophical questions: loss of faith in human beings, the world as a hell, the human propensity to lie. The kaleidoscopic structure of its narrative, the way the basic events of rape and murder were altered by different witnesses, seemed to place the film squarely within the modernist tradition of art. Parker Tyler wrote an essay in which he invoked comparisons with cubist and futurist painting in order to explain the film's temporal and spatial structure.[67] *Rashōmon* has become an enormously powerful and symbolic cultural entity, which engages, then as now, diverse currents of history, philosophy, and art criticism.

The reader who is interested in the range of interpretations the film has received should consult the existing anthologies of this criticism. What I would like to do is to explore the kind of experimentation Kurosawa attempted in this film and then to consider whether *Rashōmon* can genuinely be said to represent a modernist form of filmmaking. The story is set in the twelfth century, at the close of the Heian period when the country's central government and court authority were being undermined by the growth of autonomous political and military powers in the provinces. To the members of the court aristocracy, the class whose devotion to artistic pursuits had produced such classics as *The Tale of Genji*, the times were foreboding. Pestilence, fires, earthquakes, rebellions by warrior monks, violent crime in the capital city of Kyōto, all seemed to be signs of the dissolution of order, of a world teetering on the brink of chaos. It seemed to be the period known in Buddhist prophecy as "the end of the law," when human life would fall to its point of greatest degeneracy. In the film, three characters take shelter from a driving rain beneath the ruined Rashōmon gate, which had guarded the

25. The bandit (Toshirō Mifune) and the warrior (Masayuki Mori): characters "going astray in the thicket of their hearts." *Rashōmon.* (Museum of Modern Art/ Film Stills Archive)

southern entrance to the capital. The gate is in disrepair and is the haunt of beggars, murderers, and thieves. As the priest (Minoru Chiaki), the woodcutter (Takashi Shimura), and the commoner (Kichijirō Ueda) wait for the rain to stop, they tell the story of how a noblewoman (Machiko Kyō) was raped in the forest, her samurai husband (Masayuki Mori) killed, and a thief named Tajomaru (Toshirō Mifune) arrested for the crime. Much of the film relates, through flashbacks, four versions of the crime, as told by Tajomaru, the woman, the spirit of the samurai through a medium, and the woodcutter, who was an unseen witness to the events.

The intercutting of flashbacks to create a nonlinear narrative and the insistence on the subjectivity of memory prefigures such later, seminal films as *Hiroshima Mon Amour*, but there are also precursors. In its examination of the refraction of events through a consciousness that embodies them in a narrative, *Rashōmon* does little that was not already done by Welles in *Citizen Kane*. Furthermore, as compared with *Kane*, or with the work of Alain Resnais, or with Joseph Losey's *The Go-Between*, the temporal structure of Kurosawa's film is not overly complex. There is never an uncertainty about whose narrative frame we are in, and there is none of the deceitful play in which Welles engages when he has characters narrate events they could not possibly have witnessed. Kurosawa is not really concerned to investigate the cinematic representation of temporality, as were Welles and Resnais. Hence, the overall clarity of the narrative frames and voices. We always know where we are within them. It is *what* is recalled that is problematic, not the mode and form of its presentation. It is the content of the frames, the events enunciated by the voices, that shift and provide the film with its ambiguity. What has made *Rashōmon* a tantalizing film is its refusal to validate any of the witnesses' stories as a true account. There is simply no way to know who is telling the truth. In this ambiguity Kurosawa has found a narrative expression for his own pessimism about what Conrad referred to as the human heart of darkness. Kurosawa has remarked that "What dwells at the bottom of the human heart remains a mystery to me."[68] *Rashōmon* is the fullest expression of this mystery in all his work, a thoroughgoing attempt to penetrate the depths of the heart and a celebration of the inability to do so. The moral of the film is quite straightforward, and Kurosawa has expressed it with characteristic directness:

> Human beings are unable to be honest with themselves about themselves. They cannot talk about themselves without embellishing. This script portrays such human beings—the kind who cannot survive without lies to make them feel they are better people than they really are. It even shows this sinful need for flattering falsehood going beyond the grave—even the character who dies cannot give up his lies when he speaks to the living through a medium. Egoism is a sin the human being carries with him from birth; it is the most difficult to redeem.[69]

The extensive patterns of light and shadow in the film were meant by Kurosawa to suggest a kind of spiritual and emotional labryinth. "These strange impulses of the human heart would be expressed through the use of an elaborately fashioned play of light and shadow. In the film, people going astray in the thicket of their hearts would wander into a wider wilderness, so I moved the setting to a large forest."[70] Rather than being an intricately designed mystery story requiring the skills of a sleuth for its unraveling, *Rashōmon* is a cinematically straightforward presenta-

26. *Rashōmon's* forest imagery was meant by Kurosawa to embody the dark labyrinth of the human heart. (Museum of Modern Art/Film Stills Archive)

tion of the sins of egoism. The ambiguity within the film—the question of the reliability of the various stories—is psychological in nature, issuing from the characters and the reasons they may have for lying. It is not an ambiguity of form, located in the visual and aural organization of the film. As Kurosawa said, the paradoxes in the film are those of the human heart. They are not those of the image itself. This is an important point to which we shall return.

First, however, we need to understand the specific nature of Kurosawa's experiment in *Rashōmon*. As noted, the film attracted wide attention for the aggressiveness of its imagery, but this was not an empty display of bravura for its own sake. There are long sequences in the film that are structured as purely visual passages, as what Hitchcock might call "pure film," sequences that communicate narrative information and achieve an emotional effect strictly through the imagery. Dialogue is minimal in these scenes or nonexistent. The long sequence, composed of nineteen shots, detailing Tajomaru's first glimpse of the woman and the samurai in the forest, proceeds without dialogue as Kurosawa visualizes the heat of the day, the allure of the mysteriously veiled woman, and

Tajomaru's affectations of boredom that conceal his lust. Camera movement extends the frame and makes it fluid, capturing the dynamics of tension, fear, and anger, and visualizing Tajomaru's own shifting line of sight as the couple moves through the trees.

Many other scenes are informed by these principles of pure visualization. Perhaps the most striking is the sequence showing the woodcutter walking through the forest just before he finds evidence of the crime. The sequence is composed of fifteen shots, all of which are tracking shots, so that it becomes an extended essay on the capabilities of the moving camera. Kurosawa intercuts low-angle tracking shots of the trees, through which the sun sporadically peeps, high-angle tracking shots of the woodcutter moving through the forest, and extreme close-ups of the character with the camera following from both the front and the rear. These are among the most sensuous moving camera shots in cinema history, and the entire sequence has a hypnotic power. Much of this effect is due to its "silence," to the absence of dialogue and ambient sound. Fumio Hayasaka's percussive, rhythmic score is the only aural accompaniment to the images.

Other sequences, however, do include dialogue, but it is often of a very special kind. The first recollection of the priest about meeting the couple in the woods, the policeman's report of finding Tajomaru thrown by a horse and lying on the ground by a river, and Tajomaru's own account of riding the horse and stopping for a drink are all essentially silent sequences. The minimal dialogue accompanying the images is framed as a language of recollection, not simultaneous with the image and event. The dialogue is nonsynchronous and performs the same explanatory function as the title cards in a silent film, intruding upon the image to offer an account of its meaning.

Kurosawa, in fact, intended *Rashōmon* to be a kind of silent film. He attempted to recover the aesthetic of the early cinema, which he so much admired, and to fashion this film accordingly.

> I like silent pictures and always have. They are often so much more beautiful than sound pictures are. Perhaps they have to be. At any rate, I wanted to restore some of this beauty. I thought of it, I remember, this way: one of the techniques of modern painting is simplification, I must therefore simplify this film.[71]

> Since the advent of the talkies in the 1930s, I felt, we had misplaced and forgotten what was so wonderful about the old silent

movies. I was aware of the esthetic loss as a constant irritation. I sensed a need to go back to the origins of the motion picture to find this peculiar beauty again; I had to go back into the past. . . .

. . . *Rashōmon* would be my testing ground, the place where I could apply the ideas and wishes growing out of my silent-film research.[72]

Kurosawa says he kept the script short so that he would be able to concentrate on creating "rich and expansive" images.[73] During the sequence in which the woodcutter walks through the forest, Kurosawa fashions the camera's patterns of movement so that they become the architectonics of narrative and generate metaphor. The woodcutter intuitively responds to the rhythms of the forest by leaping a river, ducking a branch, crossing a log bridge. He does not recognize these objects consciously but glides over them in a mystical state. The lyrically tracking camera simulates the rhythms of his walk and the topography of the forest and is, therefore, a formal indicator of this condition. But his reverie is broken when he discovers evidence of a crime. As he finds several hats, an amulet case, a rope, and finally a body, he scuttles about awkwardly, with fear. As he makes these discoveries, the tracking shots cease. The objects have made him alarmed and rational. His thinking mind is switched on, and his sensuous, intuitive response to the forest is lost. This change is reflected in the shift from a moving camera to the stationary shots that record the discoveries of the objects and the dead man. The sequence has shifted on a formal and a dramatic level from sensuous movement to a fixed, narrowed perspective of interest, from the intuitive responses of the Zen state to the divided and rigid perspectives of the rational mind.[74]

As in the silent cinema, movement becomes the embodiment of narrative and the necessary sign of emotional and psychological states. Emotions must be externalized because they cannot be described in words. The excessively broad acting style in the film, which was a source of controversy when it was first viewed in the West, works in this manner to exteriorize emotion and give it concrete form. It is not unlike the expressionist style of performance Murnau insisted upon in *Sunrise*, when he had George O'Brien transformed into a hunched, golem-like figure to suggest an obsession with murder. The "simplified" style of silent films to which Kurosawa sought to return routinely included the kind of broad, sweeping gestures that Mifune brings to Tajomaru and Machiko Kyō to the role of Masago, the wife. But Kurosawa also treats their language in this expansive manner. As they cackle wildly, shriek, or cry, in an excessive style that Joseph Anderson has aptly termed "reverse anthropomorphism,"[75] their language is made strange by its very excess. The familiar is defamiliarized in the way the formalist critic Viktor Shklovsky meant.[76] Through these strategies—an emphasis upon purely visual sequences, a descriptive use of language with images for which it is nonsynchronous, and an acting style so excessive as to wrench speech out of a naturalistic context—Kurosawa creates a displacement between visual and verbal modes. Joseph Anderson has discussed a tendency of Japanese art he calls "commingling," a tendency "toward extreme complexity with heterogeneous, often redundant, elements brought together in complex relationships."[77] Citing a range of pictorial and narrative forms, Anderson discusses the ways in which image and written/verbal narrative and recitative may be conjoined in support of each other, in counterpoint, or as commentary on the other. Kurosawa's manipulations of image and dialogue in the film qualify as examples of "commingling." As noted, dialogue and vocalization assume a range of novel functions in the film. The two are not fused into a single chain of signification as is usually the case in narrative film. They are separated in conflict, the flamboyance of the imagery contesting with the hysteria of the performances. This displacement is, indeed, what the film is about. The rape and murder are recounted in four different ways. The physical world of events and objects is reconstructed verbally, but language is an unreliable mediator. The stories do not match. Gaps and contradictions prevail between word and event.[78] The "inner relationship" between word and reality is denied. This communicative disjunction is viewed in the film in ontological terms as a space wherein human sin and evil originate. The failure of language to grasp the world of events is a story about the human fall from grace into a world deformed by heterodoxy and multiplicity.

This apparent attentiveness to a restructuring of image–sound relationships, however, is not characteristic of the entire film. Many scenes, such as those at the Rashōmon gate that frame the narrative, are realized in conventional terms. The sound merely supports the images, and no conflict develops between what we see and what the characters are saying. The disjunction between image and verbal language is, then, at best a tendency that receives incomplete development. As noted earlier, the ambiguities that have intrigued viewers are primarily those of character, not form. It is here that we may question the film's status as a work of modernist cinema. Rashōmon seems to advance a claim that reality is essentially a construction, not an a priori, and that it is structured by subjectivity. But the material that must form the necessary basis of this construction is not specified. By contrast, the modernist tradition of narrative film, from Eisenstein to Godard, has taken semiotic material as its object of study. Investigation of the cinematic signifier is central to these films. Eisenstein's principles of montage worked to fragment the significations of individual shots and set them against each other in collision. Analyzing the means by which the cinema communicates, he concluded that the image "can never be an inflexible letter of the alphabet, but must always remain a multiple-meaning ideogram. And it can be read only in juxtaposition."[79] Godard was driven by his analysis of the image even more radically, to a "return to zero."[80] His awareness of the "magical" properties of photographic images, their power to demand a reading as the real objects they represent rather than as signifiers, and of the moral and political ramifications of this confusion, led him to reject the conventions of narrative cinema entirely. From this rejection, he attempted to pare down the elements of sound, light, and color to a zero point, from which they might be reconstructed in a way that would make them accessible to semiotic control. Kurosawa is not an analytic filmmaker in this tradition, and Rashōmon conducts its inquiry into the constructedness of reality at the level of the signified. The film deals with fragmentation and relativity in terms of the *content* of the narratives, not their structure. In *Ikiru*, as we have seen, Kurosawa would be much more successful at structuring disparities of consciousness and perception in purely formal terms, but Rashōmon's inability to do this weakens the film. The woodcutter's dismay and the priest's despair over the lies of the witnesses, their remarks that these lies are the most terrible of truths and certify the world as a hell, are not convincing because the film does not show us any basis for these conclusions. Unlike the ways in which language works in the plays of Beckett or Pinter, the semiotic material of the film does not fragment or nullify the basis of human communication and trust. Instead, it is the personalities of the characters that do this, the desire of the witnesses to present themselves in the best possible light. Once again with Kurosawa, personality becomes the locus of inquiry, this time limiting the claims of the film to speak to a tradition into which it has been placed.

An exploration of personality, and an overheated psychological atmosphere, also typify Kurosawa's only direct adaptation of Dostoevsky, produced directly after Rashōmon. Kurosawa's attempt to film The Idiot was perhaps inevitable, given his fondness for the Russian author and

given also the similarities of style and sensibility that inform their creations. In the work of both men, narrative becomes a vehicle of philosophical exploration; incident and action are charged with metaphysical
and spiritual significance. Like those of Kurosawa, Dostoevsky's narratives inflict a series of psychic shocks upon their protagonists, who are
placed within a world shaken to its foundations, in a state of disintegration.[81] For Dostoevsky, the truths of Christian life were being undermined in late nineteenth-century Russia by the European-derived evils
of capitalism, Catholicism, and socialism, all promising a false unity and
stemming from the failure of European religion. Against this, the example of a Russian Christian society and the Orthodox faith could enlighten
a darkening Europe and recolonize it spiritually.[82] Dostoevsky's perception of a society splintered by internal discord finds an analogue in the
historical circumstances informing Kurosawa's cinema, the encounter of
East and West and the cataclysm of war, which forever altered the social
coordinates. Kurosawa reproduces this generative matrix in the settings
of his narratives. He does not dramatize a "timeless" Japan, an unchanging national essence, but rather the traumas of historical transition.[83]
Both artists share an apocalyptic sensibility. What Michael Holquist has
observed about Dostoevsky is true of Kurosawa as well. He suggests that
Dostoevsky's work is structured by, and is especially sensitive to, the
historical dilemmas of national identity. Dostoevsky gave aesthetic form
to the national search for an identity secure from European influence "by
conceiving Russian historical doubts as existential scenarios."[84] We have
noted a similar process at work in Kurosawa's films, in which the problems of national history and identity are imaginatively recast in cinematic form.

Both men shared a perception of impending catastrophe and a search
for salvation, and they both rejected politics as a means of conducting
this search. Kurosawa and Dostoevsky flirted with left-wing movements
in their youth, Kurosawa joining the Proletarian Artists' League in 1929
and relaying messages for an illegal radical organization as his dissatis-
faction with Japanese society deepened. Dostoevsky in 1847 frequented
the Petrashevsky circle and subsequently became involved with a utopian attempt to liberate the serfs. Both men later renounced their earlier
commitment and in their work avoided the solutions of organized political action. Kurosawa now regards the commitment of his youth as the
product of a fashionable "fever among young people." He adds that it
was doubtful that he was a true Marxist, though he admits "I still lean
toward these ideas. I probably have Marxist ideas somewhere in me."[85]

For Dostoevsky, salvation hinged on personal acceptance of Christian faith and Christly love and led him eventually to a position of extreme conservatism and nationalism. For Kurosawa, the lures of religion and national pride were not compelling, but he could appreciate the emotional qualities, the emphasis on tolerance and devotion to others, of Dostoevsky's religious ethic. Indeed, though the ideologies motivating them are different, the heroes of director and writer are put through a similar ordeal. Their passionate devotion to a credo of individual and social reform paradoxically isolates them from others. "[B]eing possessed by their 'truth' defines their relationship to other people and creates the special sort of loneliness these heroes know."[86] Dostoevsky's conception of freedom and responsibility is strikingly applicable to what we find in Kurosawa's films:

> To the contrary, to the contrary, I say; not only is it not necessary to be impersonal, but precisely one must become individual, even in a degree much higher than that which is now established in the West. Understand me: voluntary, fully conscious self-sacrifice, free of any outside constraint, of one's entire self for the benefit of all is, in my opinion, a mark of the highest development of individuality, of its highest power, its highest self-mastery, the highest freedom of one's own will.[87]

The defense of a farming village by samurai, the construction of a park for slum children, the dedication to medicine as a means of curing the disadvantaged, all are examples of such voluntary, unconstrained self-sacrifice in Kurosawa's films. Though he leaves out the Christianizing components of Dostoevsky's philosophy, Kurosawa defines the social imperative in identical terms. What is necessary for salvation is a new, more demanding, higher form of individualism. This ethic "will lay hold of all your life, and may fill up your whole life," as Ippolit Terentyev dreams in *The Idiot* and as the heroes of *Ikiru*, *Seven Samurai*, and *Red Beard* demonstrate.

Dostoevsky's novels and Kurosawa's films render this ethic into artistic form using similar styles. Narrative time is condensed and focused into a series of crises. Bakhtin's description of Dostoevskian time is also true for Kurosawa: "Dostoevsky makes almost no use of relatively uninterrupted historical or biographical time, that is, of strictly epic time; he 'leaps over' it, he concentrates action at points of crisis, at turning points and catastrophes, when the inner significance of a moment is equal to a

'billion years,' that is, when the moment loses its temporal restrictiveness."[88] Time is structured as a crisis, not only because of the exigencies
of the historical era, but also because in the charged moment competing
moral demands collide. Prince Myshkin is forced to choose between
Aglaia Ivanovna and Nastasya Filippovna, Detective Murakami between
the examples embodied by Yusa and Satō. A dialectic of competing
voices structures the works. In Dostoevsky, Bakhtin called it "dialogics,"
while Eisenstein referred to it as a kind of emotional montage producing
"an unsurpassed dynamics of inner tension."[89] The emotional turbulence of Dostoevsky's novels, the melodramatics, the doubling of characters, the extroversion of gesture and feeling, may also be observed as
qualities in Kurosawa's films. The inner stresses and contradictions of
Kurosawa's work, as he attempts to conjoin differing cultural traditions
and sets of values, the inability to achieve closure, the style that celebrates polarities of line and movement, all this prevents the formation of
a stable and fixed authorial perspective. The ambivalences within the
films are the source of their textual richness. Similarly, Bakhtin noted
the lack of a "fixed authorial field of vision"[90] in Dostoevsky's novels,
where competing, fully formed consciousnesses do battle with each
other, sensing "their own inner unfinalizability,"[91] as Dostoevsky extends "every contending point of view to its maximal force and depth, to
the outside limits of plausibility."[92] Indeed, this sensitivity to historical
contradictions and the dialectics of their style often made final closure
impossible for both artists. The rescue of the baby at the end of
Rashōmon and the appearance of the schoolgirl cured of tuberculosis at
the conclusion of *Drunken Angel* are unconvincing attempts to nullify
the darkness that has preceded (a darkness that, incidentally, Akutagawa
was quite able to accept in his stories that formed the basis for *Rashōmon*). Similarly, Raskolnikov's religious conversion at the end of *Crime
and Punishment* cannot overcome the articulate power of his earlier
murderous act of rebellion.

In Dostoevsky, then, Kurosawa found an author whose forms and sensibilities, and the historical dislocations to which they responded, were
analogous to his own. Above all, he has valued Dostoevsky's ability to
confront directly the most wretched misery, the most sordid behavior. In
this directness, Kurosawa locates truth. "I know of no one so compassionate . . . ordinary people turn their eyes away from tragedy; he looks
straight into it."[93] This metaphor of looking straight into the heart of
darkness is a basic and recurring one for Kurosawa, who has said that "to
be an artist means never to avert one's eyes."[94] As noted, Kurosawa re-

calls his brother's command during the great earthquake to confront directly the most frightening sights. In his art, this is precisely what he has tried to do, and he has passed on the example to his characters. Sanada insists on extracting the bullet from Matsunaga's hand without the use of anaesthetic. In *Red Beard*, the older doctor commands the intern Yasumoto to watch carefully a dying man's last moments and forbids him to look away from a bloody operation. Kurosawa appreciated this quality in Dostoevsky—the intensity of vision, the heightened realism, the refusal to spare the reader the most horrific descriptions of cruelty and violence.

Many of Kurosawa's recurring concerns, then, find analogues in Dostoevsky's fiction. In addition to those already mentioned—the multivoiced quality of Kurosawa's films, the construction of narrative as a series of psychic shocks, the revelation of character through extremes of behavior and emotion, the acute sensitivity to social collapse, the work of art as an expression of historical rupture—Kurosawa shares Dostoevsky's fascination with criminality. The killer of *Stray Dog* and the kidnapper of *High and Low* are "underground" men, living precariously on the fringes of society and responding to it with profound contempt and as superhuman rebels, convinced of their own right to transgress. Both characters are presented as figures who are inhuman yet possessed of dignity, and the films make every effort to understand their points of view, as Dostoevsky does in his fiction. Finally, as noted earlier, Kurosawa shares Dostoevsky's regard for children as essentially innocent beings and for the violence done to them as an unanswerable indictment of the social world. This perception of children is developed in his autobiography, where he details a shocking encounter with a girl tortured by her stepmother,[95] and it is manifest in films ranging from *Drunken Angel* and *Stray Dog* to *Red Beard*.

Why, then, is his version of *The Idiot* so amazingly bad? Given these affinities for Dostoevsky's work and Kurosawa's abilities to visualize literary material, he would have seemed an ideal filmmaker to take on a project like *The Idiot*. The spiritual and aesthetic compatibility he felt with Dostoevsky, however, may actually have been the problem, for his version of *The Idiot* is as close to an embarrassingly poor film as he has ever come. The performances are mannered and overwrought, yet the camerawork is so restricted and conventional that much of the film comes to have the air of filmed theater. It is a difficult film to watch, a remarkable defect for as gifted a storyteller as Kurosawa. The work is largely incoherent, though this is probably not Kurosawa's fault. The

27. Toshirō Mifune (left) and Masayuki Mori as the Rogozhin and Myshkin characters in *The Idiot*. (Museum of Modern Art/Film Stills Archive)

original version was four and one-half hours, but the studio drastically shortened it against Kurosawa's wishes.[96] It is always treacherous to evaluate a film that has been so extensively reedited against the wishes of its maker. Sam Peckinpah's *The Wild Bunch* and Sergio Leone's *Once Upon a Time in America* are very different experiences depending upon whether one sees the director's or the studio's cut. Nevertheless, despite the confusion and gaping narrative holes the cuts have produced in Kurosawa's film, its deficiencies of style remain all too apparent.

The crowded interiors in the homes of the Epanchin and Ivolgin families, the images awkwardly filled with too many people, were shot by Kurosawa in a conventional, Hollywood style. Establishing shots, medium shots, and close-ups all follow with a perfectly American logic, with the consequence that a very stage-like space is preserved. The action is confined to a single set, and Kurosawa does not fragment space with the kind of angular staging and cutting he does so well and which had become, by this point in his career, one of his trademarks. Just as he eschews the use of editing to produce wild perceptual shifts, he avoids camera movement, so that his compositions, normally so fluid and energetic, become static and leaden. Forswearing montage and the moving camera, Kurosawa cannot perform the analysis of space, the dissection of a physical area and its cinematic restructuring, that is basic to his method of working. It may seem that part of the problem lay with Dostoevsky. His novels reveal a strongly theatrical organization, with overt physical action minimized, time compressed, and character explored and revealed mainly through speech.[97] Dostoevsky's characters do very little but say a great deal, and in some ways this is the opposite of Kurosawa's style. So strongly dialogue-bound an author seems to have compelled Kurosawa to work at the level of the actors' performances, not of the image. With very few exceptions, the scenes are staged as they appear in the novel, and Kurosawa relies on the close-up, as he has never done before or since, to convey the frenzied and agitated countenances of Dostoevsky's characters. But, as Richie points out, what works on the page seems simply overwrought on the screen.[98] Rather than locating the extravagant hysterics and hallucinatory emotional states of Dostoevsky's world on the faces of the actors, as Kurosawa does, it would have been much better to locate these qualities within the structure of the imagery. Adapting his favorite Russian author, Kurosawa earnestly tries to remain faithful but thereby fails to truly transpose the material. Donald Richie suggests that the source of this failure lies in Kurosawa's own identification with Dostoevsky. The critical distance necessary for a successful adaptation was not present.[99]

Nevertheless, a good start was made. The Myshkin character is rendered in contemporary terms, his illness rooted in recent historical upheavals. He has been traumatized by World War II and was nearly executed as a war criminal, and the signifier of foreignness, which in the novel was Switzerland, is now America. But the foreignness of Dostoevsky's character was also the source of his sickness, the isolation from Russia and the land one cause of his "idiocy."[100] Kurosawa loses Dostoevsky's reactionary nationalism, but unfortunately he also loses the ideological framework that certifies and justifies the action of the novel. Withdrawn from the framework of the Christian tradition, Kurosawa's Myshkin becomes simply a gentle man, without signifying the religious messianism of the novel's character. Thus, his spiritual confrontation with the material corruptions of a moneyed society is lost in the film, and indeed the social criticism of the novel is completely missing.[101] Dostoevsky sets the spirit against the flesh and Christianity against the power of money, but Kurosawa reads Myshkin only as an apostle of brotherly love and thereby dilutes his ideological significance and his expressive power. Bereft of the ideological tradition that certifies his passion, Kurosawa's Myshkin is a bland and insubstantial figure.

The legacy of Dostoevsky for Kurosawa would have to be an indirect one. Kurosawa's own style and aesthetic personality were simply too powerful to be overridden by the work of another. His attempt to subordinate his own forms to a novelistic structure could not be maintained. Moreover, Myshkin is not an especially good character for Kurosawa to attempt to handle. He is too passive, too indecisive, and far too masochistic. Enlightenment for Kurosawa is signified by behavioral aggression and physical action, just the reverse of the inhibited, recessive Myshkin. The influence of, and the homages to, Dostoevsky would be apparent in the future as matters of style, not content. The fervid embrace of melodrama in *Red Beard*, for example, its use of the brutalized child as narrative and moral pivot, its focus on disease as a moral and spiritual as well as a physical condition, place that film far more deeply within the Dostoevskian tradition than the overt imitation of *The Idiot*. As Richie observes, the best form of respect Kurosawa could pay Dostoevsky was to remain faithful to his own forms, to continue to create, not films from Dostoevsky, but films in the Dostoevskian manner.[102] And this is what he went on to do, leaving *The Idiot* behind as a necessary act of aesthetic catharsis.

A general absence of semiotic analysis prevails in *The Idiot* and *Rashōmon*, though to a far greater degree in the former. *Rashōmon*, after all, points to the signifying modes of the silent cinema. Moreover, Kurosawa does alter the tone of the Akutagawa stories and does some reconstruction of their point of view, though these are primarily alterations of content, not form. Six years later, however, Kurosawa demonstrated much greater sensitivity to the essential difference between the modes of image and language. He recognized that the process of adapting literature to the screen is one not of translation but of transformation. In *Throne of Blood*, the signifiers of word and image are no longer interchangeable, and the verbal texture of the play is transformed into a dense, elaborate patterning of image and sound. *Throne of Blood* dispenses with Shakespearean dialogue. Instead of trying to translate this poetry into Japanese, Kurosawa renders it as imagery. This has been generally recognized by the abundant literature that now exists on the film.[103] But what might be stressed is that the shift in the mode of signification—from words to images—also involves, and is motivated by, an act of cultural perception. Kurosawa's adaptation of the play does not simply move it to an analogous period of Japanese history. He transforms it according to a different cultural "way of seeing." The images that he has created are not cinematic equivalents for the play. They go beyond the source to render the thematic and emotional world of *Macbeth* through indigenous aesthetic modes. The shift of signification is not simply from one form of communication to another; it is not just the difference between word and image that is important; it is also the differences of perspective that one's native culture provides. In carrying out this analysis, Kurosawa demonstrates both his identity as a "global citizen," drawn to works of foreign literature, and his sensitivity to the Japanese heritage and the Japanese audience. Moreover, in transposing the play, he discovers a means of displacing personality as the locus of action.

Among the things that drew him to *Macbeth* was his awareness of the similarity between the play's world of war, internecine bloodletting, and treachery, and Japan's own period of civil war in the sixteenth century, when traitors were common figures. It was a world "turned upside down" when lords could not be sure of the loyalty of those they commanded.[104] Moreover, the characters seemed peculiarly suited to his kind of cinema. "The images of men who lived through the age when the weak became a prey for the strong are highly concentrated. Human beings are described with great intensity. In this sense, I think there is something in *Macbeth* which is common to all other works of mine."[105] In presenting these characters, however, Kurosawa has eliminated their moments of introspection. None of the play's great passages of self-examination was retained. Instead, Washizu (Macbeth) and Asaji (Lady Macbeth) embody the ambition, lust, and cruelty of the play in more pure and absolute terms. In J. Blumenthal's nice phrase, their brutality and ambition are "distilled to almost pure materiality."[106] By eliminating Lady Macbeth's speech in which she calls on the spirits to unsex her and to fill her with the direst cruelty, Kurosawa transforms Asaji into a figure of unmitigated evil, lacking the human dimension of Shakespeare's character because she is "endowed instead with a purely physical power."[107] Similarly, Asaji's act of handwashing is performed as highly stylized mime and lacks the elaborate verbal expressions of anguish Shakespeare permitted his character. All that remains of Macbeth's "Tomorrow and Tomorrow and Tomorrow" speech is a brief scene in which Washizu (Toshiro Mifune), with barely repressed verbal violence, bitterly calls himself a fool. These reductions are not just evidence of the "cinematic" qualities of the film. They take us into the analysis Kurosawa is performing.

The bitter disillusionment expressed in this speech, in which Macbeth despairingly acknowledges the brevity of life and the certainty of death, resonates with the Buddhist perspective, which, too, acknowledges the transience and illusory nature of material existence. "Out, out brief candle! / Life's but a walking shadow, a poor player, / That struts and frets his hour upon the stage / And then is heard no more" echoes the melancholy of the Noh play *Sekidera Komachi*: "The temple bell of Sekidera / Tolls the vanity of all creation— / To ancient ears a needless lesson. / A mountain wind blows down Osaka's slope / To moan the certainty of death."[108] The fated quality to the action in *Macbeth*, all of it foretold by the witches, was transposed by Kurosawa with a sharpened emphasis upon predetermined action and the crushing of human freedom beneath the laws of karma. As Richie has pointed out about the film's world, "Cause and effect is the only law. Freedom does not exist."[109] In Macduff and Malcolm, Shakespeare envisioned moral alternatives to Macbeth's evil, but Kurosawa's is a closed world in *Throne of Blood*, from which a moral dialectic has vanished. As Richie notes, the film is circular in structure, beginning and ending with the same imagery, a grave marker in a fog-swept and desolate landscape.[110] A chorus intones a passage about how human vanity and ambition, reaching beyond the grave, have wreaked violence and destruction throughout endless lives. The events of the film—Washizu's murderous path to power and execution by his own men—are inscribed in a cycle of time that infinitely repeats. A significant alteration to the play enforces this. Unlike Shakespeare's virtuous Duncan, the lord that Washizu murders had gained power by murdering his own lord, and Washizu's action is thus a replication of this prior act of savagery. The metaphors Kurosawa develops—the labyrinthine forest in which Washizu becomes lost, the fog through which the warriors aimlessly ride, the horse that circles behind Washizu as Asaji plots the death of the lord—embody as patterns of movement these ideas of temporal circularity and the fatedness of violence and evil.[111]

The transposition of Shakespeare's themes into a Buddhistic frame is enforced by Kurosawa's aesthetic choices, specifically his decision to call upon traditions of art influenced by Buddhist principles. We have already noted how Kurosawa dispenses with the play's introspective passages where the characters reflect upon the meaning of their actions. In place of this, he offers a presentation of character informed by the traditions of the Noh theater, which was a theater of the aristocratic and warrior classes contemporaneous with the age the film depicts.[112] Noh plays typically presented the confrontation of a wandering priest with a ghost or spirit drawn back to this world by longing and regret and were intended to dramatize Buddhist ethics. Zeami noted that his art "will

28. Washizu (Toshirō Mifune) meets his end in a fusillade of arrows. *Throne of Blood*. (Museum of Modern Art/Film Stills Archive)

serve to praise the Buddha and provide the means to spread his teachings."[113] Donald Keene suggests that the emotional qualities of the plays are embodied by the characters as absolutes, rather than as strict attributes of their personalities, and the plays aim to create an atmosphere pervaded by these emotions instead of localizing them as the expressions of specific characters.[114] This emphasis may be most clearly glimpsed in the use of masks to express a range of basic emotions. The masks worn by performers embodied stereotyped emotions and categorized the character according to type (i.e., warrior, old woman, demon). Kurosawa drew from this tradition in his film:

> Drama in the West takes its character from the psychology of men or circumstances; the Noh is different. First of all, the Noh has the mask, and while staring at it, the actor becomes the man whom the mask represents. The performance also has a defined style, and in devoting himself to it faithfully, the actor becomes possessed. Therefore, I showed each of the players a photograph

of the mask of the Noh which came closest to the respective role; I told him that the mask was his own part. To Toshirō Mifune who played the part of Taketoki Washizu, I showed the mask named Heida. This was the mask of a warrior. In the scene in which Mifune is persuaded by his wife to kill his lord, he created for me just the same life-like expression as the mask did. To Isuzu Yamada who acted the role of Asaji I showed the mask named Shakumi. This was the mask of a beauty no longer young, and represented the image of a woman about to go mad. . . . For the warrior who was murdered by Macbeth and later reappears as an apparition, I considered the mask of the apparition of a nobleman of the name of Chūjō to be becoming. The witch in the wood was represented by the mask Yamanba.[115]

The stylization of performance according to Noh convention also extended to gesture and movement. Zeami, the fourteenth-century theorist of Noh, insisted on the powerful effects that could be obtained by restraint. "[N]o matter how slight a bodily action, if the motion is more restrained than the emotion behind it, the emotion will become the Substance and the movements of the body its Function, thus moving the audience."[116] He emphasized this truth in a style built from dialectical combinations of elements, such as the necessity of coupling violent bodily movements with gentle foot movements or the reverse. Similarly, Kurosawa corrects the misunderstanding that the Noh is necessarily static: "The Noh also involves terribly violent movements resembling those of an acrobat. They are so violent that we wonder how a man can manage to move so violently. The player capable of such an action performs it quietly, hiding the movements. Therefore both quietness and vehemence co-exist together."[117]

The interiors of the film incorporate the bare stage design and minimal props typical of Noh, and when Washizu sits in an empty room to vent his despair over the foolishness of his acts, his voice resounds with fury, but the rigidity of his body contains the emotion, barely letting it escape. The structure of the film as a whole, in fact, exemplifies this dialectic between stasis and activity, alternating, as Noël Burch points out, between sequences of furious motion and frozen immobility.[118] The masklike presentation of characters, the stylization of their movements (especially evident in Lady Asaji), and the elimination of verbal introspection, typical of the Noh, displace the emotions of the film onto objects and the environment. "The things of man are conjoined, inseparably on the formal plane, with the things of nature."[119] The forest, the fog, the extraordinary landscapes Kurosawa presents are signifiers of an atmosphere charged by madness, futility, and violence. In *Throne of Blood*, feelings are not strictly the province and expression of human beings but are objectified within the environment, are disclosed within and through the world of things. Emotions are not expressed but revealed. The art of the tea ceremony, haiku poetry, Noh theater—arts influenced by Zen Buddhism—all made a virtue of the perception of emotional forms within the world of nature.[120] Suzuki, for example, discusses how the implements and objects used in the tea ceremony symbolize not only the human place in the natural world but also the feelings and emotions suggested by nature and the seasons.[121]

Thus, to interpret the imagery of *Throne of Blood* as if it were psychological in nature, as if the forest or the fog were reflections of Washizu's mind or spirit, is to miss the shift of signification that Kurosawa is carrying out. He has not retained the play's structuring of greed and ambition as qualities of personality, as attributes of Macbeth and his wife. Kurosawa's characters and images counter the Western codes of realism and psychology. The characters signify emotion but not as the expression of personality. The film detaches these emotions from the psyche, studies them as absolute forms, and permits their mediation and revelation by the landscape and the environment. Rain and wind have always been indices of human passion in Kurosawa's films, but here the catastrophes precipitated by Washizu's amoral actions make desolate the entire world. It becomes an empty region of fog and skeletons, of harsh wind and thunderstorm. The Confucian belief that the order of the universe reflected the moral conditions of a kingdom, that evil acts by ruler or ruled could trigger fire and storm, is embodied in this film, where horses go mad, crows incessantly caw, and the forest becomes a web trapping the human figure.

Kurosawa explores these landscapes in terms of the principles of sumi-e composition, another of the medieval arts influenced by Zen Buddhism.[122] This style of pen and ink drawing stressed empty space as a positive compositional element. Only one corner of the paper might be filled with the image of a fisherman in a boat, the small figure surrounded by a large blank area. "The composition of leaving a large area white and drawing persons and things only within a limited section of the space is peculiar to Japanese art. The influence of such pictures goes deep with us, and comes out spontaneously in our arrangement of composition," Kurosawa has observed.[123] These principles are apparent in

29. The painterly style of *Throne of Blood*. Bleached sky, fog, and desolate plains create a cosmic frame for this tale of human ambition and violence. (Museum of Modern Art/Film Stills Archive)

the vast, empty spaces of the landscapes that open and close the film, or in the whitening effect produced by fog or bleached sky in other sequences. In either case, the images are structured by an encompassing void that overtakes the small human figures below. The unfilled space of these images has a very special aesthetic value: it generates its own plenitude. In sumi-e, as in *Throne of Blood*, the use of mist and fog-shrouded landscapes creates "a sense of distance so extensive in height and width that what first seems a naturalistic panorama becomes a cosmic view."[124] Kurosawa's use of such landscapes should not be read as a kind of psychological symbol of the emptiness of human vanity. Kurosawa does eliminate the heroism of Shakespeare's play. The climax of the play, in which the forces of Malcolm, Siward, and Macduff rescue Scotland from tyranny, is transformed into the cowardly and murderous rage of Washizu's own men, who cut him down, thereby extending the saga of betrayal yet another act. But despite this change, a voice of moral authority is sounded within the film. It is not located in the conventional, and bloody, heroics that end *Macbeth*. Kurosawa views that as simply more of the same. The film's moral perspective emerges from the cosmic emptiness of the plains and fog themselves. Over shots of mist and barren landscapes, a chorus sounds the lesson of the narrative, a meditation on the foolishness of the thirst for blood and power, that is, the foolishness of fixation on worldly things. The spirit condemns the rounds of war and mocks Washizu's ambition. Madness may prevail in the world of the flesh, but the chorus and the fog-shrouded plains themselves speak a higher wisdom. The desolation of the images is both commentary and rejoinder to Washizu's actions. The film attempts to speak a discourse of enlightenment to the violence and power hunger of human behavior, but unlike in other Kurosawa films, here such wisdom is no longer of this world. It is incarnate in the spirits, the mists, and the cosmic emptiness from which they issue.

The coldness of the film, the absence of any moral dialectic within the world of human affairs, the aesthetics of reduction, of emotional distancing and objectification, all must now be seen as they could not in 1957: as forerunners of the resurgent pessimism in Kurosawa's late works, *Kagemusha* and *Ran*. *Throne of Blood* is the first major revelation of the countertradition to the committed, heroic mode of Kurosawa's cinema. It is not, however, a work of despair; not yet. The images are too controlled and powerful for that, and the cultural analysis it proposes too acute. With this work, Kurosawa has revealed how culture-bound is the act of seeing. By returning to the traditions of medieval aesthetics, particularly those informed by a restraint and simplicity of means—the Noh theater and sumi-e composition—Kurosawa discloses the differences between word and image, matter and spirit. Emotion becomes form, not expression, and spirituality opposes the world, the will and its murderous impulses. Nevertheless, a problem remained. If human behavior itself was deformed, if in its perverse expressions all suffering originated, what would happen to the Kurosawa hero and the larger project of a committed cinema?

In his next film, an adaptation of Gorky's *The Lower Depths*, Kurosawa again considered the problems of human vice and suffering and viewed them as ever self-perpetuating. Again, literary adaptation became a means of exploring the nature of cinema, in this case its spatial principles. Like *Throne of Blood*, *The Lower Depths* is a dark meditation upon human cruelty and venality, studying the relations among a group of slum dwellers in late Tokugawa times, many of whom have fallen from respectable trades into grim poverty. Nevertheless, Kurosawa also finds in the base and chillingly cynical behavior of the characters a rich and vibrant humor, and this offsets what would otherwise be a despairing portrait. The humor is unexpected, often dark and spiteful, but Kurosawa has glimpsed this before, in his own life. In his early twenties, he briefly lived with his brother in a tenement filled with the kind of characters found in the film, people who were unemployed, living in tiny spaces with no running water. As he adapted to the neighborhood, he began to notice its unusual qualities, in particular, the importance of laughter.

> Some of the people who lived in this neighborhood were construction workers, carpenters, plasterers and the like. But the majority of the residents had no visible means of support and no definable profession. Yet somehow they shared and depended on each other to such a degree that what should have been a terribly difficult life became surprisingly optimistic and, at every opportunity, downright humorous. Even the small children made wisecracks.[125]

He soon realized, however, that "the bright, cheerful humor of tenement life I enjoyed so much harbored in its shadows a dark reality. . . . Ugly things happened here, as they did everywhere else."[126] In Gorky's play, Kurosawa found a vehicle for exploring these contrary qualities, the tenacity of hope and humor and the ugliness of lives spent in the shadow of poverty and extinction. Moreover, the play gave him the opportunity to portray the lives of the wretched and the poor, an interest and focus that has been recurrent throughout his career. From the slums of *Drunken Angel*, *Stray Dog*, *High and Low*, and *Dodeskaden* to the slum dwellers cared for by the doctors and clerks of *Red Beard* and *Ikiru*, Kurosawa's cinema has consistently been drawn to the world of the impoverished. Here he may place in sharp terms his fundamental preoccupations, for poverty exposes the problematic of commitment. As we have seen, *Stray Dog* and *Ikiru* are explicitly concerned with the renunciation of compassion, a focus carried out at the levels of theme and form. The issue will recur again in *Red Beard*. In each of these works, pity is set against commitment and is viewed as self-indulgent, as treacherous and dangerous in an oppressive world. Both Gorky and Dostoevsky shared this fascination with exploring how noble impulses and good intentions may lead to disaster. Dostoevsky's "idiot," Prince Myshkin, wreaks havoc in the lives of all around him.

Gorky's exploration of the duplicity of compassion is developed through the character of a pilgrim named Luka, who encourages the slum dwellers to pursue their dreams and fantasies, who preaches a gospel of love and tolerance, but who deserts them all at the first sign of trouble. In his wake, characters are dead, despairing, or arrested. Gorky later complained that he felt the play's point of view was weakened by not having someone to represent a real alternative to Luka and his message. He wrote:

> In the play there is no opposition to what Luka says. The basic question that I wanted to pose was: what is better, truth or compassion? What is more necessary? Should compassion be carried to the point where it involves deception, as in Luca's case? . . . Luka represents compassion to the point of deception as a means of salvation, but there is in the play no representative of truth to oppose him.[127]

What is more important, truth or compassion? Herein lies a moral contradiction to which Kurosawa's cinema has always been sensitive. Enlightenment, as in Watanabe's project to build a park, entails action, not pity. Pity is too easy, enlightened action far more difficult. Counterposed to this austere ethic in many of the films, however, is an alternative appreciation of the power of dreams and illusions to secure a kind of salvation. Like Dostoevsky, and like Gorky in this play, Kurosawa has often returned to the character of the dreamer and offered the example of escape through illusion from an unbearable world. After his early romantic works, though, Dostoevsky came to appreciate the dream as the ethically irresponsible creation of an isolated consciousness.[128] Kurosawa, by contrast, has treated such characters with affection and warmth. The couple in One Wonderful Sunday, Hiruta's dying, tubercular daughter in Scandal, the starving boy Chobo in Red Beard, the denizens of The Lower Depths and of Dodeskaden, all ease the misfortune of their lives with visions of peace, salvation, or beautiful and majestic lands. For Kurosawa, the dreamer is the antithesis to Sanada, Watanabe, and Niide. The power and appeal of illusion contest with the insistence upon a direct, sober confrontation with the world, and this dialectic holds a key to the internal disintegration of his works. In The Lower Depths, as he does in Dodeskaden, Kurosawa permits himself to explore at length the texture of fantasies that bind shredded lives. While Gorky was concerned that no spokesperson for the truth existed in his play, Kurosawa is not bothered by this. The world may be a place of death and dissolution, but dreams are sufficient unto themselves.

Unlike in *Throne of Blood*, dialogue is important and pervasive in this adaptation. Kurosawa experiments with an ensemble mode of performance, modulating the characters so that they assume a unified, rhythmic whole, much like the wonderful nonsense song they sing at two points in the film. As always, however, Kurosawa is intent on visualizing the emotional dynamics that connect them. The action is confined to a single room and the yard outside, but the treatment of space "opens up" this small area to an extraordinary degree. Though the setting is quite faithful to the restricted area of the play, the effect is not at all "stagey." Unlike *The Idiot*, this film demonstrates that one may be faithful to a literary work dominated by dialogue and featuring no overt action without forfeiting the qualities of cinema. Kurosawa is able to overcome the kind of theatrical perspective one often senses in films adapted from plays largely by his reliance on the jagged editing of asymmetrical compositions. Throughout these chapters, we have been noting Kurosawa's affection for unbalanced frames, for spaces fraught with visual tension and implicit violence. *The Lower Depths* is perhaps the supreme example of this principle. Kurosawa uses the long take in many scenes, and physical action is static, but the frames are activated, unstable, explosive. The disjunctive images create a montage structure both within the frame and from shot to shot that propels the film along with Eisensteinian explosiveness. *The Lower Depths* is an extremely kinetic work, but the action is perceptual and cinematic, not physical. The camera is arranged to stress the linear chaos of the room, placed at extreme angles to the floor or to the sliding screens. As in *Ikiru*, objects and architecture assume a malevolent presence, separating and trapping the human figure. The characters sit in groups, but each person faces a different direction, and Kurosawa stresses the utter isolation of foreground and background activity. The most extravagant example of this compositional montage occurs during a scene wherein a group of characters recline outdoors while the prostitute tearfully tells of her imaginary lost love.[129] Kurosawa holds this frame for a very long time, emphasizing the stress of its linear design. Six characters are arranged as verticals, horizontals, diagonals, some with their backs turned, some barely visible in a hidden corner of the image. The group is together, indulging in fantasy, yet each character is isolated in his or her own space. The tensions set up by the different spatial fields threaten to burst the image.

30. Spatial fragmentation and the stress of linear form in *The Lower Depths*.
(Museum of Modern Art/Film Stills Archive)

This compositional violence becomes the analogue of the hidden emotional cruelties that organize the characters' lives. *The Lower Depths* is built on a paradox. Physical space is limited and shared by all yet is fractured into little pieces, like the psyches of its inhabitants. In psychological terms, there is no common space. Like illusion, emotional trauma is antisocial. It isolates and mocks the possibility of community. The compositional design of the film models this paradox, demonstrates the contrary alignments of physical and psychological space, of the theatrical "set" and its cinematic transformation. Dreams may be aesthetically appealing, but they can also be lies, and they may sow dissension. Kahei's compassionate words indirectly provoke a clash that leads to murder and betrayal. *The Lower Depths* evokes a world where the fear of death and dissolution is paramount and where the spirit may be buoyed only by fantasy and spiteful wit. As the 360-degree pan that opens the film announces, this world is sealed, self-enclosed in a way that defeats all hope, all action. Heroism has ceased to be a possibility. Dreams are the toxin of heroic action. Trapped at the bottom of a slag heap, the only sound from above that these characters can hear is the caw of a distant crow.

How have we reached this point? How have the films managed to move from the force of Sanada's and Watanabe's engagement with the world, and the confidence of their success, to the unmitigated desolation of *Throne of Blood* and the world of pain and dreams in *The Lower Depths*? Where are the necessary mediations, the dilemmas Kurosawa's cinema must have faced in order to ripen into such unrelieved pessimism? This darkness would emerge in triumphant domination of the style and tone of the final works, those ranging from *Dodeskaden* to *Ran*, films that almost seem the products of a different filmmaker. In the previous chapter, Kurosawa's struggle to forge a committed cinema was seen to be overwhelmingly difficult, given the model of individual heroism from which he worked. The films of the immediate postwar years were fraught with tensions and contradictions between the quest of the hero for ethical purity, personal isolation, and social rebellion and the contrary demands of the social structure, the incontrovertible fact that the self is not peripheral to the social order but is structured by it. We need to examine these contradictions more closely because they clearly reveal the defeats that stung Kurosawa's project and that are responsible for the emotional detachment and the relinquishing of an aggressive aesthetic in the late works, which are films of resignation that surrender the challenge of engagement. The following two chapters attempt to show how Kurosawa reached this juncture.

5 Form and the Modern World

"Petroleum resists

the five-act form;

. . . Even to dra-

matize a simple

newspaper report

one needs some-

thing much more

than the dramatic

technique of a

Hebbel or an

Ibsen."

—Bertolt Brecht[1]

The necessary mediations governing the passage from the willed optimism of the early films (*No Regrets, Drunken Angel*) to the ethic of resignation and despair that pervades the late works are two-fold. One set of factors is related to the question of history, to which Kurosawa's work has always been acutely sensitive due to the turbulent socio-cultural matrix within which it was formed. In his period films, he has confronted the structures of the past and the marks that time has left on the culture, but this has been a difficult and painful confrontation. What emerged as the lesson of history was counter to the project of his cinema. Beset by repeated ina-bilities to synthesize his heroes and their mission with the contemporary world, Kurosawa turned to the past in search of spaces in which these char-acters could act, hoping that a transfigured past would disclose a path through the present. But this did not happen. The interrogation revealed time as a destabilizing force, intensifying the alienation from a committed stance that the conflicts in ad-dressing the contemporary world had already en-gendered. The inquiry into history yielded a con-frontation that disturbed and subverted Kurosawa's attempts at a cultural and historical synthesis. In the next chapter I describe in detail the coordinates of this interrogation and the reasons for its break-down.

The other set of factors must be located in the general shape and design of Kurosawa's forms, in the narrative and visual structures he has cho-sen to use in addressing socio-political issues. This chapter explores these forms and the ques-tion of their applicability to the kinds of issues that have captured his dramatic and social interest. As we have seen in the chapter dealing with the immediate postwar films, Kurosawa was drawn to the plight of a shattered society and was both fascinated and repelled by the squalor and corrup-

tion of the black market and the gangsters that thrived in this environment. But the economics of the postwar world remain peripheral to the
real focus of films like *Drunken Angel* and *Stray Dog*, which is centered
on individuals, on doctors, cops, and thieves. Black market corruption
and profiteering are used metaphorically to stand for a general social
malaise against which the hero's determination could be pitted. This was
a malaise of passivity and resignation, the metaphor a means of disguis-
ing the cultural codes of behavior against which Kurosawa's early cinema struggled. That the environments of these films are not treated in
socio-economic or political terms both displaced the real objects of
Sanada's and Murakami's anger and made possible their small success in
healing a patient or in capturing a thief. As long as the structures of oppression were themselves limited, were confined to a local black market
ruled by a petty gangster or to the depredations of one individual un-
hinged by the war, then the means of fighting back were quite clear:
capture the thief, depose the gangster. The sump was a potent symbol
in *Drunken Angel*, but it was sharply bounded because the film could
offer the country as refuge for spiritual and psychological healing. At the
end, the bar-girl who loved Matsunaga is headed there with his ashes.
Though Sanada remains behind to fight the sump, its evil influence
could be eradicated by an official reclamation effort, like Watanabe's in
Ikiru.

In contrast to such narrowed definitions of the social environment,
the heroes in other films are confronted with far more massive, truly
structural systems of oppression. The energy of Kurosawa's efforts to
apply his forms to social problems in the contemporary world inevitably
led to confrontations with problems of a magnitude far beyond the
reformist capabilities of the individual hero. The problems of atomic
war and the nuclear economy, of the corporate state and its tentacles
of power, and of the contradictions between extreme wealth and poverty
bound into a single social system presented Kurosawa's visual and narrative forms with challenges of great proportion. *Record of a Living Being*
(1955), *The Bad Sleep Well* (1960), and *High and Low* (1963) chronicle
the attempts to meet this challenge. These are films of extraordinary
internal strife and tension, marked by aesthetic and ideological contradiction, in which Kurosawa's forms struggle to adjust to new arenas of
content.

A discussion of this struggle points beyond Kurosawa's cinema to
more general issues, which are far from resolved, of the appropriate rela-

tions between form and content within a politically committed cinema. These issues have fueled debates that have raged for decades, and it is worth pausing for a moment to establish this background since it will be relevant to understanding the nature of Kurosawa's contemporary political films. The controversy centers on opposing views of art and its relation to social and political processes. In instrumentalist theories, art is viewed much as an apparatus that can be "taken over" by groups or classes and used to communicate new agendas.[2] After the Russian Revolution, Lenin and Trotsky both advocated the absorption by proletarian culture of the aesthetic models and conventions of bourgeois art, only they were to be used to embody the new social realities. Existing forms and conventions, this position suggests, can be used to express new content. In the cinema, political filmmakers like Costa-Gavras (Z, *Missing, Music Box*) or Gillo Pontecorvo (*Burn!*) have employed various codes from the Hollywood cinema, such as narrative linearity and the use of stars, but they have informed them with leftist perspectives. Jack Lemmon discovers fascist Chile, for example, in *Missing*, and Marlon Brando plays a nineteenth-century imperialist in *Burn!*. Politics are placed inside the film at the level of content, and the advantage is alleged to be the accessibility to a mass audience that the use of popular forms and conventions permits. To some extent this is true. Undoubtedly, *Missing* helped communicate the brutality of Pinochet's dictatorship to sectors of the public for which it had been a nonreality. On the other hand, as critics of this approach point out, form does structure content. The problems of Chileans are displaced by Lemmon's empathic presence as a distraught father searching for his son, thus, with perverse irony considering the reasons for Allende's downfall, making sense of the Chilean debacle by converting it into an American tragedy dealing with the sundering of a family.

In contrast to instrumentalist views that tend to deny the primacy of form, transformative views of art emphasize this primacy and have played a much more active role in shaping traditions of political cinema.[3] Counterposed to the positions of Lenin and Trotsky was the work of the Formalists in literature and of Eisenstein and Vertov in film, both emphasizing the nature of the artwork as a construction that transforms, rather than reflects, the materials of social reality. In calling for a materialist approach to form, Eisenstein argued that the structure of film form communicates ideology, that, for example, the "structure that is reflected in the concept of Griffith montage is the structure of bourgeois society."[4] Brecht, whose work has been a central influence on subsequent attempts to shape a radical cinema, emphatically denied that existing aesthetic forms could be occupied like so much territory by groups contesting the society that had shaped those forms:

> Literary works cannot be taken over like factories; literary forms of expression cannot be taken over like patents. Even the realistic mode of writing, of which literature provides many very different examples, bears the stamp of the way it was employed, when and by which class, down to its smallest details. With the people struggling and changing reality before our eyes, we must not cling to "tried" rules of narrative, venerable literary models, eternal aesthetic laws.[5]

Thus Brecht urged the necessity of exploring new forms that might more accurately and acutely embody the social phenomena of mass industrial society, whose characteristic institutions, such as the petroleum industry or the stock market, defied conventional means of dramatic representation. Like Eisenstein and the Formalists, Brecht urged attention to the semiotic or symbolic distinctness of the artwork and to the determining importance of form.

For Brecht and the filmmakers who have worked from his tradition, politics enters the artwork through the structural relations of its materials. Thus, Godard, Bertolucci, Pasolini, Jancsó, and others have been interested in charting paths away from Hollywood codes and, sometimes, in responding directly to those codes. Their attempts to capture historical realities have been predicated upon an expansion and experimentation with cinematic form. This is because, as Dana Polan points out, "Historical reality . . . is not a mere signified, a content to be seized up by cognition."[6] It enters and shapes the signifier, which must be reworked to permit new ideologies and perspectives to be manifest. Here lies the ground for the critique of Hollywood cinema as a "transparent" mode that effaces its own signifiers, the traces of the work that produced it. For the tradition of cinema inaugurated by Brecht and whose main influence has been Godard, a degree of self-reflexivity has been essential. The structure of form has been disclosed so that the film may be seen as bearing the marks of its production, inviting the viewer to assume a reflective and critical stance that precludes his or her being overwhelmed by the spectacle, which Brecht had cautioned against. Godard, Pasolini, Glauber Rocha, and Nagisa Ōshima foreground the structure of their forms so as to invite the viewer into this new relationship with the film and with the material world that lies outside the theater. These are strategies for avoiding what Fredric Jameson has characterized as the meaning of the commodity form, the obliteration of "the signs of work on the product in order to make it easier for us to forget the class structure which is its organizational framework."[7] For this aesthetic tradition, it is not enough simply to make films that have a revolutionary content. Walter Benjamin wrote that what must be changed is the apparatus itself, that is, the institutions and forms of cinema and the other arts. Author, reader, and spectator must all become producers and collaborators.[8] The reconfiguration of form, then, permits not just the grasping of new social realities, or of old realities seen anew, but a reshaping of the spectator's relationship with the artwork as well. For Brecht, this threefold transformation—of form, history, and spectator—was the essence of realism, that is, of a committed aesthetic.

The controversy between instrumentalist and transformative views of art, and the issues they presuppose, is extremely complex, and this cursory treatment can only summarize their barest outlines. But it is important to grasp the essentials of this debate because of Kurosawa's own ambiguous relationship to its opposing terms. Kurosawa, like Brecht, has sought to fashion a committed art, but unlike the German playwright, he has resisted radical formal experimentation and, above all, a self-reflexive cinematic voice. In shifting his attention to the political problems of an advanced industrial society, in dealing with issues like atomic war or class conflict that have a systemic origin rather than an individual one, Kurosawa did not rethink or rework any of his existing forms. He simply applied them to the new contexts. As such, *Record of a Living Being*, *The Bad Sleep Well*, and *High and Low* provide a basis on which to evaluate the competing claims of the aesthetic traditions outlined above. Previous forms are infused with a new, politically far more explicit content. What happens when these new dramatic interests are encased in the old forms? Can they be taken over and used to express the new focus? Or does a collision result, in which form and content are set in opposition, each vying for supremacy over the other?

Record of a Living Being emerged from the personal concerns about nuclear weapons shared by Kurosawa and his composer-friend Fumio Hayasaka, whose own death from tuberculosis occurred during the production. The film was to be a testament to their responsibility as artists for the well-being of the society in which they lived and worked. Kurosawa recalls the genesis of the film:

> While I was making *Seven Samurai* I went to see Hayasaka, who was sick, and we were talking and he said that if a person was in danger of dying he couldn't work very well. He was quite ill at the time, very weak, and we did not know when he might die. And he knew this too. Just before this we had had word of the Bikini experiments. When he had said a person dying could not work I thought he meant himself—but he didn't, it turned out. He meant everyone; all of us. Next time I met him I suggested we do a film on just that subject.[9]

As Kurosawa worked with his screenwriters, the conviction formed that they were all making the sort of film that, "after it was all over and the last judgement was upon us, we could stand up and account for our past lives by saying proudly: We made *Ikimono no Kiroku*."[10] Perhaps as an influence from Hayasaka's own situation, *Record* is concerned with the issues of illness and death: the terminal anxiety of society under the shadow of the bomb, the pathology of individuals who live with it daily, and the possibilities of mass death that it constantly portends. The film portrays a world on the edge of the apocalypse, which is sensed by the protagonist Nakajima (Toshirō Mifune), who develops an overpowering fear of the bomb and consequently attempts to move his family to Brazil where he irrationally believes they will be safe from radiation. *Record* chronicles Nakajima's increasingly frenzied efforts to relocate his family and, failing at that, his psychological collapse and confinement in an asylum. Yet these fears are social in essence, even though the film chooses to reveal them through the pathology of the individual. Nakajima's personal irrationality contains a deeper social wisdom. The personal concerns of Kurosawa and Hayasaka were grounded in a mass public panic that occurred in 1954, when Japanese fishermen were dusted by radioactive ash from a nuclear detonation at Bikini. Their catch went to market, however, and triggered a scare about fish contamination, helping generate a reawakening of popular opposition to the bomb. *Record* reflects this climate of fear and uncertainty and projects it into the character and behavior of Nakajima, but the film uneasily negotiates the twin impulses that lie behind its creation: the personal reflections of the filmmakers and the sociological phenomenon of a terrorized populace grown afraid of its environment. While the topic calls for a political analysis, this is deflected by a focus on the psychic costs of living in the shadow of the bomb.[11] The film is split between its two voices, the social and the psychological, and while wishing to speak in the former, it never fully relinquishes the latter.

31. Anxieties of the nuclear age: Nakajima (Toshirō Mifune) contemplates the apocalypse in *Record of a Living Being*. (Museum of Modern Art/Film Stills Archive)

The contestation of these voices is apparent at the very beginning of *Record of a Living Being*. The credits appear overtop a series of high-angle long shots of the city. We see pedestrians crossing the street and boarding streetcars. Intersecting patterns of linear movement create a strong geometry of design in many of the images. Pedestrians cross the frame in one direction, offset by streetcars traveling in an opposing direction, both planes of movement bisected by the vertical lines of an additional set of tracks running down the center of the frame. By flattening space and thereby heightening its linear features, the telephoto lens accentuates the geometry of the image. These spaces, formed by networks of intersecting movements and lines, are social grids, through which the inhabitants of the film, and the culture, move. The long shots of the city opening the film describe the coordinates of these grids and thereby define an essentially social focus at the outset. But no terror is visible. As Joan Mellen points out, these people are oblivious to the threat to their lives.[12] The long-shot setups enunciate a distanced perspective that is the perfect analogue to the complacency regarding the bomb, which everyone but Nakajima shares. The social space is contaminated by that complacency, and the film observes what happens when that complacency is challenged by an individual who rejects the threat of atomic annihilation. Both the bomb, and the committed hero, are inserted into these grids, and the film studies the subsequent destabilization. It does so, however, by veering from a social to a psychological focus.

The sequence of long shots ends when the camera pans with a passing streetcar to reveal the dental clinic of Dr. Harada (Takashi Shimura). The camera then tracks through the window as Harada receives a phone call summoning him to Family Court, where he acts as a mediator in family disputes. Here he will meet Nakajima and launch an inquiry into the basis of his fears. Harada is a character who formalizes the query of the narrative and who acts as a foil for Nakajima, prompting his self-revelation. From now on, the narrative focus, and the problem that fascinates Harada, will be on learning the causes of Nakajima's extraordinary fear, which neither his family nor anyone else can grasp. Harada tells his son that he doesn't understand Nakajima, whose fear is shared by all Japanese but which for him has assumed such overpowering proportions. Harada thus articulates the enigmatic code of the narrative, and the political analysis of the film will turn on offering a credible account of Nakajima's "illness." The political rebel is defined at the outset as a puzzle, a problem around which the text of the film is organized. The film immediately alienates its own perspective. Political rebellion, rather than the target of that rebellion, becomes the object of inquiry.

Nakajima's family members have pressured his wife into filing a petition requesting that the court declare him incompetent. His plans to relocate the family in Brazil threaten their livelihood, which is centered in the foundry that the family operates. To sell the foundry, as the old man plans to do, would deprive them of their income, and no one wants to become a farmer in South America. Moreover, Nakajima has several mistresses and children by them whom he wants to take to Brazil as well. This adds a stinging insult to what his children perceive as the general insanity of the proposal to relocate. They tell the court that their father is despotic, selfish, and crazy, and that they need to be protected from his whims. The bulk of the film centers on this conflict, as the family members maneuver to have him declared incompetent and Nakajima fights to preserve his autonomy. His children cannot see that his obsession with moving stems from his love for them and his desire to protect them from the bombs. This family relationship is of crucial importance both at the narrative level and for the kind of analysis the film develops, and we will return to the point shortly.

It is important, first, to consider the film's peculiar presentation of the hero, which is so formalized that it verges on the self-reflexive. *Record of a Living Being* is almost a film about the making and unmaking of a Kurosawa hero and, in this degree of self-consciousness, shows clearly how close Kurosawa will come to inquiring into the meaning and limitations of his chosen forms without ever actually abandoning them. The inquiry is pursued at great length, even to the point where it causes the forms to break down, but Kurosawa does not reassemble them in a new configuration. Instead, he participates in their destruction, ending the film at the moment of maximum formal dissociation. The effort to address the problems of the nuclear age was inseparable from an investigation of the means by which to do so, but this did not entail a search for new means. It ended the old ones but did not point in new directions. Thus, there is something deathly about *Record* that is unrelated to its topic or to the facts of Hayasaka's illness.

The film's presentation and analysis of its hero may be approached through a grasp of its visual design, since, as always with Kurosawa, the structure of the imagery formalizes deeper thematic and metaphorical dimensions of meaning. *Record of a Living Being* is the dialectical opposite of the film that preceded it, *Seven Samurai*. By contrast with the celebration of movement in that film, its charging of every image with kinetic energy, *Record* is a film of stasis and blocked energy. Its visual design is thrombotic, surrounding the characters with dense spaces and asphyxiating enclosures. The scenes at the family court, where Harada first meets Nakajima and learns of his obsession, are distinguished by an extraordinary density of space within the image. The court meets in a tiny office, into which is crowded the three mediators, Nakajima, his wife, two sons, two daughters, and one son-in-law. Kurosawa films the scene using multiple cameras, so that the cutting produces very little in the way of conventional continuity, accentuating the sense of clutter and tight space. In addition, the extremely long lenses used in filming produce a claustrophobic quality in the interiors as well as in the exteriors by compressing space, and Kurosawa magnifies this restriction of area and perspective by using extremely low angles in many of the exterior scenes that narrowly circumscribe the available view.

The reduced and narrowed spaces of these images formalize the plight of Nakajima and define his dilemma as one of an inability to move or act. In the office of the Family Court, he is beset by family members quarreling about his money and his will, surrounded on all sides by hostile relatives about whom, quixotically, he deeply cares. The family blocks his ability to sell the foundry, even to liquidate his capital. He is hemmed in by invective at home and by the courts that freeze his assets. *Record of a Living Being*, unlike all Kurosawa's other films, is about a hero who cannot act and who therefore suffers the tortures of the damned. Kurosawa's characters define themselves through action, externalize their morality through behavior, and his forms participate in this externalization, camera movement grounding the energy of the characters' protest, the jagged editing describing the fragmented structures of the social world that, paradoxically, offer the hope for success. In *Record*, by contrast, space and form constrict. They immobilize Nakajima and prevent him from carrying out his plans. The court asks him if he fears the bombs, and he replies he has no fear, saying (repeating the Kurosawa credo of direct vision) that it is cowards who tremble and close their eyes to the danger. But when the court decides in favor of his family and impounds his assets, effectively defeating his plans to move, Nakajima is transformed. Harada meets him on the street some time later and sees a trembling, anxious man. Nakajima scornfully tells him he is full of fears now that he has been rendered helpless. As they speak, the roar of trucks and trains sounds like bombs, and exhaust fumes fill the air like fallout, making palpable the source of Nakajima's unease.

Record of a Living Being is a meditation on what sustains the Kurosawa hero and on the consequences of its withdrawal. Blocked from physical action, Nakajima retreats into the insanity of which his family has long accused him. In an irrational act, he burns down his foundry, believing that with it gone, the family will be free and willing to migrate to Brazil. But this act only intensifies the constriction of space that besets him. The tight confines of the court offices are replaced by the tiny recesses of a jail cell and, finally, by the isolation and despair of the asylum, the family with its restrictive wishes definitively succeeded by its state equivalent, the prisoner's bars. Immobilized forever by the power of the state, from which he had attempted escape, Nakajima in despair resorts to the only kind of movement left him, psychic movement. In his mind, he travels to a secure place on some other planet, where he hallucinates the burning of the Earth, which Kurosawa simulates by filming directly into the sun. As in many of his other films, dreams become a substitute for the lost possibilities of real political action.

The space and energy of Nakajima's protest have been absorbed by the family and defused by it. This is made clear at a structural level during a scene outside the court office. As Judge Araki reads the family petition, its text is superimposed overtop a close-up of Nakajima's face. As the superimposition is maintained, the camera tracks and pans to reveal a line of family members seated to the right of Nakajima. The space of the images has shifted to integrate Nakajima, isolated by the passion of his protest, into the body of the family that will prove so effective in containing that protest. The next cut extends and deepens this integration. The camera draws back from Nakajima and the family members behind him to a position farther down the hall. The new frame reveals the remaining relatives, with Nakajima situated in the distance between the two rows of hostile offspring. The petition is still superimposed over the image, which thereby describes the dual grounds of his deadlock, his engulfment and the absorption of his protest by the family and the court acting on its behalf. Space, which is usually mobilized by the energy of the hero's protest so that it becomes the signifier of that rebellion, is now the enemy, foreclosing the possibilities of movement, blocking the imperative to act so that, with nowhere to go, this imperative turns inward, becoming poisonous, and ending in dysfunctional hallucinations. In its narrative and spatial design, *Record* reveals with great intensity the breakdown and destruction of the Kurosawa hero.

This fate is rooted in the nature of Nakajima's protest, which, as Judge Araki observes, is directed against a problem that is too big for an individual to solve. We need now to consider the specific relation of this destruction to the political analysis of the film. The film not only permits but necessitates Nakajima's defeat. Though the bombs terrify him and he regards their invention as a terrible development, his immediate struggle is directed against his family, not against nuclear weapons themselves, nor against the state-industrial complex that administers them. It is a curious sort of protest, and it manifests itself not in political anger but in a desperate attempt to flee Japan. In his struggle against the family, the film counterpoints two different discourses. Nakajima speaks a language that venerates life, not death, and the responsibility for preserving it. As his relatives bicker about the loss of their fortune if they move to Brazil, he tells them that life is very precious, but his son Jirō responds that everyone dies sooner or later. In a rare moment of political anger, Nakajima replies that he doesn't mind dying but he hates to be killed. Jirō's remark manifests a resignation that is echoed by other characters in the film. Harada asks his son how he can be so calm if he is afraid of the bombs, and the boy replies, with a shrug, that it's because you can't dodge them. Araki, the court mediator, tries to mitigate Harada's feelings of responsibility for Nakajima's breakdown by saying that the old man's misfortunes are really nobody's fault, except for the bombs themselves.

Coursing through all these remarks, offered by different characters at various points in the film, is an abdication of responsibility and a cloaking of fear with protective complacency. This is the other voice that counterpoints Nakajima's insistence upon personal action and accountability.

But this complacency is not merely a self-justifying and protective attitude. It also has a material basis and function. The family members who oppose Nakajima all fret and worry about the loss of their fortune, and this is counterposed to his concern for their lives. Even the mistresses and their children scheme to be included in his will after he suffers a collapse from the frustration of trying to beat the court. Recognizing the importance of the foundry in their lives, Nakajima burns it down, trying to remove the material basis of their resistance. The space of the family has not merely absorbed the energy of Nakajima's protest, but it has itself been absorbed by the dominant structures of state and society. The irony of an advanced industrial economy is that political or social rebellion carries heavy material costs. Nakajima cannot merely rebel from an act of conscience because he also has to consider the fate of his family, which is threatened with ruin or dispersal by this rebellion. The punishment for social protest may be financial ruin. That all the relatives are worried about their incomes, and use the threat of this loss as evidence of Nakajima's despotism and insanity, is not merely an index of their individual selfishness. It, too, is a political response, but one that seeks to recoup the threat and example of Nakajima's protest and convert it into socially acceptable terms. Nakajima can stop protesting and preserve his family, or he can continue to rebel and destroy it. The discourse of money is a substitute for empowerment. Denied control by the state over their political survival, the relatives speak a language of financial survival. Through the material incentives its economy offers, the state binds individuals to its policies and defuses their protest. When Nakajima torches his foundry, he believes he has solved his problems, only to realize that he has destroyed the livelihood of his workers. The economic interdependencies of industrial society convert his rebellion into a means of victimizing others. Society protects itself by setting, economically, everyone against all. The discourse of money thereby speaks, and enforces, policies and attitudes of resignation.

Thus, the nuclear bombs become domesticated, capable of being tolerated, even forgotten. Moreover, the nuclearization of culture is internalized by the family, which becomes mobilized to quarantine the society against protesters. The domestication of the bomb, its absorption into the rituals of daily life to the point where it becomes invisible, is brilliantly visualized in a sequence that counterpoints Nakajima's frenzied anxieties against the calm reactions of a mistress who simply does not see what he does. Nakajima is visiting her, sitting on the floor while she hangs laundry outside. He is trying to persuade her and her father to come with him to Brazil and, ironically, given his own agitation, trying to make her feel more comfortable around his legitimate family members. As he speaks, a group of planes roar by overhead, and Nakajima responds with visible discomfort. These planes make palpable within the film the otherwise unseen U.S. military presence and the controversial security arrangements between the United States and Japan, which, long a disputed aspect of Japanese political culture, would generate massive protests by 1960.[13] Hearing the planes, Nakajima looks around nervously and then continues his conversation. In a moment, the planes screech by a second and then a third time. The clothing outside flutters as if in their wake. Each time Nakajima trembles with fear. Then a silent flash of lightning bleaches out the image, and Nakajima scrambles away from the sliding screen. He rushes to the baby and crouches over it protectively. The baby begins to cry in distress. As the delayed thunder rolls over the house, the mother grabs the baby from Nakajima, who now cowers on the floor. A dust cloud swirls across the yard outside, followed a moment later by a rainstorm.

Each of the sensory events in this sequence—the roar of planes, the flash of lightning, the crash of thunder, the cloud of dust, and the rain—is separated by a delay and a silence laden with expectation. Like the cultural silences that surround the bomb, as something about which no one speaks, these silences are threatening and electric. The patterns of weather that they punctuate—the wind, the dust, the rain—become sinister within a context of nuclear war, since these are potential carriers of fallout. Of course, it is only a muggy summer day, and Nakajima's anxieties are leading him toward madness. The sequence, therefore, might seem to work primarily as a description of his fevered state of mind. But it does more than this. It visualizes the bomb's penetration of the culture, its insinuation into daily life. Planes roar by, followed by a flash of light, a dust cloud, and a storm, just as if a real bomb had been detonated. But Nakajima's mistress sees none of this. She reacts only to the cry of her baby and snatches it away from him, unable to understand why he is terrified. The bomb deforms the senses as the price exacted for living with it. Once the senses are closed, that is, depoliticized, the bomb fuses

with daily life, and the signifiers of the holocaust are innocently transformed into the signs of a muggy summer day and a random group of
planes crossing the sky.

The structure of this sequence discloses the space of politics within
the film. It is, literally, the absent and the unseen. The planes are never
glimpsed, only heard, and the bombs that they may be carrying remain a
distant threat. Though Nakajima said he did not mind dying but hated to
be killed, the film does not disclose who does this killing or the institutions that guide it. *Record of a Living Being* deals with nuclear phenomena on a second-order level of transformation, in the guise of the family,
its economic worries, and the pervasiveness of eerie weather patterns—
oppressive heat, fiery lightning, torrential rain—that, as Richie notes, are
implicitly apocalyptic.[14] The bomb pervades the culture and saturates the
air with a sweaty fear no one will acknowledge while being, itself, unseen. Because the film does not admit, or even acknowledge, the institutional structure of atomic war production, its roots in the organization of
state and economy, the bomb remains merely an ethical, not a political,
problem and therefore something potentially addressable by the individual hero. But what makes *Record* a fascinating film is its awareness of
that which it represses. Though the narrative centers Nakajima in opposition to his family, not to the state, and though it insists he remain isolated in his rebellion, the gradual disintegraton of his protest is evidence
of the textual work of repression, of its denial of the transindividual nature of the problem. Nakajima's inability to move is a structural symptom
of the deadlock that besets Kurosawa's own analysis, confined as it is to
individuals and ethical questions of personal responsibility. Nakajima's
immobility reproduces the quandary of Kurosawa's cinema in its efforts
to come to terms with power and oppression as institutional structures.

Institutions have always been the enemies in Kurosawa's films, but
the isolation of the hero that this enmity breeds prevents an organized,
collective response to social oppression. Thus, though popular movements against the bomb existed at the time the film was made, Nakajima
never stands a chance of joining them. "Kurosawa falls short of counterposing to Nakajima's quixotic plan a more effective means of approaching the threat of nuclear war. Lacking this dimension, the film seems
incomplete as if something remains to be said."[15] With the path toward
a really political analysis foreclosed, the film must repress the bomb itself, disclosing its threat connotatively, as in the sequence with the
planes. And the only movement possible for Nakajima is a centripetal
one, a movement toward greater rigidity and immobility and the collapse

32. Nakajima cannot escape the social space of his family. *Record of a Living Being*. (Museum of Modern Art/Film Stills Archive)

of his rebellion. With Nakajima confined in the asylum, hallucinating a burning Earth, the film ends with a sequence that inverts the "happy birthday" shot from *Ikiru*. In that film, as Watanabe descended the stairs clutching his white rabbit, bolstered by the determination to build the park, he passed a young girl going up the stairs, while her companions sang "happy birthday" ostensibly to her but really for him. Now, at the close of *Record of a Living Being*, the same actor, Takashi Shimura, as Harada, again descends a corridor, away from Nakajima's cell, while the foundry owner's young mistress climbs the corridor on her way to see the old man. She passes Harada, and they both pause, he on the way down, she on the way up. The long lens so compresses space that the shot is rendered almost abstract in design, and the characters seem to hover in midair, their movement slowed, almost frozen. As they leave the frame, a final fade-out ends the film. The corresponding sequence in *Ikiru* promised liberation, unleashed energy, and movement, but this sequence embodies stasis, confinement, and hallucinations of oblivion. In this final image, the narrative itself freezes, irresolutely, unable to find a way of linking Nakajima's failed protest with alternate political strategies that may promise greater success. Nakajima's immobilization infects the narrative itself, the movement of which is finally arrested, as the political and social dilemmas that motivated the film ultimately elude it. By inflecting the social rebel with the stigma of psychosis, the logic of the text, founded upon a general denial of politics, must end by imprisoning him and thereby circumventing its own inquiry. Nakajima has been cannibalized by the very forms of the film.

An important component of those forms has not yet been fully considered. We have seen how the general visual design of *Record of a Living Being* emphasizes the restriction of space and how this resonates through the film's content and narrative structure. We have not yet discussed, however, the technical basis for this restriction. It is worth pausing a moment to explore this basis, which lies in the use of "long" or telephoto lenses. Lenses of long focal length are one of the centerpieces of Kurosawa's cinematic style, and we should consider their effects upon his work.[16] These lenses begin to assume significant compositional functions as early as *Stray Dog*, when he adopts telephoto perspectives to film the devastated middle-class household where Yusa has robbed and murdered. They are important features of style in *Rashōmon*, *Ikiru*, and *Seven Samurai* (where they create the impression of being in the midst of the battles by bringing the action "directly into the laps of the audience"[17]) and will come to assume an even greater role in the films that follow. Their presence and effects overwhelmingly shape the articulation of space in *Record*. Consideration of the stylistic importance of these lenses for Kurosawa will also extend our understanding of his handling of movement. His choreography of on-screen motion is a function of the use of long lenses, so that a discussion of compositional principles will also have to include their effects on the organization of character and camera movement.

Before the films of the 1950s, when the long lens begins to disturb the spatial fields with its distinctive characteristics, space on-screen exists for Kurosawa in a manner that is not fundamentally distinct from its usage in the dominant tradition of narrative cinema, that is, as a volume in which characters may be situated and through which they may move. The spaces within his frames have depth in which the characters are oriented. Kurosawa, however, will use camera movement and cutting to disturb these spatial fields, to charge them with visual tensions, so that they begin to fragment and to observe principles of discontinuity. Kurosawa's images jolt and bang together, but they do so in a way that still preserves the character of space as a volume. In this respect, they are not fundamentally different from the design of Hollywood films, where principles of continuity cutting also structure relations of physical depth within the image. In the films following *Stray Dog*, however, a new visual aesthetic begins to emerge and to grow more marked. This aesthetic is created by using the lenses of long focal length, and it is joined to the principles of montage cutting.

To understand this new aesthetic, we must first grasp certain properties of these lenses. They permit a filmmaker to effect a compression of depth within the image because they make distant objects appear much closer than they actually are. The spatial field thus becomes squeezed together, and the "longer" the lens, the greater the apparent contraction of depth. In films shot with moderate or short focal length lenses, the illusion of spatial depth is primary, but in Kurosawa's films, once the telephoto lens becomes a dominant feature of style, this is no longer true. His filmic space in works like *Record of a Living Being* tends to exist on a two-dimensional plane, a horizontal–vertical axis, rather than strictly in an illusionary three dimensions. His frames are defined by relations of height and width, which frequently take primacy over those of depth. Depth relations are still suggested. Indeed, object occlusion or overlap still functions within the frame as a depth cue, but the force of this cue is mitigated by the perspective realignments achieved with telephoto lenses. The illusion of three-dimensional space, basic to the tradition of narrative cinema, becomes for Kurosawa a planar conception of space. For him, space is a plane, not a volume.

One can no longer speak of movement *through* space in the way one can with films by other directors, for space no longer exists within the frame as a volume within which to inscribe the movements of a character. When a horseman gallops toward the camera in one of Kurosawa's films shot with long lenses, that movement becomes dislocated. The horseman does not travel through a depth of space toward the camera, but instead his actions are suspended from spatial considerations; or more precisely, a spatial context defined by depth perspective no longer serves to contain the movements of the character. This estranges our perception of motion from the kind of filmic context in which it normally occurs. The result is a heightening of sensation. The motion begins to vibrate in two dimensions rather than flow in three. The movements become hypnotic because they appear so strange. Highly stylized, abstracted from a conventional spatial context, they are thereby intensified. The expressive characteristics of these lenses are linked to the intent of Kurosawa's cinema, which is to study on-screen movement by heightening its presence. The long lenses transform motion from the object of the camera's gaze to the subject of the film. By creating movement as subject, the lenses work as an analytic tool.

The conversion of space into a plane has a number of interesting consequences. Perhaps the most obvious is that it aligns Kurosawa, with his painterly interests and training, with a tradition of composition in Japanese art that stresses a compression of pictorial planes. Painting in this tradition emphasizes surface values and a decorative treatment and eliminates overt depth cues from the image, for example, by using clouds to whiten large areas of the picture and thereby confuse a sense of scale.[18] In a sumi-e drawing, much of the compositional space is left deliberately empty. Similarly, by flattening an area of space, Kurosawa's lenses prevent it from being filled, that is, from being treated as a volume. While Kurosawa's space does not have the mystical values that sumi-e space does, it does perform a similar operation. Both are hostile to an orientation to space that regards it as a mere container of objects.

In addition to this proximity to an aesthetic tradition, another consequence of the long lens for Kurosawa's work is its intensification of linear features of composition and movement. These have characterized his work since *Sanshirō Sugata*, but the long lens creates a magnification of their effect. Kurosawa organizes movement to produce a dialectical relationship with the effects of the lens. He mitigates and modulates the space-compressing effects of the lens by using patterns of movement to suggest multiple planes of space. Linear patterns of movement create internal areas of differentiation within the frame, open the frame up in a way counter to the effects of the telephoto lenses. The opening of *Record of a Living Being* has already been mentioned, where pedestrians and streetcars cross the frame in opposing directions, in planes of space perpendicular to the camera's axis of view. The opposing movements set off these two planes of space, one containing people, the other containing the streetcars. The shot organizes zones of movement so that a spatial field, foreground and background areas, is established in tension with the telephoto lens, which works toward compressing and therefore dissolving foreground and background.

This organization of converging lines of movement is typical of Kurosawa and occurs throughout his films. One could multiply examples. He often defines planes of movement perpendicular to each other. For example, in *Yōjimbō* the hero crosses the frame from left to right in the foreground, while the villain advances toward the camera from the background, as the telephoto lens produces the illusion that they are about to crash into each other. In *Drunken Angel*, when Sanada and Matsunaga walk through the city, they advance directly toward the camera as a crowd of people rushes across the frame in the foreground, perpendicular to the plane of their advance. This shot does not feature a telephoto perspective, but it illustrates how basic this choreography of movement is to Kurosawa's cinema. Such linear arrangements of movement have a metaphorical function: they serve to distinguish the hero from his antagonist or from the masses of ordinary people for whom heroic action is always out of the question. Often, Kurosawa will visualize this distinction in terms of directly opposing zones of motion, as in *Record of a Living Being* when Nakajima rides in a car across the frame to the left through a crowd of people that is moving to the right. Again, this pattern of movement is featured in nontelephoto shots as well, as in *Seven Samurai* when Kambei, crossing the frame to the right as he returns from watching the master swordsman in a duel, is engulfed by a crowd rushing to the left, in the direction he has come. This way of visualizing movement is one of Kurosawa's visual signatures, but it assumes a special function in relation to the telephoto lenses. The long lens accentuates the fundamental linearity of Kurosawa's organization of composition by reducing space to vertical and horizontal coordinates. This gives movement the urgency and importance it has in his cinema. It holds at bay the space-devouring power of the lenses, precariously opens up the frame, and holds in check the drift toward compositional freezing and immobility that the lenses threaten. As always, movement for Kurosawa is life. It is that which creates space.

Two additional components of Kurosawa's mature style must now be considered since they, in addition to the telephoto lenses, play important roles in the other films to be studied in this chapter. The fundamental linearity of Kurosawa's cinematic system emerged early and established the formal basis that facilitated the later integration of telephoto lenses. Similarly, the two additional elements—the use of multicamera filming and the cinemascope (anamorphic) frame—are extensions of already-existing aesthetic principles. Kurosawa routinely covers a scene with three or more cameras, stationed in different places, rolling simultaneously. This multicamera approach, which he uses to overcome the actor's acute consciousness of a single camera's position and which he claims first to have used in *Seven Samurai*,[19] extends the fragmentation of his images. It anticipates his principles of montage editing by placing these principles incipiently within the phase of shooting. The multiple cameras permit Kurosawa to cover an event from a variety of vantage points and thereby to splinter its temporal and physical coordinates in a unique manner. By cutting among these different perspectives, the continuity of the physical event can be broken down. Kurosawa treats the continuous event that transpires before the cameras as an object of analysis, its coordinates opened up and displayed through simultaneous, multiple perspectives. The event "explodes" in a manner not unlike the approach of cubist painting, where contesting perspectives deform the familiar surface of an object. "[M]oving around an object to seize several successive appearances, which, fused in a single image, reconstitute it in time" was the description of cubism offered by the artists Albert Gleizes and Jean Metzinger,[20] but it might serve as well for the effects of Kurosawa's multicameras that reconstitute the event before them with a similar analytic attention. Again, we see how Kurosawa translates time into space. The temporal continuity of the event before the cameras is reconstituted as a succession of frequently jarring spatial views. As in *Record of a Living Being*, these may be perceptually confusing because of radical alterations of the angle of view and the orientation of screen direction. The event dissociates, not because, as in Eisenstein's work, action is omitted or overlapped, but because of the collage of fragmentary perspectives. As in a cubist picture, the multicameras produce a planar assembly of slivered images.

The anamorphic frame accentuates the planar quality of these images by enabling Kurosawa to emphasize the horizontal axis of the composition. Objects and characters can be spread out along the extended width of the frame, thereby heightening the linear features of the image.[21] For example, in *Red Beard* Kurosawa films the four doctors taking their meal so that they are lined up, facing the camera, across the width of the frame, with a wall close behind them, emphasizing the geometric quality of the composition. In *Dersu Uzala*, during the scene in which Arseniev and Dersu are trapped on the ice during a storm, the flatness of the images, produced by the telephoto lens, is accentuated by the landscape itself, an empty plain of ice that furnishes few depth cues to the eye. But, in addition, Kurosawa repeatedly inserts Arseniev and Dersu into the shot from the very edges of the image and has them walk across the frame at right angles to the camera's gaze. The 'scope frame, enabling Kurosawa to maximize the planar nature of his space, was the last of the major formal devices to be integrated into his filmic system. He first employed 'scope with *The Hidden Fortress* in 1958, and thereafter continued to use it on his next five films.

These elements taken together—the telephoto lens, multicamera film-ing, and 'scope composition—form a coherent visual system that elabo-rates a unique conception of space. This system will be fully deployed in *The Bad Sleep Well* and *High and Low*, as well as in *Yōjimbō*, *Sanjurō*, and *Red Beard*, which will be covered in the next chapter. The attributes of this system—the two-dimensionality of space, the analytic treatment of movement, the dialectic between space and motion, and the conver-sion of time into space—challenge the continuity codes and the stable, centered spaces of the Hollywood cinema. Departures from the carefully coded "realism" of Hollywood films, however, should not automatically be validated as a liberating maneuver. What counts is the use made of the alternate forms, the ends to which they are put. So, again, the question returns of the adequacy of Kurosawa's forms to the tasks he has set them. As the remainder of this chapter will suggest, the subversive potentials of this visual system, which counters the continuity codes of Hollywood production, are recouped and reorganized by narratives that substitute ethical dilemmas for political ones and displace structural relations of power onto individual personalities. The effort to come to terms with the nuclear threat in *Record* produced a fissured analysis, the contradictions of which simply swallowed the hero. We should now consider *The Bad Sleep Well* and *High and Low*.

A series of period films and experiments at literary adaptation fol-lowed *Record of a Living Being*, and *The Bad Sleep Well* is Kurosawa's next attempt to describe his perception of the ills of contemporary Japan. *The Bad Sleep Well*, like the subsequent *High and Low*, addresses the economic basis of political and social freedom. Economic problems—gross inequities of wealth, the black market, unemployment—are either explicitly or implicitly present in virtually all Kurosawa's contempo-rary-life films. These films repeatedly equate economic injustice with political injustice, and it is tempting to regard this aspect of his work as an inquiry into some of the motivating assumptions of the initial Occu-pation reforms, that is, into the relations between economic and political freedoms. As noted earlier, the Occupation initiated a program of re-forms intended to decentralize economic power, based on the view that Japan's big businesses, the zaibatsu, had been instigators of the war and collaborators with the militarists. While the prewar zaibatsu were viewed as having played an important role in the modernization of the country, they were also regarded by many as having hindered the devel-opment of a strong middle class in which trends toward political liberalism could be rooted and as having been symptomatic of a historic tradition where democratic controls on economic power were lacking.[22] Thus, Occupation intentions to "democratize" Japan tied economic to political reforms. "[D]evelopments in the field of economics had such a vital bearing on the process of democratization that the future of democracy in Japan may really depend largely on how successfully the Occupation achieved its final economic objectives."[23] This equation of political and economic democracy, tied to a view that hitches democratic development in Japan to the success of the Occupation reforms, raises a problem: official Occupation policy changed in its later years toward a stance that was more favorable to big business, the so-called reverse course of the Occupation. Moreover, the Japanese government revised many of the reforms once the Occupation had ended. Kozo Yamamura points out that immediate national needs for economic recovery and growth could not be reconciled with scap's initial policies of economic democratization.

> The emerging Japanese policy was to sacrifice the "democratic" elements of the scap policy, such as a competitive market structure and "just and equal" tax laws, for the sake of rapid recovery and growth. In brief the original scap policy was incongruent with the rapid growth the Japanese government desired. . . . [G]rowth and economic democracy, as envisioned by scap, failed to coexist in postwar Japan.[24]

Revision of scap economic policies, however, did not necessarily mean the stunting of democracy in Japan. Many scholars have pointed to the existence of vital currents of popular social protest and corresponding efforts by the state to adjust its policies.[25] In this vein, Gerald Curtis concludes a recent study of the postwar state structure with a strong affirmation of Japan's postwar democratic accomplishments.[26]

Kurosawa's productions during the postwar period of rapid economic growth—*The Bad Sleep Well* and *High and Low*—take a contrary view. They are extremely critical of concentrated economic power, of big business, and seem to share the same set of assumptions that motivated the initial round of Occupation reforms (i.e., that political freedom will remain a fiction as long as economic democracy does not prevail). *The Bad Sleep Well*, in particular, castigates the corrupt partnership between corporate and government officials and implies that such a partnership is no basis for political freedoms. "I don't think in any other country there is so thick a wall separating people from government officials and agen-

33. Compulsions of a tortured Kurosawa hero (Toshirō Mifune). *The Bad Sleep Well.* (Museum of Modern Art/Film Stills Archive)

cies," Kurosawa has said.[27] Expressing these views, however, was not to be easy, neither in terms of studio politics (Kurosawa reports having an acute sense of how far he could go in these films[28]) nor in terms of form. Like *Record of a Living Being*, *The Bad Sleep Well* is almost allegorical in its exhibition of the internal stresses and contradictions that beset his work as it attempts to assimilate a new and more complex arena of social relations and content. The film represents Kurosawa's thought at its limit, extended beyond its capabilities in attempting to deal with issues that are not amenable to the solutions of the individual hero. The film reveals the breakdown of this thought and the forms that sustain it, as they are shaken apart by the stresses of adapting to dimensions of content that elude them. Once again, Kurosawa demonstrates his willingness to participate in the disintegration of his forms rather than abandon them for alternate approaches. As with *Record*, these deformations are most apparent in the narrative structure and the presentation of the hero. *The Bad Sleep Well* documents a suicidal attempt by Nishi (Toshirō Mifune), secretary to the president of a powerful housing corporation, to destroy the company and its top officials.[29] His reasons are initially mysterious. Married to the president's daughter, he works from inside, manipulating top officials into betraying each other and disclosing evidence of their crimes.

The film deals with the corruption of big business, if not, strictly speaking, of the zaibatsu, whose organizations, ownership patterns, and mechanisms of control did not survive the war.[30] The housing corporation receives a kickback from the Dairyū Construction Company in exchange for awarding Dairyū a valuable contract. During the wedding ceremony that opens the film, in which the president of the housing corporation, Iwabuchi (Masayuki Mori), marries his daughter to Nishi, the police converge upon the reception to arrest Wada, a high-ranking official of the corporation connected with Dairyū. This is not, however, the company's first scandal. Five years ago, one of its officials jumped to his death from an office building. The death was ruled a suicide, but suspicions linger in the press that the man was killed to ensure his silence about the corporation's illegal activities.

The film was intended by Kurosawa to engage the system of power in contemporary Japan and reveal its abuses. The economic and political problems examined have an institutional basis. The abuses of power that the film documents are vested in a system that shields high government and business officials from public scrutiny and thereby encourages their corruption. This is why the bad can sleep well, because they may act in secrecy and with impunity. The top officials at the housing corporation—Iwabuchi, Moriyama, and Shirai—are referred to by the press as the "scandal trio." The reporters know these men are engaged in graft and racketeering but cannot get close enough to them to prove anything.

The circles of power in the corporation are closed to the queries of outsiders like the press, so the narrative of the film is designed as a probe, as a gradual revelation of the criminality of the scandal trio. Itself an investigation, the film is concerned with acts of detection and ways of seeing. As in *High and Low*, Kurosawa attends to modern technologies of surveillance and documentation: microphones, tape recorders, cameras. These are thrust into the faces of the corporation executives or the police investigators by a press eager to uncover new scandals. The arrest of business officials is attended by the furious popping of flashbulbs. At his press conferences, Iwabuchi is surrounded by cameras and microphones. Despite the heightened observational powers these technological extensions of the senses make possible, however, the structures of political power and social class remain invisible. The reporters and the police are quite helpless, the corporations secure in their ruthlessness, and only the lone avenger Nishi dares to attack them. In shaping its narrative this way, the film suggests that social reality is refractory, that relations of class and social power assume a myriad of forms and are disguised beneath public rituals and ceremonies. The bad do not identify themselves as such. The film thereby identifies an obstacle to its inquiry. A single mode of seeing will be insufficient to disclose the complex matrix of power within which Iwabuchi and his henchmen operate, for that matrix may not itself be personified. A recording of Iwabuchi's press conference or a photograph of his top officials cannot say very much about structures of power. This is why the newspaper headlines announcing the scandals, appearing as montages throughout the film, are not very informative. To pursue its inquiry, the film will have to develop a complex mode of seeing that is dialectical and does not depend upon strategies that individualize the problem or attempt to represent it directly, as do the journalists in their attempts to interview and photograph the executives. But, while we admit the necessity for such an alternate strategy, can the film develop one?

Kurosawa begins to move in this direction with an opening sequence that establishes the multilayeredness of social reality and implicitly clarifies the institutional bases of power. The film begins with the wedding of Nishi to Iwabuchi's daughter and, as Richie points out, is a sequence of sustained brilliance rare even in Kurosawa's work.[31] As a public ritual, the reception is highly formalized and gathers together Iwabuchi, his top company officials, representatives from Dairyū, and emissaries from government and political circles. The proxemics of their positioning in the room describe the networks of political and economic power in Japan, that which Nishi has dedicated himself to opposing. The room makes visible through ritual display the institutions that control contemporary society. Representatives of these institutions toast the bride and groom and make speeches about the harmony of state and corporate goals and the soundness of their enterprises. The interrelationship between corporate and state managers is directly disclosed. Outside the room, however, other agents of social power are grouped. The police have gathered in the hall and send messengers into the auditorium to summon the officials they are arresting. Behind the police are the reporters, who smell a scandal brewing but who watch from a distance. Through the design of this sequence, Kurosawa spatializes the nexus of social control, clarifying by the physical separation of these three groups—business leaders, police, and press—the autonomy of the power elite. The inner room where they are grouped remains inviolate, the police and press compelled to wait outside.

Thus, the opening of the film defines the challenge to Kurosawa's inquiry by disclosing the systemic coordinates of the problem he wishes to address. This sequence is distinguished by a fundamentally social focus, but it must compete with the old forms, that is, with a narrative centered on the protest of the individual hero. The executives' toasts are interrupted by a mysterious event. A wedding cake arrives sculpted in the form of the building from which the official leaped to his death five years ago. A large flower hangs in the window from which he jumped. With fanfares on the soundtrack, the cake is wheeled down center aisle, astounding everyone in the room. It is positioned directly behind Iwabuchi, who scowls but remains otherwise impassive. The cake's sinister presence subverts the outward harmony of the wedding ritual and hints of darker things to come. The structural perspective announced at the opening of the film is disrupted by a melodramatic enigma: who sent the cake and why?

Soon, more mysterious events occur. The police receive information from someone in the firm that assists them in their investigation. A large portion of the kickback from Dairyū disappears from its safe deposit box, and Iwabuchi is led to suspect Shirai, one of his top executives. It transpires that Nishi is engineering these events to sow dissension among Iwabuchi and his associates, prior to uncovering the evidence of their conspiracy in the death of the official five years ago. That man was Nishi's father, and Nishi has launched his program of subversion as a personal vendetta against the three officials—Iwabuchi, Shirai, and Moriyama—who arranged his death. But he also indicates that his mission has a broader social purpose. It's not only for my father that I punish these men, he tells Itakura, a friend who collaborates on his plan of subversion, but for all the people too helpless to fight back. Nishi's mission to destroy Iwabuchi and the company is meant to benefit everyone in Japan who suffers from the greed engendered by huge and unregulated concentrations of economic power. As Richie points out, however, when the wedding cake arrives in the reception hall, the focus of the film begins to shift away from the institutional and structural coordinates defined by the opening sequence.[32] In place of a detailed socio-economic focus, the film offers a revenge drama (modeled somewhat on *Hamlet*[33]) enacted by the hero against three powerful individuals. The institutional focus shifts into a design that centers on personalities and character. By transforming the problem of economic democracy into a very different concern with the crimes of three men, the film denies its initial political focus and, by apparently narrowing the scale of the opposition, permits the narrative to employ the individual hero as protagonist. The shift of focus is compelled to regenerate the old forms, but the repressed content never entirely disappears. The old forms cannot absorb it, and it returns to subvert them.

In *High and Low*, Kurosawa would be very careful to ensure that the form of the film create a series of shifting perspectives, dialectical in nature, whose movements would disclose the structural relations of wealth and poverty. In *High and Low*, these are not embodied in characters but in the formal organization of the film. By contrast, in dwelling on the revenge drama and the problem of fathers, *The Bad Sleep Well* tends to psychologize the social issues. Kurosawa does, however, tantalizingly and briefly demonstrate in one later sequence the kind of dialectical focus not otherwise employed. The sequence explicitly shows the power of the kind of complex seeing Brecht called for. After his release by the police, Wada attempts to kill himself under Iwabuchi's instructions but is prevented from doing so by Nishi. To show Wada that he owes his superiors nothing, Nishi takes him to his own funeral, where Wada sees his wife and daughter grieving and Shirai and Moriyama comforting them and bowing before the shrine.

Overcome by what he sees, Wada cries that after such a fine funeral he really must die. Then Nishi plays a tape recording for him in which Shirai and Moriyama callously discuss how they must kill Wada before he betrays them to the police and joke about how, after doing it, they will need to spend the evening with a young girl. Kurosawa stresses the dialectical nature of these competing perspectives by cutting among close-ups of Wada's shocked face, close-ups of the spinning reels on the tape recorder, and telephoto long shots of the funeral. We see Moriyama and Shirai displaying their public personas, as we hear their venal private nature on tape. Wada views their decorous behavior at the funeral, hears their cynical words on tape, and is confronted by Nishi's denunciations of them. A sound montage accompanies the competing images. The taped conversation is mixed with the banal music from Nishi's car radio and the solemn chanting of the priests at the funeral. This polyphonous sequence thus establishes multiple layers of perspective. Image and sound collide as Kurosawa demonstrates the kind of seeing necessary to reveal social reality. Wada is shocked and embittered by what he sees and hears, and Nishi is able to recruit him. By creating a rich collage of pictures and sounds, by studying the means and media of electronic representation, by demonstrating how aesthetic form can invert the meaning of the event (the funeral) it depicts, this sequence demonstrates the potency, and the importance, of dialectic perception. As Brecht said, a photograph of the Krupp factories does not tell us very much about those factories. It is not the single mode of representation that counts, that which is seen in an unmediated fashion, as Wada first sees his funeral, but the formal context in which the representation is integrated. Nishi creates a context that alters Wada's relationship to the ritual by disclosing the true social determinants of its participants' behavior. This sequence is so remarkable, and the kind of perception it announces so powerful, that it seems almost to belong to another film.[34] Kurosawa does not extend its implications to the sequences that follow, and it would not be until *High and Low*, with its obsession with electronic technologies of surveillance, that he would again pursue this kind of mediated perception.

Instead, as in *Record of a Living Being*, politics is displaced onto the family. It is possible that Kurosawa intends the model of human relationships developed here to function as did the model in *Drunken Angel*, where the Matsunaga–Okada relationship embodied a political critique cautioning against antidemocratic behavioral codes. In other words, to the extent that the prewar zaibatsu maintained a "family" structure of ownership, Kurosawa may intend the film's family focus to serve as a socio-political metaphor. But instead what happens is that political inquiry becomes defused by the structures of melodrama. Nishi has married Iwabuchi's daughter so he can insinuate himself into the old man's confidences and thereby gain access to other top officials. Yoshiko is lame and must hobble about on crutches. Nishi cannot but respond to her with pity and, over time, with love. But this creates his dilemma, for he comes to feel ashamed about using her. Paradoxically, as he gets closer to exposing her father, his feelings for her dilute the passion for revenge. The film comes to center around the question of whether it is right for Nishi to betray Yoshiko. The action is absorbed into the space of Iwabuchi's house and centers on the members of his family, as Nishi tries to balance his love for Yoshiko against his desire for vengeance. To ensure this desire, Nishi attempts to harden himself into a cold, relentless avenger by stoking his hate. He carries a photograph of his father's smashed corpse that shows the manner of death. He periodically looks at this picture, infusing himself with hatred. He tells Itakura, the friend who assists him in his plot, that it is hard to hate evil, but that to fight it he must become evil himself.

The passion of his protest is transformed into a negative energy by the problems he confronts, which outstrip his capacities. In his determination to embrace evil, Nishi emerges as one of the darkest of Kurosawa's heroes. The revelation of his identity as an avenger is visualized as an emergence from hell. Nishi stands on the rim of a volcano, cloaked in mist and vapor, a dealer in death. Wada has come here to commit suicide. Nishi initially prevents him from jumping in by asking him if he doesn't want revenge. But then he throws him to the ground, almost down into the fiery pit, and shouts, does he want to die? The shot then cuts to newspaper headlines announcing Wada's suicide.

The images create an intentional ambiguity, but it happens that Wada is not dead. Instead, his "death" has been arranged by Nishi who wants the company to believe the accountant is gone. He then uses Wada as a ghost, making him appear before Shirai in order to terrorize him into giving up the identity of the man who ordered the murder of Nishi's father. Nishi takes Shirai to the office window from which his father had jumped and, in a sequence of exceptional brutality, alternately threatens to push him out the window or poison him, finally pouring the poison down Shirai's throat himself. It is not really poison, however, just a calculated psychological torture, but it is enough for Shirai, who lapses into madness. Nishi, disappointed, says he could have used him more.

Wada, horrified by the spectacle, tells Nishi he's a terrible man. Nishi agrees and later says he's not bad enough, that he should have thrown Shirai out the window. He tells Wada he should have been glad to see Shirai suffer, since Shirai and Moriyama plotted his own death. The darkness of Nishi's quest, and the inhuman behavior he takes upon himself, decisively remove this Kurosawa hero from the coordinates of the earlier films. Nishi attempts to place himself above human emotions, to purge himself of pity and love. This represents a dark twist on the theme of *Stray Dog*, where the emotional austerity practiced by the detectives was intended as a means of protecting society against people like Yusa. The struggle against compassion was necessary to prevent Murakami from dwelling on his similarities to Yusa. It enforced a separation that made possible the apprehension of the thief. Now, in *The Bad Sleep Well*, the fight itself is in question, both in terms of the scale of the opposition and because the heroic quest is tainted by its own darkness and destructive compulsions. This transformation provides one illustration of the evolution that has occurred in Kurosawa's work since *Stray Dog*. The possibility of alleviating social ills no longer seems so certain as it once did, and the scope of social evil has infinitely expanded. In place of the thief Yusa, Nishi battles giant corporations representing thievery that has become institutionalized. Wada tells Nishi he is afraid of the outcome. Echoing Judge Araki from *Record of a Living Being*, he says Nishi is fighting against enormous powers. Nishi agrees but stubbornly insists on the primacy and capability of individual heroism by saying that the only reason they have this power is that no one challenges them.

Nishi refuses to give up the terms of Kurosawan heroism, refuses to blunt his sense of outrage and social justice, but the film will no longer permit the success of this kind of individual action. The film organizes its destruction, eliminating individual heroism both as a political response and as an aesthetic form. Nishi is killed by Iwabuchi before he can go public with his evidence. Yoshiko, unable to believe her father is truly bad, tells the old man where Nishi is hiding, thus proving once again what Richie has noted as the deadliness of compassion in Kurosawa's world.[35] Iwabuchi and his henchmen overpower Nishi, drug him, place him in his car and the car on the railroad tracks, where it is smashed by a train. Nishi is eliminated by the narrative of the film, which, by doing so, affirms the omnipotence of huge economic octopi. The film ends with Iwabuchi receiving another phone call from the unseen Mr. Big, to whom he reports and who endorses his actions. Mr. Big makes somewhat explicit Iwabuchi's ties to political power, but, as noted, Kurosawa felt constrained from developing this idea any further within the film.[36] As it is, the intensity of Nishi's protest has not even bruised the institutions of power. It is clear that individual heroism is an inadequate form of protest against the corporate state. But, to a fascinating extent, the film also makes clear that it is an inadequate aesthetic strategy. Nishi's visual and narrative presentation bears the strain of his pathological mission. The film deforms the hero in novel and unprecedented ways, and this deformation is symptomatic of textual disintegration, of the film's own dissociation in its attempt to reconcile Nishi's heroism with Iwabuchi's institutional power.

Kurosawan heroism was once founded upon the primacy and autonomy of the self, but the institutions of power in an advanced industrial society have engulfed the space where the heroic individual once stood, as they engulf Nishi. In *The Bad Sleep Well*, the self is fragmented, torn asunder, rendered spectral and ghostly. The hero becomes schizophrenic under the pressure of his quest, his identity fraudulent and based on deceit. Above all, no integration of the splintered self is possible. What once grounded the aesthetic form of Kurosawan heroism has come unstuck. Nishi is not Nishi. Nishi is someone else, he tells Shirai.

In order to conceal his background as Furuya's son so that he could marry Yoshiko and gain access to Iwabuchi, Nishi switched family registers with his friend Itakura. Nishi is really Itakura, and Itakura really Nishi. The Kurosawa hero is doubled and fatally split apart. Assuming a false identity, he embarks on the role of the avenger. His shadow self accompanies him throughout the narrative, and when Nishi is killed, so, too, in a sense is Itakura. When Nishi is smashed by the train, his death obliterates Itakura's identity as well. Itakura can never become Nishi again, his real self, because the imposter died in his car. As Itakura, the real Nishi can say nothing. "Nishi" died in Nishi's car, thereby sealing the doom of both selves. Itakura rages in impotent despair on the floor of their hideout, beneath the ruins of a munitions factory bombed during the war.

An earlier sequence in the film established this location and its special relation to Nishi and Itakura. In that sequence, huge piles of stone and skeletal buildings were seen to surround their hideout, visually marking the area as a special one, and it was separated from the other locales of the film by an aural marker, a loud, musical crescendo that accompanied the initial establishing shots of the rubble. This formal separation, however, is also a temporal one. This is an environment of the past to which Nishi and Itakura have returned, when they needed refuge from Iwabuchi's henchmen, solace from the depradations of contemporary Japan. Here, as high school students, they were mobilized during the war. Bearing the scars of war, this landscape represents not only their personal past but the national past as well. They gaze at the ruins and reminisce about their youth and how time has changed everything. Japan is now a very different place than it was during the war, they reflect. As they contemplate these differences, they stand amid the rubble, framed in old, familiar ways. This return to the past has placed the characters back within the landscapes of Kurosawa's early films, to the bombed ruins of *Drunken Angel, One Wonderful Sunday, The Quiet Duel,* and *Stray Dog,* within a time when the capacity of heroic action to regenerate society seemed a real possibility. The imagery returns them to an aesthetic era in which a belief in the omnipotence of the self provided the organizing principle. Anticipating their own imminent triumph over Iwabuchi, about to release the incriminating evidence, Nishi and Itakura journey back through Kurosawa's cinema as the narrative attempts to recover an earlier optimism and heroic commitment. But their efforts will be defeated, the project of the past foreclosed. Nishi will be killed, and Itakura will remain to haunt this landscape as a ghost, spectral heroism confined

34. Disturbances of the modern urban environment. *The Bad Sleep Well.*
(Museum of Modern Art/Film Stills Archive)

in the eclipsed landscapes of the past, just as Wada has haunted the contemporary landscape as another ghost, terrorizing Shirai with his noc-
turnal appearances. I don't know who I am, Wada confessed earlier,
whether I'm living or dead. The self has become problematic, not only for
the hero, whose integrity is rent by a schizophrenic double, but also for
those with whom he associates. Wada, too, is killed by Iwabuchi, which,
as Itakura says, was easy because he was already supposed to be dead.
The self is a phantom, like Wada, able to witness its own funeral, or like
Nishi, awaiting its extinction.

Nishi's manner of death is organized by the narrative as a displacement. He dies off-screen, and the details of his abduction are reenacted
by Itakura, whom Yoshiko finds in the factory ruins afterward. All that
remains of Nishi are his smashed flashlight, a whiskey flask, and his
overcoat lying on the ground. See how hard he fought for his life, Itakura
cries, showing her how they held him down, injected him with alcohol,
and carried him outside to the car. If Nishi was ghostly before, appearing
initially from the vapors of a volcano, now the only traces that remain of
his presence are the scattered objects on the ground. His death, by being

unseen, opens a gap in the narrative that is never filled and upon which the film concludes. This gap is the space left by the collapse of Nishi's protest and by the aesthetic forms that embodied it. With that space irreparably opened, the film ends, having pursued the logic of its forms to their point of disintegration. Nishi's protest was driven by his passion for social justice, but the failure of that protest has left a legacy of despair and withdrawal. Nishi's betrayal by Yoshiko's naiveté ensures that the energies of his rebellion are effectively contained by the evil Iwabuchi family, as the structures of melodrama engineer his downfall and generate a scenario of failure. Itakura rages with frustration about the injustice of Iwabuchi's triumph. Now all Japan will be fooled, he cries. Is this right, he asks with a maniacal scream, the energy of his outburst absorbing something of the spirit of Nishi's rebellion, except that it is transmuted into impotent rage. The narrative structure has crushed Nishi and excluded Itakura from responding. The corporate powers remain triumphant, untouched and even protected by the formal design of the film. *The Bad Sleep Well* emerges, finally, as a work that searches for the outer boundaries of Kurosawa's cinema and that, having found them, chooses to stay resolutely inside, even as the walls come crashing down.

Interestingly, as if in recognition of the dead end he reached in this work, Kurosawa remade *The Bad Sleep Well* the following year as *Yōjimbō*, another revenge drama in which Mifune again plays a subversive outsider, another alienated avenger without a secure name or identity, using stealth and secrecy to orchestrate the downfall of corrupt businessmen and gangsters. The difference here, however, is that *Yōjimbō* is a period film, and Kurosawa is able to permit his hero some measure of success because of changed historical circumstances. The samurai hero confronts the structures of capitalism in their infancy and is thereby able to triumph. Richie briefly alludes to a similarity between the businessmen of *The Bad Sleep Well* and *Yōjimbō*,[37] but the latter film has not generally been recognized for its structural relations to the former one. It is clear that Kurosawa is reworking, through a retreat to the past, the issues that *The Bad Sleep Well* had been unable to resolve. Kurosawa's strategies in *Yōjimbō* will be discussed in detail in the next chapter.

The attempts to probe contemporary social problems in *Record of a Living Being* and *The Bad Sleep Well* had ended in deadlock. By translating a structural focus into an individual one, by relying upon a single protagonist whose struggles were meant to symbolize a larger social process, the films launched a psychological and ethical inquiry that could not come to terms with the problems of the nuclear and corporate state. The linear narrative with a hero at its center generated only one mode of seeing and did not provide an adequate formal means for investigating social phenomena. Instead of displacing those phenomena onto individuals, a mode of seeing was necessary by which they could be grasped at a more appropriate level of analysis. Instead of a focus on the hero shaping events, it would be necessary to look at how events and a socio-economic system structured the individual. But this could not be done using the forms employed in *Record of a Living Being* and *The Bad Sleep Well*. Another visual and narrative structure would have to be found. In *High and Low* Kurosawa does precisely this, abandoning the unidirectional narrative and the protagonist at its center in favor of a highly formalized narrative design that shifts among multiple voices, permitting an analytical, not merely a descriptive, inquiry.

The film's narrative is elegant, disciplined, and highly controlled. Kurosawa's insistent command of its form is similar to the control he practiced in *Ikiru*. Both films adopt shifting levels of perspective in place of a single context or vantage of perception. The act of seeing is foregrounded in *High and Low* in two ways. As Richie writes, "references to seeing in the film are many and varied."[38] The film is obsessive in its study of electronic technologies of surveillance and communication, and its narrative is cast as a detective story, begining with a baffling and seemingly perverse crime and then laboriously tracking down the identity and motive of the criminal. Perception is a matter of technology and narrative, and it is central to *High and Low*. The film, like so many of Kurosawa's other works, adopts a polyphonous form of address, so that a complex play of associations develops about the acts of seeing and the social knowledge that they imply. The film is about seeing and not seeing, and the irony that is implicit in the use of surveillance and communications technologies is that they serve to conceal rather than reveal social reality. Despite their use of radios, telephones, tape recorders, motion pictures, and still photographs, the police remain unable to perceive the structural relations of wealth and poverty that triggered the crime. As in *Rashōmon*, *Ikiru*, *The Bad Sleep Well*, and many of his other films, social reality is badly splintered. Its truths and the relations of power and resources that structure human life remain veiled. *High and Low* attempts to peer into this dark well of social life, to uncover the structures that alienate and reify human existence. In doing so, it takes its clue from that sequence in *The Bad Sleep Well* in which Nishi brought Wada to his own funeral and created a multiplex context with which to confront the executive with the truth of the ritual and his own relation to it.

The film's narrative centers on a kidnapping and the hunt for the criminal. It is broken into two sections, each very different in tone, focus, and formal structure. By manipulating these sections, and by contrasting the social perspectives that they develop, Kurosawa fashions a dialectical inquiry in which each section is generated by the other in a relation of opposition. In a brief coda, in which the kidnapper and his victim finally meet, the narrative oppositions—and the class tensions that they have announced—are provided with a potential for synthesis, of a resolution of the socio-economic conflict that has driven the narrative and split it into two. If this synthesis be possible, if some mutual recognition between kidnapper and victim can occur, that is, some awareness of how each has created the other, then Kurosawa's experiment at healing his forms may, in fact, succeed. We must now trace the narrative design of the film, the two perspectives each section describes, and the structural meaning of the coda and what it shows us of Kurosawa's attempt to address the problems of contemporary Japan.

The first section of the film, more than an hour in length, is confined to the house of a wealthy shoe manufacturer named Gondō (Toshirō Mifune). His home perches majestically on a hill overlooking Yokohama, directly above a depressed shantytown where the kidnapper lives. All the action is restricted to this location, with most of it taking place in Gondō's living room where, as the film begins, he plots and schemes to gain control of National Shoes, the company for which he works. He has borrowed against his home and property to finance the takeover, gambling his fortune and future in a bid for power. He relishes such dangerous games and tells his son, playing a Western outlaw with the chauffeur's boy as sheriff, to hide and wait for the sheriff and then ambush him. Gondō draws a parallel between the secret ambush and his own stealth at taking over the company. Attack or be attacked, he tells Jun, his son.

Human relations in Gondō's house occur under the sign of marketplace economics, in which a predatory ethic becomes the only sensible one to practice. Gondō plans to outwit his fellow executives in gaining control of company stock but finds his efforts eventually betrayed by Kawanishi, his closest aide, who tells the other board members of Gondō's plan in return for being made an executive. Responding to these ethics of predation and betrayal in Gondō's business world, his wife tells him that success is no good if you lose your humanity. The first section of the film details Gondō's recovery of this humanity, which reemerges when he finds himself unable to allow the chauffeur's boy to be killed.

The kidnapper has mistakenly abducted Shinichi, believing the boy to be Gondō's son, and the ethical dilemma organizing the first section centers on whether Gondō remains responsible for paying the ransom even though the child is not his own. Initially Gondō refuses, but eventually he pays, learning the familiar Kurosawa lesson of the responsibility of each for all. If this process of moral regeneration, however, were all that this section of the narrative offered, *High and Low* would not be the extraordinary film it is. Instead, Kurosawa limits and distances this ethical conflict by resolutely maintaining a focus on the socio-economic relations that have generated the conflict as their own camouflage. Whereas in *Record of a Living Being* and *The Bad Sleep Well*, the hero's travails were central to the narrative, in *High and Low* the narrative is reorganized so that scenarios of individual heroism are refused.

As the film develops, Gondō becomes increasingly less central to the plot. For much of the latter half of the film, he does not figure at all. But even during the first section, while the action is confined to his living room, Gondō is subsumed within an ensemble design, his own potential centrality to the narrative continually offset by other groups of characters who, through movement and composition, establish a visual patterning that circumscribes his own position in the frame. This patterning establishes a social nexus that displaces Gondō both narratively and visually by ensuring that he remains only one compositional element within an extraordinarily complex series of framings. These other groups include the police, led by Inspector Tokurō (Tatsuya Nakadai), Reiko, Gondō's wife, Aoki, the chauffeur, Jun, Gondō's son, and Kawanishi. All these characters join Gondō in anxiously awaiting the kidnapper's calls as Kurosawa in a masterly maneuver deploys the various groups across the width of the 'scope frame. These sequences are among the finest he has created and stand as peerless examples of what can be done with the anamorphic frame. Despite the deliberate restriction of action and locale, Kurosawa invests the scenes with an explosive energy that is the result of multicamera cutting, which continually alters the axis of view and requires an ongoing perceptual reorientation by the viewer. As the groups of characters wait for the calls, their positions shift through a series of carefully choreographed permutations, which Noël Burch accurately identifies as "one of the most highly developed variation structures in Kurosawa's work."[39] The complexity of these variations is intensified by the movements of the cameras, which are also shifting to offer a series of novel framings. The event and its observation become disjunctive, as the film begins to enunciate its concern with the disparity be-

35. While the police and his wife look on, Gondō (Toshirō Mifune) prepares the luggage that will carry his fortune to the kidnapper. The multiple areas of composition visualize an impacted social space. *High and Low*. (Museum of Modern Art/Film Stills Archive)

tween sight and that which is observed. Though the action is tightly restrained to a small physical space, the cameras open up this space by offering a series of differently placed but simultaneous perspectives and by amplifying, through the montage cutting, an impression of movement and visual energy that is purely formal since the physical event itself contains very little. The energy resides in the images, not in the event.

The analytic capabilities of the multicamera technique are conjoined to a social analysis that integrates Gondō within the institutional spaces of family, corporation, and police, all of whom have representatives within the room. The 'scope frame, the telephoto lenses, and the multicameras all define the coordinates of these group relations and their primacy, thus diffusing an overweening focus on the individual hero. Kurosawa manipulates the positions of Gondō, the police, Kawanishi, and the chauffeur, among others, to stress both the density of the social fabric and its relational nature. Let us examine more closely how Kurosawa uses the multicameras and the anamorphic frame to describe the conflicting demands these groups make upon one another. He plays particularly upon the relations between Gondō and Aoki, alternately separating and then bringing them together as the groupings within the frame change. Aoki has special significance as the father of the kidnapped boy and, for Gondō, as the unwelcome reminder of his obligation to pay. When Gondō realizes that Shinichi is missing, he goes to the sliding glass door at the right of the frame, while Aoki is placed at the left frame edge, so that an extraordinary distance separates them. Aoki is standing in the hallway outside the room. As Gondō cries that it is Shinichi who has been abducted, Aoki slowly comes into the room and pauses, still at the other end of the frame from Gondō. Then as Aoki cries for his son and rushes to the glass door at the right of the frame, Kurosawa anticipates his movement by cutting to a telephoto shot from outside this door. The new perspective flattens Aoki and Gondō into the same plane of space by shifting the horizontal axis of the composition from the previous shot by nearly ninety degrees. The shift of perspective from an image stressing Aoki's and Gondō's separation to one stressing their proximity plays upon the ambivalence of their relationship, Gondō unwilling to pay but disturbed by Aoki's grief and Aoki desperate for his son but ashamed to ask his employer directly to meet the ransom demand.

The shifts among multicamera perspectives announce these ambivalent social allegiances. The kidnapper calls a second time to tell them he realizes he has the wrong boy but still demands payment. As the phone rings, a detective races across the frame to the left to monitor the call on the upstairs phone. Kurosawa pans quickly to follow his movements but interrupts the pan to freeze the camera upon a countervisual and dramatic element: an image of Aoki immobile in the doorway. The succession of movement by stasis is arresting. Kurosawa then begins to develop the dominant rhythm of the sequence, alternating isolated figures with group shots. In the next shot, Kawanishi, Gondō, and Tokurō gather around the phone as Gondō answers, and Aoki hovers standing in the background. Time is elided by a wipe and the conversation is heard as it is played back on the police tape recorder. As the kidnapper talks, Gondō walks away from the recorder into the background of the shot, as Kawanishi, Reiko, Jun, and the police huddle together in the foreground. Again, Aoki haunts the edges of the frame, a nagging presence, placed on the extreme right edge of the image. Kurosawa then contrasts this ensemble shot with a framing of only Gondō and Aoki, at opposite edges of the image, the anamorphic frame stressing their visual separation as they face in different directions. Kurosawa then goes back to the previous group shot and then cuts again to the shot of Gondō and the chauffeur. This time their solitude is broken by Kawanishi, who walks into the frame between them. He urges Gondō to ignore the ransom and complete the takeover attempt. He is, therefore, a disrupting influence both visually and narratively. Kurosawa interrupts his plea by cutting back to the group shot, with Gondō and Aoki in the background. Kurosawa then returns to the isolated framing of Gondō, Kawanishi, and Aoki as Gondō repeats his decision not to pay. As he says this, however, the composition is altered: he crosses to the police and his family, who are gathered around the tape recorder, attempting to reintegrate himself with them as he declares his opposition to Aoki. Then, as the shot continues, he walks away from them, moving into the background as Aoki walks in a counter-direction to leave the frame on the left.

I hope this description suggests something of the complexity of framing and choreography of movement that typifies the entire first section of the film. As Reiko, Aoki, Kawanishi, and the police impose conflicting demands upon Gondō, some urging that he pay, others not, Kurosawa uses his multicameras to capture and concretize these tensions in terms of a shifting visual field as the various groups compete to make their demands felt. The cameras capture social process itself, defining Gondō's reduced range of options as a function of the social construction of his position within the narrative and its visual construction within the frame. The individual is clearly shown to be embedded within a network of institutional roles and expectations. The individual hero has explicitly become an interactionist self. Gondō is defined in successively different ways, by the options that compliance with Reiko and Aoki, Kawanishi, and the police hold forth. The density of character positioning within the frame visualizes this impacted social space.

In a sense, this sequence recapitulates the opening of *The Bad Sleep Well*, where Kurosawa began to explore the coordinates of institutional power before replacing this with a psychological portrait of a single family. In *High and Low*, by contrast, he sustains the social focus throughout. The social space of Gondō's apartment does not exist in a vacuum, though Gondō behaves as if it does. He gazes down on the city as if he were royalty, lives in air-conditioned comfort to escape the heat that chokes Yokohama, and can banish the city by simply closing his curtains. In his wealth, he has dissociated himself from his surroundings, but it is precisely this arrogance that has enraged the kidnapper, who strikes at Gondō from the stifling heat of the overcrowded city below the hill. The kidnapper's calls disrupt Gondō's carefully arranged world and

36. Tokurō (Tatsuya Nakadai) tracks the kidnapper as the police mobilize for the hunt. *High and Low*. (Museum of Modern Art/Film Stills Archive)

shatter his complacency. Each call is more insistent than the last, until Gondō finally pays and is ruined. Through the urgently ringing phone, the class and social realities denied by Gondō erupt into his world and destroy it.

The dialectical focus of the first section, achieved by cutting among the competing views afforded by the multicameras, is reframed in the second half of the narrative in terms of the splintered perspectives of the world outside Gondō's home. The second section details the hunt for the kidnapper by the police and the laborious sifting of clues that gradually yield his identity. As Richie has pointed out, the first section is the high, heaven, the second the low, hell.[40] The differences between them are socio-economic, differences of class. The two are connected, with elegant self-consciousness, by a bridge, in both a literal and a structural sense. Gondō pays the ransom by dropping it out a train window during a brief, incredibly furious sequence whose raging energies collide with the stasis of the scenes inside his home. As the train thunders over a bridge, the kidnapper retrieves his money by the river below, and the film passes into its second major section. Gondō is eclipsed as a major character and moves to the periphery of the action, as the police department mobilizes for the hunt.

Kurosawa announces the narrative break with typical grace. The "bridge" sequence ends with Gondō embracing the rescued Shinichi, and the image fades out. The second narrative section commences when a fade-in reveals Gondō's house, viewed for the first time from the outside, in a low-angle shot taken from the bottom of the hill. Kurosawa then cuts back even farther as we see two policemen viewing the house through binoculars from a phone booth. The cops remark that the kidnapper was right, the house does seem to look down on everyone. As they leave the frame, Kurosawa returns to an image from his early films and gives us another sump. His camera pans the refuse-littered surface of the water and picks up a reflection of a man walking. The camera tilts up to reveal the man's back, and a series of shots show him from the rear as he goes down several alleys and up into a tiny apartment. It is the kidnapper, and at last we see his face as he reviews newspaper clippings covering the case.

Both sections of the film are structured differently, and these differences permit Kurosawa to surmount the psychological framework that he had applied to contemporary social problems in previous films. The spatial restrictiveness of the first half has already been discussed as well as the role of multicamera filming in visualizing the social field. This restrictiveness was linked to Gondō's own class blindness, perched on his hill and confined to his wealthy home, oblivious to the city below. By contrast, the second section is conceived as a tour of that city, executed as a series of descending socio-economic steps as the police gradually tighten their net about the kidnapper. As in *Stray Dog*, the narrative progresses through a mélange of contemporary milieus: train stations, hospitals, junkyards, bars. These are places the kidnapper has frequented, and we accompany the police through these environments. Through this tour of the city, Kurosawa constructs a montage of contemporary Japan, that is, of the world from which Gondō and the corporate hierarchy of National Shoes have detached themselves. The final stop is a foul ghetto frequented by junkies, lighted and photographed to accentuate its grotesquerie. The kidnapper visits this ghetto seeking a human guinea pig on whom to try a lethal dose of heroin. This vision of poverty and suffering constitutes the most extreme antithesis to the orderly and comfortable world of Gondō. But how does Kurosawa's film orient itself to these two extremes?

The structure of the film offers us a clue. The narrative is bifurcated, its sections connected by a bridge. But there is another mediator as well: the kidnapper. He is a medical student who is enraged by the contrast between his impoverished surroundings and Gondō's heavenly estate. He comes to hate Gondō and abducts the boy as a means of venting his wrath and ruining the executive. His is not a political rebellion but an action born of existential desperation and a consuming fury. Thus, when at the end he tells Gondō of his reasons for the crime, he cannot pose them in political terms. The kidnapper sees Gondō, the "high," only in terms of a personal relation founded on hatred, while Gondō, until the end, remains blind to the "low." For each character, vision is defined as a social perspective, and in each case it is incomplete, myopic, or occluded. Social reality, the existence and structure of class relations, is veiled, mystified to the sight of both an executive living at the heights of the society and a criminal who is aware of profoundly unequal standards of living.[41]

The film attempts to confront this mystification by studying images, reflections, and technologies of perception. The film's obsession with perception and images is overwhelming. In addition to the technologies of surveillance—the radios, tape recorders, cameras, and hand-drawn pictures employed by the police—Kurosawa's images, as Richie notes,[42] stress a myriad of reflecting surfaces: windows, mirrors, water, sunglasses. The kidnapper is first glimpsed as a reflection on the surface of refuse-littered waters. In his apartment, he looks at newspaper headlines and photographs describing the loss of Gondō's fortune and his ruination. Then, as he looks out his window through binoculars at Gondō's house, Kurosawa cuts directly to a sequence in which the police and Gondō view the motion pictures and still photographs taken from the train.

Human events and relations are mediated by these images and instruments of perception, or, as Richie puts it, reality is "counterfeited."[43] The kidnapper exists for the police only as a voice on magnetic tape and a grainy image photographed from a speeding train. The photographic enhancement of tracings left on a notepad by the kidnapper's accomplices leads directly to his exposure. He, in turn, studies Gondō through his binoculars and newspaper photos and headlines. The irony is that although these media and recording technologies permit the police to capture the kidnapper, they cannot disclose his motive, the perception of wealth feeding off poverty that enraged him. For all these mechanical enhancements of the senses, the characters of the film remain blind to the structure of social reality. In this sense, the electronic mediation of human relationships slides into a structure of alienation. It is the image of Gondō's house, not who he is personally, that triggers the crime, just

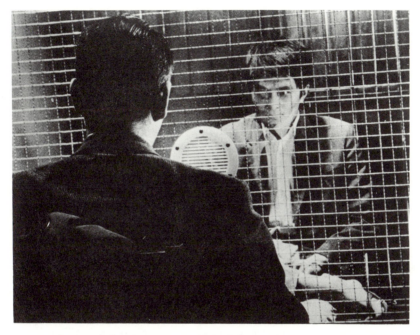

37. Space as social metaphor: a window of glass and wire separating them, Gondō confronts the kidnapper who has tormented him. *High and Low*. (Museum of Modern Art/Film Stills Archive)

as the image of the expensive dress in *Stray Dog* drove Yusa to rob and kill. The fruits of conspicuous consumption are toxic to the social body. ·

Although the characters of the film remain oblivious to the social and economic divisions in Japanese society that have set Gondō and the kidnapper in opposition, the structure of the film visualizes these very divisions. The bifurcated narrative formalizes them, and the "bridge" that mediates the two sections is purely ironic. For no reconciliation is possible. When Gondō and the kidnapper finally meet in prison just after the kidnapper has been sentenced to execution, they face each other separated by a wire-and-glass barrier. The kidnapper taunts Gondō and asks him if he rejoiced at the death sentence. Gondō asks, with weary resignation, why they must hate each other. Gondō's question, as well as his decision to pay the ransom for another's son, might seem to typify a humanist dimension within Kurosawa's work.[44] But the structure of the film defeats the question because it concretizes socio-economic divisions into a series of visual and aural barriers separating the city's inhabitants. Not only are all relationships mediated by images and recorded sounds, but the two sections of the narrative drive a wedge between Gondō and the kidnapper, which is replicated by the glass-and-wire wall now between them. The humanism of Gondō's question is a substitute for his failure to perceive the very real reasons why the kidnapper should hate him, his inability to understand the relation between his air-conditioned palatial home and the cramped, stiflingly hot dwellings of the poorer residents in the city below.

As if to mock his apparent belief in the essential equality of all people, who should therefore have no business hating each other, Gondō and the kidnapper exchange images.[45] As they converse, the reflection of each man in the glass occasionally overlaps the face of the other. But these compositions do not make a statement about the equality or common humanity of the characters, any more than the bath of mud at the end of *Stray Dog* implied the equivalence of Murakami and Yusa. Both films stress the necessary differences between the men, *High and Low* translating them into its own formal operations. *High and Low* offers, finally, structures of separation, not humanistic reconciliation, a vision of contemporary society rent by inequalities of wealth and social standing and the pathologies these breed. The two sections of the film remain sundered in opposition, and the synthesis that their antagonism might have yielded fails to occur. Gondō learns nothing from the kidnapper at the end, and the criminal remains unrepentant even in the face of death. He mocks Gondō bitterly and has a final nervous breakdown, prompting the police to haul him away. As his screams fade, an iron grate slides down behind the glass window, sealing off Gondō from his antagonist and the perception of class structure that this confrontation might have offered. As the final credit falls, Gondō is sitting in the dark, facing the iron grate, haunted by his failure to understand, by his inability to reach an accord with his persecutor, but most of all by the necessity that his question "Why must we hate each other?" evoke only more hate. The final frame is an image of stasis, of blockage, of eternal confrontation between the high and the low. Gondō will be sitting here forever.[46]

Again, the movement of inquiry and enlightenment has been arrested. In *High and Low* Kurosawa is able to discard many of the formal structures that impeded his inquiries in *Record of a Living Being* and *The Bad Sleep Well*. Alternate forms were found to replace them: a radicalizing of narrative structure, a discarding of protagonists and scenarios of individual heroism, a self-reflexive attention to images and vision, and an attempt to reflect in the structure of the images the coordinates of the social field. What Kurosawa uncovered with these new forms were entrenched structures of alienation and social opposition, embedded in relations of class and economic structure. In the film, no hero exists to oppose them, and their power is thereby amplified tenfold. Though Nakajima and Nishi were ultimately defeated, the passion of their protest remained to animate and haunt the films and to imply the necessity of rebellion against corporate corruption and willed mass suicide. The spaces of *High and Low* have been evacuated of such passion, and Gondō can only sit in bewilderment, immobilized by the antagonistic social energies. The deadlock the images describe is intensified by the absence of individual heroism. Its removal subjected the narrative and the images, and Kurosawa's inquiry, to a final reification, a hardening that symbolized the intensifying resistance of the contemporary world to the solutions that had seemed so compelling in the ashes of war.

6 History and the Period Film

[T]he historical

process cannot be

understood with-

out a permanent

element of nega-

tivity, both ex-

terior and interior

to man.

—Sartre[1]

Kurosawa's contemporary films are attempts to redefine the cultural boundaries of modern Japan by dramatizing the emergence, out of the ashes and wreckage of war, of a new type of individual, whose example is tested in confrontations with contemporary ills ranging from tuberculosis to atomic war. From the outset, however, the optimism of this project had to contend with a kind of epistemological and ethical inertia, a suspicion that the world might not be amenable to change and that the hero might be torn apart by the very energy of his protest. Such, as we have seen, were the fates of Nishi and Nakajima. The problems of the contemporary world seemed intractable, and the power of the social structure manifested a malevolence that could undermine and destroy the efforts of the heroes. The result was a pattern of qualified affirmation founded upon small demonstrations of heroic success: a schoolgirl cured of tuberculosis, a thief apprehended, a playground constructed. But organized political responses to oppression are rarely portrayed in Kurosawa's cinema.

Throughout the films, we can observe shifting tensions between the self and the group as Kurosawa recognizes, from differing vantage points, the difficulty of separating self from culture. The films constitute a series of responses to the particularly sensitive dilemma of how and where the autonomous individual may be positioned in relation to more traditional cultural norms. Kurosawa's conviction about the sanctity of the self has sometimes entailed a failure to consider the power of society and the realities of the social construction of the self. Thus, the films will stubbornly affirm Sanada's heroic credo while demonstrating why it will not work, or else they will chronicle, as in *Rashōmon*, a world of social dislocation interiorized by the psyche and rending the possibility of human interconnectedness and cooperation. In the latter case, only a wish-fulfilling fantasy solution can lift the storm clouds. Without a thorough analysis of society—something like that proposed by Brecht—a political solution founded on mythologies of individual heroics is doomed to failure. Kurosawa's dilemma has been a belief that the individual might snip the interactionist linkages with social groups in the obsessive pursuit of a quixotic goal.

Other major Japanese directors, such as Yasujirō Ozu or Kenji Mizoguchi, have not shared this problem. Neither one has a strong feeling for the need, in Ozu's case, or the capability, in Mizoguchi's case, of the individual to reject social demands. Ozu's cinema locates its characters within patriarchal traditions, even if, as Bordwell and Satō point out, the films critically or sadly observe the loss of patriarchal authority in modern Japan.[2] If some of the young people stray, refuse marriage partners, or seek careers of their own, there is often the reassuring presence of Chishu Ryū to which we are returned at the end of a film. Bordwell's recent portrait of Ozu presents the director as a more critical and this-worldly filmmaker than does Donald Richie's earlier account.[3] Bordwell writes that Ozu's films of the 1920s and 1930s become "liberal protests against the failure of the state's social responsibility."[4] Even so, though the films may at times question tradition and/or modernity, as in the scenes in which Ryū and his friends sit in bars and bitterly observe the pointlessness and boredom of their lives, these men would never embark on Watanabe's journey. Since, for Ozu, security ought to be found within the established social groupings—family, work associates—his characters need never break from them.

By contrast, Mizoguchi's work is critical of medieval and patriarchal institutions and reveals a concern for the social status and misfortunes of women. As Audie Bock points out, however, this does not necessarily entail a "feminist" perspective in the Western sense of the term. Mizoguchi's portrayals of the social oppression of women "do not necessarily imply a political concern with the improvement of women's status in society," Bock suggests, because an aesthetic of resignation prevails in his work that tends to legitimize human suffering.[5] At the end of Ugetsu Monogatari, the camera slowly cranes upward, not in protest over the horrors wrought by civil war, but rather in gentle release from the cares and sufferings of corporeal existence. "These enclosing moments of Zen-like space remove the viewer from the exhausting human passions and remind him of his role as spectator at a performance and as contemplator of life."[6] Even though Mizoguchi is aware of the horrors of violence to the body and spirit, his characters do not undertake organized opposition to oppression. As in Ozu's tender, elegiac accounts of the passing of old values, a contemplative aesthetic prevails.[7]

Kurosawa, by contrast, was far more sensitive to culture as a material force, a field sustaining multiple tensions. (In this respect, his work has been underappreciated. Its attention to culture as a dialectic field prefigures the kinds of social examinations later carried out by the Japanese New Wave.) His films investigate these tensions, probing for ideological fissures and weaknesses, and constantly shift their mode of analysis. If, in the contemporary films, Kurosawa places himself in the fray, fully engaged with the exigencies of the synchronic moment, in his period films he has adopted a far more analytic and philosophical stance, appropriate for a diachronic inquiry. Kurosawa's period films announce a series of investigations into the meaning of the past, its structure and texture, and its relevance to the modern era. The past is very much alive for Kurosawa, and his admiration for Mizoguchi is founded on that director's fidelity to details of historical realism.[8] In particular, Kurosawa feels a special bond to the samurai world, and so it was perhaps inevitable that this world would play such a large role in his films. He observes that memories of his past and his childhood tend to be colored by a martial spirit.[9] As a youth, he studied swordsmanship, with long treks to the school punctuated by meditation at the Hachiman shrine. He relates an amusing incident in which, pelted with rocks by a group of children carrying bamboo swords and poles, he faced them down like a little warrior, charging them with his wooden sword and flailing away with all his might, rather as Mifune does at the conclusion of *Yōjimbō*.[10] But all chance for glory vanished when an adult appeared to back the children up, carrying an even larger pole, so the young samurai had to make a hasty retreat. During the summer holidays of his third year in middle school, Kurosawa fished and swam and spent time in a forest, living what he called a "kind of mountain samurai's existence."[11] Studying his family's genealogy chart, he was delighted to discover he had a famous warrior for an ancestor. His brother he compared to a "masterless samurai," referring to the awe and respect people had for him.[12]

But perhaps it is his fantasies that best illustrate the special bond he feels with the samurai tradition. During the apprentice days at P.C.L., while he was on location in the Hakone Mountains with director Eisuke Takizawa, an encounter with the landscape seemed to transport him back to an earlier time:

> In the morning as we rode along in our car in the wan light of pre-dawn, we could see the old farmhouses on both sides of the road. Farmers dressed as extras, wearing their hair in topknots, clad in armor and carrying swords, would emerge from these houses, throw open the huge doors and lead out their horses. It was as if we had really been transported back into the sixteenth century. They would mount and ride along behind our car. Rolling along past massive cryptomeria and pine trees, I felt that these, too, were part of that ancient era.
>
> When we arrived at the location, the extras led their horses off into the forest and tethered them to trees while they built a huge bonfire. The farmers gathered around the fire, and in the dim forest their armor caught gleams of light from the roaring red fire. It made me feel that I had stumbled on a band of mountain samurai in the woods.[13]

Kurosawa's intense feelings for premodern Japan, his perceptions of himself and his family in these terms, disclose a view of the past as a living, sensuous reality. In his most recent films, this past has entirely displaced twentieth-century Japan. The major films that take the past as their subject—*Seven Samurai* (1954), *Yōjimbō* (1961), and *Red Beard* (1965)—shift their focus away from the modern world in an urgent search for affirmation, for a self that is not badly torn and splintered, and for a social world that does not grind its members to bits. This is a search for the continued viability of the project initially announced by the early postwar films, and the stakes are high. For Kurosawa's ethical project to persist, the past must disclose possibilities of freedom and humane action not immediately accessible to the present. Therefore, the relation of these films to the contemporary works is quite important. We should consider how these films visualize the past and how they use it as a medium for imaginative play because in their workings we can locate the necessary transitions between the affirmations of *Stray Dog* and *No Regrets for Our Youth* and the despair and renunciation of *Kagemusha* and *Ran*. These are the pivotal films, incorporating the affirmative power of Kurosawa's heroic mode with the visions of apocalypse and disintegration familiar in the late works. The confrontation with history was evidently a traumatic one.

Seven Samurai is one of Kurosawa's most celebrated works, perhaps his best known film, and certainly the one most directly influential on the Hollywood cinema, helping inaugurate through its translation into

The Magnificent Seven a series of Westerns dealing with groups of gun-fighters.[14] As Joseph Anderson has discussed, however, the Americani-zation of Kurosawa's film entailed a domestication of style, the substitu-tion of dialogue and pedestrian camerawork for its essentially visual qualities, the vitality of its cutting and imagery.[15] What is always impres-sive about *Seven Samurai* is its boundless energy, the speed of its track-ing shots, the aggressiveness of its wipe-linked transitions, and the daz-zling use of multicamera perspectives. The film is an exercise in kinesis, in the realization of a cinema defined as pure motion. As Richie points out, Kurosawa "insisted that the motion-picture be composed entirely of motion."[16]

It is also one of his most richly textured philosophical works and the first of his period films to be set during an era that has come to have special meaning for him and which he has largely made his own. This is a period of time known as the Sengoku Jidai or the time of the civil wars, a century-long period of strife and turbulence during the sixteenth cen-tury when the military class struggled within itself for control of land and political power. In addition to *Seven Samurai*, *Throne of Blood*, *The Hidden Fortress*, and *Ran* are set during this era, and *Kagemusha* studies the transition from this political chaos to the advent of national unifica-tion. The Sengoku period has been characterized as an age of change, a time when the Japanese world had turned "upside down" as the bound-aries of class or vassalage became unstuck as "persons in inferior posi-tions challenged those in authority and often took mastery over them."[17] Kurosawa is attracted by these fluid class boundaries and the new poten-tials for human realization they offer, as well as to the social and eco-nomic changes characterizing the era. "The troubled times of Japan's civil wars provided the lower classes with both the occasion for inde-pendence and the opportunities for self-advancement. While the feudal wars brought destruction and turmoil, they served also to encourage so-cial mobility and widespread economic growth."[18] The changes of the sixteenth century have been compared with the Meiji period in terms of a comparable release of cultural energies and restructuring of society.[19] The economic and political growth of the Sengoku period is viewed as a harbinger of the development of a national political structure and the bureaucratic apparatus to administer it.[20] In this interplay between forces of change, sometimes experienced as forces of destruction, and the longer-term course of national growth that developed from them may be found a source of Kurosawa's fascination for the Sengoku period. He may have experienced it as a felt parallel with his own turbulent wartime and postwar eras, when so much overt destruction was coupled with undeniable energies of creativity and national development: a new Constitution, rapid economic growth, and a stable political system presided over by the long-dominant Liberal Democratic Party.

Before the emergence of a national political structure through the efforts of the trio of "Great Unifiers"—Oda Nobunaga, Toyotomi Hideyoshi, and Tokugawa Ieyasu—political fragmentation and bloody regional struggles prevailed.[21] The behavior of the warriors during this period contrasts with the idealized portrait that emerges in the codes of *bushidō*, which were systematized at a much later date, during the Tokugawa period (1603–1867), by Yamaga Sokō.[22] His samurai were meant to stand—in their temperance and loyalty, their self-discipline and austere unconcern for wealth and power—as models and leaders for all the other classes.[23] Sokō was writing for a time when the samurai had become administrators, and he was trying to rationalize their current social function and reconcile it with their more manly past. The distance between the idealized warriors of Sokō's efforts at ideological reconstruction and the violent struggles of the Sengoku Jidai are important for Kurosawa's films because he has drawn from both terms of this legacy. The samurai of *Throne of Blood* and *Ran* manifest the greed and thirst for power of the historical past, while the heroes of *Seven Samurai* glorify the ideals of the ideological past. The exploits of these seven samurai are, however, developed within, and are carefully contrasted with, an age of political disintegration and class warfare.

Kurosawa has pointed out that most samurai films tend to be set during the Tokugawa era, when the warrior's code and social function were different. "I think I'm the only one who has ever made films about the sixteenth-century civil wars."[24] As noted, one of the things that interests the director about this time is the fluidity of class boundaries, particularly the relationship between samurai and farmer. During the Tokugawa period, the classes were separated, and the behavior appropriate for each was explicitly formulated. By contrast, during the civil wars peasants were often conscripted to serve as soldiers, and many samurai were small landholders, subsisting by farming. Kurosawa has noted these differences:

> I think there's a misunderstanding not only on the part of Westerners, but on the part of younger-generation Japanese as to what a Samurai is. In fact, the profession of the warrior began around the eleventh or twelfth century and most of the films that

you and I see are set in the seventeenth or eighteenth century, a period of peace when the professional warrior had an entirely different code of ethics and way of behaving. This was imposed by the Tokugawa Shogunate of that time and its atmosphere is entirely different from that of the period I'm much more interested in, which is the late sixteenth century. . . . The warrior class had much more freedom at that time; a peasant could still become a warrior then.[25]

Relations among the classes and the permeability of class lines are central to *Seven Samurai*. The story is structured by alliance and enmity among three groups: farmers, samurai, and bandits. A small peasant village suffers depradations from a gang of brigands, who come twice a year to loot rice, horses, and women. The farmers overhear the bandits planning to return in the spring, and after consulting with the village patriarch, they decide to resist. Agrarian uprisings at the time, often quite violent, were not uncommon, but Kurosawa deals with resistance by the agrarian class in a manner that permits him to juxtapose different social types: the farmers hire samurai to work for them. The samurai plan a defense of the village, erect fortifications, and lead the peasants in battle against the bandits.[26] The film is sometimes interpreted as a study of revolution, as a kind of political statement about how a vanguard group (the seven samurai) can lead a mass to overturn its reified social consciousness and assume a new political destiny.[27] But *Seven Samurai* is far more ambivalent than this about the nature and meaning of class. The work may be regarded as an inquiry into the social preconditions and political foundations underlying the contemporary films. *Seven Samurai* is a film about the modern works, an attempt, by moving farther back into history, to uncover the dialectic between class and the individual, an effort to confront the social construction of self and to see whether this annihilates the basis for individual heroism.

At first glance, the film seems to affirm all the familiar elements of the heroic mode. Kambei (Takashi Shimura), who will become the leader of the samurai, is introduced performing a selfless act. By posing as a Buddhist monk, he rescues a child held captive by a crazed thief in an episode that, as David Desser has pointed out, is apparently modeled on a Zen anecdote.[28] He receives no pay or acclaim for this act. It is, simply, the correct way to live, as Sanada and Watanabe also discovered. Moreover, an apparent rejection of social codes seems essential to its success. To fool the thief, he has to put aside his long sword and cut his topknot (both are signifiers of samurai status) and shave his head so that he will look like a priest. Kambei becomes heroic, it would seem, only through the dissolution of his class identity. His determination to accept the farmers' plea for help is a recognition of his responsibility for them. They have given him their best by feeding him rice while they are eating millet. He tells them that he will always appreciate their sacrifice, as he holds a bowl of rice in the center of the frame, the first of many times when rice will function as a vector of communication.

Kambei's decision is an exceptional act of conscience far beyond the capability of the ordinary samurai. The farmers have already approached many warriors (one warrior, glimpsed in passing, is played by a very young Tatsuya Nakadai[29]) who are either drunken fools or worthless thieves, absconding with their rice. Kambei's luck is, initially, not much better. The first warrior he attempts to enlist immediately asks which clan they are fighting for. When told their employer is a group of farmers, the man haughtily refuses, proclaiming the unworthiness of the enterprise for his ambitions. Only seven warriors are capable of lending their skills to a cause promising no reward or glory. When told that they may die this time, Kambei's old friend, Shichirōji (Daisuke Katō), smiles with a valiant warrior's acceptance of the honorableness of violent death.

Also in keeping with the heroic form of Kurosawa's cinema is the presence of a master–pupil relationship. The youngest samurai, Katsushirō (Kō Kimura), becomes Kambei's disciple, and the film studies the young man's traumatic encounters with battle, violence, death, and sexuality. The elder warrior possesses the superior wisdom of an enlightened master adept at the art of inner perception, a seeing with the spirit, not the eyes,[30] and Katsushirō eagerly seeks the opportunity to learn from his presence. During the match between Kyūzo (Seiji Miyaguchi), the supreme swordsman, and a loud, blustering samurai, Katsushirō's attention is drawn to the vehemence of the latter, while Kambei instantly recognizes the silence and repose of Kyūzo as the signs of true mastery.

Also customary is the film's view of individual choice as a function of social crisis. The farmers are afraid of the bandits but perhaps even more afraid of the samurai. Some, like Manzō, prefer to negotiate with the brigands rather than hire samurai, who may, after all, loot their village and rape the women as the bandits threaten to do. Manzō points to the reality of class hatred when he asks the village patriarch whether samurai will fight for them just for food, which is all the village can offer. The elder replies that they should find hungry samurai. Even bears come out of the woods when they are hungry. The social cataclysms of the age, the defeat and destruction of warrior clans in battle, have dislocated many samurai, who are unemployed, hungry, searching for work and a lord to serve. Joan Mellen has suggested that the film implies that only such extraordinary conditions make possible the emergence of these seven heroes.[31]

Kurosawa translates the sociological dislocations of the era into visual terms, realizing what would otherwise be the abstractions of a historical period as the concrete material of form. Four farmers have been sent in search of samurai, but before Manzō, Rikichi, Mosuke, and Yohei meet Kambei, they room in a hovel with a group of worthless ruffians, a blind musician, and a drunken, penniless samurai. He has lost his money to the ruffians, and they beat him up. Clearly, it is an ominous era when scruffy laborers trounce warriors for daring to draw their weapons. Yohei begins to cry and plead with the others to return home. They know nothing about samurai. The strong ones are beyond their control, and those who seem willing are weaklings. The farmers meditate on their misery, and the laborers laugh at them with contempt for their poverty. The farmers are out of their element, the ruffians hold sway, and the samurai is a disgrace. The three groups are isolated in the frame or are compositionally separated by a ceiling beam or other obstruction. By cutting among the groups with baroque changes of angle and moving the camera to reverse screen direction and to prevent the repetition of previous compositions, Kurosawa constructs a centerless area of spatial fragmentation, where one's perceptual moorings are continually being cut loose and buffeted by compositional crosscurrents. Instead of the repetition of camera positions, each is unique and offers a novel, and often bewildering, vantage on the action. The scene contains nineteen different camera setups and only five repetitions of a previous setup. Some of these repetitions, however, are deceiving because they begin with a familiar framing but then use camera movement to shift to a new position. The room becomes a signifier of destructured social space through a cinematic rendering that undermines the formation of a coherent spatial field.

This collapse of perceptual coherence is the tremor left within the film from the emergence of a novel code that alters and reworks the shape and position of individual heroism. Kambei's selflessness, the master–pupil relationship, and acts of conscience as a register of social decay are familiar elements subjected to a kind of alchemical transformation that changes their very nature. To see how the change occurs, let us look at the terms of this new code, which are manifest at the level of form, in cutting, framing, and the general orientation of space in the film. A key moment revealing the presence of this transformational code occurs early, just after the farmers overhear the bandits planning to return in the spring. A long shot shows the circular huts of the village, and as Kurosawa cuts to closer views, a circular gathering of peasants appears within the space of the village (established in the previous shot), equating the peasantry with the architectural form of the village and the abstract idea of community it embodies. The peasants have assembled to plan their response. The dominant tone is one of despair and resignation. A woman, framed in an astonishing close-up of her behind so that she becomes pure volume, pure geometric shape, wails about the burdens of war, land taxes, and drought.[32] Manzō is more resigned, saying that suffering is the peasants' fate and that it's useless to try to change it. Rikichi, on the other hand, consumed with anger and shame (it is later learned that the bandits have taken his wife), rebels against this passivity. Why don't we kill them, he asks, precipitating a small panic among the villagers. He and Manzō quarrel over this plan, and Rikichi, frustrated at the submissiveness of his neighbors, breaks rank, leaves the group that encircles him, walks off a distance and sits down. Of all the peasants, Rikichi will suffer the most and fight the hardest against the bandits, and he comes the closest to embodying the courage and fortitude of the samurai. Under other conditions, he might have become a Kurosawa hero. But instead the framing reinscribes him within the group. As soon as he walks off, alone, Kurosawa cuts to a new composition with Rikichi in the foreground and the group behind him, with the telephoto lens flattening the image to eliminate his separation from the others. The extreme compression of space places him back among the peasants by creating an illusion that no area of separation exists. Then, as the frame is held, Mosuke suggests they consult the patriarch, and the group rises and engulfs Rikichi. Rebellion and rejection of the group with its norms of submission to a history conceived as fate have been countered by a framing and structuring of space that restores the rebel to the domain he has sought to leave.

This important sequence is one of many in the film that articulate a new conception of space, in which compositional relations and patterns of movement work to contain and confine characters within structures of social power. When the samurai arrive at the village, the farmers hide, afraid to greet them. Insulted and angry, the samurai consult with the elder in his mill, and Kambei points out the injustice of the farmers expecting the samurai to do something for them while behaving in this fashion. The other samurai stand in angry silence, and Manzō, Yohei, Rikichi, and Mosuke are embarrassed at the behavior of their neighbors.

Inside the mill are representatives of the two hostile classes, but instead of cutting back and forth between them, isolated in separate frames, camera movement is used to counterpoint the emotional rift. The sequence begins with a close-up of the patriarch, but then the camera tracks around him to include Kambei, Shichirōji, and Heihachi (Minoru Chiaki) in the frame as well.[33] The scene then cuts to a shot of three other samurai, Gorobei, Katsushirō, and Kyūzo, but the camera begins tracking again so that the patriarch is included with them in the frame. Then the image cuts to a medium shot of Manzō and Mosuke, and the camera tracks back to include Kambei and the elder within the frame. In each of these three shots, the characters all face different directions and assume varying orientations to the camera so that the space is a hostile one and indicates the tensions of the moment. Yet in each of these shots, the composition has focused on an individual or class in isolation and has then shifted to integrate them with the other members of the social world. The cinematic energy of the film, framing and movement, communicate the social ties among characters, denying their isolation. In this respect, *Seven Samurai* is a reversal and refutation of the example of *Ikiru*, arguing against the possibility of solitary, existential heroics. There is simply no space in this film where a hero can stand as an individual. That space is constantly being transformed into social terms where isolation and individualism are regarded as pathologies.

When Mosuke and a band of men try to desert the common defenses of the village and guard their own homes, Kambei forcibly returns them to the ranks of the villagers. The camera has stressed the solidarity of the group effort through a circular track around the periphery of the villagers, assembled to hear the final instructions of the warriors before the bandits are due to arrive. The samurai tell the villagers they must move in pairs, not as individuals, for safety. Mosuke, angry because his home lying outside the village must be abandoned for the sake of the community's survival, breaks this circular movement with a tangential flight. After forcing him back in line, Kambei tells the others that everyone must work together as a group and that those who think only of themselves will destroy themselves and all others. Kambei's words are extraordinary, given the ethical context established by Kurosawa's contemporary-life films, where the hero is expected, as a matter of course, to define an individual path. But here the material of the past discloses no spaces in which the individual can move, no spaces not already inhabited by groups and their demands. The self must be an interactionist self or cease to exist. When, during a meal, Katsushirō and Kyūzo attempt to save their rice for an old, starving peasant whose misfortune is known only to

38. Kambei (Takashi Shimura), flanked by Gorobei (Yoshio Inaba) and Katsushirō (Kō Kimura), declares that the farmers and samurai must struggle together as one. *Seven Samurai.* (Museum of Modern Art/Film Stills Archive)

them, Kambei demands to know what they are doing. Information must be the property of the group, and private knowledge is a threat to its security. When Kikuchiyo (Toshirō Mifune) abandons his post to go into the bandits' territory to get one of their guns, Kambei lectures him about his irresponsibility. Going on your own merits no reward, he says. In war it is cooperation that counts. Freedom thus becomes the prerogative of the group, as a new ethical model emerges in this film. "The limits of individual freedom of action are fixed in such a way as to ensure that the activity of the individual will not breach group limits. . . . Loyalty towards the group forms the basis on which individual activity is carried out."[34]

Kambei's restoration of Mosuke to the group observes the same principle governing the reframing of Rikichi earlier as well as the terms of Kambei's own initial appearance. The cutting of his topknot and the donning of a priest's clothing had seemed to be signs of a relinquishing of class identity necessary for humane action (the saving of a child). They have sometimes been interpreted in this fashion, but as Kurosawa has pointed out, Kambei is really fulfilling his samurai heritage, which specified the warrior as a guardian of the welfare of the other social orders.[35] Once again, a reframing has occurred. What has appeared to be the abandoning of class has actually been behavior in accord with social dictates. Here we may grasp the new code shaping the space and narrative of the film. It is the awareness of class as a determining force, structuring the social field and constraining the individual's range of choice and behavior. *Seven Samurai* is a film about the primacy of groups, the untranscendability of class, and by implication the fiction of individual heroics. Heroism is possible, but only through merger with groups. "Only through collective struggle is survival possible or can society itself be sustained."[36] As Kambei says, by themselves a handful of samurai can do nothing against forty bandits. But united, samurai and farmer become a ruthlessly efficient fighting machine. The dialectic of individual and group rises to a new level in this film, with a power accorded the group it has never before possessed in Kurosawa's films. Samurai and farmer face each other across a gulf of animosity and hatred, but the possibility of their union, thinkable only in this time of social disintegration, holds extraordinary potential. It offers the vision of a different reality, of a transcendent future, an escape from war, oppression, and class conflict. The union of these groups creates an opening in time, a gap in history, through which an alternate future might be attainable, the millennium grasped. "The renewed world is no mere improvement on the present. It implies a total break, a total discontinuity with the relative conditions we now endure."[37] Fulfillment of this chiliastic dream will depend on the outcome of the samurai–farmer alliance and what it symbolizes: realization of an organic community in a world rent by class division. If successful, it will mean the negation of history, the surmounting of time and class. In this respect, *Seven Samurai* offers a millenarian model of political reform and the quest for social justice, which has its roots in religion and the radical realignments of perspective announced by peasant revolts.[38]

> Before the age of modern science, in the medieval and early modern periods, it was far more common for the restructuring of a new order to proceed not in logical terms but on a religious or apocalyptic plane. The masses, for example, as if exorcised from being possessed by foxes, would suddenly intuit a new vision of the world, make a mental leap, and rise up to challenge the present order. This kind of religious apprehension of the world lay behind most of the popular rebellions and peasant wars of the medieval period.[39]

39. The weight of the dead and the promise of community in *Seven Samurai.* (Museum of Modern Art/Film Stills Archive)

Within the terms of the film, history has brought the peasantry only suffering and an experience of existence as an unending, essentially undifferentiated flow of miseries. War, famine, drought, taxes, banditry, all the dislocations of the period have been internalized by peasant culture to form a consciousness of resignation, a hatred of the oppressor, and a vicious taking of vengeance when possible. Through their bloodlust and war-making, the samurai are responsible for much of the misery of the farmers, and a sudden shift in the film's mode of analysis makes this clear. Kikuchiyo, the most buffoonish of the group of samurai, discovers a cache of armor and weaponry hidden in Manzō's house, and in a scene of great emotional power he confronts the samurai with these weapons, which the peasants have stripped from the bodies of warriors they have murdered. Kyūzo quietly remarks that he would like to kill all the farmers in the village, prompting an explosive outburst from Kikuchiyo, who points out that the farmers may be greedy and tricky, but it is the samurai who made them that way by raiding their villages and stealing their crops. With tears of rage and shame in his eyes, he defends the farmers' right to resort to trickery to survive. The violence of his rage, and the truth of his words, humble the samurai, who are moved by his speech. Kambei guesses the truth. "You are a farmer's son, aren't you?" he asks. Kikuchiyo, embarrassed, runs out of the hut. The samurai take no revenge; they merely renew their pledge to help the villagers. No one protests because they are all implicated in the crimes Kikuchiyo described. Had circumstances been different, had they come to this village as part of a warlord's campaign, they might have torched the dwellings and taken the crops. Instead, the vicissitudes of the time have placed them in this peculiar position whereby they commit a kind of historical suicide. The bandits are samurai, fallen on hard times, and by destroying them, Kambei and his compatriots are annihilating their own class, creating for the seven samurai a profound temporal displacement that subsequent imagery will note. As the pivotal character, the farmer who aspires to be a samurai, who tries to cross class lines, Kikuchiyo becomes, like Rikichi, a character mediating relations between the groups.[40] There is, however, little doubt about Kikuchiyo's fundamental social identity. The framing consistently isolates him from the rest of the samurai, who are clustered together as a group, and establishes a proximity with the peasantry. Often he will confront the samurai to expose, through the contrast with his own buffoonery, the nature of their identity and, in the scene with the armor, their complicity in sustaining a system of economic exploitation. The mediating characters, Rikichi and Kikuchiyo, enable the film to forge a dialectical analysis of class, defining samurai and peasant in terms of a relational opposition.[41] The strife of the era works to sustain and deepen this opposition, but the film asks how inevitable this conflict is and, by posing this question, defines the decisive philosophical moment of Kurosawa's cinema. Its outcome will be far-reaching, for it will determine the manner in which history is experienced and understood by later films: as a field of potentialities, loosely structured vectors of action, open to human intervention; or as a frightening teleological process, unyielding and implacable, justifying a notion of karma or fate.

Despite its epic qualities, the film admits a tragic view of existence, and this creates an opening through which the latter experience of history emerges, briefly, but with great power. It is felt in the sequence with the peasant Kuemon's grandmother. This is a brief scene, omitted from shortened versions of the film, but it is central to Kurosawa's interrogation of the past. We first learn of her through Katsushirō, who begins saving his rice for someone in the village. When Kambei demands to know who it is, the scene shifts to a hovel inhabited by a decrepit, terribly ancient woman. She seems to be a hundred years old, her face almost obscured by slabs of wrinkled flesh hanging lifelessly from the forehead and cheekbones. The samurai bring her their rice, and Kambei remarks, as her moaning fills the hut, "This is terrible." The grandmother's family has been killed by the bandits, and she longs to die, to escape from the trials of her life. Death, the sooner the better, is the sole relief she can anticipate. But an awful thought occurs to her: what if, in the next world, there is great suffering, too? Heihachi, moved by her condition, tells her there is no misery in the next world. But she is not convinced. In this gnarled, dispirited peasant woman, the vicissitudes and misfortunes of the laboring class are given flesh and a quavering voice. In the midst of this epic adventure, a voice of despair has sounded, articulating a fear beyond comfort, a horror that land taxes, civil war, poverty, and violent death reach beyond the grave, in the next rounds of existence, deforming human life and potential and making of time an endless cycle of suffering. History looms as a relentless force, demanding privations against which there is no recourse, not even in death. This is a history defined by scarcity, by the lack of sufficient food and resources, transforming earthly existence into a hell. In a world of scarcity, Sartre points out, every human being is necessarily an enemy to all others since each, by laying claim to insufficient resources, threatens the others with extinction. Class becomes a means of structuring this competition and enmity and of deciding who will go without.[42]

The events of the film are driven by the need to overcome this lack, by the efforts of the three groups to control the sources of food and labor. The bandits regularly take the village's crops and animals, and the farmers are initially afraid the samurai will do the same. They hide much of their food, and only after the two classes have begun to trust each other, in the respite between battles, do the farmers dare bring out this hidden food and sake and make a gift of it to the warriors. Every event in the film hinges on this basic question, informing and organizing the narrative: who will control the rice fields? It is rice that structures the relations among the classes, that has brought the bandits like a plague to the village, that signifies and seals Kambei's initial acceptance of the farmers' plea for help, that mediates relations among the samurai and the village children, and that finally remains in the possession of the peasantry in the film's last, powerfully symbolic sequence. George Sansom points out that the samurai wars of the middle ages are comprehensible as attempts by powerful warlords to gain control of the country's most valuable rice lands, parlaying this control over resources into political power.[43] Much of the land in Japan is composed of hills and mountains, unfit for cultivation and lending a special urgency to the bloody quests for control of the alluvial plains. Kurosawa forms his narrative from this situation but adds a bitter, poetic dimension: the irony of the samurai's adventure lies in their desertion of attempts by their own class to gain hegemony. In this desertion lies the force of their moral example, but against the currents of the age they are powerless. As Northrop Frye has observed about the tragic hero, there is something against which he, no matter how great, is small. "This something else may be called God, gods, fate, accident, fortune, necessity, circumstance, or any combination of these, but whatever it is the tragic hero is our mediator with it."[44] It is against the view of time announced by Kuemon's grandmother that the samurai take their symbolic stand and embody the possibility of an alternative. But will the film permit them to succeed?

As the counterforce to the social schisms of the age, as the ideal illumined by the actions of the samurai, the film posits the possibility of the organic community, free of disintegrative rifts and competitions, whose members are fused with a common project and common goals. The warriors and the farmers are battling for the dissolution of class, for an ideal of human cooperation. As they work together to make the village defensible against bandit attacks, seemingly intractable suspicions melt away. Kikuchiyo, Kyūzo, Katsushirō, Heihachi, and Shichirōji give their rice to the village children and joke with them. Katsushirō and a village girl, Shino, fall in love. The farmers share their hidden food with the samurai. Kambei cradles and plays with a village baby in the mill while her mother watches. This is the familiar Kurosawa insistence that true human action must carry a socially beneficial aim, that heroism is measured by the rectification of social oppression. Here, however, the symbol of that rectification is not an isolated park or a diseased individual but an entire community, which becomes transformed morally and economically, its members bound by trust and a sharing of resources. This community is an oasis of life in a surrounding region of darkness and death.[45] Outside the village lie destruction and nothingness, a terrible void. No one is permitted to venture beyond its secured borders. Like the Teutonic knights in another battle epic, Eisenstein's *Alexander Nevsky*, the bandits are not fully individuated but instead tend to be presented as an irrational, destructive force.[46] They hide in the darkness and attack from three directions under cover of night, and they use their guns to pick off samurai and villagers. (The guns, initially purchased from the Portuguese in 1543 and then replicated by Japanese technicians, will come to alter the social codes of samurai warfare by making obsolete the skills of a brave swordsman.[47]) When Rikichi, covered with mud, ventures past the village borders in pursuit of fleeing bandits, he is transformed into a hellish phantom, his features unrecognizable by torchlight. Kambei tells him to halt and has to ask who he is. From the surrounding darkness and violence, he snarls his name, but it is not the Rikichi we have known. The young couple who leave the security of the village to rescue their father from the mill are killed by bandits, and their baby, the one Kambei had cradled, is barely rescued by the samurai. The fight against the bandits is a struggle to keep evil out, to eradicate class itself, to prevent the transformed relations of samurai and farmer from relapsing into the former condition of hatred and schism. The village contains a fragile moral experiment that must be guarded by force of arms because its example may be so easily crushed.

Heihachi's flag becomes the emblem of these new relations. On it, samurai and village are represented as graphic symbols, and the flag infuses the groups with its symbolic meaning during their moment of deepest despair. When everyone has gathered on the burial ground to mourn the death of Heihachi, the first samurai killed, Kikuchiyo raises the flag, and the entire assembly is galvanized by its image. But its presentation in this sequence is subtly ambiguous and points to the outcome of the social experiment. As the sequence develops, the shots begin to omit the samurai and to concentrate on the farmers. The image cuts from a close-up of the flag fluttering against a bare sky to a long shot of the entire group on the hill and then to a medium shot of only the villagers as they contemplate the banner. A medium shot of the flag follows and then another medium shot of the villagers. Then the camera tilts down the length of the flag, passing the circles representing samurai and stopping on the character standing for the village. It lingers on this character, and then the image cuts to a close-up of the patriarch and several farmers. A long shot of the entire group on the hill follows, then another tilt down the flag, with the camera again lingering on the symbol for village. The structure of this sequence stresses the farmers' relations with the banner, not those of the samurai. By lingering over the flag's symbol for the peasantry, the film visualizes it as the enduring class and the samurai as a transitory group, made peripheral by the flow of time. (This idea is also expressed by the guns—all the samurai who die are killed by firearms that render their prowess with swords useless.)

This imagery implies the ultimate failure of the alliance, and indeed the bitterly ironic, and justly famous, conclusion of the film returns the farmers to their rice fields and a ceremonial replanting while the surviving samurai are clustered below the mound of graves. The framing separates the two groups, and the final camera movement of the film links the samurai visually to their fallen comrades, to a world of the dead.[48] Displaced by history as a vanishing class, and by the structure of the film during the symbolic raising of the flag, the warriors have won the fight with the bandits only to confront a more comprehensive defeat. They remain noble, viewed by Kurosawa as true heroes, but they are vanquished by the structures of time and class. Paradoxically, the organic community is destroyed in the moment of victory. With the bandits gone, the farmers no longer need the samurai, and class disparity and exclusion reappear. Shino rushes past Katsushirō to the rice fields, and he dares not follow her because their romantic alliance is socially forbidden. The framing groups him with the other samurai.

But, more important, at the last moment the film seems to rethink its own analysis and to transform its allegiance to the ideal the alliance embodies. The film climaxes with imagery of true classlessness as the logical culmination of the moral development the narrative has been observing. The final battle is a supreme spiritual and physical struggle, and it is fought in a blinding rainstorm, which enables Kurosawa to visualize an ultimate fusion of social groups. Their efforts forged by common praxis, samurai and peasant become a single team, a fearsome, efficient force defending their community. As such, they are indistinguishable, covered alike with mud and fighting with equal desperation. But this climactic vision of classlessness, with typical Kurosawan ambivalence, has become a vision of horror. The battle is a vortex of swirling rain and mud, slashing steel, thrashing, anonymous bodies, and screaming, dying men. The ultimate fusion of social identity emerges as an expression of hellish chaos, against which the final relapse into native ritual and class separation feels a relief.

The film seems to short-circuit its inquiry, and we must look for the answer to this in Kurosawa's own conflict-ridden relationship to the normative power of groups. Throughout its length, the film embodies a belief in the centrality of class exploitation to the medieval world and searches for an alternative, but an end to class differentiation would also mean an end to heroes, to those extraordinary individuals whose supremacy to the masses has constituted a moral example that has been central to Kurosawa's narratives. To abandon the hero would mean to abandon the cinema of postwar commitment. It would also entail for Kurosawa the substitution of another view of time and history, one predicated on the inevitability of social disintegration and failure of individual will. Contestation between these two alternatives structures *Seven*

40. Kikuchiyo (Toshirō Mifune) and Kyūzo (Seiji Miyaguchi) in the final battle, a vortex of rain, steel, mud, and death. *Seven Samurai*. (Museum of Modern Art/ Film Stills Archive)

Samurai, though the end of the film, with its imagery of class exclusion and the death of the heroic tradition as historical necessities, seems to assert the primacy of time as teleology, to offer "an epiphany of law, of that which is and must be."[49] The inquiry into the viability of the transcendent community has failed to disclose a basis for its construction. The space of the past has not furnished a terrain on which the social rebel may stand. Permeated with group norms and obligations, the individual is structured by the social fabric. Class and its determinants are inescapable, and heroism is possible only in terms of the idealized codes of class ideology, the samurai as embodiments of the highest expression of bushidō. Instead of furnishing the basis for existential heroism in the modern world, history demonstrates structures of closure, binding the medieval individual to the circumscribed codes of his time, and making infirm the ground on which the modern rebel fights and his actions as substantial as the movement of a shadow.[50]

Seven Samurai's unexpectedly rigorous and honest confrontation of the limits to individual action posed the fundamental problem for Kurosawa's cinema: how to create an opening in time to admit the emergence of heroes. Perhaps in recognition of how difficult it would be to solve this dilemma, Kurosawa did not return again to the problem for some time. Instead, he attempted to maintain the scope of his heroic cinema as if its viability had not been questioned. As we have seen, he continued to construct contemporary heroes, in *Record of a Living Being* and *The Bad Sleep Well*, and to set them against social problems. The failures of Nakajima and Nishi, however, indicated the difficulties of this maneuver. *Seven Samurai's* demonstration of the power of the social order to structure the individual could not be ignored. Though Kurosawa might pretend otherwise, the dilemma would not go away but would remain to subvert his work. Even the return to the warrior tradition did not, at first, necessitate a reformulation of this problem. *Throne of Blood* explores only one half of the dialectic revealed by *Seven Samurai*, taking the despairing, deterministic perspective enunciated by Kuemon's grandmother and making it the basis of an entire cinematic vision. When history is articulated as it is in *Throne of Blood*, as a blind force, the need to find the basis for responsible action is no longer relevant. Heroism ceases to be a problem or a reality. Toward the same end—the elimination of competing voices within the text—*The Hidden Fortress* (1958) substitutes a fairy tale logic for *Throne of Blood*'s nightmare world. The film, intended by Kurosawa as a lightweight entertainment, deals with the efforts of a princess and a loyal general, Rokurota (Toshirō Mifune), to restore the fortunes of their clan. As Richie observes, the film is a kind of big-budget remake of *Tiger's Tail*, with expensive sets and more action, which again inverts the codes of period film heroism by presenting the action through the eyes of a pair of flea-bitten commoners who help Rokurota transport the clan treasure across enemy territory.[51] The film is visually impressive, constituting Kurosawa's first use of the anamorphic frame, but the overall tone remains a frivolous one. The film renders the social basis for heroism unimportant because no effective challenges to it exist. No force in the world could thwart Rokurota Makabe from his luminous destiny, but on the other hand, he could never constructively mediate the wrenching dislocations of his social world in the manner of a Kambei or a Watanabe. His example is stirring but essentially rhetorical.

It was not until *Yōjimbō* that Kurosawa once again took up the challenge of dialectical historical inquiry. The period has shifted. The time is now the late Tokugawa era, but the structural problem is the same: the relation between the heroic individual and the historical moment. Here, however, instead of directly engaging the exigencies of the past, instead

41. The violence of the sixteenth-century civil wars in a fairy tale context. *The Hidden Fortress*. (R5/S8 Presents)

of trying to think them out and work through their contradictions, Kurosawa demonstrates an entirely different strategy, which needs to be seen as the response, finally forthcoming, to the unanswered problematic posed by *Seven Samurai*. History will be conjured up only to be refused. The sociological turbulence of late Tokugawa times will be portrayed with Kurosawa's usual fidelity to detail only to be annihilated by the hero. History becomes the enemy in this film, which performs an elaborate rite of exorcism, removing temporality from the moral landscape in order to purge the world of the terrors glimpsed by Kuemon's grandmother.

To see how this is carried out, we need to grasp the film's peculiar, self-conscious presentation of its protagonist. *Ikiru* had elaborated an intense, searching, and quite serious Brechtian experimentation with form, through which the film studied its own construction of the hero and spoke to the viewer about this. By contrast, *Yōjimbō* substitutes a giddy cackle in place of *Ikiru*'s sobriety but constructs an equally Brechtian hero and then watches with delight as he rips through the curtain of history with his sword.[52] Sanjurō, the samurai hero, is a character displaced by his time, a period when a rising business class threatened the logic of existing social relations as the economy shifted to money, not rice, and to ties mediated by the exchange of commodities and the rationalizations of profit, not personal allegiances and obligations.[53] Samurai became dependent on the money economy, and many fell into debt.[54] Nevertheless, the official Neo-Confucian ideology urged the samurai to live frugally and scorn money. In the *Conversations at Suruga-dai*, Kyūsō Muro cautioned that "to cherish in one's heart or even to speak of overfondness for one's life or the worship of money may be suitable for the merchants, but it is hardly so for the samurai."[55] Muro's *Conversations* voices concern over the destruction of traditional values by the growth of a mercantile class and condemns the spread of the "money-grubbers" and their evil ways.[56]

Yōjimbō gives this moral outrage a comic twist by exaggerating the magnitude of the corruption that Kurosawa, like the Tokugawa Neo-Confucianists, seems to feel the business class represents. Sanjurō (Toshiro Mifune), a rōnin (a samurai without a lord to serve), roams the countryside, looking to use his sword in return for a bowl of rice. He wanders into the most venal town imaginable, where rival gangs of gamblers are battling for control and where he is greeted by a dog carrying a dismembered human hand in its mouth, one of Kurosawa's most famous and blackly humorous images. The struggle for power among the gamblers is also a contest between two rival merchants, one of whom is aligned with each gang. Kuemon (Takashi Shimura), the aging, dissipated sake brewer, has thrown in his power with Ushi-Tora, while the silk broker has allied himself with Seibei, Ushi-Tora's antagonist. Sanjurō proceeds to manipulate one gang against the other by promising each his services as a bodyguard, hoping that they will all end by annihilating each other, which, in fact, they do.

In its vision of a town controlled by the avarice of competing merchants, who have enlisted gangsters to maintain their markets and who recognize with primitive intelligence that the best advantage is gained by murdering one's competitors, the film uses the past in order to criticize the present. In *Yōjimbō* the merchants embody the future, and the town is offered as a microcosm of the contemporary corporate state, which had been castigated in *The Bad Sleep Well*. "The dreadful town in *Yōjimbō* is contemporary Japan."[57] But Kurosawa is not interested in mere factual reconstruction. He is out to elaborate an alternate mythology, a fantastical account of how history might have, should have, turned out, if only the temporal process had included a moral component to ensure, with a kind of Malthusian logic, the destruction of evildoers once they become too numerous. *Yōjimbō* presents the apocalypse of the business class, the incarnation of every traditionalist's most fervent dream, and, as Joan Mellen points out, its drama of samurai against merchant, its portrayal of a world rent by greed, controlled by thugs, but brought down by San-juro's sword, constructs a fable about the end of capitalism.[58] The mer-chants are destroyed by a member of the class they ultimately made extinct, as Kurosawa permits himself an outcome that the actual devel-opment of events did not allow. As such, the film has a fairy tale quality, a "once upon a time" tone, that is the source of its humor as well as its self-reflective meditations.[59]

Sanjurō is explicitly offered as a wish-fulfilling figure, as a formal con-ceit necessary for the imaginary destruction of the business class, which, from an ideological perspective, incarnated a set of values contrary to the ideals of samurai life. He strides into the town, is greeted by the dog, and is menaced by Ushi-Tora's thugs. He stops for some sake at an inn run by Gon (Eijiro Tono), who tells him about the situation in town. Gon de-spairs over the violence and brutality rampant in the streets as Ino (Daisuke Katō), Ushi-Tora's brother, returns with more hired killers. Gon tells Sanjurō that only swords can settle things here and that he'd best leave if he doesn't want the violence to get him, too. The coffin-maker next door hammers away throughout the scene, the only artisan profiting from all the killing. The hammering provides the same dark counterpoint as does the dog earlier, establishing the essential evil of the world, an evil that, to Gon, seems omnipotent. He believes that nothing can stop the gangsters and merchants or halt the future their actions are ushering in. Sanjurō sees it differently. He smiles and tells Gon that he'll stay, that he gets paid for killing and likes this town. He adds, however, that he'll make sure all these criminals are stopped. Think about it, he says. It would be better if they were all dead, he mutters reflectively as Masaru Satō's music rumbles ominously. Like other Kurosawa heroes, Sanjurō has decided to enter the battle, to meet the world's evil head on, but unlike them, he has no ethical reason for doing so, no ideal to which he commits. His involvement lacks the moral dimension that inhered in their behavior. He decides to destroy the gamblers and merchants simply because it would be amusing. He offers no other reason. The abstract character of his decision, its absence of content, establishes its basically formal nature. It foregrounds Sanjurō's stature as an artifice, as a charac-ter Kurosawa dreams up for the express purpose of eliminating gang-

42. Sanjurō (Toshirō Mifune) enjoys the carnage from his watchtower perch in *Yōjimbō*. Director Masahiro Shinoda criticized Kurosawa for this imagery. (Museum of Modern Art/Film Stills Archive)

sters. He has stressed this point: "I was so fed up with the world of the Yakuza. So in order to attack their evil and irrationality, and thoroughly mess them up, I brought in the super-samurai played by Mifune. . . . Only such a samurai of the imagination, much more powerful than a real samurai, could mess up these gangsters."[60]

Gon replies to Sanjurō's declaration with disbelief, telling him it's impossible, that he'll never do it. The samurai smiles and remarks that he can't do it alone, indicating that he'll need Seibei and Ushi-Tora to do his work for him. But the remark is also a self-reflexive one, signifying his own immateriality as a historical figure, his status as a construction embodying Kurosawa's fervent wishes for an end to economic corruption and organized crime. He cannot do it alone because he needs the force of Kurosawa's desire as an energy from which to materialize. What makes *Yōjimbō* such a remarkable film is its emphasis upon Sanjurō's artificiality and its giddy celebration of the power of the wish. Throughout, the samurai functions as a kind of surrogate director, arranging and manipulating events as if he were structuring a screenplay and organizing a narrative.[61] He first sells himself to Seibei, who, elated, announces a noon raid on Ushi-Tora. When they assemble in the street, Sanjurō leaves Seibei and announces his desertion to Ushi-Tora's group. Then he climbs a watchtower, the better to view the showdown he has precipitated. The gangs converge hesitantly, displays of bravura alternating with outbursts of cowardice, as Sanjurō mirthfully watches from above. The expected annihilation is interrupted, however, by a messenger who announces an official inspection, so everyone puts down their swords and pretends all is well. Later, when the official is gone, Sanjurō renews his program of manipulation, provoking an angry outburst from Gon, who scornfully tells the samurai that he is behaving as if this was all part of a show he wrote. Sanjurō agrees but modestly adds he authored only half of it.

The film manipulates point of view, however, in such a restrictive manner that it is as if Sanjurō were the complete author. The first shot defines the film's strategy in this respect. In a long shot, a range of mountains looms in the distance, and no human figures are visible in the landscape. It appears to be a fairly conventional, impersonal establishing shot. But then Sanjurō strides into the frame, filmed from behind and in such close terms that his back dominates the image, obliterating the distant mountains. Perspective is reversed, as foreground dominates background, Sanjurō looming over the snow-capped crags. Then a long sequence follows as the samurai walks, in synchronization with Masaru Satō's music, while being filmed from behind. Again the view is so close that the surrounding landscape is largely obscured. The mountains, the empty roads, the deserted fields, and the locations established at the opening of the film are mediated by the presence of the hero, revealed only as he moves through them. His first encounter with the town is another exercise in perspectival restriction. As he walks through the main street, only one conventional long shot is used, clearly situating him within the much larger space of the town. This is the first shot of the sequence. But after this, every shot narrows perspective to an extraordinary degree. As he walks through the street, Sanjurō is filmed from behind at such close quarters (deceptively close, since a telephoto lens is employed) that his back occupies nearly all the frame. The low angle of view further magnifies his visual dominance. The narrowness of the anamorphic frame is exploited to conceal the details of the town. Because of the great width of the frame, the town's buildings can be seen on either edge of the screen, where Sanjurō's back does not hide them. But very little of the architecture is actually revealed. The narrowness of the frame, its lack of height, prevents this. An almost claustrophobic response is elicited. The parameters of the conventional, "objective" long shot that opened this sequence have been reversed: vision is restricted, character dominates architecture, and point of view structures space.

Sanjurō's visual centrality also defines the design of the narrative. It, too, becomes his extension. No event or character is witnessed unless he is also present to see them. When he offers to join Seibei's side, the boss excuses himself and confers with his family in private. Orin, his wife, urges that they kill the samurai rather than have to pay handsomely for his services and nominates their son as the executioner. Have to kill a few or the men won't respect you, Seibei tells the boy. The three huddle in a concealed room, but we are privy to this conversation because Sanjurō, suspecting something, has come down the corridor to listen. None of this conversation, however, is overheard until the samurai establishes himself at the location. Later, an early morning meeting between the gangs appears to transpire without Sanjurō's knowledge, until at the end of the sequence, he climbs down from the watchtower where we learn he had been all along. Near the end, Ushi-Tora's massacre of Seibei and his gang is initially experienced as an off-screen event because Sanjurō is not there. Gon is smuggling him out of town in a wooden box. We hear, as he does, the screaming and dying. Anxious to see the massacre, Sanjurō has Gon carry him closer, and they move from place to place, trying to get the best view. Only when Gon places him next to the flaming building and Sanjurō peers out of his box does the camera show us the event. Throughout the film there is no disparity between what Sanjurō knows and what we know, unlike in *Ikiru*, where gaps in perspective are played upon and magnified. But the restriction of point of view in *Yōjimbō* manages to create a similar Brechtian self-reflexivity by establishing the reciprocity that must exist between Sanjurō and the narrative. As the character is Kurosawa's fantasy projection, the narrative is the projection of the character, a chain of events that he arranges and creates so that, in turn, he may act.

In addition to this inflection of the protagonist, the constructed, artificial nature of the film is also emphasized through its extreme visual angularity.[62] *Yōjimbō* features some of Kurosawa's most geometrical compositions, with an extreme visual formalism heightened by the anamorphic frame and the telephoto lens. The width of the 'scope frame, in particular, is used to accentuate compositional frontality to a degree far beyond what can be accomplished with the standard format. When Seibei tells his four strongest men that they will raid Ushi-Tora's gang at noon, the men, plus Yoichirō, Seibei's son, are displayed side by side across the width of the frame. Similarly, the film's many confrontations in the street feature compositions in which whole gangs of twenty to thirty men are arranged laterally across the 'scope frame, the linearity of the compositions heightened by the flattening of perspective achieved with the telephoto lens. Kurosawa will often accentuate the frontality of such compositions by adding highly stylized movement, by inserting characters laterally into the frame so that their movement occurs in a plane perpendicular to the camera's axis of view. The camera will be set up in the center of the street, its axis parallel to the street, and then a character will enter the frame, bisecting the street and the camera's view by ninety degrees. This often necessitates a highly artificial pattern of movement, clearly unlike the way a character would normally walk.

Such compositional linearity is exploited to best advantage during the first of two sequences in which Seibei and Ushi-Tora's gangs swap prisoners. Kurosawa creates a series of reciprocal, symmetrical compositions that establish, in visual terms, the fundamental moral similarity of the two groups. I would like to describe this sequence in some detail because it so clearly shows the extent of the visual formalism prevailing in the film. Seibei's gang has kidnapped two of Ushi-Tora's henchmen, who could implicate their boss in a contract killing, and Ushi-Tora has kidnapped Yoichirō to exchange for the two men. The sequence begins with a high-angle long shot of the empty street, which runs as a diagonal across the frame. Hansuke, the town official, announces the time, and, in the first example of what will become a prevailing pattern of reciprocal imagery in the sequence, Seibei enters the top of the frame, at one end of the street, traveling laterally from right to left, while Ushi-Tora enters the bottom of the frame, traveling from left to right. The next two shots are reciprocal images of each other. A medium long shot of Seibei, perspective flattened by the long lens, presents him in the center of the frame as he asks Ushi-Tora if he is ready. Ushi-Tora answers in the next shot, framed identically to the previous one, the visual similarity so strong that only the change of clothing alerts us to the cut. Then two of Ushi-Tora's men, with Yoichirō bound in ropes, cross the frame from the right at a 90-degree angle to the axis of view, as in the next shot, a reverse-field cut, two of Seibei's men bring their prisoners across the frame from the right, at a 90-degree angle. Then a cut takes us to an overhead long shot of the street, as both groups of prisoners begin to move forward at the same time, at the top and bottom of the frame. A medium shot follows, showing Seibei's bunch advancing directly toward the camera in a frontal framing. A reverse-field cut presents Ushi-Tora's group moving forward in an identical composition. Then a cut takes us back to the overhead long shot of the street, but even this framing has a duplicate. The next cut is to another overhead long shot, but one that violates the 180-degree axis of action, so that the street now inclines diagonally in the opposite direction. At this point, the extraordinary symmetrical properties of the sequence are broken as it concludes when Nosuke (Tatsuya Nakadai), Ushi-Tora's brother, pulls out a gun and executes Seibei's prisoners. Kurosawa, however, has one more flourish to display: the entire sequence finds its symmetric duplication in the one that immediately follows, presenting *another* swap of prisoners by the two sides and utilizing the same patterns of linear movement and compositional reciprocity.

This, however, is no empty exercise in form. The sequences are structured as a series of mirror images. Shots become mirrors of each other, compositions reverberate as twins. Each gang is a reflection of the other, and their mutual gaze defines an unremittingly savage and corrupt world, where crime feeds on itself and endlessly reproduces. Filled with reflections of such violence, the world becomes a kind of perverse funhouse, as the extremity of the evil grows so radical that it becomes comic. The gangs are filled with misshapen giants who carry oversize hammers instead of swords, with wildly tattooed sociopaths who brag about having done everything bad and who delightfully anticipate being hanged or decapitated when they are caught. Misshapen and ugly, the gangsters scuttle about with crustacean-like movements. These human-animals are animated by a misanthropy that displays an even more striking "reverse anthropomorphism" than *Rashōmon*. Those who are not criminals or merchants are helpless and must hide indoors to escape the violence endemic in the world outside. Actions of fleeing and hiding are repeated so often that they become a major structural element of the narrative. Gon peers out of his inn to view the sordid episodes in the street, not daring to venture outside. Hansuke, the official, comes outside only after first looking to make sure nobody is being killed. A farming couple, representatives of a sociologically "normal" life, undergoes brutal victimization by Ushi-Tora. The woman is used as Kuemon's concubine, and the man is forced to live near them but beaten if he tries to see her. The couple has to flee the town to survive.

The world of the film is so dangerous that one can only cower indoors and hope that the violence will not spill over inside. It is a world without sanctified spaces, unlike in Kurosawa's other films where Sanada's

43. Evil unleashed, as the violence of the gangsters and their merchant backers consumes the town. *Yōjimbō*. (Museum of Modern Art/Film Stills Archive)

clinic or the village defended by the seven samurai offers the vision of an alternative, regenerative human community. The zone of darkness inhabited by the bandits in *Seven Samurai* is now everywhere. Violence, and the organized forces that maintain it for profit, is coextensive with space. Against all this, Sanjurō is largely helpless. He spends most of the film hiding indoors with Gon and must rely on trickery and guile for success rather than on direct confrontation. Eventually, the gangsters discover his motives and beat him terribly. Escaping, Sanjurō finds refuge at Gon's inn, but it offers no safety. Ushi-Tora and his men burst in, looking for him, and Sanjurō survives only because Gon has hidden him in a corner. Sanada in *Drunken Angel* was able to face down and expel the gangsters during a similar invasion, but here all zones, all dwellings, all human relationships are infiltrated, deformed or destroyed by the alliance of merchant and gangster.

How, then, may Sanjurō hope to prevail? The answer is easy: by destroying the world. The conclusion of *Yōjimbō* offers a raging apocalypse of violence, fire, and death. With a madly escalating logic of mutual destruction, Ushi-Tora torches the silk stores, and Seibei retaliates by puncturing Kuemon's sake vaults, precipitating a general conflagration from which only Ushi-Tora and nine of his men survive to claim the town. But nothing is left: Kurosawa pans humorously across the smoking buildings and through the dusty streets littered with corpses to reveal a despairing coffin-maker. There are now so many bodies that he is out of business. Sanjurō and his machinations have precipitated this final onslaught, but who better to do it in such a world than this stigmatized figure? Through his alienation, the film clearly admits how artificial, provisional, and ultimately ineffective is the solution Sanjurō offers. The social dislocations of the era have cast him loose, have made him a rōnin, a man of the wave, a piece of flotsam drifting where he will. Dirty, shaggy, unshaven, always scratching, his soiled appearance violates samurai etiquette, as does his habit of asking for money. He is repeatedly identified with dogs. In the opening scene, two peasants see him and remark that the smell of blood brings the hungry dogs. A hound crosses his path in town, and Ushi-Tora's men contemptuously call him a dog. The social moment is so bleak and unsparingly corrupt that the hero cannot escape tarnishing and becomes transformed into a literal outcast, bearing the marks of his stigmata.

A wonderful moment occurs early in the film that stresses this transformation, making it explicit. Sanjurō sells his services to Seibei, who immediately announces the noon raid, but the old bodyguard, Homma, is offended by the new recruit's higher pay and wants to avoid participating in the raid. He slips out the back, hops over the fence, and runs off, but not before pausing and waving to Sanjurō. Homma has a familiar smile. It is Susumu Fujita, the star of *Sanshirō Sugata* and *No Regrets for Our Youth*, as Homma, waving to Toshirō Mifune. The moment becomes self-referential, a scene in which the two heroes, past and present, of Kurosawa's cinema meet. As Fujita says good-bye to Mifune and takes off down that road, Kurosawa's cinema bids farewell to its youthful, idealistic hero in favor of the alienated persona incarnated by Mifune. It is also a farewell to a more innocent conception of the past, as an era that could nurture Sanshirō's childlike optimism and spiritual commitment. From now on, the force of history would be felt in terms incompatible with these conditions.

With the self-reflexive acuity and delight so typical of this film, as if to acknowledge the transformation and disintegration of the heroic persona, Sanjurō is equated with the dead, just as he had been with the dogs. After he is beaten by Ushi-Tora, Gon smuggles him out of town to a graveyard that has a temple nearby where he can recuperate. In the twilit cemetery, Sanjurō smiles grimly at Gon, who, startled, remarks that he looks more dead than alive. When Sanjurō returns to town for the final fight, he carries a dead man's sword, given him by the coffin-maker. The sword of the samurai had always been his most symbolic possession, emblematic of his soul, and under no conditions was he ever to part with it.[63] For Sanjurō to fight with the sword of a corpse is tantamount to being a corpse himself. It is his most alienated moment, but it is only thus that he can defeat the forces of time. The visually flamboyant battle takes place in the main street, as huge clouds of dust swirl around the combatants. Sanjurō faces ten men, one of whom carries a pistol. The winds that stir the dust are like those that announced Nosuke's first appearance in the film, when he pulled the gun from his kimono. These winds have brought firearms to the town along with the culture of the West, which will end the warrior tradition. The merchant class will control the country and consign the samurai to the graveyard and to legend. But not yet, not while Kurosawa may invoke his own imperatives. Historical reality is carefully established in the film, attention given to the rise of a money economy and the introduction of firearms, only to be refused, finally, and attacked. The hero is capable of beating a pistol and besting ten men in a massacre that "is a wish-fulfilling fantasy."[64] It is possible only because Sanjurō is a phantom of the imagination, and Nosuke realizes this. Before he dies, he promises the samurai that they will meet again, at the gates of hell. History has been surmounted but only through the hero's loss of unity. Sanjurō is both hero and dead man, solution to historical dilemmas and artistic fiction. Looking around the town, piled high with corpses, he remarks that now it will be quiet here. It is the quiet of the tomb. Capitalism has been defeated but only at the cost of destroying time and the world. The many fires and deaths in this film are purifying agents. If Sanjurō is finally the instrument that cleanses an exploitative society, if we thrill to his prowess in battle and respond enthusiastically to all the destruction he wreaks at the end, we are also reminded of his need to go into hiding like the helpless characters lest the forces of history and his social context really destroy him and make impossible an imaginary solution. In the last shot, Sanjurō strides away, his dark form made insubstantial by the telephoto lens, like a shadow flitting across a wall.[65]

Yōjimbō is structured by a commitment to what Freud termed "the omnipotence of thought," an attitude toward the world that "according to our understanding of the relation of reality to thought must appear like an over-estimation of the latter. Objects as such are overshadowed by the

44. Preparing for the showdown, Sanjurō arms himself with a dead man's sword. *Yōjimbō.* (Museum of Modern Art/Film Stills Archive)

ideas representing them; what takes place in the latter must also happen to the former, and the relations which exist between ideas are also postulated as to things."[66] This is the principle underlying magic, Freud suggested, a belief in the power to remake reality according to the contours of the wish. The extraordinary deformities afflicting the characters in the film, the gallery of monsters that Sanjurō confronts, are the result of objects becoming "overshadowed by the ideas representing them." The nightmarish terms defining the world of *Yōjimbō* result from this displacement, as Kurosawa permits his disdain for gansters and merchants to overwhelm their world and wipe it clean, much as a Tokugawa Neo-Confucianist would have liked to do. Furthermore, in its fantasy gratifications, *Yōjimbō* may be read as an allegory about Kurosawa's own notorious and well-documented confrontations with studio executives and marketing representatives, whose commitments to profit helped usher in the "dark ages" of Japanese film. Sanjurō is offered as a subversive director, manipulating the scenes from his watchtower, whose plans are counter to the scenarios plotted by the gang bosses. In this respect, *Yōjimbō* might be regarded as the precursor to a very similar film by a director influenced by Kurosawa. It performs the same cathartic function as Sam Peckinpah's *Bring Me the Head of Alfredo Garcia*, another film that sets the corrupting influence of lucre against the purifications of ritual violence as it constructs an allegory in which the criminals become symbolic incarnations of film producers and investors. Like Kurosawa's hero, Peckinpah's protagonist also rises from the grave to wreak vengeance on the businessmen who hired him. Both directors, acutely sensitive to the corrupting influences of money (Kurosawa would return to this theme again in *High and Low*), sought solutions in these films through the intervention of a supernatural hero.

Kurosawa followed the adventures of this hero in one more film, *Sanjurō* (1962), in which the rōnin falls in with a group of earnest young samurai trying to root out corrupt officials in their clan. It is a more delicately funny film than *Yōjimbō*, with much of the humor emerging from the studied contrast between Mifune's dirty, shaggy samurai, always asking for money, and the stereotypically noble, virtuous behavior of the young men. But the film, compared with its predecessor, is considerably more static, and the humor, while more subtle, is also far less radical in intent. *Yōjimbō* is global in ambition and adventurous in style, fusing the comic and the grotesque without diluting the power of either. In *Sanjurō*, by contrast, Kurosawa's concerns are much more modest. He gently mocks the conventions of samurai films, satirizing the pompously feudal behavior of their characters,[67] but he does not extend the political, historical analysis of *Yōjimbō*. Indeed, the use of history in *Sanjurō* is less radical. It merely provides a general backdrop for the action and does not receive the critical treatment that the other films examined in this chapter provide. Before moving on, however, it is worth noting that both *Sanjurō* and *Yōjimbō*, in the explicitness of their violence, helped inaugurate a new level of gore in samurai films. The severed arm and the geyser of blood erupting from a slain samurai's chest—two of the most memorable images from the films—helped change the way other directors filmed swordfights. There is a celebration of the bloodiness of violence in both these films, which is why, in *Sanjurō*, the attempts to condemn such violence, by including a character who criticizes it, do not really work. Afterward, however, Kurosawa backed away from such celebratory explicitness and attempted to dissociate himself from it:

> For the final sword fight in *Sanjurō* between the two men, I had the blood gushing as an experiment. It was the first time it was ever done in Japan. Having done it once, I have no desire to

45. Sanjurō vanquishes his foe and alter ego (Tatsuya Nakadai). This scene is a key moment in the visualization of violence in the samurai film: moments before, Sanjurō's sword has cut so deeply that his foe's chest erupts in a geyser of blood. *Sanjurō*. (Museum of Modern Art/Film Stills Archive)

do it again. I feel that other Japanese filmmakers who have looked at these two films and perceived that they were interesting, have totally misunderstood what was interesting about them: it wasn't the one blood scene. It was the character of Sanjurō. And the decision to take the blood and guts and exploit that in their films is a misunderstanding of what makes an audience like a film as well.[68]

Kurosawa would never again celebrate violence as he did in these two films. Affirmations, even those of violence, were becoming increasingly foreign to the spirit of his work. The bloodshed in *Ran* is certainly explicit, but it is infused by a despair and melancholy that turn it to horror.

The way out of the dilemma posed by *Seven Samurai* was found in *Yōjimbō* to lie in fantasy. History would be invoked only to be laughed out, and through this laughter the hero would be incarnated. The self-referential use of fantasy as a formal element here points toward its more extensive use in *Dodeskaden*. At the end of *Yōjimbō*, Sanjurō strides away into a void, his sword having eliminated the terrors of a corrupting world. Sanada had a crowd into which he could vanish, to which he could bring his reformatory efforts. By contrast, the ethic of *Yōjimbō* is one of isolation, a celebration of alienation. From here, Kurosawa could take the logic of his cinematic project only one step further, an extension that would represent both its culmination and the initial moment of its dissolution. Unable to work through the mechanisms of closure that the past wielded against the moral project of his cinema, Kurosawa sought solace in a time and space conceived in mystical terms. The attempt to escape what Mircea Eliade called the "terror of history" led to the search for an antihistory, for transcendence, an attempt to freeze the flow of time and lift its burden of suffering. In doing this, Kurosawa was thrown back on his last resource. The contemporary world mocked the efforts of his heroes, and the past refused to disclose a space for the social rebel. There were no cities on the hill. Only antihistoric space remained as refuge, but if one entered it, one might never return. The path to a committed, political art might be lost forever, and this, indeed, is what happened. This was the risk, and it came true. Kurosawa entered this space to make *Red Beard* and never found his way back. In the films after this, all the heroes would be dead, and the laws of karma would be irrevocable.

Red Beard is a unique film in Kurosawa's oeuvre, and to discuss it adequately we must now change the terms of the analysis. In no other film is there the sense of dual reality, of different planes of being. Watanabe's dedication to the park in *Ikiru* is founded on his realization that all that counts is what one does in this life. Unlike the films of Ozu, Bresson, and Dreyer, which, it has been suggested, belong to a tradition of "transcendental style,"[69] Kurosawa's work has always exhibited an exclusive commitment to the surfaces of the material world. *Red Beard*, however, is the exception. This is a deeply spiritualistic film. It postulates the existence of a world beyond the senses, one that may be grasped, indirectly and emotionally, during brief moments of exceptional insight. Suffering and death are the subjects of the film and the vehicles of this revelation. The inquiry is a new one that goes beyond the surfaces of phenomenal reality, and this may be what Kurosawa meant when he said he wished with this work to push film technique to its limits.[70] This kind of cinema poses enormous problems for critical discussion. The temptation is to bow down before the sublime image, of which *Red Beard* contains many, while pronouncing the inexplicability of all really great art.

There will be points in the discussion that follows where the mystery of an image will have to be noted. The aesthetics of the film are informed by, and point toward, such mystery. What is basic to our purpose, however, is to understand how Kurosawa came to adopt such a novel perspective, how the narrative and imagery of the film structure a sense of mystery, and what this new orientation is responding to. In brief, we will see that this new spiritualized aesthetic is the substitute for the failure of a materialist cinema.

Red Beard was nearly two years in production, and Kurosawa has remarked that on this film he worked harder than ever, wanting to make something so magnificent that people would be compelled to see it.[71] The setting is again the Tokugawa era. For three years the young doctor Yasumoto (Yūzō Kayama) has been studying the secrets of Western medicine at Nagasaki. Filled with arrogance and self-satisfaction over his status as a member of the nation's professional elite, planning to become the Shogun's own doctor, he is distraught to learn that he has been assigned to work in a public clinic, where only poor people will be his patients. Dr. Niide (Toshirō Mifune), nicknamed Red Beard, runs the clinic, and the film studies Yasumoto's tutelage under Niide, his confrontations with sorrow, illness, death, and his own moral growth into a public-spirited, dedicated physician. Keiko McDonald points to the centrality of the master–pupil relationship in this work.[72] Through it, Kurosawa returns to the explicitly didactic cinema of the early postwar years, but with the infusion of a new perspective and aesthetic. Yasumoto is to be a model for all young Japanese, as the film demonstrates—one final time, in supreme terms—the nature of responsible living.

The film appears to be loose and shapelessly structured. It is long, over three hours, and filled with a multitude of characters and subplots. Where the narrative of Seven Samurai, an even longer film, was oriented by and developed toward a single goal—defeat of the bandits—and featured the kind of tight narrative construction typical of Hollywood productions, Red Beard moves in many directions simultaneously as it explores the lives of the clinic patients and their past and present suffering. Moreover, the unifying idea of the film is an other-worldly one, and its attempt to illuminate truths of the spirit can only be indirect. These must be suggested, not explicitly observed, because they are far more intangible than the defense of a village. For these reasons, Red Beard has sometimes been regarded as a formless work[73] when, in fact, its structure reveals a tight organization. It has the massiveness and sprawl of a nineteenth century novel because of a comparable effort to assimilate and

46. Yasumoto (Yūzō Kayama) learns the secrets of life and death from Niide (Toshirō Mifune), in the supreme master–pupil relationship of Kurosawa's cinema. *Red Beard.* (Museum of Modern Art/Film Stills Archive)

convey a comprehensive vision of life. In this respect, the film is an anachronism. In the international cinema of the 1960s, a modernist sensibility was emerging, marked by a restlessness and self-referential complexity of form. Works by Godard, Antonioni, and Resnais, as well as by members of Japan's own New Wave,[74] broke new ground by challenging the conventions of narrative cinema, among them the direct, unmediated presentation of character and narrative and its corollary, the spectator's identification with a character placed in melodramatic situations. Kurosawa, by contrast, does not engage in self-conscious formal experimentation, as he did in *Ikiru* and *Yōjimbō*. He evokes the simplest human experiences and relationships and does so in outmoded terms by calling upon a nineteenth-century sentimentalism, the kind associated with the novels of Dickens or Dostoevsky.[75] The film has often been decried for its melodrama,[76] and it *is* melodramatic, but no more so than the experiences of Oliver Twist or Raskolnikov. As with Dickens and Dostoevsky, Kurosawa's melodrama is a consequence of the urgency of his vision. His symbiotic involvement with his material, the vehemence of his stance, generates this emotional excess, the extraordinary intensity by which states of evil and innocence are portrayed, and their striking polarity. Indeed, he has admitted that in writing the script for the film, he constantly thought of Dostoevsky,[77] and the influence of the Russian novelist may be at its greatest in this film.

The narrative studies Yasumoto's progressive moral development and is organized by the stages of this education. At first his brashness leads him to perceive the clinic as an awful place to work, low in prestige and offering no real remuneration. Tsugawa, the doctor whose place he will be taking, tells him the clinic is terrible, the patients are all slum people who smell bad and are full of fleas and lice. Yasumoto smells a foul stench. The smell of the poor, Tsugawa tells him, as Kurosawa cuts to a shot showing a cluster of wretched people huddled along one corridor, waiting for medical attention. The lighting and framing present this group as an undifferentiated mass, alike in their misery. Niide later tells Yasumoto that without the effects of poverty, half the people here wouldn't be sick. The clinic patients are slum dwellers, starving families, individuals who, through misfortune, have fallen to the bottom of society and can no longer care for themselves. Poverty is omnipresent in the film, afflicting all the patients, and it is encountered whenever the doctors venture outside the clinic.

Kurosawa, however, demonstrates a new attitude toward these oppressive conditions, a result of the defeats encountered by the previous films in their attempts to find political and social solutions. He now constructs poverty as a mythic condition and as an interior one, not as a political problem. The poor on whom Yasumoto gazes are silent, inert, submissive in their suffering. They display no anger or brutality, only resignation and sadness. Poverty has become a mental condition, inducing helplessness and humiliation and stripping people of their dignity. (The terms of this analysis of poverty belong to Konstantin Mochulsky, who pointed to its relevance for Dostoevsky's novels.[78] It seems clear that Kurosawa has taken it over from the Russian novelist.) Niide tells Yasumoto that there are really no cures. People say poverty is a political problem, but politics has never done anything for the poor. Has a law ever been passed to get rid of poverty, he asks, adding that the problem is much deeper than that. There is always some story of great misfortune behind illness, he says.

These words are central to the film. They indicate that Kurosawa has now given up entirely on the effort to grapple with the social context. Without that effort, none of the previous films would ever have been made. But the tension between personality and environment, embedded in those films as a true dialectic, has now become an antithesis. Withdrawal from society has fostered a total focus on the psyche, whose vicissitudes are regarded as far more important. One of the patients at the clinic is a madwoman who seduces men and kills them with a hairpin. She had been raped repeatedly as a child, but Niide says that she was born with her insanity. Many other people have had bad experiences without turning out as she did. This harsh judgment, encountered in an earlier form in *Stray Dog*, has several consequences. First, it indicates the historical limitations constraining Niide's medical practice, which operates at a time when the psyche had not yet been articulated as the focus of a separate discipline and was accounted for in terms of hereditary factors. Second, however, and more important, it discloses the extent to which illness is now conceived in strictly metaphysical terms. Sickness is regarded as the outcome of misfortune, not of social factors. The perception of misfortune is now firmly embedded within an appreciation of time as that which inevitably brings trials and sufferings to one's life. Suffering is spiritualized in *Red Beard*. It is an interior condition. A grasp of its secrets is the prerequisite for cure and the basis for the reversal of time, the cancellation of history, that is the project of this film. This is what Yasumoto has to learn in decisive encounters with three of Niide's patients.

Yasumoto's arrogance is due to his confusion of medical technique with true healing. His error is a belief that curing is something done to bodies. His first encounter is with the madwoman, who seduces and nearly kills him by playing on his desire to cure her. He responds to her exhibition of distress out of an overwhelming belief in his own abilities and must be rescued at the point of death by Red Beard, under whose shadow he wakes up in the next scene. Yasumoto's education is to proceed by a series of emotional shocks, and the madwoman has delivered the first. Others, however, are soon forthcoming. Assisting in his first operation, performed under horribly primitive conditions, Yasumoto cannot bear to confront the open wound of the patient, and Niide commands that he not look away, stating the essential Kurosawa credo that one bear to face the unbearable. The young doctor, however, cannot yet do this, and he faints. The antidote to his arrogance is the realization that pain is more than a response to damaged tissue. A gold-lacquer craftsman named Rokusuke is dying of liver cancer, and Niide tells Yasumoto to watch him carefully. The room fills with the awful sound of the old man choking and gurgling his last painful moments, and Yasumoto, horrified, backs into a corner and falls to the floor. He later tells the clinic's other doctor, Mori, that he finds it amazing that Red Beard could call a man's last, wretched moments solemn, but Mori replies that Niide looks into their hearts as well as their bodies. He says he is frightened by the pain and loneliness of death, but not Niide, whom he wants to be like some day. It is precisely this pain and loneliness that Yasumoto must absorb and make his own if he is to adapt to the spartan life at the clinic.

Death, and the suffering that precedes it, is the limit challenging Niide's work at the clinic. It is the boundary against which the doctors continually battle, and the effort to counter suffering must engage the mystery of death. Yasumoto grasps this mystery when Rokusuke's daughter comes to the clinic and tells the sordid, humiliating story of her marriage to her mother's lover and rejection of her father. Old Rokusuke died without saying a word because he had been condemned to silence and isolation by his daughter. But now she wants to atone. Did he die in pain? Niide says he did not, and she exclaims that it had to be that way or else life would be too unendurable. Yasumoto, recalling the agony of the old man's last moments, is shocked at Niide's lie. He had watched the moment of death closely, but its threshold yielded no secrets. Nothing was revealed, until now. Kurosawa cuts from Yasumoto to a strange image of Rokusuke, framed in profile, his throat contorting in pain but without the sounds of choking that we remember. A curious calm pervades the image. Rokusuke stares upward and is lighted from above, giving his face a beatific cast, and the burst of music on the soundtrack, consonant chords, seems to negate the fact of his pain. This is the first of several extraordinary images that convey a sense of transcendental wonder, of connection to an inexpressible depth or truth of being. In such images, the familiar becomes momentarily strange and disturbing. Is this image that Yasumoto recalls fact or fantasy? Its ontological status is not clear. Now, however, that Yasumoto has learned from the daughter the reasons for Rokusuke's pain and silence, his death is transfigured. It evokes awe and becomes a spiritually charged event as its physicality is diminished, a lack of importance symbolized through the absent sound.

From Rokusuke, Yasumoto learns the truth of Niide's words about misfortune lying behind suffering. But Kurosawa is interested in the manner by which such misfortune may be negated and surmounted, and he establishes the way through the example of Sahachi, another dying patient whose last moments Yasumoto observes. Sahachi relates another long narrative that has emotional misery as its core. He married a woman promised to another man. Feeling ashamed and sinful over breaking the

47. Niide and Yasumoto carry the battered child, Otoyo, to the safety of the clinic. Human suffering increases in a darkening world. *Red Beard*. (Museum of Modern Art/Film Stills Archive)

other engagement, she kills herself. Believing that he caused her suffering, and that of the other man as well, Sahachi buries her next to the clinic and devotes his life to working for others. Sick as he is, he works to buy eggs and fish for the other patients. He embodies the Dostoevskian example of universal responsibility, of each for all. Working too hard, he has grown more ill and is now dying. The other patients are distressed beyond comfort. To them he is a saint, thinking only of others, never of himself. These are, of course, the familiar terms of Kurosawan heroism, but here that heroism has become transmuted into acts of everyday kindness. It has attained a simplicity and purity it never before possessed. Sahachi dies, but he has inspired Yasumoto. The young doctor finally dons his clinic uniform, which he has until now refused to wear. At this point he is given his first patient to cure, a girl named Otoyo, who has been savagely beaten and brutalized by the owner of a brothel.

Just as heroism has become transformed into acts of everyday charity, the perception of human suffering is also altered. No longer analyzed in social terms, it is now, simply, evil. Otoyo is the eternal Dostoevskian child, whose brutalization calls into question the existence of God and

morality. I don't understand it, Red Beard says. Why does such a child
have to suffer so? The task faced by the Kurosawa hero is now one of
fighting metaphysical evil, and this can be done only by conquering
time, by creating a transcendent space where time is abolished. Through
Yasumoto's efforts to heal Otoyo's mind and body, Kurosawa describes
the specifics of this task. The young doctor nurses her in his room, sealing it off from the rest of the clinic. An extraordinary privacy and inti-
macy develops between them as Kurosawa shows, through pantomime
and carefully controlled music, Yasumoto's efforts to care for her. He
nurses her to health and then falls ill himself, and she, with perfect moral
symmetry, nurses him. The room, and the clinic that surrounds it, becomes a container of healing power and, as such, is set off against the
surrounding world.

The visualization of this division draws on what is, for Kurosawa, a
novel conception of space. Virtually all his previous films featured
highly angular compositions and the accentuation of patterns of movement conceived as metaphors for states of individual enlightenment or
networks of social obligation. The essential feature of this design was
visual instability, and Kurosawa explored various means toward this
end. The choreography of oppositional patterns of movement was one
such technique, whereby he might answer a camera movement in one
direction with a wipe traveling in another direction and a character in
the new frame moving in yet a third direction. Strongly linear patterns of
movement prevailed in which Kurosawa would contrast motion toward
or away from the camera with movement bisecting the frame in a horizontal plane. Motion might be implicit within a static frame, achieved
through a tense compositional arrangement of diverging lines and
planes. Or he might alternate, as in *Stray Dog*, between scenes of frenzied
activity with fast cutting and lengthy, static scenes filmed in long takes.
But whatever particular formal strategy he might explore in a given film,
he usually avoided repeating previously established camera setups, so
that the viewer, constantly reoriented by a succession of novel perspectives, came to inhabit a screen space that was in a continual state of flux,
always shifting, never familiar. This visual strife must be seen as the
essential signifier of Kurosawa's own committed position, as the correlative of his involvement with the exigencies of the social and historical
moment. The fragmented space of his films is the appropriate visualization of the fractured social periods that most of the works study, but this
splitting, while generating the moral dilemmas faced by the heroes, also
grounds the possibility of their success. Again and again, the films have

postulated that social crisis contains both the danger of chaos and violent collapse as well as the opening for alternatives. The undermining of a stable screen space and the dissolution of the culture during a moment of historical transition are different components of the same chain of signification.[79] They demonstrate the urgency of Kurosawa's involvement with his culture and his time and the depth of his optimism. Only as all that is familiar disintegrates may the outline of a better world be glimpsed. Like Dostoevsky, Kurosawa has always been an artist of the apocalypse. Like Dostoevsky's, Kurosawa's characters hover always on the brink of spiritual catastrophe, of a trial that will test them to their utmost, take them through fires that will either consume or purify. Frequently, as in *Rashōmon*, *Seven Samurai*, *Record of a Living Being*, and *Yōjimbō*, the entire world is threatened with conflagration. It is only by meeting this energy of destruction with another energy, with another power, that the apocalypse, individual or social, may be avoided. The instability of screen space, its fracturing through linear design or choreography of movement, unleashes this counter power and signals the reformatory impulse of Kurosawa's cinema.

All this has changed in *Red Beard*. In place of explosive visual energies attesting the seriousness of the struggle, and the real danger of its being lost, Kurosawa now works with an aesthetic of restraint and reduction. *Red Beard* is a film of stillness and quiet, of physical remove and isolated spaces. The film's narrative is built around the contrast between the space of the clinic and the surrounding world, and the imagery describing each region is starkly different. This visual design works "to impose on the present world a kind of mythical or eschatological geography."[80] Inside the clinic, where healing power is manifest, characters sit in repose, contemplatively taking their meals, studying books, mixing prescriptions, or earnestly seeing to the health of their patients. Very little medicine, however, is actually dispensed. Healing, instead, comes through inhabiting the special space of the clinic, a region of quiet, stability, and security so different from the outer world. Otoyo's cure comes through the provision of a secluded, comforting, supportive space where her emotional scars may heal. Kurosawa explores an alternate style in order to describe this space. Characters in the hospital converse in long, uninterrupted shots and are framed in symmetrical, balanced compositions. Many sequences are recorded in a single shot, with frontality accentuated as characters sit facing the camera, arranged side by side across the anamorphic frame, parallel to the wall behind them. These shots are virtually motionless, as an aesthetic of stasis emerges in Kurosawa's cinema not unlike that of Ozu's. Most important, space is stabilized, either through balanced compositions that are prolonged by the long take and the absence of character or camera movement, or through the repetition of camera setups. During the scene where Rokusuke's daughter tells Niide and Yasumoto about her father, Kurosawa cuts among close-ups and two-shots of all the characters, but he continually returns to previous and familiar setups. Spatial orientation is assured, not challenged. Moreover, Kurosawa generally obeys the 180-degree axis of action, so that screen direction is a constant. Spatial relations become harmonized and predictable in a way they never were before.

By contrast, the outside world is a place of strife and violence. It is glimpsed only briefly when Yasumoto and Niide visit the out-patients, when Yasumoto goes looking for Otoyo after it seems she has run away from the clinic, or when flashbacks visualize the contents of Sahachi's memories. During these periods, the landscape is ripped by severe winds churning huge clouds of dust, pummeled by harsh rains, or torn apart by earthquakes and landslides. This turbulent region is where Otoyo has been brutalized, where Sahachi lost his wife, and where Rokusuke and his daughter lived lives of misery. Gripped by severe elements and destructive human relations, the world outside the clinic is a place of visual and emotional trauma. Kurosawa's camera emphasizes this destructiveness, recording tempests of earthquake, storm, and human violence. Against the horrors of this engulfing space the tiny area of the clinic is set in defiance, with the doctors venturing outside to reclaim the most brutalized individuals to their care. The contrast of these spaces is a contrast of stillness and chaos, of restraint and excess, of compassion and violence, but most of all, of the sacred and the profane. The sanctified space of the clinic can be maintained only in isolation from the surrounding world. The distinction is between "two provinces of being: a common, generally accessible province and another, sacred, precinct which seems to be raised out of its surroundings, hedged around and guarded against them."[81] Violation and invasion from outside must be vigilantly prevented. When the madam of the brothel visits the clinic attempting to return Otoyo to a life of prostitution, the entire hospital, doctors and staff, unite in opposition to chase her away.

This division of the world into two regions, a protected zone of stasis and sacred relations and a degraded region of passion, violence, and flux, also works toward a separation of time and history from human affairs. Outside the clinic, in disintegrating landscapes, history prevails. It is the region of temporality and narrative, containing the deforming experiences of the madwoman, Sahachi, Rokusuke and his daughter, and it is illuminated and disclosed through their memories. It contains the past, now identified with trauma, from which the clinic is in retreat. Its contents can be released only by extreme disturbances, such as Rokusuke's death or the landslide that unearths the skeleton of Sahachi's wife. The encounter with the past is a convulsive one, and, in response, the film uses the sacred space of the clinic and its own narrative structure to conquer history and reverse time. Otoyo's cure is nothing but such a reversal, an attempt to undo and reconstruct the damage wrought by the temporal world. She is young and her past carries less weight than did Sahachi's and Rokusuke's, and the effort is successful. The passage of the seasons parallels both Otoyo's cure and Yasumoto's education, and the film begins and ends before the gate of the hospital, enforcing a circular design. The ending of the film is a beginning. Deliberately avoiding a climax, Kurosawa concludes with Yasumoto's decision to remain at the clinic, and the final images present his return with Niide to the gate and to the patients beyond. It is the commencement of another story. Such a structure, capped with the film's final images of melting snow, the coming spring, a marriage ceremony, and a renewal of dedication to the clinic's mission, regenerates time with an iconography describing returns and beginnings. This, then, is the refuge to which Kurosawa was driven in his meditations on the past, toward a cancellation of its legacy. The film, to use Mircea Eliade's description of myth, confers "a cyclic direction upon time, annuls its irreversibility:" "Everything begins over again at its commencement every instant. . . . No event is irreversible and no transformation is final. . . . Time but makes possible the appearance and existence of things. It has no final influence upon their existence, since it is itself constantly regenerated."[82]

Death itself may even be reversed. A young boy, Chōbō, whom Otoyo has come to love, and his family have taken rat poison to escape from chronic starvation. They are brought to the clinic, and the boy lingers near death. Niide and Yasumoto can only, helplessly, pronounce that he will live if he lasts until morning. He begins a final convulsion, as if he is about to die. Determined to save Chōbō, Otoyo and the clinic cooks call his name into a deep well, obeying an old superstition that since wells lead to the center of the earth, a dying person may be called back through them. As they chant his name, Kurosawa tilts down the length of the well to the center of the earth, and as a tear falls on the water below, Niide announces that Chōbō will live. This is the final event of the film, before the brief coda treating Yasumoto's marriage and return to the

48. As Niide and Yasumoto try to save Chōbō, they confront the mystery of death and the limits of medical knowledge. *Red Beard*. (Museum of Modern Art/Film Stills Archive)

clinic, and therefore it assumes a structural importance. It radically proposes an ultimate power to the force for good. It completes the logic of the film as a whole, which demonstrates not just the annulment of time but the creation of a positive karma, in which the inevitability of suffering is repealed. The optimism of this project is evident in the film's proposal of a chain of good will, of the ethical example of a life dedicated to healing and cure, spreading from Niide to Yasumoto, to Otoyo, and even taken up by all the cooks in the clinic. Richie points out that Kurosawa suggests the force for good may be so strong as to be contagious.[83] But, as Barbara Wolff notes,[84] what should be added is the Buddhistic basis for this proposal. A thirteenth-century treatise on moral and behavioral precepts had admonished that it "is wrong to be kind to those who treat you well and unkind to those who treat you badly.... If you are good to the bad, then the bad may reform."[85] Karma proposed an equivalence through time of good fortune for good deeds and of misfortune for evil deeds. A reward for kind behavior was sure to come, if not in this life then in the next. "[T]he Gods and Buddhas will rejoice at your good deeds and you will be rewarded in your next existence. Try always to improve your karma by returning good for evil."[86] Eventually, a steadily improving karma would result in the attainment of enlightenment, of Buddhahood, resulting in the transcendence of time and suffering.

Kurosawa reconstructs this doctrine of positive karma, but he offers it as a possibility in *this* life by releasing his enlightened characters from the constraints of time and history. Here is the basis for the film's aesthetic of stillness and restraint. In contrast to earlier films, satori, enlightenment, has already been achieved. The visual energy of the preceding films was generated by the effort to attain this enlightenment, by the vehemence of protest against crushing social exploitation. Near the beginning of *Red Beard*, when Yasumoto rebels against Niide and runs out of the clinic, the frame is energized in the old fashion. Kurosawa records his flight in a series of rapid tracking shots, but they are the only ones in the film. Otherwise, calm and quiet prevail as Kurosawa resorts to the stable, static frame. Stasis was broken by movement, by the energy of Yasumoto's protest, but the film dramatizes the elimination of this protest and the return to stillness. There are no cures, really. Yasumoto comes to agree with Niide's rejection of politics and, with it, the material world. In place of the lost politics, only the comforts of a withdrawn and contemplative stance remain.

The film's ideal is a monastic one, and this retreat symbolizes Kurosawa's own flight from his postwar commitment. Kurosawa has pointed out that *Red Beard*, although a period film, expresses his views of contemporary Japan:

> I think that the terrible reality that I describe in *Red Beard* is exactly that of Japan today. How to explain the contrast, the discrepancy between what one sees, the appearance of prosperity and the deep reality? Of course, if you only look at the economic expansion of the last few years, all the misery of the people is evaded or hidden. The people no longer believe in politics or the administration. The economic expansion will not last. The current prosperity is based on misery and will collapse.[87]

As Niide observes in the film about politics and the poor, Kurosawa despairs about the possibility of alleviating these conditions of social oppression. "If we had a climate of catastrophe, there would still be some hope. But in reality things are kept the way they are. The tragic, disastrous, strange things just continue."[88]

This new, disenchanted view of the perpetual nature of suffering and exploitation helped transform the material of the films from *Red Beard* on. Discussing Kurosawa's recent films, Audie Bock notes their "didactic remoteness." "The shantytown atmosphere of *Dodeskaden* is hard to find in contemporary wealthy Japan, and the man in unspoiled nature represented by Dersu is hard to find anywhere in the world."[89] Viewing Kurosawa's most recent films, one feels that the hopes for social reform have indeed died.[90] Paradoxically, however, this deepening pessimism, beginning to surface in his work of the late 1950s, has accompanied the eras of Japan's rapid economic growth, the state's growing assumption of policies of social welfare, and the development of broad-based movements of social protest centering around such issues as revision of the Japan–U.S. mutual security treaty, industrial pollution, and the government's efforts to construct the Narita airport.[91] Noting the appearance of citizens' movements in the 1950s, and their rapid growth in the 1960s and 1970s, Ward concludes that the presence of popular protest movements in Japan has opened democratic spaces within the state and has resulted in a populace that is far more participatory and politically involved than in the past.

> Of greater fundamental importance, however, was the gradual emergence of local and national interest group associations and citizens' movements with goals that required political action if they were to succeed. During the 1960s and 1970s these grew rapidly in numbers . . . and exploited the institutions of Japan's new democratic political system on behalf of their particular causes. . . . The result today is a far more politically informed, involved, and participant population than existed in the Japan of the 1920s or 1930s.[92]

This tide of popular activism is relevant to *Red Beard* and to the films that followed because of its glaring absence from their narratives and concerns, because of the adamant refusal by these films to believe that society could be made better. The growing reluctance of Kurosawa's work to engage topical issues came to be seen as a kind of opportunism, a penchant to blow willy-nilly with the prevailing wind. Masahiro Shinoda found the image of Toshirō Mifune atop the watchtower in *Yōjimbō*, watching the conflicts below with amused detachment, to be an apt metaphor for Kurosawa's own position. Shinoda wondered if Kurosawa, and the generation of filmmakers to which he belonged, would "choose any political positions ultimately to make their films enjoyable."[93]

Shinoda's verdict, of course, casts a pall over Kurosawa's work, even the clearly engaged films of the immediate postwar years. For the next generation of Japanese directors—the New Wave—the evasiveness of Kurosawa's political vision, its miring in "humanist" values, was a thing to be avoided. As evidence of the consequences of such evasiveness, Niide's speech in *Red Beard* dismisses the relevance of politics not just for the poor but also for those contemporary Japanese who were then in the streets demonstrating on behalf of causes that were deeply felt. Other filmmakers chose to be inspired by these currents of protest. Desser ties the emergence of the Japanese New Wave in the 1960s to the massive protest movements surrounding the revision of the U.S.–Japan security treaty in 1960.[94] By contrast, with evidence readily at hand of democratic protest in modern Japan, of real spaces where farmers or fishermen could confront or defy the policies of the state, Kurosawa chose instead in his work to retreat to the past and to mythical spaces. The resurgent pessimism of the late films is defiant indeed.

As a measure of this defiance, Kurosawa discarded the analytic capabilities of his montage aesthetics in favor of the authorial detachment afforded by the long take and the long shot. From now on, he would use this style to contemplate the world from a distance, and it would be a world grown increasingly eccentric, a world of dreams (*Dodeskaden*), of arcadian paradise (*Dersu Uzala*), and of crushing despair (*Kagemusha*, *Ran*). Politics was dead, as was hope for the future. With a celebration of life as a dream and effort as illusory, and a certification of helplessness and fatalism, negativism suffused the remaining films and confirmed the flight from commitment.

Irretrievably/

Gone are the days

of glory—/My

dream has van-

ished!/Surely the

day will soon

come/when I

leave this

brushwood hut.

—*The Tale of*

the Heike[1]

Yasumoto's return with Red Beard to the clinic was scored with triumphal music derived from Beethoven and Brahms, and, as Joan Mellen points out, the end of this film marked the close of the major, most important part of Kurosawa's career.[2] It was the climactic expression of the themes and forms he had been pursuing since the 1940s. Four years of inactivity followed *Red Beard,* of abortive projects, of failures to secure funding for future films, and of growing tensions with younger filmmakers whose experimentation and radical questioning of form seemed also a rejection of the tradition of cinematic realism and social commitment that had nourished Kurosawa. The ripening of alternate, nontransparent, politically and cinematically self-conscious modes of filmmaking in the works of Ōshima and others seemed to leave Kurosawa's cinema far behind and to reveal its boundaries in such a way that they appeared hopelessly narrow. Kurosawa's manipulations of form in *Ikiru* had been at least implicitly Brechtian, and the cinematic experimentation in *Throne of Blood,* in which he infused cinema with the performance and compositional styles of Noh theater and sumi-e painting, had turned on an analysis and celebration of traditional aesthetic values. By contrast, Ōshima's subversion of form was explicitly political and, like Godard's cinema, frequently used overtly Brechtian devices to counter the illusions of mimesis. The gulf between Kurosawa's cinema and the countertendency represented by other modernist filmmakers seemed unbridgeable. The generational rift pained him. Of his inability to communicate with newer generations of directors, he has observed: "I would like to be friends with them, but for some reason they avoid me. Some say that my style is old-fashioned, and others say I'm just an old man and not worth paying any attention to. As far as I'm concerned, aging is not a matter of chronological age but of talent and how you are able to exercise it."[3]

Following the failure of his participation in 20th Century Fox's production of *Tora! Tora! Tora!*, Kurosawa could not finance another project until he joined with three other directors to form an independent company, Yonki no kai (The Four Musketeers). The other partners were Keisuke Kinoshita, Masaki Kobayashi, and Kon Ichikawa, and the company was conceived to rejuvenate the cinema as a director's medium. Kurosawa describes its mission, and its fate, this way: "We wanted to form a group to become the 'nucleus' of Japanese film. We wanted to make films without having to fight for them at every step. We set out quite idealistically, thinking if we added D'Artagnan to the Three Musketeers, we'd have Four Musketeers. We thought it was a way to rescue Japanese cinema. The association foundered on the fact that we all had strong individual personalities."[4]

Dodeskaden (1970) was the company's first and only production, and it was a commercial failure. The company folded, and it would be ten years before Kurosawa would make another film in Japan. *Dodeskaden* came at a critical juncture in his career. In *Red Beard* he had pursued the logic of his cinema to its completion, while the countertradition exemplified by Ōshima, Shinoda, and others was pushing the cinema in a different direction from that in which Kurosawa had taken it. After the prolonged inactivity, the damage to his reputation following the *Tora, Tora, Tora!* disaster, and the challenges from the antirealists, *Dodeskaden* could not help but carry an inordinate amount of symbolic weight. It was an old master's return to the medium and perhaps it might even constitute a response to the radical forms of the Japanese New Wave. What kind of film would Kurosawa make?

Dodeskaden, an episodic portrait of slum dwellers, was shot on a budget of under one million dollars and in a quick twenty-eight days,[5] an amazing feat for a man who had become one of Japan's most expensively budgeted directors. Kurosawa admits that he made the film "partly to prove I wasn't insane," that is, to quell rumors that his legendary perfectionism had not reached pathological proportions.[6] The quickness of the shoot may be responsible for some of the film's peculiarities.[7] It looks like no previous Kurosawa film, and apart from a few tracking shots and an occasional use of the telephoto lens, it lacks Kurosawa's stylistic signatures. Moreover, it represents his first return to the standard screen format, the first film since The Lower Depths in 1957 not shot in 'scope. The disjunctive editing and angular compositions that have typified his work have been softened by an emphasis upon long takes and a more balanced arrangement of characters within the frame. Screen space is no longer a function of perceptual disturbance. The work of composition and camera movement assumes a minimal presence that is quite rare in his cinema and that differs from the accomplishment of Red Beard. A deliberate restriction of montage aesthetics prevailed in that film, too, but Kurosawa's framing stressed frontality and linearity, thereby preserving a stress upon the artifice of the imagery. The formal structure of Dodeskaden manifests neither of the dual stylistic impulses of his work. Neither the blunt, aggressive energy of the montage aesthetic nor the austere reductiveness of geometric, immobile, frontal framings typifies its design.

Nevertheless, the film is visually experimental, though this is not a matter of camera placement or editing. It is Kurosawa's first film in color and an attempt to understand this new formal element. In Dodeskaden, he discards the constraints of the naturalistic environment and celebrates a gaudy expressionistic style, full of hot primary colors, in which clothing, buildings, and the landscape itself glow with a full spectrum of wild hues. Kurosawa has painted his sets, the faces of his actors, even artificial backdrops representing the sky, the sun, and the moon to give them a lurid glow appropriate to the cartoonish, hallucinatory quality of the film. He had been reluctant to use color, believing that he did not understand it. With the cameraman Takao Saitō, who shot Dodeskaden, however, he felt he had met someone whose research in color technique accorded with his own evolving understanding.[8] Having decided to use the new element, Kurosawa applied it with such intensity that it became the dominant component of form. The aggressiveness and self-consciousness so lacking in his camerawork and cutting are manifest in the deployment of color. "Dodeskaden was a kind of color experiment for me. It was my first color film and I tried all kinds of things— even painting the ground, not to mention the sets. To deal with these characters in their very restricted setting, I had to use color as much as possible to bring out this setting. I was consciously being very experimental there."[9] The design is feverish, deliriously intense, often comically exaggerated. Among the characters are two laborers and their wives, who live across the street from each other. Each family's clothing is coordinated with the colors on the front of their houses. The worker from the red house wears a red sweater, the one from the pale yellow house wears a pale yellow sweater and headband, and his wife sports a sweatshirt with black bands like those that diagonally cross the front of their home. There is nothing subtle about this, but it becomes funny when the wives and husbands switch partners. Returning from an evening of drink, the husbands are not sure which house to enter, bound to observe the tacitly agreed infidelities but confused by the mismatch between their clothing and the color of their new residences.

Color structures the design of entire scenes, as in the one in which a young girl is sexually violated by her uncle as she lies across a bed of violently red flowers. Kurosawa's use of color is not gratuitously experimental, for the amplification of hue creates an ironic counterpoint with the reduced conditions of life, the minimal levels of food and clothing characterizing this neighborhood. In this gap between material subsistence and aesthetic extravagance, between economic marginalization and stylistic transgression, both the social critique of *Dodeskaden* and its contemporary despair may be located. The film constructs a critical social allegory, but it merges imperceptibly into an aesthetic that is indifferent to social conditions. In this ambiguity, the film locates and celebrates the power of fantasy, both of the artist who fashions imaginary worlds and of impoverished people whose only escape lies in a realm of dreams. Kurosawa explores that area between poverty of the flesh and the heated ruminations of the spirit where the imagination dwells.

The title of the film is a form of onomatopoeia. It is meant to be the sound of a trolley and is the obsessive cry of an adolescent boy who imagines himself a trolley driver. He compulsively drives his make-believe trolley around a slum neighborhood, whose denizens constitute the cast of the film. As in *The Lower Depths*, Kurosawa studies the conditions of life among those excluded from society, who manage a precarious existence on the periphery of the human world. But whereas poverty in the earlier films raised the challenge to a hero of responsible living, here the world is completely self-enclosed, its coordinates defined by despair, dreams, and drunken revelries. In addition to Rokuchan, the trolley boy, the group of slum dwellers include Katsuko, a young girl made to work endless hours by a lazy, drunken uncle whom she supports and who rapes her; Hei, a mysterious shell of a man with dead eyes who speaks to no one; Ryō, a good-natured fellow who takes in his wife's illegitimate children as if they were his own; Tamba, a gentle man who behaves compassionately toward others; and a beggar and his son who live in the decaying frame of a car and alleviate their starvation with visions of a celestial house they are constructing in their imagination.

49. His spirit buoyed by fantasies, Rokuchan drives his imaginary trolley through the slums. *Dodeskaden*. (Museum of Modern Art/Film Stills Archive)

The ensemble nature of this cast affects the structure of Kurosawa's narrative and the kind of social space it delineates. As the film opens, Rokuchan inspects and then drives his make-believe trolley into the center of the neighborhood, and his path intersects the movements of one of the drunken workers. The worker is standing on the invisible rails, and Rokuchan blows his horn to clear the tracks. Then, as he crosses the frame from left to right and exits, the worker walks in the opposite direction to rouse his comrade. Instead of following Rokuchan as he makes the circuit with his trolley, Kurosawa tracks with the worker to his friend's house and continues with them as they set off for work. The paths of two characters central to the film—Rokuchan and the drunken worker—have crossed, but these people do not know each other except dimly, by sight as residents of the same general neighborhood. The coordinates of the narrative will be arbitrary in this way, structured as a series of accidental encounters.

As the workers depart, they pass a group of washerwomen working around a ground-level spigot, and Kurosawa now lingers on the women, as an official with a grotesquely funny facial tic passes them, pausing to twitch uncontrollably. Both the women and the official will be regular characters, but the only ties that bind them are the polite and distanced codes of neighborly recognition. The movements of the characters describe a series of randomly intersecting lives. The paths of Rokuchan, the workers, and the official cross the same terrain but at different moments and in varying directions. In Kurosawa's previous films social space had been rigidly structured, and its formalized norms had to be subverted by the hero. But the hero ultimately did not prevail against the social structure. It diminished and finally extinguished the space in which he moved. In *Dodeskaden*, Kurosawa finds a social space that is open and permeable, free of confining social duties and group norms, but this openness is also an emptiness in which the laws of structure are replaced by the free form of random encounters. The social space is open because the condition of poverty has replaced and leveled the characters' former roles and positions. For Kurosawa, the linear narrative was a structure of commitment.[10] It had chronicled the growth of subjectivity and moral consciousness, was focused and directed by the hero's obsessive goals, and was set in motion by his activity. Because everyone is blighted by their poverty in *Dodeskaden*, because the human figure has become as expressionistic a feature of the landscape as decaying cars, because abandonment by society has obliterated the possibility of heroism, narrativity—as a symptom of all this—breaks down. The narrative becomes diffuse and nonlinear and organizes the lives of its characters as a series of tangents, briefly and arbitrarily interconnected. Unlike the way in which it functions for Brecht or Ōshima, the nonlinear narrative here signifies an entropic condition. The destructuring of social space in this film is doubly symptomatic: of the cultural abandonment of these slum characters and of Kurosawa's own disengagement from the social fabric. The rigidity of social codes in the earlier films was a mobilization generated in response to the rebelliousness of the Kurosawa hero, whose behavior elicited an authoritarian response from the social hierarchy. By contrast, the permeability of social space in the slum neighborhood of *Dodeskaden* and the absence of rigid social roles and class tensions are the symptoms of the withdrawal of Kurosawa's previous authorial voice.

The path of his departure may be traced through dreams and fantasies, but as these inevitably carry the imprint of the world in their design, they are imbued with a darker reflection and allegory of contemporary Japan. The film opens as it closes, at Rokuchan's house. He and his mother are praying to Buddha, and Rokuchan asks Buddha to take care of her because she seems worried and sad. The windows are covered with drawings that he has made. They are all of trolleys and dramatically reveal the extent of his obsession. Blocking the windows, these brightly colored pictures obliterate the outside world. The room is sealed by dreams, its space defined by the imagery of Rokuchan's visions. In this weird, private world, he and his mother appeal to Buddha for salvation rather than to the self, as previous Kurosawa characters would have done. Concerned to dispute the rumors of his own madness, Kurosawa ironically fashions a hallucinatory world whose main character is himself mad.

Rokuchan tells her he has to go to work, that the maintenance crew is not reliable. He pantomimes a routine in which he dons a driver's uniform and steps outside into a bleak, gray, metallic landscape whose desolation so strikingly contrasts with the gaiety of his drawings. It is a depressing industrial landscape, a slag-heap littered with corroding automobile frames, rusting slabs of metal, and mountains of unidentifiable rubbish. It stretches to the horizon. No trees are visible. No birds sing. Rokuchan walks to an open space, where he has parked his trolley. He begins an elaborate routine in which he inspects the machine, starts its engine, and then drives it down a path through the refuse, shouting "dodeskaden." As he goes through this ritual, the film affirms the power of his hallucination by providing a realistic aural accompaniment to his motions, much like Kurosawa had done with the imaginary symphony in *One Wonderful Sunday*. We hear the trolley door open and its engine start. Rokuchan may be demented, but that dementia is very dear to Kurosawa, and he affirms the logic and humanity of its delusions by allowing the soundtrack to validate them. Rokuchan's delusions are absorbed by the film's form and become real, a strategy Kurosawa extends as the boy begins to drive. In a series of reverse-field cuts, Kurosawa tracks and zooms to simulate the imaginary trolley's motion as Rokuchan races across the blasted landscape. Eventually the path of his travels takes him into the shantytown where most of the characters live, at which point Kurosawa leaves him to examine them.

This sequence has laid bare the ethics of the film. Rokuchan's fantasies of color and motion are developed as a response to the horrifying industrial world that has stripped his own life of sensuality and freedom. Confined to a tiny home in the midst of an auto graveyard, Rokuchan imbues his life with vitality and pleasure through his imagination. In the first shot of the film, we see him standing in the doorway, watching a distant trolley pass, its reflection visible in the glass next to him. Affluent Japan, a world where people really ride trolleys, is distant and unattainable, and he is captivated by its image. Kurosawa regards Rokuchan's visions as evidence of the power of art to transform life. David Robinson reports Kurosawa as saying that Rokuchan "symbolizes the artist, the cineaste who creates entirely by the power of his imagination."[11] If Rokuchan's visions are meant to stand for the transformative powers of art and the cinema, then the character's isolation and his peripheral relationship to modern Japan must resonate with Kurosawa's own position in the film industry at this time. As the boy races across the inhuman landscape, a group of schoolchildren call him "trolley-crazy" and throw things at him, expressing contempt and persecuting him in a way that Kurosawa may have understood only too well.

More important, however, the brief appearance of the well-dressed schoolchildren stresses the alienation from the developed Japan of the shantytown dwellers. Contemporary Japan, where people ride on trolleys, possess shiny cars, and eat at restaurants, may as well be another world for these slum people, so remote is it. The beggar-boy who lives with his father in the shell of an abandoned car remarks that he once saw pictures of foreign lands, and it is he who, in another sequence, passes indifferently the shiny cars in town. The outside world is foreign. It is Other and exists only as photographs seen once, the reflections of a passing trolley on a window, hostile schoolchildren throwing stones from a distance. Kurosawa does not engage this world of commodities and commerce. He turns away from it, permitting it to exist only as a tracing on the periphery of the slum dwellers' lives.

Nevertheless, tradition survives as cultural nostalgia. The father living in the abandoned car constructs a dream house in his imagination, consulting with his son on its design. As they plan the gate, the fence, the swimming pool (much as the oppressed couple in One Wonderful Sunday had dreamed about the features of the restaurant they wanted to own), Kurosawa cuts in fantastically colored images of these structures done in rococo, Spanish, and British styles. But they decide their house must not be of stone, like foreign houses. We Japanese, the father pronounces, couldn't adapt to stone houses. They are too cold, and we love to live in the midst of nature. For this reason, he says, the Japanese have designed wooden houses, sensitive to climate and weather. The boy, who sleeps in the frigid car, agrees that he doesn't like stone houses, either. The father talks of national and cultural differences as if they still existed as realities in his life. He celebrates love of nature in a world where it has become extinct. He and his son live surrounded by steel and concrete, but the old cultural identity lingers on as a ghostly memory.

The only tree in the film is a dead one, gnarled, leafless, and stunted, and a woman reflects that when a tree is dead it is no longer a tree.

Dodeskaden evokes a nightmare landscape, where rotting automobiles become homes, where fish are poisoned and bring death to the beggar-boy, and where nature has been supplanted by corroded, rusted steel. Conjuring the dream house for his son, the father remarks that the gate will be green, but first it must be painted red as an anticorrosive. Dreams for these people function in just this way, as protection from an acidic world. "Frequently within several hours they live through a paradise of love or an entire life, huge, gigantic, unheard-of, wonderful, like a dream, magnificently beautiful. . . . [R]eality produces an onerous impression, one hostile to the dreamer's heart, and he hastens to withdraw into his own inviolable golden nook."[12] The words are Dostoevsky's, but they aptly describe Kurosawa's validation of fantasy as balm for a consciousness oppressed by the industrial landscape. As Joan Mellen perceptively notes, for Kurosawa, "the imagination as a value in itself offers moments morally superior to and more authentic than the brute facts of 'real life.'"[13] Nevertheless, it was not always this way, as decades of Kurosawa's committed films clearly demonstrate. Now, though, in *Dodeskaden*, consciousness has been severed from the world to drift in hallucinatory rapture. Where once it contested experience, now it flees from it. The cultural heritage of nature veneration, the aesthetic celebration of snowfalls and moonbeams, has become irrelevant to a world that has obliterated nature itself. The gaudy, stylized design of the film must be seen in this allegorical dimension. The decaying dwellings covered with a rainbow of colors and the wildly hued ground and faces of the characters evoke a poisoned environment, glowing with radioactivity, weirdly colored by buried chemicals that have ruptured the ecosystem and returned to disfigure humans and dwellings alike. By the late 1960s in Japan, pollution had emerged as a major social problem. "Since [the nation's] rapid growth policies stressed chemical and heavy industrialization, pollution of the environment proceeded with a vengeance."[14] Citizen protests against industrial pollution were rapidly growing, and a widely publicized series of lawsuits dramatized the ills of "itai-itai" disease, Minamata disease, and others.[15] It is in this context that the wild color design of the film should be viewed. It evokes a landscape of make-believe but also of pollution and its terrors. Mellen reports that Kurosawa remarked to her in 1972 that he wished to make a film about pollution.[16] In a sense, *Dodeskaden* is that film. Against a backdrop of real world misfortune and antipollution political struggle, however, the es-

50. The horror of life in an industrial wasteland. *Dodeskaden*. (Museum of Modern Art/Film Stills Archive)

cape into dreams carries the taint of poison, however much Kurosawa may want to validate the magic of fantasy. The dreamworld of *Dodeskaden* is grotesque and disfigured. As his boy lies dying from the toxic fish, the father cannot stop dreaming of his enchanted house. As he lowers his child's ashes into the ground, he visualizes the swimming pool, finished at last. Dreams are not just balm for the savaged spirit, they also embalm it.

Kurosawa answered the stylistic experimentation of the New Wave filmmakers with a grandly antirealistic film, but in place of Ōshima's political analysis Kurosawa offered a condemnation. *Dodeskaden* signals both Kurosawa's horror over modern Japan, contaminated by its own progress, and his withdrawal from it.[17] *Dersu Uzala* (1975) is therefore the logical sequel to this film. If modernism has destroyed the ecosystem, *Dersu Uzala* observes the moment of its eclipse and mourns the destruction of the wilderness as a violation not just of nature but also of the human world. Before he could make *Dersu Uzala*, however, a film that is his farewell to heroes, Kurosawa passed through a grim period in his own life during which the future of his career seemed to be in serious question (see Chapter 1 for a detailed discussion of this period). "After *Dodeskaden*, I had some very dark moments when I thought about what the prospects were in Japan, and I realized that if I wanted to go on making films, I would never get out of debt."[18] Depressed over the critical and commercial failure of *Dodeskaden*, unable to secure financing for future films, and plagued by health problems, Kurosawa attempted suicide in 1971. Afterward, he began a slow process of spiritual recovery, aided by an accurate diagnosis of his health problems and by an offer from Mosfilm to make a film in Russia. Looking back on this period, Kurosawa has reflected: "I think I was suffering from some kind of neurosis, but I also had a bad case of gallstones, and it wasn't until long afterward that it was diagnosed and successfully operated. I didn't realize until after the surgery that I had been in pain for years, and I'm sure it had been affecting my spirits."[19] The intense, hallucinatory design of *Dodeskaden*, the overheated, interior world of the psyche where much of the action transpires, the fragility of the spirit wounded by an implacable world, all are symptomatic of this period of pain and depression. The isolation of the characters and the schism between their consciousness and the world are analogues of Kurosawa's own desperately unhappy situation. Rokuchan's room, its windows that provide access to the outside covered with the images of his artwork, is a magic space, secure and safe from the terrors of the spirit, where kindly Buddha will intervene with his healing powers. The ambiguity with which the film views Rokuchan's visions lies here. They are both a form of madness, the products of a dysfunctional mind, as well as a means of transcendence. When the spirit is in flight from the world, the illusions of art cease to be lies. They provide a means of salvation, Kurosawa suggests, obstinately believing in the power of his craft to sustain, if no longer a comprehensive project of social reform, then at least himself.[20] The ambitions of assisting in a task of national cultural reform have contracted, along with the spirit, until only the prospect of personal, psychological survival remains, as a compelling necessity. *Dodeskaden* is a chronicle of this contraction. The expressionism of form, the antirealism, and the exploration of color provide vectors for creative movement while the real avenues of social and political power remain closed. Kurosawa has not only retreated from contemporary Japan. He has accompanied Rokuchan to that tiny room of the imagination. It is this flight, coupled with its celebration of fantasy, that makes *Dodeskaden* such an unsettling work. The fairy tale euphoria Kurosawa seeks to communicate as his camera gazes rapturously at the drawings is profoundly disturbing.

If, in *Dodeskaden*, contemporary Japan has become a slag-heap, its landscapes grotesque and oppressive, its trees and fish dead and poisonous, then the possibilities for moral commitment and social reform have already been foreclosed. Dreamers replace heroes, and art exists to provide escape for the battered consciousness. *Dodeskaden* studies an industrial and cultural catastrophe that has already occurred. It is a post-apocalyptic film, chronicling the human effort to subsist in a world rendered uninhabitable. Though four years of inactivity followed before Kurosawa would work again, his next film is also concerned with these issues, but it develops them with a complementary focus. *Dersu Uzala* inverts the time frame and terms of analysis of *Dodeskaden*. Whereas *Dodeskaden*, with much gaiety of spirit, conducts a wake for a deceased culture, *Dersu Uzala* sadly tends the patient during its last moments of life. What has vanished from the world in *Dodeskaden*—the spirituality of nature, providing the moral basis for human conduct—is cherished and grasped by *Dersu Uzala* in the very moment of its passing.

The film represents a double removal for Kurosawa, a removal from both the contemporary world and his own culture. He made the film in the Soviet Union on invitation from Mosfilm, and it is set in the early decades of this century. The offer to make a film in Russia rescued Kurosawa from the despair and inactivity that followed the completion of *Dodeskaden* and gave him the chance to realize this project he had long cherished ever since discovering the diary of the Russian explorer whose exploits the film chronicles. Now he had a chance to make the film. As for working in Russia, away from Japan, Kurosawa seemed cavalier about issues of cultural isolation. "If I couldn't direct in Japan, why not? Cinema is an international language."[21]

The need to work was so compelling that it simply overpowered the desire to make Japanese films for a Japanese audience. Besides, Kurosawa considered himself a "global citizen." Moreover, this project, filmed on location in dense Soviet wildernesses, would give him an opportunity to exercise his passion for incorporating nature as an element of the drama. That passion is apparent in many of his films, wherein the cycle of the seasons, climate, and weather conditions are active participants in the drama. The oppressive heat in *Stray Dog* and *Record of a Living Being* is omnipresent and becomes thematized as a signifier of a world disjointed by economic collapse and the atomic threat. The narrative of *Red Beard* is structured by the passage of the seasons. Even in his first film, *Sanshirō Sugata*, the montage dealing with the abandoned clogs is punctuated with imagery of snow and rain. Rain in Kurosawa's films is never treated neutrally. When it occurs in *Rashōmon*, *Seven Samurai*, *Throne of Blood*, *Red Beard*, and *Dodeskaden*, it is never a drizzle or a light mist but always a frenzied downpour, a driving storm. Kurosawa's sensibility, like that of many Japanese artists, is keenly sensitive to the subtleties and beauties of season and scenery. He remembers the sounds of his boyhood, of Taishō-era Japan, and points out that they "all are related to the seasons."[22] During his youth, Kurosawa recalls that when he read novels he had trouble comprehending human behavior and motivation but was highly responsive to the evocation of natural scenery. "At that stage of my life I didn't understand very much about people, but I did understand descriptions of nature. One passage of Turgenev I read over and over again, from the beginning of *The Rendezvous* where the scenery is described: 'The seasons could be determined from nothing more than the sound of the leaves on the trees in the forest.'[23] He adds that "Because I understood and enjoyed reading descriptions of natural settings so much at this time, I was influenced by them." He does not specify the nature of the influence, but perhaps that is because it is already so apparent.

Dersu Uzala gave Kurosawa the chance to make this interest the primary subject of a film.[24] In this film Kurosawa studies the Siberian wilderness whose magnificence dwarfs the scale of human action and ambition, thus reversing the terms by which the other films had proceeded. A celebration of love for nature and respect for all its forms, which the beggar in *Dodeskaden* had pointed out as part of Japanese tradition, but which was impossible for him to realize in his world of steel and rust, is the organizing principle of the film. Nature veneration is rescued for art by Kurosawa from the ravages of the modern world, but to do it he has to move back in time to discover an unmapped, uncharted region. The film constructs a great arcadian myth about the human fall from grace consequent upon the loss of the wilderness and the personal ethic that it grounded. The magnificence and inhuman dimensions of the vast Siberian forests are indifferent to the facts and scale of human life, yet paradoxically they offer a path to an enlightened form of living. The film charts this path and defines the terms of a code of living that Kurosawa finds deeply compelling but which he can no longer locate in modern Japan. Herein lies the source of the film's profoundly melancholy tone. It is a work in which Kurosawa mourns the death of all that he loves.

In the film Kurosawa studies the friendship between the Russian explorer Arseniev, who is surveying and mapping the Ussuri region on the Pacific seaboard, and Dersu Uzala, the hunter and trapper whom he meets and who becomes his guide. As they traverse this area, Kurosawa gives his images an epic scope. To do this, he returns again to the anamorphic frame after having used the standard screen ratio in *Dodeskaden*. He uses the wide space of the 'scope image to portray the enormity of the mountains and forests of the region, exploiting the breadth of the frame to capture the boundless spaces of the landscape. The imagery of mighty forests, vast rivers, and huge mountains of ice has a serene and forbidding beauty. But he also studies the human world, using the anamorphic frame, as in *High and Low*, to delineate group allegiances. Kurosawa deploys characters across the width of the frame in clusters and positions that define them in social, moral, and psychological terms. When Dersu and Arseniev converse by their fire, they sit in the foreground on the right of the frame while the soldiers camp in the upper left background, the two groups separated by a gnarled tree that leans diagonally away from an embankment across the center of the image.[25] The wide-screen image permits Kurosawa to achieve a separation between these groups impossible in the standard format, and he insists on this separation by extending the length of the shot. This composition translates the social coordinates of Dersu's isolation and of Arseniev's ability to mediate that isolation into contours of cinematic space. It is a strategy that Kurosawa will use again at other points in the film.

The spatial design of *Dersu Uzala* is, however, basically not one of fragmentation, despite such compositions. As in *Dodeskaden*, Kurosawa employs the long take and the sequence shot and thereby respects the integrity of space within the frame. The analytic cutting, the reverse-field framing, and the 180-degree perspective violations typical of his earlier style are conspicuously absent, except as occasional occurrences. In this period of his work, they are no longer the organizing principles they once were. Instead, Kurosawa pulls back with his long lenses to observe images of quiet and stasis, which work as extended tableaux, devoid of the kinetic energy that editing or camera movement can supply. Indeed, Kurosawa's camera is largely stationary. Whereas in *Rashōmon*, *Seven Samurai*, and *Throne of Blood* forests were treated as places of mystery and sensuality where he executed tracking shots of a grace and power unsurpassed by any other filmmaker, the forests of *Dersu Uzala* are not rendered with such fluid poetry. Here the camera pans only to follow figures. The only extended tracking shots in the film occur as Arseniev and his party race along a riverbank to rescue Dersu, who is trapped out on the river. But these shots are slow, languid, and anemic by comparison to those of *Throne of Blood*, probably Kurosawa's best, where the camera races with breathtaking speed through the forest to follow the galloping samurai Washizu and Miki. *Dersu Uzala* is a film about the invasion of the forests, about the restriction of Dersu's freedom to roam the hills, and its formal structure emphasizes the compositional beauty of the painterly image over the excitement and pleasure of movement. This conjoining of long takes, long shots, and telephoto lenses, however, also creates an aesthetic of detachment. The pictorial tableaux are frozen with a beautiful immobility that grows even stronger in *Kagemusha* and *Ran*, and this aesthetic design becomes a means of preventing intervention into these worlds, either by a stubborn, rebellious protagonist or by Kurosawa himself. His perspective is becoming one of observation, not participation, and the gradual freezing of the images testifies to this change.

The narrative of *Dersu Uzala* is divided into two major sections, set in 1902 and 1907, that deal with separate expeditions which Arseniev conducts into the Ussuri region. In addition, a third time frame forms a prologue to the film. Each of the temporal frames has a different focus, and by shifting them Kurosawa is able to describe the encroachment of settlements upon the wilderness and the consequent erosion of Dersu's way of life. As the film opens, that erosion has already begun. The first image is a long shot of a huge forest, the trees piled upon one another by the effects of the telephoto lens so that the landscape becomes an abstraction and appears like a huge curtain of green. A title informs us that the year is 1910. This is as late into the century as Kurosawa will go. After this prologue, the events of the film will transpire even farther back in time and will be presented as Arseniev's recollections. The character of Dersu Uzala is the heart of the film, his life the example that Kurosawa wishes to affirm. Yet the formal organization of the film works to contain, to close, to circumscribe that life by erecting a series of obstacles around it. The film itself is circular, opening and closing by Dersu's grave, thus sealing off the character from the modern world to which Kurosawa once so desperately wanted to speak. The multiple time frames also work to maintain a separation between Dersu and the contemporary world. We must go back farther even than 1910 to discover who he was. But this narrative structure has yet another implication. It safeguards Dersu's example, inoculates it from contamination with history, and protects it from contact with the industrialized, urban world. Time is organized by the narrative into a series of barriers, which enclose Dersu in a kind of vacuum chamber, protecting him from the social and historical dialectics that destroyed the other Kurosawa heroes. Within

51. The explorer Arseniev and Dersu, the last Kurosawa hero. *Dersu Uzala.*
(Museum of Modern Art/Film Stills Archive)

the film, Dersu does die, but the narrative structure attempts to immortalize him and his example, as Kurosawa passes from history into myth.

We see all this at work in the enormously evocative prologue. The camera tilts down to reveal felled trees littering the landscape and an abundance of construction. Roads and houses outline the settlement that is being built. Kurosawa cuts to a medium shot of Arseniev standing in the midst of the clearing, looking uncomfortable and disoriented. A man passing in a wagon asks him what he is doing, and the explorer says he is looking for a grave. The driver replies that no one has died here, the settlement is too recent. These words enunciate the temporal rupture that the film studies. It is the beginning of things (industrial society) and the end of things (the forest), the commencement of one world so young that no one has had time yet to die and the eclipse of another, in which Dersu has died. It is his grave for which the explorer searches. His passing symbolizes the new order, the development that now surrounds Arseniev. The explorer says he buried his friend three years ago, next to huge cedar and fir trees, but now they are all gone. The man on the wagon replies they were probably chopped down when the settlement was built, and he drives off. Arseniev walks to a barren, treeless spot next to a pile of bricks. As he moves, the camera tracks and pans to follow, revealing a line of freshly built houses and a woman hanging her laundry to dry. A distant train whistle is heard, and the sounds of construction in the clearing vie with the cries of birds and the rustle of wind in the trees. Arseniev pauses, looks around for the grave that once was, and murmurs desolately, "Dersu." The image now cuts farther into the past, to 1902, and the first section of the film commences, which describes Arseniev's meeting with Dersu and their friendship.

Kurosawa defines the world of the film initially upon a void, a missing presence. The grave is gone, brushed aside by a world rushing into modernism, and now the hunter exists only in Arseniev's memories. The hallucinatory dreams and visions of *Dodeskaden* are succeeded by nostalgic, melancholy ruminations. Yet by exploring these ruminations, the film celebrates the timelessness of Dersu's wisdom. The first section of the film has two purposes: to describe the magnificence and inhuman vastness of nature and to delineate the code of ethics by which Dersu lives and which permits him to survive in these conditions. When Dersu first appears, the other soldiers treat him with condescension and laughter, but Arseniev watches him closely and does not share their derisive response. Unlike them, he is capable of immediately grasping Dersu's extraordinary qualities. In camp, Kurosawa frames Arseniev by himself, sitting on the other side of the fire from his soldiers. While they sleep or joke among themselves, he writes in his diary and Kurosawa cuts in several point-of-view shots from his perspective of trees that appear animated and sinister as the firelight dances across their gnarled, leafless outlines. This reflective dimension, this sensitivity to the spirituality of nature, distinguishes him from the others and forms the basis of his receptivity to Dersu and their friendship. It makes him a fit pupil for the hunter.

Dersu is an extraordinary individual in the familiar terms of Kurosawa's cinema, yet he also represents a new departure for Kurosawa. His presentation skews the terms of the social analysis proposed by the earlier films. His actions are informed by the generosity of spirit and the sensitivity to the needs of others that have been persistent hallmarks of Kurosawa's protagonists, except that here these attributes are sanctioned as requirements for survival in the wilderness. Though ultimately engaging a project of social reform, the enlightened behavior of the other heroes emerged as a personal, existential decision. It rejected and rebelled against established social hierarchies and roles. Herein lay the quixotic aspect of their behavior. It was not sanctioned by society, yet it aimed to benefit others. Few people were even capable of recognizing it for what it was, yet the heroes were dedicated to a vision of service to the human community. By contrast, Dersu's wisdom is completely asocial. His home is the hills. He roams the forests in the company of beasts and is ignorant of and indifferent to the ways of society. In earlier films Kurosawa would have viewed such isolation as selfish, but now he regards it as a kind of purity. "In this ideal [of a retreat to nature and solitude] there is the sharpest antagonism between the world of men and the world of nature. Only by fleeing to the bosom of nature can one escape the contaminations and sufferings of human troubles."[26] Wisdom is now possible only by severing all ties with society. The pristine quality of Dersu's impulses, his generosity, and his innocence of human evil are the result of a life removed from human intercourse. The coordinates of his wisdom are established by the natural environment, the beneficence of his actions by the logic of survival. As Kurosawa points out, "I couldn't have portrayed the character of Dersu without showing the nature in which he lives—without it he wouldn't exist."[27]

When he first appears in Arseniev's camp, Dersu accepts food because he is hungry. That day he shot a stag but it escaped. One of the soldiers mockingly asks why, if he is such a great hunter, he missed his shot, adding that soldiers never miss. Dersu angrily replies that if you shoot all the beasts, we'll go hungry. For Dersu, all that happens in his chosen environment is part of a natural balance and is therefore meaningful. He missed the stag so there would be food for another day. Later, discovering a shack during their wanderings, Dersu repairs its roof and asks Arseniev to leave salt, matches, and rice inside. Arseniev asks if he plans to return, and Dersu says no, he leaves the provisions for others who will find them and will not go hungry. As Dersu repairs the hut, the other soldiers watch curiously while joking aimlessly among themselves. Their relation to this shack, to the environment, to time itself is different from Dersu's. They live in the present and are themselves helping to usher in the historical future. Their mapping of this region will assist the development of settlements. Their orientation to time is a linear and a unidirectional one, and they can feel no connection to this dwelling. By contrast, for Dersu, time is nonlinear. Past, present, and future constantly interpenetrate and fold back upon one another. He understands the shack's history, he knows by reading signs that it was constructed three days ago by a Chinese man who traveled this way, and he projects a future for it by repairing its present condition and leaving the food. For

Dersu, the fixation of modern men upon progress, their unidirectional orientation to the future, is a mark of ignorance. Dersu's world is timeless, that is, it is freed of the epistemological frames erected by industrial culture. Past, present, and future all coexist with stability and in equilibrium. Arseniev's party represents the mapping of nature and, thereby, its attempted subjugation, whereas for Dersu wisdom entails a necessary cooperation with the ecosystem, for one is part of it. If Dersu leaves food to ensure the survival of others, the chances are good they will do the same for him.

With this logic, Kurosawa finds in the natural world a basis for his ethic of individual responsibility. Arseniev admires Dersu and remarks that he was a fine man because he provided for the needs of complete strangers, people he would never see. Later, Dersu, Arseniev, and the soldiers camp at another shack to wait out a storm. When it is over and they move on, a rainbow lingers over the dwelling, as if to sanctify Dersu's presence and example. Dersu's magnanimity is nourished by his perception of the essential spirituality of nature. He talks to the fire and to wind and water as if they were people. A soldier laughs and asks him why, and Dersu replies because they are alive. Angry fire, water, and wind are frightening, he says. They are powerful men. A strong breeze suddenly appears, whipping leaves across the frame, as if in answer to his words. Earlier, in a magnificent image, Dersu and Arseniev stood on a vast plain, framed between the moon on their left and a fiery setting sun on their right, humans and celestial bodies alike flattened by the long lens into a single plane of space. It is an image of great mystery and serenity. As they contemplate the heavens, Dersu explains that the sun is the most important man because if he dies everything else dies, too. He initiates Arseniev into the secrets of the universe. The other Kurosawa heroes were in touch with important social and moral imperatives, but Dersu is connected to cosmic truths, and it is Arseniev's blessing to have known him briefly.

But like those other heroes, Dersu is alone, except that his isolation is mitigated by his orientation to time. He tells Arseniev that he once had a wife, a son, and a daughter, but they died of smallpox. He burned them along with his home. One evening, Arseniev finds Dersu alone by a river, singing in the firelight. Dersu tells him that it was here that he lost his family. He dreamed recently that they were all in a tent, shivering in the cold and hungry, so he came here to give them some food. Though long dead, his family and their past remain a part of his world, needing food and shelter that Dersu is still careful to provide. Despite this, however,

Dersu's isolation is terminal. There is no one to follow his example and lessons. The film is about a failed master–pupil relationship. It has no chance to develop because Dersu's wilderness, which sustained his code, is being torn down and because Arseniev is himself of the city, where he has a home and family, and will not abandon its comforts. Unlike the hunter, Arseniev is a fallen man, compromised by his urban tastes.

Dersu lives beyond the need for human contact, an effective analogue to the position of Kurosawa's cinema at this point, having withdrawn from the imperative to participate in the work of reshaping society. In this film, sociality has given way to a supreme hermeticism. In a sense, Dersu's destruction is a corollary of his contact with the modern age. "[P]rogress and civilization are enemies of the nobility of men like Dersu."[28] He and Arseniev, however, love each other, and their parting at the end of the 1902 expedition is filmed by Kurosawa with great feeling. They go their ways through the snowy landscape, a railroad track between them, but pause, each calling the other's name in affirmation of their bond. These are calls across time, between two worlds, forever sundered and one in eclipse. The second part of the film makes explicit this decline. Arseniev returns to the Ussuri region in the spring of 1907 and again meets Dersu, who once more serves as his guide. Overjoyed to see his friend, Arseniev tells him that he is just the same, but he is wrong. Almost immediately, ominous indications of Dersu's fate begin to appear. Walking through a foggy landscape, Dersu discovers that he has lost his pipe, a sign of his diminishing acuity, and retraces his path to find it. He sees tiger tracks and realizes that one is stalking them. In the eerie, fog-shrouded forest, Dersu shouts for the tiger to leave them alone, which it does, for now. But this tiger will reappear, and Dersu will come to know it as an emissary from Kanga, a spirit the Goldi worship, who is telling Dersu he may no longer remain in the forest. The tiger's first appearance follows immediately upon the reunion of Dersu and Arseniev, and it returns with the coming of autumn. It blocks their path, and Dersu shoots at it. It runs off, but Dersu is convinced it will die, and he drops his rifle in terror, distraught at the rupture with the natural world he has precipitated. In his world, to kill a tiger is very bad. Thereafter, he grows sullen and angry, rejecting the friendly overtures of the soldiers, and he begins to go blind. He can no longer see the wild boar to hunt, nor even hit a glove set up as a target. How will I live in the forest now, he frantically cries to Arseniev. On New Year's Eve, the tiger returns again for him, huge and spectral as a shadow that leaps across Arseniev's tent, its growls merging with the wind. Dersu frightens it off by throwing flaming pieces of wood, but he now realizes that his bond with the forest is broken. With resignation, he accepts Arseniev's offer to live in his home in the city.

The last act of the film traces the breaking of Dersu's spirit in the city, where he cannot shoot his gun, pitch a tent, or chop down a tree. He quarrels with officials over these restrictions. How can people live in boxes? he asks Arseniev, echoing the comments of the beggar in *Dodeskaden* about stone houses. That character had no choice over the kind of environment in which he lived. Dersu, by contrast, has been empowered by his life in the hills, has known the alternative to modern, urban life. Now, in Arseniev's home, he can only sit in despair, staring at the tiny flames in the stove that remind him of the hills he once roamed. Finally, Dersu asks to be allowed to return to the forest. Arseniev relents and gives him a new rifle of the latest design, which he says can be aimed easily even for one with poor eyesight. But Dersu never makes it back. He does not die in the forest naturally, of exposure or by an animal seeking food. He does not even fully escape the city. Its taint haunts him. He is killed by someone for the rifle, and Arseniev is summoned to identify the body. He buries Dersu in a secluded place next to huge cedar and fir trees, and he sets Dersu's staff on the grave as a marker. He stands by the mound, as he had at the beginning, and murmurs "Dersu." Thus the film completes its cyclic structure. The grave and the marker will not last. They will be obliterated by the encroachments of civilization, so Kurosawa leaves them as they were, not in the present (1910) but still in the past. He never returns to the time frame of the prologue but ends with a close-up of the staff. The effect is of an attempt to escape time by remaining within the inner frame of the narrative. We never leave the space of Arseniev's nostalgic memories. They secure Dersu against the world that destroyed him. Condemned to live out the future, Arseniev can only look back and mourn what has been lost. He buried something of himself here, in this grave, as has Kurosawa. Dersu may be gone, but he was still the best man and the last hero.

Kurosawa's cinema has passed from the eccentric dreams of the outcast Rokuchan to the heroic isolation of Dersu, a passage that registers the rapid decline of its committed project. *Dersu Uzala* is a funeral oration for that project, an attempt to transpose what were once historical and sociological grounds for commitment onto a mythological plane. The film's structure is simple and direct, without the dense formal complexity that distinguished the earlier films. In its loose, episodic narrative, unlike that of *Dodeskaden*, isolation produces not madness but enlightenment. Grace is achieved not in art but in nature. But this nature, and the myth of a life before the fall that it expresses, is ideological. *Dersu Uzala* embodies an idea of nature that in the West is familiar from the romantic tradition. Nature is transcendent, culture merely a dross upon it. But the romantics were in flight from industrial civilization, and their nature worship proved an ideological dead end. As a form of social protest, it was eminently cooptable. The same problem plagues the film. While Kurosawa has attempted to venerate the unspoiled wilderness and by implication to criticize social life, the conception of nature he employs is but a cultural category. Attempting to escape culture, he falls back into it. Dersu and his wilderness remain an aesthetic fiction, compelling but duplicitous.

The film's allegory seeks to explain and justify Kurosawa's own social and aesthetic withdrawal, and Dersu's indifference to society may be viewed as a wish-fulfilling purgation of Kurosawa's tormented relationship with modern Japan and the film studios. (In this respect, it is worth noting the affinities between character and creator. Like Dersu, Kurosawa suffers from problems with his eyes, and the year of Dersu's obliteration, 1910, is the year of Kurosawa's birth.) Dersu's forests, the terrain that shapes his morality, are antihistorical spaces, where time is nonlinear and the modern orientation to progress appears a form of foolish ignorance. The film does not interrogate history or engage it but attempts to escape from it, because that history now contained not only the blight of urbanization in Japan[29] and pollution, but also the legacy of a failed cinematic project and the contemporary misfortunes of screenplays rejected and funding denied. *Dersu Uzala* spiritualizes what had been the materialist basis of Kurosawa's cinema. As the hero is removed from people and communities, the power of the hero as ethical example collapses. It is history, that old, relentless enemy, that destroys Dersu by invading his forests, and with the last of the Kurosawa heroes gone, the cinctures of time constrict with implacable force. This is what both *Kagemusha* and *Ran* study, the horrors of a world voided of humane conduct, where the coordinates of human affairs are defined by failure, treachery, violence, and death.

Like that of *Dersu Uzala*, the narrative of *Kagemusha* (1980) is preoccupied with the threat of time and is charged with an allegorical dimension. The film, a product of joint financing between Toho and 20th Century Fox, an arrangement initiated by the American directors George Lucas and Francis Ford Coppola, who were distressed at Kurosawa's in-

52. Kurosawa on location for *Kagemusha*. (Museum of Modern Art/Film Stills Archive)

activity, returns Kurosawa to his own culture and the guise of the samurai film. It had a troubled production and suffers from the loss of its original lead, star Shintarō Katsu, and his replacement after production had begun with Tatsuya Nakadai.[30] Neither here nor in *Ran* is Nakadai able to bring the kind of commanding presence and emotional power that the films require and which Toshirō Mifune could have supplied. The result is a dramatic softness clinging to the central character of each film.

Kagemusha grew from Kurosawa's fascination with the Battle of Nagashino, in 1575, wherein the Takeda clan was wiped out by an army led by Oda Nobunaga and Tokugawa Ieyasu that used muskets to annihilate the opposition. "I grew very interested in the Battle of Nagashino, which remains a question mark in history. No one has satisfactorily explained why all the taishō of the Takeda Clan should have died, while not one taishō of the Oda or Tokugawa Clans did."[31] The Takeda army was renowned for attacking as rapidly as the wind, as silently as the forest, and as mercilessly as fire, these attributes symbolized by the characters on their banner. But the deployment of firearms on a massive scale

53. Kurosawa with American directors Francis Ford Coppola and George Lucas during production of *Kagemusha*. Lucas and Coppola were instrumental in helping Kurosawa make this film. (Museum of Modern Art/Film Stills Archive)

by Nobunaga demonstrated the eclipse of an era of hand-to-hand combat, the anachronistic status of swords and lances as weapons of war. The battle was striking for the scale and thoroughness of the slaughter. By contrast, samurai warfare in preceding centuries had been distinguished by loosely coordinated encounters of small groups that prevented destruction on such a massive scale.[32] With his sensitivity to the nuances of historical change, Kurosawa recognized this event as the augury of a new era.

In the latter half of the sixteenth century, battles raged among powerful warlords for control of the capital Kyōto. The film deals with the struggle among Takeda Shingen, Oda Nobunaga, and Tokugawa Ieyasu, the latter two in alliance against Shingen. Although the film ends with the destruction of the Takeda clan, in the events that followed Nobunaga managed to forge a brief reign over the nation until he died seven years after the Battle of Nagashino. Ieyasu ultimately solidified national control, and his dynasty retained this power for two centuries, a period of lasting political stability. With the end of the Tokugawa era in the mid-

nineteenth century, the country embarked on a path of modern industrial development. For Kurosawa, the Battle of Nagashino embodied a
contest between the older cultural heritage and the currents of modernism and Westernization that would prove so decisive. The character of
Nobunaga, in particular, fascinated him. "It is clear that Nobunaga was
a genius, a much more 'modern' man than the average Japanese of that
time. According to the missionaries, Nobunaga knew that the earth was
round, and was well informed about the world situation. He was also an
active importer of new objects and ideas from abroad. That was the sort
of personality that defeated the Takeda Clan."[33]

Kurosawa was motivated by a pedagogic purpose in making *Kagemusha*: to educate younger Japanese about the past and specifically to
offer an answer to the puzzle of why Shingen's son led the clan to destruction.[34] If, however, this was the purpose, it is curious that Kurosawa
chose to present the event as he does. If his desire was to speak with a
contemporary audience, his affections in the film clearly belong to the
past. Though Nobunaga commanded Kurosawa's interest and is used as
a harbinger of the dawning modern age, the film is devoted to Shingen
and the fate of his clan, which displaces the focus away from the country's unification and eventual modernization in favor of an elegiac concern with what was lost, perhaps because the modern age has become a
source of so much distress for Kurosawa.

The tone of *Kagemusha* is distanced, almost cold, as Kurosawa explores the destruction of the Takeda clan, a destruction that is presaged
by the clan's attempt to escape the terrors of time, the foreclosure of its
future that Shingen glimpses just before his death. The clan tries to escape this future by keeping Shingen alive through the impersonations of
a double. In examining this attempt, the film participates in the revision
of Kurosawa's earlier work that the late films are collectively elaborating.
The dialectic between self and society is extinguished, along with the
prospects for human freedom. These had always been rooted in the autonomous personality, which Kurosawa had valorized over the interactionist self and the socio-economic environment, but this was an ideological move of a deeply problematical nature. Kurosawa's construction
of personality, which once embodied the optimism of the postwar years,
collided with the institutional nature of political and economic power in
the modern world. Buffeted by internal contradictions, troubled by interactionist linkages to normative groups, divorced from the kind of genuinely social perceptions that might renew it, Kurosawa's construction of
personality steadily broke apart. Now, in its wake, *Kagemusha* projects

it as an empty form by elaborating a world in which illusion and image replace enlightenment and in which personality is hollowed out and becomes a role, to be performed with great artifice, as human will and free choice are crushed beneath the weight of destiny.

During a siege of one of Ieyasu's castles, Shingen is shot by a Tokugawa sniper. Before he dies, he issues a strange will. He requests that the generals of the clan keep his death a secret from their enemies as well as from their own men. His death must be concealed for three years, during which time the army must not move from its domain. If you move to attack, he warns with clairvoyant accuracy, the Takeda clan will be destroyed. The bulk of the film studies the efforts of the generals to honor this will. They enlist the aid of a kagemusha, a double (Tatsuya Nakadai), to impersonate the late lord and thereby perpetuate the power of the clan.[35] The double is, in reality, a petty thief who bears an uncanny resemblance to Shingen. Kurosawa opens the film with their confrontation, which he films in a single long take. Nobukado, Shingen's brother who has been acting as a kagemusha, has rescued the thief from crucifixion and has brought him before the lord. Shingen is impressed by the resemblance but distressed that such a scoundrel, sentenced to execution, should be his double. Hearing this, the thief laughs rudely and angrily points out that he has merely stolen a few coins, while Shingen has murdered hundreds and robbed whole domains. Who is wicked, he asks.

In the first few minutes of the film, the critique of economic and political oppression that sustained and lifted *Seven Samurai* to greatness and which has characterized much of Kurosawa's earlier work seems to be reappearing after a long period of dormancy. The thief identifies the savagery of the warlords. Not only Shingen but Nobunaga and Ieyasu were able practitioners of slaughter. Beside such violence, the crimes of the thief are, indeed, insignificant. But the critique that is apparently developing is deceptive. Shingen replies calmly that he agrees. He is wicked, he says, but he justifies this as necessary to gain control of the country. War is everywhere, and unless someone unifies the nation, there will be endless rivers of blood and mountains of dead. The thief is impressed by Shingen's composure. The lord tells Nobukado that the thief has spoken honestly and that he should be trained as a kagemusha. Kurosawa intends that Shingen's personality, his discipline and directness, his ability to see into the hearts of others, should be so impressive that they motivate the subsequent behavior of the thief and of the entire clan. The thief not only agrees to impersonate the lord, but he goes to his death for him, as does the whole clan at Nagashino. Kurosawa explains it in these terms:

> I had to consider how this man could become so immersed in the character of Shingen that he would actually "become" him. I decided that it must be because of the strength of Shingen's own character. Then I reflected that the taishō who died in battle must also have been charmed or enchanted by Shingen. In effect, they committed suicide at Nagashino—they martyred themselves for Shingen. They must have been in love with him, if you will.[36]

The thief is drawn into the affairs of the clan, despite his initial unwillingness to act the role of the late lord. He comes to love Takemaru, Shingen's grandchild, and to admire, and be respected by, Nobukado. When he sees loyal retainers dying for him in battle, he recognizes his responsibility for the fortunes of the clan and comes to accept his role. During the battle of Nagashino, as he watches the slaughter of "his" clan, subservience to codes of fealty compels him to pick up a lance and charge to his doom. What began as an accusation of barbarity against Shingen has developed, instead, into a love affair for the lord. The film does not develop the critique but abandons it. Kurosawa is more interested in offering a melancholic meditation upon time as a process of dissolution and the world as a structure of illusion than in developing the kind of materialist inquiry into the medieval world that distinguished *Seven Samurai*. Nobunaga and Ieyasu remain peripheral characters in the film. Instead of showing the emergence of a nation, Kurosawa offers a vision of failure, the doom of the Takeda clan. Instead of the construction of durable political institutions that would last for centuries, he gives us the rivers of blood and the piles of dead.

As Shingen leaves the room after his first meeting with the thief, the soon-to-be kagemusha bows to the ground, but the lord has already gone. The thief bows before an empty presence, and Kurosawa ends the sequence with this image, thus establishing the basic metaphor of the film, the tenacity with which Shingen's influence continues to shape the clan's fortunes even after his absence. The clan's attempt to preserve the impression of their lord's health for three years permits the film to explore the nature of images and illusions, which is its real subject. Ironically, all the double need do is appear in public, at clan conferences or in battle, in order for the clan hierarchy to persist and the machinery to keep running. Enemies and retainers alike are convinced by the double's appearance and expert mimicry. Even those who know remark on how Shingen seems to live through him. Image becomes reality or almost as good. The power of illusion to compel allegiance and to shape events is graphically illustrated in a battle sequence during which the double leads the clan to protect the rear of Katsuyori, who has attacked one of Ieyasu's castles. Nobukado tells the double that he mustn't move, that he must stay on the hilltop with his troops and banners where everyone can see him. Young Takeda samurai willingly die to protect the man they believe is their lord, and Ieyasu's forces, afraid of Shingen's martial prowess and convinced that the entire clan is camped there, make only halfhearted attempts to attack. They retreat, the castle falls, Katsuyori is the victor, but, most important, the charismatic power of Shingen is confirmed along with the need for the impersonation to continue.

On the one hand, the film seems to be implying that the institutions of regional daimyo rule have become emptied of meaning, perhaps in anticipation of the greater national unity that Nobunaga and Ieyasu will help usher in. They persist only through the complicity of the clan elite in maintaining a lie, and when the lie is exposed, when the impersonator is found out, the clan is destroyed. When the thief is deposed, Katsuyori assumes control and, in spite against his father, leads the clan out of its domain to attack Ieyasu at Nagashino. On the other hand, the portrait of the respect that grows between the thief and the Takeda generals is so tinged with a mutual camaraderie, and without the class animosity that would be expected under such conditions, that the destruction of the clan becomes an event the film mourns with great feeling. As the generals cross their lances for the last time before charging Nobunaga's guns, in full awareness that their day has ended, the tone of the film becomes positively dirge-like. *Kagemusha* invigorates the doomed clan and the institutions that sustain it with feeling, with respect, and with genuine sorrow at their passing. The reasons for this must be located in Kurosawa's repeated difficulties in placing heroic action within the modern world, but they are also to be understood in terms of the allegorical inflections of the narrative.

This narrative documents the skill of the thief in playing his role. More than once, he improvises a gesture or word to allay the suspicions of retainers or mistresses, and the improvisations, though spontaneous, are true to the spirit of Shingen. In the clan's allegiance to its figurehead, the film envisions a social community's devotion to a sequence of images. Moreover, though the elite generals know the falsity of these images, the people depend on them for their meaning and orientation. Thus, the film elaborates a metaphor for the cinema itself, which, like the kagemusha, dispenses images to a willing public that tacitly acknowledges their fictive nature while yet submitting to their power.[37] The thief, like Kurosawa, is a master manipulator of these images. But eventually this character is exposed and expelled from the community, as Kurosawa has been from the Japanese film industry.[38] What follows may be regarded as a wish-fulfilling revenge fantasy affirming the social need for the artist. The clan, once it is deprived of the thief's imagery, disintegrates. Though false, these images were necessary to sustain the community. Without them, it dies. By expelling the artist, it seals its doom. *Kagemusha* may thus be read as an allegorical work that endorses the necessity of illusion for the maintenance of the social fabric. The injunction against "looking away," the moral and aesthetic imperative of direct confrontation as a means to truth, has been abandoned in the late films and their characters. The power the imposter comes to wield and the clan's embrace of his performance mock the sober vision extolled by previous Kurosawa heroes. These meanings are implicit within the narrative and may account for the film's curious attachment to the Takeda clan and feeling of remorse at its end. Like Kurosawa within the contemporary film industry, the thief does not cut his ties to the community. Though expelled, he hovers nearby, watching Shingen's official funeral and the final battle. He remains attached to those for whom he had performed.

Despite these allegorical inflections, however, the film never really interrogates the status of images, the nature of their construction, or the apparent social need for them. The film is ironic, not analytic. The visual structure of the film is sedate in the manner of Kurosawa's late works. As a sign of this diminishing formal aggressiveness, wipes, once the favorite transitional device, may not be found in *Kagemusha*. Indeed, as a pervasive feature of style, their presence is radically diminished in all the works after *Red Beard*. In *Kagemusha*, Kurosawa keeps cutting to a minimum and concentrates on creating pictorial effects within the frame. Composition stresses balance and a centering of the human figure rather than fragmentation and asymmetry. Montage, as in the other late films, is greatly restricted, appearing only as a means of constructing set-pieces: the ice storm in *Dersu Uzala*, the Battle of Nagashino in *Kagemusha*, the massacre of Hidetora's retainers in *Ran*. Once the organizing principle of Kurosawa's form, disjunctive cutting now makes only brief appearances that disturb the otherwise placid surface of the films. In *Kagemusha*, the spatial fields are quite stable, preserved through the freezing of characters into tableau-like arrangements, a restriction of camera movement, and the limiting of cutting to a functional, not a directive, role. Dislocations occur in the story, not in the images. Important events are withheld from view so that a series of ellipses punctuates the narrative. The crucial shooting of Shingen is never witnessed. It occurs off-screen. Only the report of the rifle is heard. Similarly, Katsuyori's burning and sacking of Takatenjin castle is elided, as is, with especial brilliance, the actual massacre of the Takeda clan by Nobunaga's musketeers. That event is relayed through the horrified reactions of the witnesses, and only its aftermath is visible in an epic montage of bloodied men and stunned horses struggling to rise.[39]

In this world of illusions, one can never be sure of one's senses, and this insecurity finds its structural equivalent in the narrative ellipses rather than in the actual imagery, whose epistemological status is never ambiguous. By contrast, the opening and closing sequences of a film like *Citizen Kane* establish a temporal and spatial structure that is highly suspect, incarnating the problems of personality, point of view, and observation at the formal level of the image. Similar issues animate *Kagemusha* but not this stylistic self-interrogation. The ellipses create doubt about the status of events, but by themselves they provide an insufficient grounding for the film's discourse about artifice and imagery. As in *Rashōmon*, these issues are described by the events of the narrative rather than by the structure of the imagery. Kurosawa's dramatic interests have again pushed him to the boundary defining his intuitive, nonintellectualized cinema. To go beyond this, the film would have had to admit a self-reflexive dimension foreign to Kurosawa's work (except in *Ikiru* and *Yōjimbō*). To fulfill these interests, Kurosawa needed to transgress this boundary but did not. The result is a work whose forms cannot adequately express its content. The material is full of potential that has not been realized.

The work does, however, announce a new direction for Kurosawa's cinema, which has been prepared by the renunciations of the modern world in *Dodeskaden* and *Dersu Uzala*. *Kagemusha* transforms the master–pupil relationship in a way that clearly reveals the corrosive pessimism that has sundered these more recent works from those that preceded. The scenarios in which an older and more experienced character ushered a novice into the secrets of responsible living offered a formal embodiment of the larger ethical project of Kurosawa's cinema, providing a model for the generation and transmission of reformist codes of

54. Charismatic clan leader or shadow warrior? The self as an epistemological and social problem in *Kagemusha*. (Museum of Modern Art/Film Stills Archive)

behavior. The task of social reform was placed in the hands of individuals like Kambei and Niide, as personality came to displace environment. But this ideological dominance of the psyche and of free choice over socio-economic circumstance was a willed achievement, sustained only by Kurosawa's own allegiance to the value of the self over the social order, and it could not and did not last. The late films trace a new arrangement of power between psyche and environment, a new configuration between self and society. Where once the individual could grasp events tightly and demand that they conform to his or her impulses, now the self is but the epiphenomenon of a ruthless and bloody temporal process, ground to dust beneath the weight and force of history. *Dersu Uzala* recorded the failure of the master–pupil relationship, and *Kagemusha* goes even further by revising the very terms of the model. Whereas before, the relationship created humane spaces in distinction to a corrupted social order—Sanada and Niide's clinic, the village defended by the seven samurai—now the relationship works to sustain outmoded institutions even as they are inexorably crumbling. The lie is substituted for enlightenment. As the thief sees Shingen's burial in Lake Suwa, he is overcome by a conviction that he owes the late lord a profound allegiance that, far from meaningless, has become even more compelling in death. The thief begs the generals to employ him. He walks into the lake toward the spot where Shingen is buried and says he wants to be of use to him. The relationship has become spectral and is generated from beyond the grave with the master maintaining a ghostly presence. Its end is death, not the renewal of commitment to the living that typified its outcome in earlier films. A clan general said earlier that they needed a double who would be willing to die for the clan, and this the thief proves himself capable of doing, making the supreme sacrifice as he charges across the field of corpses.

Inverting the ethical design of the earlier films, *Kagemusha* offers a discourse on the necessity of denying the self. This denial is qualitatively different from the recognition of the supremacy of group allegiances in *Seven Samurai*. That recognition did not preclude the development of outstanding individual heroes like Kambei or Kyūzo. Integrated within the group, they still remained men of superior skill and distinction. *Kagemusha's* vision, however, is radically different. Nobukado, who had played the double before, tells the thief that he often wanted to be free and truly himself but that now he thinks this was selfish. The shadow of a man can never desert that man, he says. He was his brother's shadow, and now that Shingen is gone, he feels he is nothing. As the thief leaves his mistresses, his shadow looms across the ceiling, making clear that the double is bound forever to the original lord. The master–pupil relationship has been emptied of meaning. It now exists to celebrate the extinction of self and to point its adherents toward oblivion, toward a heroic death in service to clan and domain. The clan accedes in its own suicide in order to maintain its house. The foundering of Kurosawa's cinematic project becomes translated into the narrative structure of the film.

Kagemusha thus becomes a meditation upon the inevitability of death and disintegration. That the film deals with well-known historical events gives the narrative a deterministic cast. We know that no matter what the Takeda clan does, it will be wiped out at Nagashino. All the images of the clan warriors on the march, filmed against the horizon or on empty plains so that the images take on an abstract appearance, describe a movement toward oblivion. The howling winds that surround Katsuyori and Nobukado as they watch their generals ride to doom displace these characters from the stage of earthly affairs. As the thief runs toward the muskets and is shot, Kurosawa cuts to an image of Katsuyori's empty seat, wind and dust swirling around it. In historical reality, Katsuyori survived Nagashino and was not killed in battle until later, but Kurosawa is working on a metaphorical scale. Nagashino was the bad karma of the Takeda clan and represented the crushing of its free will, the foreclosure of its ability to choose.

The attempt to sustain Shingen's life through the double reveals the duplicity of the ego, its status as illusion, as a phantom or a shadow warrior. "One might compare the ego to a cloud of fireflies in the night. What is it in reality? A gathering of fireflies. As a distinct being it does not exist. Yet one might mistake it for a distinct creature, fantastic and luminous, which lives, extends or contracts itself, and floats against the black sky. . . . The ego is merely an illusion."[40] The self can no longer ground the project of a committed cinema. Individuality is replaced by self-denial, but this is not the denial requisite for enlightenment. Rather it is preparatory for life as a shadow. This is why there is no possibility for the kind of heroism observed in the earlier films. Heroism, like the ego, is merely a false gestalt, like a cloud of fireflies against a black sky. The thief fails as a double, and the martial prowess of the Takeda clan is overwhelmed by Nobunaga's guns. In Kurosawa's films of the immediate postwar years, the cataclysm of World War II was seen as an interval, a terribly wrenching event, but one bounded by the hope for recovery and the possibility of a different future. By contrast, time is now cataclysmic in essence. The national unification that Nobunaga and Ieyasu would achieve lies outside the focus of the film, which describes instead a course of failure, death, and disintegration. Commitment to this world, whether of the artist who hopes to remake society and history or of the generals who hope to perpetuate their clan, yields only disappointment and disaster, a legacy of pain and failure. *Kagemusha* is able to soften this bitterness with a melancholy and regret that signify Kurosawa's residual attachment to his material. But in *Ran*, only bitterness remains, presaging the onset of a night without gods, heroes, or artists.

The intensification of this bitterness is a product of the culmination of many factors, among them the changes in the Japanese film industry that were discussed in Chapter 1. But we are now in a position to see this deepening pessimism as a result of the internal development of the films themselves in relation to their culture. In the ashes of war, when Kurosawa embarked upon the project of developing a socially engaged cinema that would have the autonomous self as its formal and ethical center, certain contradictions, aesthetic and cultural tensions, necessarily arose. The culture made little room for the kind of self that Kurosawa believed was necessary for national recovery. In the modern state, the corporations and governmental bureaucracies, the educational system, patterns of family life, all offered sets of hierarchies in which the individual was expected to find his or her place. Norms of behavior continued to be derived from important social groupings, and as the partnership between capital and the state deepened, the democratic opening to the autonomous and rational self promised by the reforms of the postwar years seemed to be increasingly in doubt. As noted earlier, the logic of Kurosawa's narratives and images seems to decry the "reverse course" of the Occupation-induced reforms. This is what films like *Record of a Living Being* and *The Bad Sleep Well* protest, the foreclosure of popular participation in decisions of state and economy by a small managerial elite. Yet this apparent foreclosure did not have to mean the end of topically engaged filmmaking. Even with the long political dominance of the Liberal Democratic Party and the exclusion from power of opposition parties, a lively tradition of public dissent continued. Citizen protest—focused on pollution, the U.S. military presence, the Vietnam war, and other issues—turned to "extra-institutional" channels. In their analysis of the prolonged, intense protests surrounding construction of the Narita airport, Apter and Sawa suggest that these channels are a function of the exclusion of oppositional political voices from the centers of power.

> [T]he lack of effective local government and the powerlessness of opposition parties in the face of the LDP's long dominance are two factors that help to explain why extra-institutional protest in Japan has been so bitter and violent for such a long time. . . . Even today, and especially in the ranks of the civil service, there is a distrust of opposition of all kinds.
> . . . Where party opposition is so ineffective, offended public opinion is more likely to resort to direct political means.[41]

In his work, Kurosawa could certainly have celebrated these forms of rebellion, these "direct political means." He could have tied his work to the tides of contemporary political activism unfolding around him, as did many of the New Wave directors. That might have renewed it. But the necessarily collective and social nature of political activity excluded the kind of contentious, critical individual in which Kurosawa believed. Kurosawa was an artist of crisis, and as the moment of historical rupture that gave form to his work subsided, as traditional social groupings reconstituted themselves in newly contemporary forms, the cultural ground on which his work had been built began to shift. It was like trying to rebuild after an earthquake only to find the structures you had erected skewed and deformed by yet another seismic shift. Kurosawa's works had always been marked by an extraordinary degree of internal, formal tension, but in the later 1950s this strife increased until their design split wide open and the only way of reconstituting an aesthetic strategy lay in a return to stasis, to visual rigidities and compositional hierarchies, to stiff formalized groupings that introjected within the frame the coordinates of an ultimately triumphant social arena. The substitution in the late films of the long take and static groupings of characters for montage and a fluid camera typified this final displacement of style and an attempt to realign form with culture that implicitly acknowledged the outcome of the earlier experiment.

It is in this context that *Ran* (1985) should be understood in all its fierce bitterness. Like *Kagemusha*, it, too, was an international coproduction, the result of foreign financing, this time from France, permitting Kurosawa to work yet once again. It is a film Kurosawa had long wanted to make but was not sure he ever would, given the reluctance of Japanese studios to finance so expensive a production. The film is loosely modeled on Shakespeare's *King Lear* and was inspired by Kurosawa's researches on medieval Japanese history. He became fascinated by a warlord reputed to have had three excellent sons and wondered what would have happened if the three had been, instead, bad. What happens is the destruction of their clan and domain, much as in *Kagemusha*. *Ran*, the title meaning "chaos," is a relentless chronicle of base lust for power, betrayal of the father by his sons, and pervasive wars and murders that destroy all the main characters.

The action and images of *Ran* bespeak the resurgent darkness of Kurosawa's contemporary outlook. "If you look at the situation of the world around you, I think it's impossible in this day and age to be optimistic," he has observed.[42] "All the technological progress of these last years has only taught human beings how to kill more of each other faster. It's very difficult for me to retain a sanguine outlook on life under such circumstances."[43] In *Ran* Kurosawa studies this technological, and social, amplification of violence. Once again, he uses the period of the Sengoku Jidai to construct a historical metaphor. The civil wars, the political instability, and the endemic patterns of ambition and betrayal that typified that period are used to offer a commentary on what Kurosawa now perceives as the timelessness of human impulses toward violence and self-destruction. "[S]ome of the essential scenes of this film are based on my wondering how God and Buddha, if they actually exist, perceive this human life, this mankind stuck in the same absurd behavior patterns."[44] Unlike in the earlier work, human choice is now foreclosed, behavior predestined, and the descent into chaos a certainty.

As the film opens, the aging warrior Ichimonji Hidetora (Tatsuya Nakadai), celebrating a successful boar hunt, cedes control of his clan and most important castle to his eldest son. As he tells the assembled guests, his life has been one of fighting, the lands he governs wrested with much bloodshed from other warlords. The endless rounds of war must be abolished, he proclaims. Thus, he will retain only the title of Great Lord and a thirty-warrior retinue while passing the reins of power to a younger generation in the hopes that it will do better. His eldest son, Tarō, will now be head of the clan, Jirō and Saburō, the other sons, retaining control of several secondary castles and committed to aiding Tarō in times of trouble. Hidetora intends for his kingdom to be united, with the three sons standing together, preserving the house of Ichimonji.

But none of this comes to pass. Instead of a new era of peace and cooperation among the regional warlords, Hidetora's retirement precipitates a ruthless quest for ultimate power between Tarō and Jirō. Saburō, the only son who truly cares for his father, is banished by Hidetora for minor offenses. The old man, however, soon learns his folly, as Tarō strips him of the clan's insignia and banishes him from the domain and as Jirō's forces murder Tarō and defeat his armies in battle. Jirō then assumes control of the clan, takes Lady Kaede, Tarō's wife, for his own, and dedicates himself to finding and killing Saburō. Lady Kaede, in turn, helps engineer the downfall of the Ichimonjis by manipulating Jirō into an ill-considered confrontation with other warlords, leading to his death and the fall of their castle. Lady Kaede, it transpires, is fulfilling her own plan of vengeance. Her family was killed by Hidetora following her marriage to Tarō, and now she seeks the utter destruction of Hidetora's clan. The internecine struggles and diabolical betrayals are multilayered, and the only certainty within the logic of the film is the expectation of suffering and bloodshed.

Sensing the chaos that Hidetora's retirement will unleash, Saburō tells his father that his plan of unification is folly and absurdity, pointing out that the three sons are all children of the age, schooled in violence and power-seeking. As such, how does he expect them to honor loyalty and live in peace? Hidetora interprets these words as an implicit threat against himself and the other sons and banishes Saburō. This speech, and the subsequent events it prophesies, illustrates the power that Kuro-

55. The vengeance of Kaede (Mieko Harada) precipitates the downfall of the Ichimonji clan in *Ran*. (Museum of Modern Art/Film Stills Archive)

sawa now accords to karma and the environment. The self can no longer transcend its age. Hidetora and his sons, no matter their intentions, are doomed to enact scenarios of betrayal, vengeance, and murder in their quest for power. You should know this better than anyone, Saburō tells his father, because you spilled oceans of blood.

Hidetora, indeed, is condemned throughout the film as a bloodthirsty monster and in this respect is quite different from Shakespeare's Lear, who at his worst was simply a fool, a man "more sinned against than sinning." Hidetora, by contrast, is continually haunted by his own acts of violence that rise up about him like phantoms. After a monumentally bloody battle in which Jirō attacks Tarō's forces and, in the process, destroys Hidetora's retainers, the old man flees the carnage, rushing out into a storm, much as Lear had done. On the grassy plain, he hallucinates a ghostly army of his victims, rising up to surround and condemn him. His own acts, like bad karma, return to destroy him in the form of Lady Kaede, whose machinations are largely responsible for the fall of the Ichimonjis. Moreover, Jirō's first wife, Sue, is also a victim of Hidetora. He killed her family and burned her castle in a previous campaign and, rather than putting her brother to the sword, gouged out his eyes. Sue gives her brother an image of Amida Buddha to soothe his suffering, and he tries to pray but with no effect. Tsurumaru, in some ways, represents the most explicit condemnation of Hidetora's own behavior because of the alteration of the Shakespearean source material on which his character is based. In Shakespeare's play, it was Lear's enemies who put out the eyes of Gloucester, Lear's friend, but Kurosawa has Hidetora, the Lear figure, commit the atrocity. Hidetora confronts this horror when, seeking shelter from the storm, he finds refuge in the dwelling of a blind man, who turns out to be Tsurumaru. Thrown into a frenzy by Tsurumaru's quiet suffering, Hidetora stumbles back out into the storm.

Rather than the spectacle of undeserved suffering that Shakespeare offered, Kurosawa presents, as in *Throne of Blood*, a world of bleak landscapes and repetitive violence, from which no one escapes condemnation. The characters are villains all, or else are victims, like Sue and Saburō, both of whom are killed by Jirō's henchmen. Kurosawa's view of the human character is at its bleakest and most unsparing, and history has given way to a perception of life as a wheel of endless suffering, ever turning, ever repeating. Throughout the film, characters continually remark about being in hell. A dying warrior, stuck through with arrows like Washizu, announcing Jirō's betrayal to Hidetora, proclaims that he is truly in hell. Hidetora, wandering the plains a madman, sees Sue and Tsurumaru atop the ruins of a castle he had burned and hallucinates that he is in hell. At the end, Hidetora's fool, crying over his and Saburō's lifeless bodies, rages to the gods about their pitilessness in crushing human beings like ants.

The constant reference to hell is explicitly visualized in the film's finest sequence, a montage of overpowering intensity that depicts the massacre of Tarō's and Hidetora's forces by Jirō's samurai. Much of the sequence is silent, with only a dirge-like musical accompaniment intensifying images of incredible violence. As the armies mass and rush to battle, dispassionate long shots offer images of the sun blotted out by rolling dark clouds, a samurai holding his severed arm and laughing demonically, another reeling with an arrow through his eye, masses of muskets sparking like fireflies, rivers of blood gushing down the castle walls, samurai riddled with arrows like porcupines, and quivers of flames dancing over mountains of corpses. The images accumulate in intensity, piling horror upon horror, and Kurosawa structures them in terms of a flow of movement and compositional energy as in the old Kamakura-era narrative scrolls.[45] But this is to be a scroll of hell. As Kurosawa has described it in his screenplay:

Hidetora, his strength drained from his body, slips and tumbles down the stairs like a dead man falling into Hell.

A terrible scroll of Hell is shown depicting the fall of the castle. There are no real sounds as the scroll unfolds like a daytime nightmare. It is a scene of human evildoing, the way of the demonic Ashura, as seen by a Buddha in tears.

The music superimposed on these pictures is, like the Buddha's heart, measured in beats of profound anguish, the chanting of a melody full of sorrow that begins like sobbing and rises gradually as it is repeated, like karmic cycles, then finally sounds like the wailing of countless Buddhas.[46]

This powerful sequence is among the finest that Kurosawa has created. The images have a ferocity, a dynamic rhythm, and a compositional richness that nothing else in the film attains. Ironically, Kurosawa musters his greatest energy for the bleakest and most unsparing section of the film. His cinematic gifts are fully engaged only here, in offering an expression of pure despair. Kurosawa has found hell to be both the inevitable outcome of human behavior and the appropriate visualization of his own bitterness and disappointment. This sequence is the visual centerpiece of the film, as well as being the pivot around which the narrative turns. In the world that *Ran* conjures, as well as in the film's own formal structure, the vision of hell is a logical necessity. In a world condemned, where action is destruction, where efforts of choice and will produce only pain and suffering, hell offers the energies of damnation. Motion is no longer the signifier of enlightenment. It now yields extinction.

The reductive visions of *Ran* offer a negative inversion of the terms by which the early films sought to grasp and change the world. Free choice, once the measure of heroism and the means of freeing onself from the demands of the environment, has become severely restricted and, when exercised, perverted. After Jirō's army destroys Tarō's forces and Hidetora's retainers, the castle is torched. Hidetora goes insane and wanders past the ranks of Jirō's samurai, who silently watch this spectral figure drift by. Jirō weakens in a moment of filial regard and starts toward his father, but one of his generals restrains him, reminding him that he chose this path toward absolute rulership and must not falter. Surrounded by flame and bodies, Jirō lets his father go. His choice has committed him to a path of evil, from which he is not permitted to diverge.

In a final metamorphosis, human character now admits a newly essential element, which has previously been attributed to the effects of a bad environment. Yusa, the kidnapper in *High and Low*, Matsunaga, all were regarded as having been warped, their highest impulses deflected, by social dislocations, economic collapse, or diseased, sump-ridden surroundings. Deliverance lay in making the right choices, as Murakami did, in possessing the strength of self necessary to triumph over blighted surroundings. As we have seen, however, Kurosawa's analysis lacked an energizing category other than the self, which, left in isolation by this lack, finally collapsed. A resurgent pessimism in the late works rushed in to fill the void and reconstituted human character as a structure of evil and life as a transient and predestined dance of darkness. Jirō now can embark only on a life of predation, as had Hidetora before him, letting blood run like a river and piling corpses to the sky, as Washizu in *Throne of Blood* had been advised to do. Nevertheless, the chorus in *Throne of Blood* spoke the film's moral perspective and created a frame around the bloody deeds of the characters. In *Ran*, this dialectic is absent. The frame is burst. Hell is everywhere.

Evil is now the category by which to understand human behavior. In the space of a vanished social and cultural analysis, metaphysics has appeared. What was once a materialist cinema and program of reform has become instead a transcendental lament. This is why the analysis of space, achieved through a montage aesthetic, and the cultural investigation that underlay it, became transformed into a strategy of withdrawal via the long take and the long shot. Cultural and historical spaces had become hostile to Kurosawa's investigation, and the camera withdrew. In its absence, montage, and the spatial analysis it proposed, became demonic and suited to images of violence and death, as in the climax of *Kagemusha* and the centerpiece of *Ran*. As if in acknowledgment of its materialist, Eisensteinian roots, montage as a formal structure proved incompatible with Kurosawa's growing metaphysical interests. The problems to be addressed, Kurosawa now believes, are spiritual ones. The once-compelling issues of political and social reform have been revealed as illusory, like the gestalt producing a cloud of fireflies on a moonlit night. The man whose films once proclaimed that willpower could cure all human ailments now professes that the world is impervious to reform and the artist shackled in his or her ability to compel such change. "I believe that the world would not change even if I made a direct statement: do this and do that. Moreover, the world will not change unless we steadily change human nature itself and our very way of thinking. We have to exorcise the essential evil in human nature, rather than presenting concrete solutions to problems or directly depicting social problems."⁴⁷ Kurosawa adds that he did not think in these terms when he was young and that is why he could make such films then. "I have realized, however, that it does not work. The world would not change."⁴⁸

The contrast with the earlier conception of the hero could not be more striking. Yet what appears as so sharp an antinomy has, in fact, been continually unfolding, a progression through contradiction, both within the forms and in their relation to an evolving culture. The end of *Ran* is cheerless indeed. In the final shots, the bodies of Hidetora and Saburo are being carried across a twilit plain, with a ruined castle and a setting sun in the background. Standing on the wall of this castle, etched against the horizon, Tsurumaru advances toward the edge of the precipice, feeling his way with a cane. Suddenly, he loses his balance and drops the image of Buddha he has faithfully carried. Kurosawa then cuts to an extreme long shot to offer the final image: a blind man at the edge of a precipice, bereft of his god, alone in a darkening world.

In its power and bleakness, its discourse on isolation and defeat, this last image becomes a metaphor for the predicament of Kurosawa's cinema in this transitional period. An enormous distance separates *Sanshirō Sugata* and *Ran*—one announces with exuberance an explosive cinematic talent on the verge of finding a sustaining social vision, the other reveals the exhaustion and repudiation of that vision. In the final period of his filmmaking, explored in the next chapter, Kurosawa moved away from the bitterness that was manifest in *Ran*. But he could not return to the heroic tradition and the social commitment that underlay it. His own changing outlook, and a changing Japan, had taken his work far from the spirit of Sanada, Niide, Murakami, and the other heroes.

But, though Kurosawa would leave this tradition behind, it remains the most powerful voice of his cinema. His best work speaks from this tradition, and indeed the heroes continue to live in the images he left with us. We may still take a stand with Kambei in the cold rain on the morning of that final battle or heed Niide's call never to look away. Kurosawa's initial commitment to use film to visualize the myriad intersections of self, culture, and history, to document through visual form the contradictions inherent within postwar national reform and recovery, left a profoundly articulate body of work. The vicissitudes that beset that work between *Sanshirō Sugata* and *Ran* illuminate the multiple determinants operating upon the films, primarily the logic inhering within Kurosawa's chosen forms and the ways he deployed them, and the relationship of those forms with the cultural history they attempted to visualize.

After constructing an epic cinema of heroic ambition, Kurosawa participated in its revision and dismantling during the transitional years of 1970–1985. Had he ceased filmmaking at the end of this period, these works would have remained the antithesis of his heroic films. But he continued working, and, as he had done with the heroic films, so he did with the melancholy and bitterness of the transitional years—he moved beyond these and left them behind. Entering the last phase of his life, Kurosawa found a new kind of film to make and a new use for cinema. Doing so, he redefined his work and attempted to achieve closure on his filmmaking and on the life he had lived through cinema.

8 The Final Period

"Now the moon of

my life sinks in

the sky and is

close to the edge

of the mountain."

—Kamo no

Chōmei[1]

In a burst of productivity during the last decade of his life, Kurosawa embarked upon the final period in his filmmaking, completing three films that were released in a four-year period. In a move that is virtually unprecedented in world cinema, Kurosawa redefined his filmmaking to encompass an extended late period style. Late periods are common phenomena in other arts, such as music and literature, but the peculiar conditions surrounding creativity in cinema tend to prevent its artists from having late periods.

The most important of these conditions is the sheer difficulty of making films. American director Sydney Pollack (*Out of Africa* [1985]) called filmmaking "the most enormously grueling physical exercise you can go through, because there is so much emotional strain."[2] Generating much of this stress are the economic constraints under which filmmakers must operate. Filmmaking is a business, and directors get to make movies only when they can secure funding, as Kurosawa often could not. The efforts to secure funding can be lengthy and arduous and may demand tremendous work just to get a production started. Once a production is underway, the work is intensely physical and requires great mental concentration. During postproduction the battles and the struggles against compromising the initial vision continue. When a film is released, the industry's marketing side takes over, and the filmmaker watches from the sidelines, hoping that the picture finds an audience. It is no wonder that Kurosawa once likened being a director to being a general waging war. Filmmaking is a process of continuous struggle, at best a difficult and anxiety-laden enterprise. As a result, talent burns out very quickly, and few filmmakers sustain careers long enough to have a late period.

Kurosawa continued working into his eighties. In fact, all of the films that I will examine in this chapter were made after he turned eighty. Although Jean Renoir, Luis Bunuel, John Ford, and Alfred Hitchcock all sustained lengthy careers, they made their last films when in their seventies, and none of these directors established the kind of fully elaborated late period that Kurosawa developed. Thus, even in this rarefied company, Kurosawa stands out. His case is special, and it becomes more so when one considers that Kurosawa did not just sustain a career but made his films into a record of an artist who grew old with and through cinema. As he did, his relationship to the medium, as to life, altered significantly. The works from *Sanshiro Sugata* (1943) to *One Wonderful Sunday* (1947) show Kurosawa's developing mastery of film style. The films from *Drunken Angel* (1948) to *Red Beard* (1965) belong to an age of heroism during which the ambitious use of cinema reflected the tasks of post-war reconstruction. Those from *Dodeskaden* (1970) to *Ran* (1985) define a period of melancholy and bitterness and a questioning of youthful idealism. By contrast, the final films, beginning with *Dreams* (1990), manifest a more contemplative outlook, in the twilight of life, as death approaches and recasts the shape and significance of one's days.

Thus, the last films look simultaneously backward and forward. They anticipate what is yet to come, but they do so on the basis of what has already transpired. In this regard, they are bi-temporal in theme and style. They manifest new attitudes toward life and the world and new audio-visual designs, while incorporating traces of the older Kurosawa style. This, too, is a phenomenon of late periods—the incorporation of familiar stylistic devices in a new context in which the earlier traces assume a self-reflexive form. The artist, effectively, quotes from him/herself as if to say "this I once did, this once was my signature." Examining issues of style change, the eminent musicologist Leonard Meyer[3] emphasized the way in which later styles use the past in order to make it a part of the present: "[O]nce an earlier idiom becomes a viable means of creating in the present, its 'pastness' tends to become irrelevant—merely chronological. Its implications are no longer 'closed out'; and, as the past becomes relevant and consequential, its 'pastness' dissolves. It is literally then a part of the present."[4]

Dreams (1990), *Rhapsody in August* (1991), and *Madadayo* (1993) incorporate readily familiar pieces of the earlier Kurosawa iconography in a way that integrates these later works with what has come before, even as they extend the range and scope of Kurosawa's filmmaking. In this context, Meyer's remarks about the integration of earlier design elements into later styles can work as a description of the designs in Kurosawa's last films: "These elements are juxtaposed, integrated, and combined both with one another and with newly invented material in such a way that past and present, transcending surface disparities and manifest eclecticism, inform and illuminate one another, creating a new conceptual order—a new work of art."[5] Kurosawa, then, redefined his cinema by striking out in a fresh and hitherto unexplored direction. He did not retread the old films, revisit or recreate them, as he would have done had his artistry been exhausted. Instead, he redefined and reinvented his work. In this regard, as *Dodeskaden* seems so stylistically bewildering in relation to prior films, so *Dreams* seems an amazing disjunction with the films of the transitional years. Yet what seems disjunctive is, in fact, connective. Kurosawa created anew in his final works but did so by referencing the past so as to define a final phase of his filmmaking, the existence of which changes the past by recasting and reordering the career. Where, then, did he go in his last films, and how did he incorporate the earlier formal signatures into these works?

As I suggested in previous chapters, *Red Beard* summarized and completed the kind of cinema Kurosawa had been practicing since his first picture in 1943. Nearly thirty years passed between *Red Beard* and *Madadayo*, a longer span of time than the roughly two decades between *Sanshirō Sugata* and *Red Beard*. Thus, though he made fewer films in the latter portion of his career, that interval comprised a larger part of Kurosawa's life and consequently witnessed his aging to a more considerable extent. As he aged, so did his characters: Dersu, Hidetora, the old man in the concluding episode of *Dreams*, the grandmother Kane in *Rhapsody in August*, and the elderly professor in *Madadayo*. These characters have already grown old when we meet them, and they grapple with the loss of skill, the diminution of authority, and the self-examination prompted by the approach of life's end. The contemplation of these issues becomes extremely pronounced in *Rhapsody* and *Madadayo*, and as Kurosawa's predilection for aged characters advanced with his years, his identification with them intensified with each film. As a result, Kurosawa's later films function more as psychobiography than as traditional narrative filmmaking and, as we will see, they provide a fascinating portrait of the artist as an old man, facing the end of life, and aware that his filmmaking has entered its final phase.

In this phase, he no longer aimed to use his art, as he once did, to compel social change. That objective ended with the close of his heroic mode. But as a filmmaker and citizen, Kurosawa remained concerned

56. Kurosawa directs his childhood surrogate in *Dreams*. Working in his eighties, Kurosawa took his filmmaking into new and hitherto unexplored territory. (Museum of Modern Art/Film Stills Archive)

about the state of the world. Several episodes in *Dreams*, for example, deal with themes of pollution, threats to humans and the environment posed by nuclear energy, and with the undying ghosts of war. Kurosawa presents these issues in a declamatory style.[6] He proclaims them rather than dramatizing them, and thus he observes and announces instead of engaging the viewer emotionally in a manner that could compel change. He points to these issues because they trouble him, but his mode of address indicates his conviction that little will change. There are no characters meant here to serve as role models for the audience and through whose anguished choices Kurosawa aims to dramatize the terms of personal and social transformations, as he once did. Kurosawa's declamatory mode of address is connected with other phenomena of his late authorial voice, and I will consider this mode and these phenomena more fully in a moment. Chief among them is the problem of Kurosawa's intended meanings. As we shall see, Kurosawa's manner of working in his last films was often at odds with what he claimed he wanted to say in these pictures.

Instead of richly modulated narratives, the last films are relatively unmediated registers of his personal and philosophical outlook in the twilight of his life. In respect to his career after *Red Beard*, the films fall into two distinctly different categories. *Dodeskaden, Dersu Uzala, Kagemusha,* and *Ran* are the transitional works that take Kurosawa and his audience from the heroic phase to the psychobiography of *Dreams, Rhapsody,* and *Madadayo.* In these transitional films, Kurosawa still practices a narrative mode of filmmaking, in contrast to the episodic and essayistic mode he employed in the last films. In the films of this transitional period, he expresses melancholy for the loss of premodern Japan and rage and bitterness over the human appetites for violence and self-destruction. The bleakness of this philosophical outlook and the intensity of feeling with which Kurosawa conveys it—particularly in the scenes detailing the massacre of the Takeda clan in *Kagemusha* and Hidetora's retainers in *Ran*—differentiate these works from the tranquility of the three that follow. Japanese critic Tadao Satō, a long-time commentator on Kurosawa's work, has noted these differences and the change in Kurosawa to which they point. Of *Kagemusha* and *Ran,* Satō writes, "There is a deep-rooted despair which transcends the special nature of that age [i.e., the Sengoku period]. The very darkness of these films forces us to wonder whether these dreams are not foretelling the destruction of humanity itself."[7] In contrast, for Satō the last works have a "freshness and innocence" that indicate Kurosawa "has finally reached a state of mind in which he can depict peacefulness, love, [and] the pure heart of children."[8] In Linda Ehrlich's wonderful phrase, the last films are about "the extremes of innocence," namely, childhood and old age.[9]

Kurosawa, as an artist, moved beyond the melancholy and despair of the films of 1970–1985. The films of those years define a largely anti-heroic period, generally inclined toward a repudiation of the narrative design and moral outlook of his previous work. By contrast, the final three films are not anti-heroic. They are merely and quietly nonheroic, as Kurosawa explores areas of life that are smaller, more private, and more delicate than his earlier aesthetic and philosophical outlook permitted. This shift of focus is multifaceted, with consequences for theme and formal design.

Kurosawa continued to employ recognizable stylistic hallmarks, although in many cases this usage constitutes the kind of self-reflexive quotation and borrowing that Leonard Meyer described as an attribute of late period style. Kurosawa maintained his preference for long focal

length lenses that give the composition of his films such uniquely stylized attributes, chiefly the reduction of spatial depth. The magnification of distant objects and the consequent compression of foreground
and background spaces causes the piling up of objects in these areas.
The opening shot of *Dreams*, for example, is a telephoto long shot of a
Taishō-era house with a gate. A boy runs toward the foreground of the
composition, but the optical distortion created by the lens so flattens
the space of the shot that he seems to remain very close to the house. In
the next moment, though, Kurosawa uses movement to provide a depth
cue that offsets the effects of the telephoto lens. The boy's mother enters the frame and moves about in the area between the child and the
house. Her movements define a mid-ground area of the composition
which, in turn, clarifies the true distance between the boy and the
house. This mid-ground area did not have a perceptual presence in the
shot prior to her entrance because of the way the telephoto lens had
flattened the compositional space. Her appearance dramatically
realigns the spatial relationships of the composition and abruptly
changes the viewer's perceptual organization of the scene. Kurosawa's
telephoto lenses treat space as a plane rather than a volume. In some
shots and scenes—notably "The Peach Orchard" episode of *Dreams*—
Kurosawa allows the space to remain as a plane; in others, like the
opening shot of *Dreams*, he uses movement or editing to reconfigure it
in a more three-dimensional way.

Near the beginning of *Madadayo*, Kurosawa introduces Tokyo in
1943 with an establishing shot of a street filmed in extreme telephoto
perspective. The camera frames the street so that the roadway, on a
slope, crests in the lower third of the frame. So compressed is the space
of the shot that the lines of the street appear to run vertically in the
frame rather than as a recession into distant space. The telephoto lens
has so distorted the composition that normal cues of depth perspective
are reconfigured as measures of verticality. Height within the frame
conveys the measure of distance. In the next moment, Kurosawa cuts to
another long shot of the street, viewed from the same angle, but with a
normal lens and a drastically different rendition of space. The normal
lens does not magnify distant objects and thus does not compress and
flatten perspective. The viewer is wrenched out of the peculiar space of
the previous shot and forced to reassess the positioning of the roadway,
its occupants, and the surrounding buildings, all of which appear to be
much smaller and further off than they had seemed to be in the telephoto composition. The optical relationship of these shots is clearly

dialectical, based on a conflict between what Eisenstein would term matter and its representation by the differing optical characteristics of chosen lenses.

This is one of Kurosawa's most recognizable signatures as a filmmaker—his fondness for using movement, editing, and mise-en-scène to resolve the spatial ambiguities caused by telephoto lenses and to force viewers to reassess their cognitive organization of the compositions. But this formal design no longer correlates with the dramatic and narrative context in which it used to appear. In his earlier work, the radical realignments of perspective were formal translations of Kurosawa's belief in the value of sudden shocks as a path to enlightenment. Kurosawa's heroes matured by undergoing a series of moral and physical traumas in their efforts to regenerate self and society, and in his autobiography he correlated this outlook with his own personal history and maturation. The perceptual realignments, occasioned by his disjunctive editing and use of mise-en-scène elements in opposition to telephoto distortion, were stylistic registers of Kurosawa's broader social project, embodying at the level of visual form the engaged cinema he was constructing.

But the contrasts in Kurosawa's mise-en-scène between telephoto distortion and other compositional elements persist in the last films as an isolated formal attribute, no longer related to a program of cinema with ambitions for self and nation. The stylistic signature lingers, though the engaged stance of the filmmaker has abated. The films no longer study a rough road to enlightenment. Kane, the old woman in *Rhapsody in August*, is a character already formed and completed and faces no significant moral challenges or choices. The same is true for the elderly Professor in *Madadayo*. The "I" character, Kurosawa's surrogate self who appears throughout the episodes of *Dreams*, is a passive observer of the strange things that transpire around him. He does not initiate any activity, nor does he change as a result of what he sees and experiences. Whereas, in his younger days, Kurosawa was committed as a filmmaker to the unformed protagonists whose trials and traumas taught them the lessons of responsible living, his later films deal with individuals whose lives are largely completed.

In addition to the telephoto lens and the peculiar compositional uses to which he put it, Kurosawa continued in his last films to use another signature element—multiple axial cuts. In this case, though, the device survived in an even more vestigial form than the mise-en-scène dialectics. The axial cuts have always been among the most striking and unique of Kurosawa's signatures. Beginning with his first film, Kurosawa loved to intercut two or three shots, whose compositions were exactly aligned with the axis of view established in the initial camera position. Each succeeding shot, though, brought the viewer closer to a significant character or object. The camera's angle of view remained the same across the shots, but the cutting propeled the viewer into the scene in a highly dramatic way. The optical changes from shot to shot felt like jump cuts, though they were not. In *Sanshirō Sugata* (1943), when Sanshirō kills his opponent in a judo match, Kurosawa shows the reaction of the dead man's daughter in a rhythmical series of three axial compositions. She first appears in long shot as part of a crowd, then in medium close-up, and finally in extreme close-up, the montage producing a series of perceptual jolts as the image is dramatically, repeatedly enlarged. With similar effect, axial cutting pushes the viewer closer to the burning millhouse in *Seven Samurai* after the initial bandit attack, and to the broken lock on the casket Sanjurō will use to elude his captors in *Yōjimbō*.

The first edit in *Dreams* is an axial cut. Kurosawa moves from the long shot of the boy standing outside his house to a medium shot using matched axial perspectives. But the cutting here does not occur within a narrative crisis point or other dramatically significant moment. Thus, the editing does not carry the explosive qualities of the device as used in *Sanshirō Sugata* or *Seven Samurai*. A similarly vestigial usage occurs in *Rhapsody in August*. Kurosawa employs the familiar cuts during the scene in which the grandchildren find Kane sitting quietly with an elderly neighbor who, like Kane, lost her husband in the Nagasaki bombing. Kurosawa here presents a fully elaborated, three-shot axial pattern that begins at a distance and then brings the viewer in close to the action. In the first shot of the series, the grandchildren peer through a window at Kane and her friend. Next come medium shot and medium close-up framings of the women, along the camera's axis of view. The cutting is rhythmical and carries the viewer toward Kane and her friend, but the axial design, as in *Dreams*, persists here in a dramatic context that does not seem to warrant or motivate the device. The cutting does not serve to concentrate visual attention upon a dramatic or emotionally salient element of the narrative, as it did to such striking effect in *Sanshirō Sugata*, *Seven Samurai* and *Yōjimbō*. As defined in the film, Kane's friend remains an anonymous and insignificant character. She performs no function in the narrative (indeed, the narrative itself is minimal and diffuse) and, except for her tie to Kane, she is completely undefined.[10]

Why, then, does Kurosawa use axial cutting, once one of his most exciting narrational tools, to bring the viewer into closer proximity with this scene? He does so as a means of acknowledging the heritage of his filmmaking style, its foundational designs and, by acknowledging that heritage, of bringing the past into the present and making it live again. In these passages, Kurosawa quotes his own style, not because he wants to recreate it or do it in any fully elaborated sense, but as a way of remembering and acknowledging. Because he has already in earlier films fully elaborated these motifs, he need not do so now. A brief citation can suffice to evoke the previous, more elaborated usage. The fragment embodies the whole from which it has been derived. In this way, the axial cuts, and other vestigial elements of style, point beyond these last films to the larger body of work and to the lifetime of creativity incarnated in that work. Doing so, they open a place for these later films within that corpus of work. Thus, these devices are not meant to perform the dramatic or narrative functions they once did. Instead, they are now about themselves. They assume an iconographic status as shared symbols passed by the filmmaker to his audience, symbols that recall the history of this relationship and of the films that have brought it into being.

As Kurosawa moved to a more contemplative stance in his last films, his method of filming continued the shift away from disjunctive editing so pronounced in his post-*Red Beard* films. At the end of his career, he filmed scenes in a few extended takes and covered the action with three cameras, two at right angles to one another and a third in an axial position. Long shot, medium shot, and close-up framings were a function not of camera position but of the lenses employed. As a result, his last films are visually quite placid and lack the pyrotechnics of editing or camera moves that his earlier work possessed. Moreover, his characters forsook activity for stillness and contemplation. They do not act but, instead, sit and talk. The decline of physical activity in favor of contemplation and conversation in the final films no doubt mirrored Kurosawa's life experiences at an advanced age and the psychological changes that accompanied them. In his mid-sixties, he was trekking with his cameras through Siberian forests filming *Dersu Uzala*, and ten years later in *Ran* he was staging epic battles. But this could not persist, even with his extraordinary level of energy. Thus, his last characters, in *Dreams*, *Rhapsody* and *Madadayo*, enjoy the privilege bequeathed by their long years—sitting and talking. Thus, to examine these films is to behold works of inwardness and quietude, qualities not so prevalent in the earlier and more extroverted films.

Kurosawa's tremendous international influence made possible the inauguration of his final creative period. The major studios in Japan had drastically cut back on the funding and production of films, with devastating impact upon the last decades of Kurosawa's career. In 1990, for example, the majors produced only fifty-eight films.[11] Kurosawa had not made a film totally financed by a major Japanese studio since 1965. *Dodeskaden* was an independent production; *Dersu Uzala* was financed and filmed in Russia; *Kagemusha* was cofinanced by Twentieth Century Fox; and *Ran* was partly financed by French producer Serge Silberman. In keeping with this pattern, overseas funding again proved essential for the continuation of Kurosawa's career. Three powerful American directors—Steven Spielberg, George Lucas, and Francis Coppola—fans of his work, interceded for him with the Hollywood industry and helped secure funding from Warner Bros. for *Dreams*. The film carries the credit, "A Steven Spielberg Presentation," and it features special effects work by Lucasfilm's Industrial Light and Magic. In providing this support, the American cinema acknowledged the enormous debt it owed Kurosawa, a debt incurred through the influence of his pictures upon its filmmakers and genres.

In some ways *Dreams* was a natural project for Kurosawa, even as it signaled a new direction for his filmmaking. Kurosawa had long been fascinated by the role that fantasy and hallucination play in human life, especially in helping to ease the pain in lives torn by hopelessness, despair, and poverty. In *One Wonderful Sunday* (1947), for example, the despair of the young couple wandering amid the rubble of post-war Japan is alleviated by their dreams of opening a coffee shop of their own. At the end of the film, Kurosawa makes their fantasies concrete. To amuse his depressed girlfriend, the young man pretends to conduct the first movement of Schubert's Unfinished Symphony. As he does so, Kurosawa gives the imaginary symphony tangible form by putting its music on the soundtrack. In *Scandal* (1950), the tubercular daughter of the corrupt lawyer Hiruta (Takashi Shimura) escapes from her illness into a dreamworld, where she imagines herself healthy. Kurosawa's most elaborate exploration of these issues occurred in *The Lower Depths* (1957) and *Dodeskaden*, which portray the bleak lives of slum dwellers living as social outcasts. The characters escape into luxuriant mental worlds that Kurosawa views ambivalently: they provide comfort but also accompany suicide and madness.

In these earlier works, Kurosawa shares Dostoevsky's sensitivity to the ambiguous gifts of the dream world, springing as they do from the ruminations of the isolated consciousness. On the one hand, dreams might produce exquisite pleasures and perceptions and provide access to a wellspring of creativity that eludes ordinary consciousness. On the other hand, the dreamer might come to prefer the seductive appeal of fantasies to the bland or unpleasant facts of daily existence. Dostoevsky wrote of the "indescribable pleasures" afforded by dreams such that "the moments of sobering are horrible."[12] Of the dreamer, he said, "Imperceptibly the talent for real life begins to be deadened within him."[13] Dostoevsky recognized the charms of the dream world as well as its relationship to an onerous reality, its function as an escape from the unbearable. Kurosawa shared Dostoevsky's perception of this duality. During the period of his heroic films, however, Kurosawa adopted the spartan injunction of facing reality rather than pursuing the pleasures to be found in an escape from it. He never permitted his heroes, those characters intended to be role models for the post-war Japanese audience, to indulge in the comforts of fantasy. Instead, Kurosawa's prescription for post-war Japan was a sober and clear-eyed confrontation with social ills.

Kurosawa's ambivalence about the dream world was most apparent in his artistic credo of bravely confronting unpleasant truths, which became a central political and artistic metaphor in his earlier films. As I suggested in Chapter 3, this credo derived from the example set by his brother Heigo. When he and Akira viewed the devastation of the Great Kanto Earthquake in 1923, Heigo forbade him to look away from the horror. In Akira's youth, Heigo assumed the role of a spiritual guide and teacher, and Kurosawa was deeply impressed by his brother's unconventional manner of living, one that transgressed the boundaries of normal social life. Heigo was a key influence on all of the Kurosawa heroes who do the same.

Kurosawa internalized Heigo's commandment and, as I have discussed in previous chapters, it emerged in the films as an important center of visual and narrative meaning. The injunction against averting one's eyes was the essential behavioral code for Kurosawa's heroes, as well as his general prescription for post-war Japan: confront social illness and oppression and, with fortitude, overcome it. In this regard, Kurosawa's use of narrative was most significant, an inseparable part of his reformist filmmaking. The linear narratives of his films symbolized the terms of Kurosawa's social commitment, setting his heroes upon spiritual and personal journeys that led to confrontations with social ills such as crime, poverty, disease, class injustice, corporate corruption, and state nuclear terror. The dream world was allocated as a privilege for the peripheral characters, not the heroes, as a balm for those for whom the heroic quest was inaccessible. Foreclosed from following the heroic example, the peripheral characters were permitted, instead, to escape into hallucinatory reverie.

The dreamworld, then, stood in tension with the heroic narratives of Kurosawa's finest work and with the general social commitment that informed his filmmaking until 1965. By contrast, in *Dreams* Kurosawa shifted in his regard for the dreamworld so as to favor the other term of its dual nature, its connection with creativity and a life-force. Dreams, he had now come to believe, are wellsprings to the genius that lies within the brain and the heart of all human beings. A dream, Kurosawa said in connection with this film, "is the fruit of pure and earnest human desire. I believe that a dream is an event created in the uninhibited brain of a sleeping person, emanating from an earnest desire which is hidden in the bottom of his heart while awake. . . . A human is a genius while dreaming."[14] Thus, in this shift of perspective, *Dreams* revised and recast the terms of Kurosawa's heroic mode. It reallocated virtue from the struggle with material circumstance to the mysteries of inner consciousness.

To explore these mysteries, Kurosawa avoided narrative almost entirely, save for its suggestion via a recurring character who appears in the dream episodes. This character is Kurosawa's surrogate, who embodies the director's presence inside the various dreams. (The term "dreams" must be used loosely. Few of them have the bizarre time-space properties of true dreams. They are too literal for that, each episode fixed in a stable locale and period.) The film is a collection of eight vignettes that are loosely ordered according to the issues they examine and that correspond to dreams Kurosawa claims to have had on a continuing basis. The movie, though, has no structural features that determine this ordering, and the vignettes could be reshuffled into a different order. Thus, the picture does not have the holistic design possessed by Kurosawa's narrative works. It does not have the strengths which narrative proffers, chiefly the ability to achieve a structural unity through variety and to show change in a way that makes possible the development of a moral perspective. Instead, Kurosawa worked here in a serial fashion, moving from dream to dream and starting over again with each new episode. There are recurring issues in the film, but no narrative to tie them together. As a result, the searching thematic analyses performed throughout this book on Kurosawa's other films are more difficult to conduct with *Dreams*. A small-scale film, it is an anthology of essays rather than a unified and integrated work.

While it was very unusual for him to move in a nonnarrative direction (only *Dodeskaden*, of his earlier films, comes closest to a nonnarrative design), Kurosawa, significantly, did not abandon the social commentary that he once used narrative to develop. As noted earlier, several episodes address the topics of environmental pollution and the terrors of the nuclear age. His interest, though, in looking outward at the world was conjoined with a countervailing emphasis that would, over the course of these three films, come to outweigh it. This attention was the inward-looking and contemplative effort to come to terms with mortality. Kurosawa used *Dreams* as a means to explore various attitudes toward death and dying. More than anything else, this interest defines the singular project of his last period. In the episodes of the film that address this issue, one finds a catalog of attitudes from Kurosawa's earlier work as well as a strikingly new outlook, one more serene and less anxious. Symptomatic of this is the new use to which Kurosawa put the dream mode. For Kurosawa, dreams were not just fonts of creativity, roadmaps to an alternate consciousness. They were also a portal to those regions where life shades over into death and makes this transition in a variety of ways, enabling the dreamer, and the filmmaker, to study and to master the experience of life nearing its end.

The first dream, "Sunshine through the Rain," recasts the quest narratives of Kurosawa's earlier films in terms that are less socially inflected and more poetic, mystical, and suggestive. The episode also introduces the psychobiographical elements that many subsequent episodes will include, as well as Kurosawa's next two films. The episode does not originate from a dream but rather from a story that Kurosawa's mother used to tell him about fox weddings that occur in dense forests during rainstorms while the sun is out. Kurosawa remarked, "I really believed that there were these fox weddings in that kind of weather. My mother told me that if I ever saw one something terrible would happen to me."[15] In his screenplay, Kurosawa identifies the setting of the dream as his own home and the boy in the dream as himself (figuratively, if not literally). "Now I have become a little child. As a boy of five, I stand beneath the roof of the traditional Japanese gate in front of our house watching the rain."[16] The set in the opening scene is a reproduction of the house in the Koishikawa district of Tokyo in which Kurosawa lived as a child, with the family nameplate drawn by the artist Shusetsu Imai. Kurosawa thus envisioned himself as a player in the drama, and as the episode develops into a quest narrative, the journey is inevitably inflected with personal significance.

In the scene, the boy stands beneath the gate during a driving rainstorm, the kind of heavy, loud rain that typically falls in a Kurosawa picture. Before he goes out to play, his mother warns him that it can be dangerous if he discovers a fox wedding in the woods. Naturally, he goes to the woods and there discovers a procession of foxes, actions that Kurosawa films with a series of tracking shots. The camera movements, though, are slow and short, as is the norm in his late films, and lack the extraordinary speed and fluidity of the tracks in his earlier pictures. The result, consistent with his late film style, is a marked deemphasis upon movement in favor of the static frame. In his eighties, Kurosawa worked and created to a different pace than in his youth. Taken as a whole, the rhythms of his filmmaking, established by cutting, camera movement, and the choreography of action within the frame, had slowed and become more methodical. The average length of Kurosawa's shots is quite long, the inclusion of montages is rare, and camera movement is languid and unobtrusive when it does occur. The furious dynamism of his youthful films would be quite out of place in these twilight works and had become quite foreign to his manner and method of working. Bearing witness to these changes of rhythm is a rare experience in cinema for the reasons noted at the beginning of this chapter. Few artists age significantly in cinema, and fewer still make the films that bear the marks of this aging.

In the next action that occurs in the episode, the foxes see the boy, and he runs away. Returning home, he is told by his mother that an angry fox has visited the house and left a knife with which the boy is to kill himself to atone for his transgression. She tells her son that she cannot let him into the house until he goes and begs forgiveness from the foxes, lest they harm him or he be forced to carry out their wishes with the knife. Denied readmittance to his home, the child is thrust out into the world, alone like so many Kurosawa protagonists have been, and embarks upon a life's journey in the film's striking final image, one of several special effects provided by Industrial Light and Magic. In long shot, the boy walks away from the camera, through a field of brilliantly hued and illuminated flowers and toward a majestic rainbow arcing over distant mountains. The rainbow announces the advent of regions unknown, awaiting this solitary boy, as the concluding image presents once again the essential Kurosawa vision, of the self cast upon a lonely voyage of discovery. The knife that the boy carries and the act of suicide to which it is associated, however, temper the sense of impending mystery and adventure evoked by the rainbow. Like so many Kurosawa characters, the boy does not opt for suicide, yet he carries the knife and with it the potentiality of exercising that option. Kurosawa had once attempted suicide, and his brother Heigo did kill himself. Thus, this personal history inflects the episode's conclusion, and if the boy does not use the knife, neither does he leave it behind before embarking on the journey. Over even this most majestic and poetic of the film's episodes, the specter of death hovers, as a subtle yet palpable presence.

The next episode, titled "The Peach Orchard," introduces what will be a recurring theme and issue in the film, the loss of purity and beauty in the modern world because of human folly. Here Kurosawa presents the issue in terms of the aesthetics of beauty, inhering in peach blossoms and the costuming of china dolls, while other episodes frame it in terms of environmental pollution and the belief that science can improve upon and overcome nature. Except for a few occasions in the film, Kurosawa explores these issues in a deeply felt but quietist manner.

In the episode, the young Kurosawa surrogate encounters a large group of china dolls that has come to life and is gathered upon a multitiered hillside denuded of the peach trees that once grew there. The dolls tell the boy that they will never again visit his home because his family, foolishly, has cut down all the trees. The boy objects that he loved the orchard in bloom and begins to cry because he will see it no more. Moved by his tears, the dolls, which introduced themselves as the spirits of the peach blossoms, begin a dance, and the orchard reappears for the boy in all of its beauty.

Kurosawa films the scene with a telephoto lens that flattens the tiered hillside into a single plane of space. He intercuts shots of the boy and the dolls using his familiar reverse-field cutting method, in which he crosses the 180–degree axis of action so that the visual field of each shot is the precise reverse of the one that preceded it. As a result, the sequence exhibits a very familiar visual design. Eventually, the dolls' dance ends, the vision disappears, and the boy is left standing in a desolate field surrounded by the mangled stumps of the peach trees. The aesthetic of beauty here is also an aesthetic of loss. The boy wanders through the field until he finds a single remaining bush. Its pretty blossoms are a nostalgic reminder of the beauty that is gone forever from his life, and Kurosawa ends with a freeze frame of the boy's face. Kurosawa's use of the freeze frame is quite singular. In this context, it serves to emphasize and preserve forever in time the boy's sobering contemplation of beauty and loss, the intertwined attributes of the episode.

The issue of loss is broached in the next episode in terms of life itself. In "The Blizzard," Kurosawa explicitly explores the approach of death, personified in the character of a snow maiden who appears, it seems initially, to comfort a fallen traveler. A deadly blizzard overwhelms a four-man mountaineering team. As they try to make their way back to camp, the howling winds and driving snows exhaust them, and they succumb to fatigue and despair. Through the bleakness of the snowy landscape and the undifferentiated nature of the characters, about whom the viewer learns nothing save that they live and work in this place, Kurosawa develops an abstract parable of the existential dangers that life holds. Cut off from their camp, the men trudge wearily through a snow-blind landscape that is inhospitable to life. Kurosawa's stylized soundtrack conveys only the howling winds and gasping breaths of the travelers. As his three companions collapse beneath the snow, their leader, the adult Kurosawa surrogate (played here and in the remaining episodes by Akira Terao, who played Tarō, one of Hidetora's treacherous sons, in *Ran*) incarnates the virtues of Kurosawa's earlier heroes. Fired with determination and willpower, he pleads with his companions not to give up hope, to continue on and, above all, not to sink into the snow and sleep because there lies death.

But he, too, grows tired, and as he collapses the snow maiden descends and wraps him in a glittering blanket. She is beguiling, her movements tender and gentle, and to convey death's soothing embrace Kurosawa eliminates all ambient sound, replacing the howling winds and gasps of the men with a lovely vocal solo. But this death—the extinction of the self in an icy and empty world—is to be refused. It is an unwelcome death because it represents a crushing of the self by unendurable circumstance. The Kurosawa surrogate struggles to rise, and his efforts disclose the true evil of the snow maiden and the death she brings. She transforms into a demon, now holding down her victim, forcing him into oblivion as the harsh sounds of the storm return. Life is worth struggling to keep, even in such abysmal circumstances, Kurosawa suggests, as he had throughout the heroic mode. The character struggles free, the demon departs, and the storm abates, revealing to the men that they were only feet from their camp. Tenacity and persistence find their rewards. In what seems to be the bleakest episode yet, Kurosawa finds affirmation, finds it when things are at their worst, as

57. The snow demon's cruel face emblematizes the terrors of death's approach. (Museum of Modern Art/Film Stills Archive)

he had done throughout his heroic films by insisting that its value lies in its connection to adversity.

The preoccupation with death is placed in a historical and artistic context in the next two dreams. "The Tunnel," shows the continuing legacy of the Second World War for Kurosawa and his cinema, as for Japan itself. The Kurosawa surrogate is now an officer who has fought in the war. At the entrance to a dark tunnel, another of those nasty Kurosawa dogs greets him, the kind that trotted out of the town in *Yōjimbō* with a human hand in its mouth. Here, the dog has a pack of hand grenades on its back and barks the sound of gunfire. Warily by-passing the dog, the surrogate walks through the tunnel, and as he exits, it disgorges the ghosts of the Third Platoon, which he commanded during the war and which had been completely wiped out. After a tearful meeting, he urges them to return to the past and to rest in peace.

The episode presents the war as a nightmarish experience that will not die and that has violently wrenched the individual from the moorings of family, friends, and society. One of the privates, for example,

Noguchi (Yoshitaka Zushi, who played Chōbō in *Red Beard* and Roku-chan in *Dodeskaden)*, looks at a light gleaming in the distance and murmurs that this is the home of his parents. He is overwhelmed with despair at his isolation from home and family. Although Kurosawa escaped service in the Pacific and commenced his career during the war years, the conflict and its aftermath haunted the landscapes and the characters of *No Regrets for Our Youth, One Wonderful Sunday, Drunken Angel, The Quiet Duel*, and *Stray Dog*. Kurosawa repeatedly referred to Japan's period of militarism as a Dark Age, and he wrote about his own experiences as a filmmaker during that time with intense bitterness, likening life in Japan during those years to living inside a jail cell.[17] Thus, though Private Noguchi is a fictionalized character for Kurosawa, the anxieties expressed in the episode are especially strong. The spirits do not understand that their bodies have died, and the dog of war reappears to growl and bark gunfire at the end of the episode. Though it has been a long time since Kurosawa's filmmaking responded to the exigencies of war and the task of national recovery, the episode shows that this most profound and important stimulus to Kurosawa's filmmaking had not been forgotten by the filmmaker, left behind, or put to rest.

"Crows," the next episode, is the most fascinating and intriguing of the film. In it, Kurosawa explores a wealth of personally salient issues. These include, again, the approach of death, the resonance and lingering presence of suicide, his own career as a painter with its ambitions and uncertainties, and the kinship and humility that he feels with and before the art of Vincent van Gogh. (Kurosawa had long wanted to make a film on the life of van Gogh.) This time, Kurosawa places the issue of impending death within the context of career and art. In this case, its threat is not, as in "The Blizzard," the extinguishment of the self in a merciless world but rather the loss of opportunities to engage in artistic creation, which for Kurosawa made life meaningful. As Kurosawa explored various aspects of death in *Dreams*, he adopted different attitudes toward the experience, using his art in a cognitive way to access the emotional components of the experience and a repertoire of responses to it. Thus, in a continuing way across the film, Kurosawa introduces the issue, subsequently drops it, and then reprises it as a variation on a theme. In this regard, the episodic structure of the film worked for him better than would a narrative structure. It enabled him to try out different approaches to the phenomenon of life's end, as he might were he a writer composing a series of discrete essays. It structurally equipped him to work with variety rather than with the unity of design to which a well-constructed narrative generally points, and this variety suited the exploratory nature of his inquires in *Dreams*. Not until the end of *Madadayo* did Kurosawa achieve a fitting and moving closure on the issue.

As the "Crows" episode begins, the Kurosawa surrogate, wearing Kurosawa's trademark hat, gazes in a museum upon van Gogh's paintings, particularly "Wheat Field with Crows," thought to be the final canvas van Gogh completed before killing himself. Perhaps because the pull of van Gogh's art for him is so strong, the surrogate finds himself suddenly and mysteriously inside the landscape of the painting. He meets the artist (played, in a bit of ultra-weird casting, by director Martin Scorsese) at work in a wheat field and is given a brief tutorial on the nature of art and creation.

Van Gogh asks, impatiently, "Why aren't you painting?", and proceeds to describe his ferocious appetite for creating and the extraordinary labor that it requires, terms that are readily analogous to Kurosawa's own experience. "I consume this natural setting, I devour it completely and whole. And then when I'm through, the picture appears before me complete. But it's so difficult to hold it inside." As with himself and his own work and his personal tastes that favored things forceful and intense, Kurosawa evokes the artist here as a powerful engine, driven and laboring, and art as the outcome of this difficult effort. "I work, I slave, I drive myself like a locomotive," van Gogh confesses, and Kurosawa intercuts tight close-ups of a locomotive with images of the painter at work. The desaturated color of the close-ups places them as poetic images within the sequence. True art, for Kurosawa, requires Herculean efforts; it does not come easily. He depicts van Gogh as a painter totally committed to his work and consumed by the will to create, as was Kurosawa. But the enemy of creation is death, which ends the artist's opportunity to work. "I have to hurry. Time's running out. So little time left for me to paint," van Gogh exclaims and hurries away. These are resonant anxieties for an eighty-year-old filmmaker. If the episode portrays van Gogh in an overly romanticized fashion, these worries were real.

When van Gogh departs, the Kurosawa surrogate is left to wander through the landscapes of van Gogh's paintings in a sequence that features more special effects work by Industrial Light and Magic. The surrogate trapped in the paintings makes explicit Kurosawa's reverence and respect for van Gogh. But it also implies that, had he not elected the cinema as his chosen forum, Kurosawa might have been lost as a

58. The Kurosawa surrogate (Akira Terao) receives art lessons from master painter Vincent van Gogh (Martin Scorsese). (Museum of Modern Art/Film Stills Archive)

minor talent in mediums not his own that were already claimed by true giants, condemned, in effect, to wander inside their forms. Eventually the surrogate finds himself back in the wheat field and glimpses van Gogh disappearing over the horizon amid a circling flock of crows, about to complete his art and meet death. Kurosawa's next syntax is exquisite. As the painter vanishes, Kurosawa cuts outside the painting, then zooms out to reveal the surrogate back at the museum and gazing at this painting. On the soundtrack, two wails of a locomotive are heard, the first loud and insistent, the second softer and more distant. In the next moment, it can no longer be heard. At that, the surrogate removes his cap, and the episode ends with this lovely evocation of creation, death, the artistic legacy, and the acolyte's reverence for it. Kurosawa, this master of cinema, humbly placed himself, if not his work, before one who had lived and died in the medium that was Kurosawa's first love.

The next two dreams are closely related to one another and are animated by Kurosawa's anxieties about cultural and technological modernization. As I suggested in Chapter 1, these were formative concerns for Kurosawa and his generation. The anxieties about whether Japan could modernize while still remaining essentially Japan helped produce a cultural perception of modernity in ambivalent and, at times, negative terms. In Kurosawa's films, modernity brought the political values of democracy and individualism, but it was also there in the imagery of ghettoes, poverty, night clubs blaring raucous Western jazz, corporate corruption and the eclipse of the warrior ideal, and in the later works there most of all in the loss of nature and the poisoning of the environment. The contradictions of modernity came to seem irresolvable and, as Kurosawa grew older, he became more nostalgic over what he felt had been lost. *Dersu Uzala* turns to the early part of the century to study natural man who exists outside of urban culture. *Kagemusha* and *Ran* both look back to Japan's past and away from the modern period that Kurosawa found so distressing.

In "Mt. Fuji in Red," Kurosawa evokes the disaster of a nuclear holocaust, as he had done in rather different terms in *Record of a Living Being*. In this dream, a series of exploding nuclear power plants cause even Mt. Fuji to begin a meltdown and, as the terrified populace of Japan flees to the sea, radioactive gases sweep over the tiny island nation. As one character remarks, however, Japan is very small and bordered by the ocean; there is nowhere to escape. The dream ends with the complete annihilation of the Japanese except for a few remaining characters, including the Kurosawa surrogate who is last seen, as the dream ends, futilely trying to beat back the toxic gases. Throughout this dream, Kurosawa employs the visual rhetoric of his friend Ishirō Honda, who served as a creative consultant on the film and who is better known for his own series of Japanese science fiction films, such as *Godzilla, Rodan,* and *Mothra.* The process photography and the shots of fleeing crowds recall similar, well-known sequences in Honda's films and make explicit the connection between Honda's popular monsters and Japanese nuclear anxieties, particularly, at the time, a sense of being held hostage to the political needs of the United States in its Cold War struggle with the former Soviet Union. Those characters still alive as the episode ends curse their political helplessness and the duplicity of industry executives who insisted that the nuclear plants were safe.

"Mt. Fuji in Red" begins with impressively artificial images of the explosions surrounding Fuji, but the episode quickly loses its inherent drama and becomes flat and uninflected. The problem here, and in the remaining two episodes of the film, is not only that Kurosawa had become overly didactic, hammering away at his points. He was, arguably, entitled to do this after a lifetime of magisterial filmmaking; he had earned the privilege of speaking directly to his viewers. The real problem is a fatal one for his work as a dramatist, and that is the near-total loss of irony. It besets this episode and those that follow in *Dreams* and afflicts virtually all of *Madadayo*. Without irony, Kurosawa cannot shape his material and give it the shadings and nuances that would enrich it. Most of all, he lost that extraordinary feature that his best filmmaking possessed and that I referred to in Chapter 4 as a dialectic of competing voices, through which Kurosawa unfolded powerful moral dialogues within the films. As Bakhtin observed about the novels of Dostoevsky, Kurosawa's characters sense "their own inner unfinalizability" in narratives that extend "every contending point of view to its maximal force and depth."[18] Kurosawa's sensitivity to historical ruptures and the psychological and social crises to which they give rise readily found expression through this dialectical design; this sensitivity has vanished from his last films. The exquisite ironies of his mature work, such as Watanabe sinking into his deepest pool of despair as his coworker sends a windup toy rabbit across the table, have no counterpart in the last films. Kurosawa here speaks directly, simply, without urgency and, critically, without drama. Donald Richie's remarks about *Madadayo* really apply to all three of Kurosawa's last films: "There is no irony in the film since nothing is compared to anything else; all is straight-forward presentation. Everything is apparent."[19] This declamatory mode represents a striking change in Kurosawa's dramaturgical style, one that was, perhaps, not for the better. Kurosawa had been an extraordinary dramatist, and he excelled at making social and philosophical issues manifest in the behavior and actions of characters. *Seven Samurai* is about the utopian possibility of human community, *High and Low* about the reasons why this fails, but never in these films are such issues stated baldly or directly. They are implicit within the shifting ironies of the narratives. By contrast, in *Dreams*, *Rhapsody*, and *Madadayo*, Kurosawa adopted a didactic style in which virtue (e.g., veneration for nature) and vice (e.g., pollution and human folly) are explicitly and repetitiously proclaimed, giving the films a preachy quality. As the characters in the films became more passive, the moral tone of the works became more insistent.

This didacticism resulted in part from a change in Kurosawa's screenwriting practices. *Dreams* was the first film he wrote by himself, and he continued the practice of sole authorship with his subsequent films. By contrast, his earlier pictures were invariably written in partnership

with two or three other people—Hideo Oguni, Masato Ide, Ryuzō Kikushima, Shinobu Hashimoto, and others. This collaboration helped reign in
Kurosawa's predilection for stating rather than showing. The funeral wake
in *Ikiru* has some of these attributes, and at the end of *The Bad Sleep Well*,
the social criticism becomes bald and maudlin. It is remarkable that so
dynamic and skilled a narrative filmmaker as Kurosawa had this other
proclivity, and in this regard the success of his earlier work is a reminder
of how crucial collaborative filmmaking is. Kurosawa's screenwriting
partners drew the best from him, helping to make him a better filmmaker.
But, in his last films, without the safeguard of collaborative scripting,
Kurosawa replaced narrative with declamatory episodes and created a
central character with whom he identified directly and without irony. I
shall have more to say about this lack of irony later in the chapter.

The didactic and unmodulated tone of "Mt. Fuji in Red" carries over
into the next dream, "The Weeping Demon," which is the weakest segment in the film. This is a post-apocalyptic dream. The end of the
world has come. Nature has been destroyed; all birds and animals are
dead. The Kurosawa surrogate wanders a blighted landscape, coping
with loneliness. He encounters a single-horned demon that points out
monstrous, seven-foot-tall dandelions, the result of nuclear toxins released into the environment. The demon complains to the surrogate
that nature has vanished from the earth, that people have poisoned the
environment with pollution and radioactivity. The creature shows the
surrogate a colony of fellow demons. They writhe in pain in a pit filled
with bones and blood red water. The surrogate's horned guide explains
that these were once human beings. They were government officials
and millionaires, but they have now become demons because of their
environmental sins and are suffering through a kind of hell. Kurosawa
intends that the demons' disfigurement is an objective correlative of
this destruction of the earth, but it is difficult to see how the one is
connected to the other. Furthermore, the camera work is flat and unin-
teresting, and the images of giant, brightly colored, monstrous dandelions dotting the hillside, as well as the horned demons themselves, are
unpersuasive vehicles to carry the didactically expressed despair about
pollution and economic corruption.

In the final episode, "The Village of the Watermills," Kurosawa
evokes the virtues of living in balance and harmony with nature. Thus,
this episode is counterpoised to the previous two, which had shown
the consequences of violating nature. The surrogate crosses a river and
finds himself in a peaceful, bucolic village where he meets a gentle,

elderly man (played by Ozu-favorite Chishu Ryū). As he will do in his next film, Kurosawa evokes here what he has come to believe are the virtues of pre-electric living. The old man explains that this village has no electricity, that the villagers rely upon candles, oil lamps, and fires for illumination and heat. To the amazed surrogate, the old man asks why the night should be as bright as day, as it is in cities and elsewhere in the modern electrical world. Then you cannot see the stars, he says. He chides the materialism of modern Japan, saying that people have become too dependent on their conveniences and have forgotten they are part of nature. Scientists, especially, think they can improve upon nature, but instead land, water, and air are all being destroyed, and without them no one can live.

As he speaks, animate nature surrounds him—the brook gurgles, the wind rustles the trees, and birds sing and call. Kurosawa shows what he believes is perishing and thus the episode is extremely nostalgic. He notes about this vignette, "The theme here is nostalgia—nostalgia towards the loss of Mother Nature and, with it, the loss of the heart of mankind. Therefore, the images of nature in this sequence must be extremely vivid. It must be so powerful that nature's energy must burst forth from the screen."[20] The gentleness of Chishu Ryū's persona pervades the episode, which accordingly lacks the anxieties that the two previous segments so strongly evoked.

Kurosawa concludes this dream, and the film, with yet another evocation of death. This time, though, the attitude is celebratory and joyous, regarding death as the natural conclusion of a centered and balanced life. The old man explains that no one likes it when death claims the young, but for the old, living in harmony with nature makes even death a friend. In the concluding moments, the village celebrates the passing of a ninety-nine-year-old woman with a parade, dancing, and music, a procession that the old man joins and leads. Kurosawa shows it as a festive and happy occasion, and he now presents the prospect of life's end with a wisdom and maturity not evident in the other episodes, which tended to greet the occasion with varying degrees of trepidation. Before the old man goes off to join the parade, he merrily tells the surrogate that he is 103 years old, a good age, he says, to stop living. He adds, though, an important acknowledgement—he says that being alive is good and exciting. After trying out a variety of approaches and attitudes toward the twilight of life, Kurosawa ends his film here, with the dance, the song, and with the old man's pleasure at living but readiness to pass on.

59. The old man (Chishu Ryū) leads a joyous procession celebrating mortality with music and dance. (Museum of Modern Art/Film Stills Archive)

As Kurosawa himself lived on through the Dark Age of modernity, his dream self, the surrogate, was not permitted to remain behind in the village. He leaves its confines, crossing over the bridge that spans the brook and exits from the shot. The film, therefore, concludes by emphasizing the disjunction of past and present. The camera holds its framing of the village, the trees, and the sparkling water as the end credits roll. The dreamer has gone on, but the images remain with the village, this place, for Kurosawa, of memory and joy and truth. The episode ends here but, given the film's serial structure, it does not provide a conclusion to *Dreams*. Indeed, the film's serial structure has not warranted conclusion. As a compendium of issues and concerns, *Dreams'* episodic nature suited Kurosawa's initial foray into the terrain that would define his last artistic phase. To elaborate this phase, however, in his next films he returned to a narrative form. Thus, *Dreams* stands as an experimental work for Kurosawa, one that, given his subsequent return to narrative, may have been somewhat unsatisfying, but which nevertheless enabled him to find aesthetic and philosophical alternatives to the terms of his previous work.

As he did so, good fortune came his way and facilitated his efforts to master cinema's secrets by defining it anew. Breaking with the long hiatuses between productions that had afflicted his career, Kurosawa found backing and launched immediately into his next project, *Rhapsody in August*. This film was the first Kurosawa work in over two decades to be solo-financed by a major Japanese studio (Shochiku), and it elaborated the themes and motifs that Kurosawa had broached in *Dreams*. It placed the disjunction of past and present, not in a dream but within the historical context of the atomic bombing of Japan. In a tale of generational disparities, Kurosawa examines the legacy of the war years for those Japanese who survived them and for the younger generation who did not directly experience the trauma. *Rhapsody in August*, therefore, furnishes clear evidence that Kurosawa's filmmaking continued a degree of social engagement up until its end, even though the politics of *Rhapsody* are curiously evasive, an attribute that gave rise to no little controversy when the film was released. The main character is another aged individual who harks back to a more premodern Japan. Kane is an old woman who lost her husband in the atomic bombing of Nagasaki and who has continued living on their property since his death. He was a schoolteacher working in the city on August 9, while Kane was at home where the low mountains that separate their home from Nagasaki shielded her from the blast. Afterward, she could not find her husband's body amid all the rubble and, while she survived, her mind and her heart remained fixed on the past.

The narrative of the film, slight as it is, investigates the bomb's legacy by juxtaposing the experiences of three generations, those like Kane (and Kurosawa) who are pre-war, those born in the 1940s, and the youth of today. By juxtaposing the behavior and outlook of these generations, Kurosawa investigates the legacy of the bombing for Japan and tries to envision possibilities for transcending it. He said, "What I would like to convey is the type of wounds the atomic bomb left in the heart of our people, and how gradually they began to heal."[21] As the film opens, the annual August ninth memorial service for the bombing victims approaches, and Kane is visited by four grandchildren who serve to accentuate the cultural and social disparities between the old and young generations. The kids wear shirts emblazoned with the names of American colleges. They object to her food, complaining that the beans, pumpkin, and chicken are so smothered in soy sauce and cooked to a pulp that they can't tell what they are eating. Without rancor, they exclaim on the strangeness of a house that lacks a television and other modern conveniences. And, most significantly for Kurosawa, they know little of the war's history, particularly the bombing of Nagasaki and how it has affected their grandmother and others of her era.

Despite the youngsters' historical ignorance, Kurosawa's presentation of this generation is sweet and affirmative. The children are good-hearted and, though they are unaware of the older Japan that Kane represents, they are receptive to the stories and tales that she tells them. Kane awakens in the grandchildren a desire to learn more of their family history and of the bombing, and Kurosawa shows them becoming more historically sensitive through their contact with the older generation. In this regard, Kurosawa advances the theme of generational reconciliation that he will again broach in *Madadayo*, and that he felt keenly in his own experience as an older Japanese, and an older director, who wished to connect with young people. In its hopefulness, this approach and attitude is counterpoised to the dark parable of generational rupture in *Ran*, a film that came from a more difficult period in Kurosawa's career.

However, though *Rhapsody* acknowledges the potential for the youth of modern Japan to connect with its roots, Kurosawa is more unsparing of the middle generation, raised during the war. This is the generation that grew up amid the massive influx of Western culture that followed the war and the American occupation and benefited from Japan's postwar economic "miracle." Kane's children, now grown adults, are depicted as greedy and shallow opportunists. As the film begins, they are in Hawaii visiting a wealthy but ailing uncle, Suzujirō. He is Kane's elder brother, whose existence no one suspected until he wrote to her from Hawaii. Suzujirō represents a lost generation of Japanese, those who assimilated to the West and who, in the film, are symbolically forgotten. He emigrated from Japan to Hawaii in 1920 and made his wealth in the pineapple business. As part of this lost Japan, Kane regards him with ambivalence, and she does not wish to accept his invitation to visit. Suzujirō is now American, she believes, and though Kane denies feeling animosity for America, he is no longer Japanese to her. Even the grandchildren, looking at a photo of Suzujirō's children, remark that they are all American.

Her children, though, do not share Kane's ambivalence about things American. They are bedazzled by Suzujirō's palatial house and by the huge pineapple plantation, and they drool at the prospect that their newfound relative might have jobs for them. Kane calls her children "miserable" for being so seduced by money. Worse, though, than this, they behave as historical opportunists. In Kurosawa's generational par-

60. Surrounded by her grandchildren, Kane receives an unexpected letter from Hawaii. (Museum of Modern Art/Film Stills Archive)

able, they willingly forget the past in order to survive and prosper. In Hawaii, they fail to tell Suzujirō that his brother-in-law, Kane's husband, perished in the bombing. When the grandchildren wonder why their parents concealed this from Suzujirō, Tateo, the eldest grandchild, says, "To put it nicely, it was consideration. To put it badly, it was calculation. To put it straight, it was that Hawaiian family's money." Kurosawa believed that this disconnection from the past was a generational response to the horror of the war. He said, "The people who survived Nagasaki don't want to remember their experience because the majority of them, in order to survive, had to abandon their parents, their children, their brothers and sisters. They still can't stop feeling guilty. Afterward, the U.S. forces that occupied the country for six years influenced . . . the acceleration of forgetfulness, and the Japanese government collaborated with them."²² By contrast, Kane's ties to her past and the open-mindedness of the grandchildren represent, in symbiosis, the grounds for a cultural healing of the war's trauma.

The film's politics, then, such as they are, exist in the family portrait and the differing responses by its members to the war. These politics, therefore, are metaphorical and poetic. Kurosawa does not deal with the history of the war, nor with the debates surrounding the Bomb, especially those questions about whether a second bombing—of Nagasaki—was necessary. While deliberate and, as we shall see, to an extent carefully considered, these omissions create problems arising from the film's ambiguous point of view and Kurosawa's uncertain control over the perspectives and voices embodied in the narrative. In this respect, the film Kurosawa made is not the one he professed wanting to make. The film's preview screening aroused considerable animosity in the American press, and angry reporters grilled Kurosawa about his intentions. Was he, they asked, blaming America for dropping the Bomb? Wasn't the film's reticence about Japan's role in the war simply a manifestation of that nation's traditional reluctance to acknowledge its role as an aggressor? Japanese scholar Tadao Satō noted that Western reporters were especially keen to know why Kurosawa showed Japanese damage from the Bomb but did not acknowledge Japan's attack on the U.S. or its aggression in the war, conditions which had motivated the bombing.[23] Satō wrote, "This one-track response was the most noticeable aspect of the press conference following the preview showing of *Rhapsody in August*."[24] He speculated that it was not just the latent and unresolved political tensions between the U.S. and Japan that caused the hostility; it was also Kurosawa's own popularity in the West. "For Americans, this might be an especially strong reaction because they feel that the Japanese director whom they most respect is expressing resentment toward the U.S."[25]

Two aspects of the film were especially inflammatory. One occurs during the extended scene in which the grandchildren visit the Nagasaki memorials to the bombing victims. The tone of the scene is mournful, evoking the tragedy of the event, and in this regard it manifests the elegiac tone that Donald Richie has identified as the fundamental characteristic of Japanese films that address Hiroshima/Nagasaki, a tone which Kurosawa's earlier *Record of a Living Being* so bravely eschewed.[26] A montage shows the memorials contributed by other nations, and a substantial number of these are from former Eastern Bloc and communist countries: Czechoslovakia, Poland, Bulgaria, China, Cuba, and the former USSR. Shinichirō, the youngest grandchild, points out that there is no memorial from the United States, and his elder sister, Tami, replies, "Of course not, they're the ones who dropped the bomb." The political evasions here are quite severe. As Matthew Bernstein and Mark Ravina note, Kurosawa "ignores the complex political motivations for the other countries to send memorials to victims of an Ameri-

61. In a controversial moment of international reconciliation, Kane shakes hands with Clark, her American nephew. (Museum of Modern Art/Film Stills Archive)

can nuclear weapon. The Bomb [in the film] exists outside of history."[27] Given the film's lack of political complexity and Kurosawa's failure to engage the history of the war, the sequence seems to arrogantly condemn the U.S. for a war crime and to do so by affiliating with America's Cold War opponents. While this may not be what Kurosawa intended to convey, his unsophisticated handling of the material left him open to the charges.

The second offending incident in the film involves Clark (Richard Gere), Suzujirō's son. On his father's instructions, Clark visits Japan with the intention of persuading Kane to make a trip to Hawaii. In Japan, he learns of the death of his uncle in the Nagasaki bombing, whereupon he visits the site and expresses remorse over the bombing. American critics tended to construe this as an apology for the bombing. In fact, though, Clark is exhibiting a humane response to the evident destruction and loss of life, not a political judgement about the use of the bomb. In a subsequent scene, he apologizes to Kane for not knowing of his uncle's death. Many critics found this, too, to be offensive and regarded the character's dialogue as an expression of national atonement for having used the bomb. Summarizing this negative reaction, critic Yomota Inuhiko wrote, "Many critics, myself included, thought Kurosawa chauvinistic in his portrayal of the Japanese as victims of the war, while ignoring the brutal actions of the Japanese and whitewashing them with cheap humanist sentiment."[28] But nothing in the film is so politically specific or motivated. The film's evasiveness demonstrates Kurosawa's desire to avoid engaging the historical controversies. Clark's apology is a function of the character and the narrative situation, not of some political points Kurosawa wants to score. As Bernstein and Ravina suggest, "In pressuring his aunt to come to Hawaii, he had been unwittingly demanding that she miss her husband's memorial service. His apology is distinctly 'Japanese,' in that it is concerned less with guilt and moral abstraction than with shame and a concern for human sentiment."[29]

Moreover, through Kane, Kurosawa aims to indict war itself, rather than a specific war or particular sides in a war. Kane confesses to Clark that she feels no anger toward America, only toward war itself which, she feels, will one day destroy everyone. Yet Kurosawa's clumsiness in handling the sequences at the Nagasaki shrine—their hortatory, sententious tone and lack of historical context—quite reasonably raised suspicions about the film's point of view. The problem is one of tonality and, again, the lack of irony. *Rhapsody in August* works best when it concentrates on the generational portrait of Kane's family. There, Kurosawa makes his points through what minimal narrative there is and through the mix of perspectives represented by the characters. By contrast, in the Nagasaki scenes Kurosawa abruptly switches to the kind of bald pleading that surfaced in *Dreams* in both the Mt. Fuji and Weeping Demon episodes and does so in ways that make nonsense of the characters. Escorting her siblings through the city, Tami suddenly becomes wise and poetic beyond her years, like a character from an Alain Resnais film, intoning about the mysteries of memory and forgetfulness. The Nagasaki of old is buried beneath this city, she says portentously, adding that the events here have been forgotten by people today (a claim immediately contradicted by Kurosawa's images, which show throngs gathered at the memorials). Until this abrupt switch in the film's rhetoric and in her character's function, she too had forgotten and had been merely an adolescent girl. When Kurosawa tries now to use her as the voice of conscience and history, the effect is ludicrous and unpersuasive, and it raises those questions about Kurosawa's control of social and political perspective that so troubled American critics.

Although the film points toward large-scale issues of the war's legacy for succeeding generations and the lingering tensions between the U.S. and Japan, it does so in an apolitical way and by using a very small dramatic arena. It centers on Kane and the grandchildren, the small physical surroundings that Kane inhabits, and the emotional pull that the past exerts for her, particularly in her longing for her deceased husband. Most strikingly, Kurosawa offers no realistic representation of the bombing or any glimpse of wartime Japan, despite the tremendous importance these events have for Kane and the grandchildren. These omissions resulted in part from Kurosawa's sense that it would be wrong to film them. He deliberately avoided a re-creation of the bombing because he felt the event was too momentous to grasp through art, that something of the magnitude of that experience was inaccessible to filming and especially to the audience watching such a re-creation. He said,

> It is absolutely unfilmable. That state of destruction and of such terrible human anguish does not belong to the realm of the presentable. There is no way to express it, to film it, to reproduce it. These are events that provoke only one type of reaction: to avert one's eyes. . . . It is better to have them imagined by the spectator since in the end one risks showing them in such a manner that people will turn away.[30]

Kurosawa made a reasoned aesthetic and moral decision to avoid a vulgar re-creation of the atomic blast that would only numb the sensitivities of the viewer. But, whereas a film like Alain Resnais's *Night and Fog* (1955) or *Hiroshima Mon Amour* (1959) proceeds from an identical premise, those works construct complex dialogues about what it means to bear witness, as survivor or artist, to tremendous historical traumas. Kurosawa's film does not, mainly because he no longer works as a dramatist through the evocation of a multiplicity of voices and their carefully controlled perspectives. Thus, Kurosawa does little to stimulate the spectator's imagining of the trauma, despite his wish to do so. As a result of his aesthetic choice and his mode of working, the Bomb is curiously absent from the film on these two levels, as literal and as figurative representation.

But there is yet another reason for the film's off-stage sense of history, and this has to do with the attributes of Kurosawa's late period. *Rhapsody*'s small-scale focus on Kane, and particularly on her memories of the past, entails that the historical context to which the narrative points stays off-screen. In other words, for Kurosawa at the end of his career, history was that which had *already occurred* or which might occur *elsewhere*. It was not a continuum to include the present time and space of the story, its characters, or its author. This characteristic is intensified even further in *Madadayo*. This feature of the late films exists in sharp tension with Kurosawa's desire in *Rhapsody* to talk about the wounds the bomb has inflicted on the Japanese and particularly with his conviction that, in its after-effects on their health, "the atomic bomb is still killing Japanese."[31] The social goal that he set his filmmaking in this regard does not concur well with the manner in which he now worked as dramatist and storyteller.

Thus, in keeping with his late films, Kurosawa dramatizes few events and shows little actually happening. Instead, he films characters discussing important things that have happened in the past or are happening elsewhere and off-screen. The somewhat Byzantine family history of Kane and Suzujirō is conveyed in a letter that the grandchildren read. The viewer sees none of it because it is a recollection after the fact. The trip by Kane's children to Hawaii and Suzujirō's death occur off-screen. Kurosawa dramatizes none of Kane's memories. His images do not access these, save for one fantastic moment when Kane describes how the flash of the bomb looked like the opening of a giant eye. This Kurosawa shows literally—an eye opening over the low mountains. The characters do not participate in momentous events, as did his earlier heroes. Instead, they observe and recollect things that once happened and whose effects are still felt. They sit and talk about things transpiring elsewhere. At its end, Kurosawa's became a cinema of recollection, not action, one suited to an advanced age in which activity has given way to memory.

In *Rhapsody*, though not visualized, these memories have tremendous resonance for Kane and, through her, for the filmmaker whose generation she represents. Like the village elder in the concluding episode of *Dreams*, Kane is a character displaced in time and unreconciled with the present. Her habits and experiences derive from an earlier era to which she feels profound attachment. She has no television or washing machine and believes she does not need them and, in fact, is better off without them. She is pre-electric and, like the village elder in *Dreams*, believes there is virtue in this. She does have a refrigerator, but only because Tami had begged her to buy it. Kurosawa's famous temperament is reflected in Kane, whose grandchildren say she is stubborn and, like Kurosawa, Kane is tied to the sights and sounds of old, pre-war Japan. Both felt somewhat estranged from electric living and the conveniences it proffers. In old age Kurosawa came to feel a greater connection for the world of his youth. In his autobiography, he discussed his nostalgia for the sounds of Taishō, where he spent his youth. Significantly, these were nonelectric sounds, and he lamented that, culturally, many were now lost forever.

> The sounds I used to listen to as a boy are completely different from those of today. First of all, there was no such thing as electric sound in those days. Even phonographs were not electric phonographs. Everything was natural sounds. . . . But as I sit here and write about these childhood sounds, the noises that assail my ears are the television, the heater . . . all are electrical sounds. Children of today probably won't be able to fashion very rich memories from these sounds.[32]

The aged characters in Kurosawa's late films personify the estrangement conveyed in this passage. While his work always exhibited ambivalence for modernity, this shifted toward an explicitly posed resistance and rejection. Kane's alienation from the modern, electrified world is intensified by the reawakening of her familial memories—the abrupt news that she has a sibling, Suzujirō, whom she had forgotten. These reflections upon her family occur in conjunction with the anniversary of the Nagasaki bombing; this, in turn, deepens her sensitivities regarding the loss of her husband in the flashpoint of her life and of the nation's life. Word soon arrives that Suzujirō has died, severing that link to the familial past and precipitating a general crisis for the old woman. That evening, a thunderstorm, with its bright flashes of lightening, sends her into frenzy. Like Nakajima in *Record of a Living Being* (Kurosawa again quoting from earlier work), she reacts to the storm as if it were the bomb itself, and she rushes about, covering her grandchildren with sheets to protect them from fallout. As he did with Nakajima, Kurosawa shows here how the bombing has forever altered the experience of life in Japan. Fused for Kane with the facts of her subsequent life, it becomes perceptually indistinguishable from a summer thunderstorm and thus is not a past event but one that is entangled in the present. (In *Madadayo*, Kurosawa reprises this motif. During thunderstorms, the old Professor hides under blankets because the thunder and lightening remind him of the Allies' bombs.)

Beyond their initial panic, though, as Kane and Nakajima construe lightening with the flash of bombs, her response is very different from his. This difference is symptomatic of the outlook and orientation prevailing in Kurosawa's last works compared with the period when he made *Record of a Living Being*. Nakajima's madness resulted from his heroism, that is, his attempt to resist the nuclear logic of the Cold War years. Unlike Kane, the legacy of the atomic bombing did not leave him with a mellow resignation to life and its misfortunes. It inflamed his passion to resist and to reject the probable destiny of nuclear annihilation that Cold War geopolitics forced upon him. In the terms that defined all of Kurosawa's heroes, Nakajima acted. He tried to save his family by moving it out of Japan. If the past, that is, the nuclear bombing of Japanese cities, threw its radioactive shadow across his future, Nakajima sought to escape that future by outrunning it, by escaping to a portion of the globe he believed would be safe from fallout. As with all of Kurosawa's heroes, Nakajima's impassioned effort to transform the conditions of his life defined his moral stature.

Kane, by contrast, is resigned to endure the present even as the bombing and the giant eye that loomed over the mountains haunt her. She says that she used to be bitter about the bombing but is so no longer. Her affections tie her to her grandchildren but, more importantly, to the past, to her husband and to the pre-Shōwa world that she finds inherently virtuous. That past now beckons her more powerfully than any living connection she has to the present conditions of her life and, in the film's extraordinary conclusion, she attempts to move backward through time to recover a lost world that she has never psychologically survived or lived beyond. The next day, following the thunderstorm, Kane vanishes. Her family discovers that she has laid out her husband's clothes, and Tateo says that the clock in her head is running backwards, that she is attempting to go back to Grandfather's time. A neighbor reports that Kane looked at the heavens, saw clouds that looked exactly as they did the morning of the bombing, and left for Nagasaki. The family sees her in the distance, hurrying toward the city.

In the concluding shots, Kurosawa reprises another familiar stylistic signature, but in keeping with the self-quotation prevalent in his late style, he employs it in a new context. In *Seven Samurai*, he poetically captured the power and nobility of the samurai by filming, separately and with a tracking camera, each warrior on the run and then intercutting the separate shots to create a dynamic montage. The montage commented on the prowess of each warrior, individually, and also on their fusion into a fighting group. The cutting framed each warrior separately in his own shot. During filming, however, Kurosawa had exactly matched the positioning of each warrior relative to the moving camera. Thus, when he intercut the shots, he created strong graphic continuities between the identically framed images. The montage thus isolated the warriors as individuals within separate shots and simultaneously linked them with the others (through the graphic continuities established by the framing) in a poetic statement about the dialectic between individual and group that is at the heart of the film.

In *Rhapsody in August*, Kurosawa reprises the montage of graphically linked shots of individuals on the run. The montage in this case is longer and more elaborated than in the earlier film. In *Seven Samurai*, the sequence was exceedingly brief and consisted of one series of six flash images of the samurai. Kurosawa's reprise of the design in *Rhapsody* consists of seven series of graphically related tracking shots of family members running in pursuit of Kane. A cutaway to Kane brackets each series. As in *Seven Samurai*, Kurosawa again moved the camera with an identical speed for each shot, and he centered the characters within the frame. As a result, because the compositional matches across the shots are so strong, the cuts between the images are almost subliminal. After the first two series of tracking shots show the grandchildren and their parents, the subsequent series concentrate only on the grandchildren, each series separated by the aforementioned cutaways to Kane. After the third such series, the wind inverts Kane's umbrella, and Kurosawa brings in a children's chorus singing Schubert's song "The Wild Rose," the lyrics of which had been recited by Tateo in an earlier scene, and had been visualized in a memorably poetic interlude during the Nagasaki memorial service. The chorus accompanies another series of shots of the running grandchildren, and then a slow motion reprise of Kane and the last tracking shots of the grandchildren, also in slow motion. As in other cases where Kurosawa self-consciously used earlier stylistic attributes, the designs do not grow organically from the material. The montage adds energy to the end of the film but, unlike its use in *Seven Samurai*, there seems to be no sufficient connection here between the graphical continuities and what they are expressing.

Other aspects of the sequence, however, work very powerfully and successfully to move the scene onto a poetic and nonliteral plane. Kane moves very slowly, barely trudging forward against a strong wind, while her family members run at top speed to overtake her. But they never do so, despite the fact that they are not far behind. Kurosawa

repeats this contrast six more times (before the final slow motion series), each repeat showing first Kane and then the family members moving at differing rates of speed yet never coming together. The sequence
thus presents an explicit temporal contrast between Kane and her family, a contrast that is a vivid and poetic embodiment of her temporal
and psychological displacement relative to her offspring and the modern world they inhabit and which she now wants to escape by fleeing
into the past. The final images of Kane, struggling against a headwind
that has nearly immobilized her efforts to move forward, show in memorably poignant terms her efforts to escape the history to which her
latter life has been subject, of the excruciatingly intense desire she
brings to this effort, and of her inability, pushed back by the headwind,
to recover or re-enter that past. Her desire is paradoxical. She is hurrying to rejoin her husband and to reinhabit the world she shared with
him, to be lost in that world but also to be lost to the modern era
through the atomic bombing, which cleaves these periods from one
another.

These concluding images demonstrate that Kurosawa retained his
brilliance for visualizing, metaphorically, the inner psychological and
spiritual dynamics of a character and for locating these within a social
or historical context. This is so even if, as here, the character's stance
amounts to a rejection of history, and the film as a whole is an inward-
looking, rather than outward-looking enterprise. Furthermore, characteristic of the remarkable mellowing of Kurosawa's last works, he presents
the ending without any of the tragic tonality that has characterized
much of his filmmaking and that soared to such heights in *Kagemusha*
and *Ran*. Instead, at the last moment, he deflects the sequence into a
lighthearted vein by having the wind invert Kane's umbrella and adding, on the music track, the children's chorus.

In Kurosawa's last films, this mellowness replaced the intensive, dramatic conflicts of earlier works in which he had set heroic protagonists
in conflict with traditional Japanese society (e.g., Watanabe's alienation
from his family and work associates) or with the awful mutations of
post-war culture (e.g., Sanada's battles with disease and gangsters in
Drunken Angel). Kurosawa showed the loneliness, anguish, and suffering of these heroes and the difficulties of the project of personal and
social transformation that lay before them. Instead of dramatic narrative
action that manifested the reformist project undertaken by Kurosawa
and his heroes, the last films lack overt action. They emphasize, instead, meditation and reflection as the keys to memory, and the pre-

modern past that it can access, and the movement of history off the stage and into the wings. This latter attribute, especially, is a remarkable shift in the filmmaking. Kurosawa's use of narrative in his earlier films enabled him to imaginatively reorganize the historical path of post-war Japan, in which his life was enmeshed. The attenuation of narrative in the late films signals a less impatient and rebellious outlook, one that now finds significant virtue in quietly enduring the vicissitudes and misfortunes that are an inevitable part of life.

This transformation is most striking in *Madadayo*. It is Kurosawa's final film and the last production of that remarkable burst of creativity and good fortune that enabled him to complete three films in four years. He launched into the production of *Madadayo* eight months after the release of *Rhapsody in August*. Kurosawa's affinity for the aged characters in his last films reaches its greatest intensity in *Madadayo*. The picture is based on the life of the writer Hyakken Uchida (1889–1971) at the point in 1943 when he resigned his university career to concentrate on his writing, which had proven to be popular and profitable. The war years, though, subjected Uchida to a prolonged trial. An air raid destroyed his Tokyo house, after which Uchida and his wife lived in a small, shabby hut and endured the privations of the remaining war years and then the Occupation. His students' devotion helped sustain Uchida's spirits, and to pay tribute to their beloved professor, the students initiated a yearly birthday party celebration on his sixty-first birthday. The celebrations continued for more than ten years, up to Uchida's death.

More so even than *Rhapsody*, *Madadayo* shows the rapid vanishing of history from Kurosawa's work. This is especially notable in light of its being a period film, set for the most part in the 1940s, dealing with the war and its impact upon daily life in Tokyo. On location in Gotemba, west of Tokyo, Kurosawa commissioned large-scale sets to show the destruction wrought by the Allies' bombing campaign, which transformed the city into piles of burned and blasted rubble. At Toho Studio in Tokyo, open air sets portrayed the street life of 1940s Japan. But Kurosawa then used these sets in an almost subliminal fashion by restricting his camera mostly to interiors. The sets appear only in brief shots that show the city surrounding Uchida's dwellings. Kurosawa focuses on the inner space of these dwellings and the banquet halls where the birthday celebrations are held, not on the urban environment and the social history of which it is part.

Except for a few quick shots showing Japanese and American sol-

62. *Madadayo's* portrait of the elderly professor and his adoring students embodied Kurosawa's wishes for the endurance of his artistic legacy.

diers, the war and post-war Occupation are off-screen events. The film opens inside Uchida's classroom as he tells his students that he is resigning his teaching post. Kurosawa then introduces the first exterior of Tokyo, circa 1943. A telephoto shot shows a group of Japanese soldiers carrying banners and marching toward the camera. In the next shot, the camera pans from the soldiers to a cart parked on the street—the Professor's belongings are being unloaded from the cart—and then tilts up to a house. A narrator tells us that this is where the Professor will now live. In a fluid pan and tilt, the optical movement of the shot shifts from the historical tableau of wartime Tokyo to the private, biographical space of the film's main character, living in semi-seclusion. In the scene that follows, some of the Professor's students help him unload his belongings and set up the house. As they do this, a small reminder of the war years occurs: the banners carried by the passing soldiers briefly appear through the foliage in the background of the property, and then they vanish.

Kurosawa evokes the historical frame of the war years and then moves quickly past it in order to concentrate on the private affairs of the Professor. Other points in the film's episodic structure contain notable historical elisions, as Kurosawa leaps over intervals of dramatic action. The destruction of the Professor's house occurs off-screen. Uchida hosts several students at the house one evening, and as they sing in tribute to their beloved teacher, Kurosawa cuts away to the street outside. Air raid sirens begin to sound, and the streetlights go out. As this happens, Kurosawa slowly pans left, to the exterior of Uchida's house, and employs a narrator to provide the information that will not be shown. Dispassionately, the narrator says that the house burned down in the air raid. Using a fade, Kurosawa moves to the next time and space of the film—Uchida's shabby hut where he now takes up residence. In a series of axial shots, the Professor's students arrive to visit him.

The end of the war and the beginning of the Allied Occupation are also treated as off-screen events. Kurosawa leaps over them and resumes the story at points beyond their inception. After a few scenes showing the Professor enduring life at his hut during the war, Kurosawa again uses a fade to make the leap and the elision of historical time. Two Allied jeeps drive up the rubble-strewn street and past the Professor's hut. After this quick evocation of the external world, Kurosawa moves to the private space of Uchida's dwelling, and the Professor mutters about the scarcity of food now that the war is over. American soldiers appear in one subsequent scene, where they help disperse some drunken students from one of the *Maadha Kai* ceremonies.

Despite the film's period setting and authentically detailed sets, Kurosawa reduces historical time and place in these significant ways. The glimpses of history that Kurosawa does provide are conveyed in quick, broad strokes. The Occupation becomes a jeep-load of soldiers riding in the street. This design is especially remarkable given Kurosawa's intense feelings for the war and the postwar years and because of the influence those periods exerted upon his filmmaking. Kurosawa's perception of the nation's folly in embarking upon the war, and the massive devastation that resulted, were the formative experiences that shaped his filmmaking over the next decades. Moreover, some of the events in the film have direct personal correlates in Kurosawa's life. Like Uchida, Kurosawa felt the daily presence of the air raids, and his house met a similar fate, destroyed by fire in an air raid the day after Kurosawa and his wife had moved out.[33] But, despite these affinities with Uchida's misfortunes, in *Madadayo* Kurosawa relegated the war to a peripheral and background element. This change points to the film's disengagement from the temporal flux of history and its embrace, instead, of a Buddhist outlook, accepting the passages in one's life, particularly the cosmic dimensions inherent in the inevitability of aging and dying.

It is in this context that Kurosawa integrates the *Hōjōki*. After his house burns, the Professor takes one possession to the shabby hut. It is his favorite book, the *Hōjōki* by Kamo no Chōmei, a literary diary written in 1212, recounting Chōmei's experiences living in a small hut during the late Heian period. This period was turbulent, marked by storms, earthquakes, pestilence, famine, and fires, which Chōmei describes in the first section of the work and which the Professor appreciates as analogous to the calamities of the war through which he is living. He tells his students that he feels like Chōmei, living in his hut amid a period of great flux. As he did in *Rashōmon*, Kurosawa uses an evocation of Heian-era catastrophes as a commentary on contemporary social misfortune, but, unlike *Rashōmon*, which concludes with the woodcutter's redemptive acceptance of an orphaned baby, the catastrophes of the era in *Madadayo* are not mitigated by the transforming power of individual moral choice. The Professor does not act. He merely waits out the war and finds comfort in Chōmei's Buddhist acceptance of the transience of life and its misfortunes. In a famous passage, Chōmei wrote, "The flow of the river is ceaseless and its water is never the same. The bubbles that float in the pools, now vanishing, now forming, are not of long duration."[34] Chōmei composed the *Hōjōki* during the last years of his life, as Kurosawa did with *Madadayo*. Disturbed by the ugliness and misfortune that he saw in the world about him, and disappointed that he did not get a posting as Warden of the Kamo Shrine, Chōmei withdrew from the world to live a reclusive existence in his small, mountain hut. Writing his account of this spiritual existence, he vividly described the horrors that beset the outer world, a world of foulness, evil and suffering: "All is as I have described it—the things in the world which make life difficult to endure, our own helplessness and the undependability of our dwellings. And if to these were added the griefs that come from place or particular circumstances, their sum would be unreckonable."[35]

Chōmei's response to the circumstances that disillusioned and saddened him was to renounce the world and to find solace in a monastic retreat and a life of simplicity and contemplation. The hut he designed for his last years was intentionally small, "not even a hundredth the size of the cottage where I spent my middle years."[36] This reduction in size accentuated the purity of his concentration and emblematized his forfeiture of worldly attachments. For reasons that may not be dissimilar, the dramatic space of Kurosawa's final films contracted and came to center on the spiritual issues represented by the main characters. Accompanying this contraction was Kurosawa's disinclination to engage and explore, through narrative, the outer world of history, the external events that impinge upon the inward lives of the characters. Significantly, while recounting the late Heian disasters, Chōmei omitted mention of the Taira-Minamoto warfare that erupted in 1181. Donald Keene has suggested that he may have felt a reference to politics would be incompatible with the stance of worldly renunciation that the piece represents and attempts to portray.[37] As we have seen, in Kurosawa's later films, and especially in *Madadayo*, the political world receded from view. Like Chōmei, he adopted a contemplative stance. It is most significant, therefore, that he presented the *Hojoki* as a key text in *Madadayo*. Chōmei's diary and the conditions of its inception resonated deeply for Kurosawa. Chōmei's life as a hermit, dwelling in seclusion, provided a template for the design of *Madadayo*. As a literary and religious figure, the hermit embodies a process of withdrawal from society, the antithesis of the social engagement personified by the rebel heroes of Kurosawa's earlier films.

Chōmei's withdrawal from society, however, did not produce the serenity he sought, as the second section of the *Hōjōki* indicates.[38] There, Chōmei adopted a more personal tone than in the historical chronicle that formed the diary's first section. Chōmei wrote of his self-doubt. How could he transcend his surroundings and find grace in the Buddhist concept of *mujō*—the contingency of human life—when he so loved his hut and had labored to craft an object, the diary itself, as a well-designed literary form? "The substance of the teaching of the Buddha is to have no attachments to anything. The fact that I now love my grass hut is a sin. That I am attached to my solitude is a hindrance to my salvation. Why do I write about these useless pleasures and waste precious time?" In the *Hōjōki*, Chōmei left a literary narrative chronicling this spiritual struggle near the end of his life. What Kurosawa shows, though, is the hermitage, the withdrawal, not the struggle or the self-doubt. Save for a few complaints by the Professor about the privations of life in his hut, Kurosawa does not portray a spiritual trial.

Once again, as with *Rhapsody in August*, what he shows is at variance with what he said he wanted to show. Kurosawa had planned *Madadayo*, in part, to showcase the value of the individual's pursuit of personally meaningful truth. Kurosawa's primary school art teacher, Seiji Tachikawa, made a tremendous and lasting impression on young Akira by breaking with the norms of art instruction. Years later Kurosawa recalled, "The fact that at such a time I encountered such free and innovative education with such creative impulse behind it—that I encountered a teacher like Mr. Tachikawa at such a time—I cherish among the rarest of blessings."[39] Instead of having his pupils slavishly copy the style of existing works and judging them on how well they had imitated these models, Tachikawa encouraged his students to develop their own styles. This individualism struck Kurosawa as the true way, the right way of teaching art, and the approach applied as well to other areas of life. He wanted *Madadayo* to carry this message, with particular relevance to the art of filmmaking. He said,

> I think I have had many students, teams of assistants who have remained with me, attentively, for years, as if they wished to benefit from a certain experience through our contact. It is said that, in the East, education consists of a master teaching his students a technique they must eternally repeat and reproduce. Things are different in the art of filmmaking. Here, the situation is more like Western education, in which professors teach even the youngest students to find within themselves their own truths.[40]

> It is one of the reasons I wanted to make *Madadayo*. In the end, the teacher turns to his students and says, "The only gift I can give you is to invite you to find within yourselves what is important to you. No matter how insignificant it may be to others, this thing in which you believe will give your life direction."[41]

This message, however, does not emerge forcefully in the film. What emerges, instead, is worldly renunciaton, incarnated by the *Hōjōki*, and the figure of the hermit that stands within and behind it. This, and the students' undying devotion to their teacher, are the emotional core of the film. And it was here, in accessing this emotional core, that Kurosawa responded with the astounding artistry of old. In a sequence of surpassing lyric beauty, Kurosawa offers a montage showing Uchida and his wife at their hut, watching the passing seasons. Scored with music by Vivaldi, the montage repeats a series of paired, axial framings to evoke an aesthetic for each season, as Uchida and his wife contemplate the passage of time. Sitting quietly, they watch the seasons flow

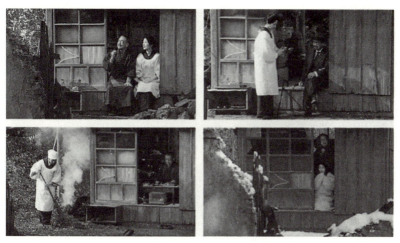

63. Kurosawa summons his magisterial artistry for a beautiful montage showing four seasons as the professor passes time at his tiny hut.

by. It is a scene of breath-stopping beauty, and it is the aesthetic and ethical heart of the film.

Concentrated in this scene and dispersed through the surrounding episodes, Kurosawa shows not the interaction of character and environment, but the seclusion of the Professor, waiting for the storms in the outer world to pass. Kurosawa explores in *Madadayo* not the flux of history, the war, or the individual's pursuit of truth, but a phenomenon at once more fundamental and more personally connected to his own situation: the perceptible approach of life's end. In the *Hōjōki*, Chōmei had asked, "Which will be the first to go, the master or his dwelling?"[42] This question reverberates throughout *Madadayo*. Chōmei's answer was the Buddhist recognition of the impermanence of all earthly things. Neither master nor dwelling will last. Kurosawa, though, offers a somewhat different answer: the master's legacy will not die. The latter half of the film shows the yearly parties, ritualized affirmations of the old Professor's enduring importance and value. The title of the film—and the name of the parties—derive from the recitation accompanying a child's game of hide and seek. *Mouii Kai?* (Ready?), shout the seekers. *Madadayo* (Not Yet), replies the child in hiding. *Maadha Kai?* (Not Yet?!), replies the group, impatient for the game to get underway. To revere their *sensei*, the Professor's former students hold these parties for more than a decade as the old man advances to his final year. They call the parties *Maadha Kai*, which the old man says jokingly the students all seem ready to ask him. Each year, he replies to them, *Madadayo* (no, not ready to die yet), though one day he assures them he will say *Mouiiyo* (I'm ready). The parties, therefore, mark and celebrate the *sensei's* continuance of life and his moral example while preserving a subtle recognition that his time is past and is drawing to a close. In just these terms, and with no attempt at subtlety or irony, Kurosawa identifies the old man and the parties with himself and the legacy of his filmmaking.

Each year the students toast the old man and offer glowing testimonials to his cultural importance and shaping influence on their lives. They say the Professor is like the sun. Alternatively, in song they proclaim that he is like a moon that shines over the entire nation. The testimonials go on and on, and the depth of the students' devotion and affection is bottomless. The first *Maadha Kai* scene runs on-screen for over twenty-one minutes, an interminable length that demonstrates the depth of Kurosawa's personal investment in the material. Unfortunately, the lack of irony and the failure to delineate the students as individuals (*contra* Kurosawa's stated intentions) make the scenes flat and uninflected, even while they evidently worked as a form of psychotherapy for Kurosawa. Through them, he explored questions about the value of his own work and example and how it will be received by succeeding generations. The questions, though, are not posed in a substantial way; the affirmations are too quick and forthcoming. The students' inexhaustible devotion to their Professor evidently was reassuring for Kurosawa, at least as he imagined it in this film, whose ultimate questions deal with the longevity of a master and his dwelling and not with events, like the war, that are now viewed as the ephemera of history. Through the reassurances of the *Maadha Kai* ceremonies, Kurosawa suggests that, though the master passes on, the dwelling—the work—will last.

Accordingly, Kurosawa concludes the film with a scene whose content and tonality are unprecedented in his cinema. At the seventeenth *Maadha Kai* party, the old man collapses and is taken home. That night, with some former students in attendance, he lies in bed, dreaming. The students hear him call out, *Madadayo*, as he had done throughout the years. Kurosawa then ends the film inside the old man's dream, demonstrating once again the importance of the dreamworld for this late period of his filmmaking.

64. The old professor's devoted students honor him with song at one of their yearly *Maadha-kai*

The Professor dreams the child's game of hide and seek. The dream-scape is bathed in golden light. One boy hides from his playmates and calls out *Madadayo*. They search for him in the far distance, making of the boy a familiar Kurosawa figure, solitary and alone. Struck with the golden light, he comes out from his hiding spot and gazes up at the heavens. The camera pans and tilts from the boy to the sky and reveals an expressive, poetic configuration of clouds. The imagery of the clouds lingers on screen for forty-five seconds, to the music of Vivaldi, and then the end credits begin to scroll. I was unprepared for the grace and beauty of this final scene, and viewing it in the context of Kurosawa's body of work nearly moved me to tears. The poetic cloud formation brings the work full circle, back to its beginning in *Sanshirō Sugata* and the character whose enlightenment was embodied by this imagery, and it incorporates, of course, resonance with the clouds as used in *Ran* and *Rhapsody in August*. In those films, however, the clouds were turbulent, and Kurosawa used them as a metaphor for human violence, showing it inflecting the natural world. Thus, the cloud imagery in

Madadayo links more in spirit with *Sanshirō Sugata*. As in *Sugata*, the imagery is beneficent and inspiring. In *Madadayo*, the clouds embody the release of the self into death and provide, therefore, a complimentary temporal and philosophical relationship to their use in *Sugata*, where they represent the renewal of self.

Moreover, the end of *Madadayo* astonishes by the depth of its tranquility. In Kurosawa's earlier work, death occasioned, and was accompanied by, great anxiety. Watanabe's psyche is shattered by the news of his cancer diagnosis in *Ikiru*, and he cannot accept death without first transforming his life. In *Seven Samurai*, Kuemon's grandmother, near death, is terrified that the next world may contain still more bandits and starvation and may be more hellish than her present wretched life. *Drunken Angel* ends with Sanada raging against the senselessness of the gangster, Matsunaga's, death. In *Red Beard*, the young doctor Yasumoto watches a dying man's last moments and sees nothing transfiguring, only anguish. Until Kurosawa's late period, death had been an adversary, never welcomed, always combated, and he never allowed his heroes the release of ritual suicide. There always remained too much for them to accomplish for the betterment of an imperfect world. By contrast, in *Dreams* Kurosawa acknowledged the certainty of passing, and in *Madadayo*, with his own life nearing its conclusion, he found a mellowness, a calm acceptance of the end, and visualized it as a passage of beauty. Near the close of his life, Kamo no Chōmei wrote that he no longer mixed with people or the world. "I seek only tranquility; I rejoice in the absence of grief."[43] At the end of *Madadayo*, the Professor has retreated into a comforting vision of grace and peace from which, it is implied, he will slip quietly into a final release. Death now holds no terror, brings no anguish, heralds no grief, as Kurosawa presented imagery and emotions he never before accepted or explored on film.

The ending is, therefore, also a beginning of sorts, and *Madadayo* takes its place as the culminating work of Kurosawa's final period. *Dreams*, *Rhapsody in August*, and *Madadayo* are more serene than his other films, more preoccupied with small things and with a reduction of dramatic space. In place of narrative, their episodic structure opens a new quietism in Kurosawa's work, as he searches for spiritual integrity in the self in retreat from a cataclysmic historical and social arena. As the experience of modernity and postmodernity came to seem more ominous, the pre-Shōwa past grew more appealing and seductive. But if that past could not be reclaimed or reentered, the transience of worldly things was reassuring. One sits in the quiet of a small hut as history rushes loudly past.

In a letter to his brother in 1888, van Gogh had written, "Oh, my dear brother, sometimes I know so well what I want. I can very well do without God both in my life and in my painting, but I cannot, ill as I am, do without something which is greater than I, which is my life—the power to create."[44] When all else is gone or has been revealed as illusion, the need to create remains, unassailable as long as breath is drawn. Kurosawa often remarked that he wanted to die on the set while the camera was rolling. He never got that wish, but he left three final films as testimony to his love of cinema. Had he ceased filmmaking after *Ran*, he'd have ended his career on a note of high accomplishment. But he continued to make films because there was no other alternative for him. Living, for Kurosawa, was making films; to stop one was to stop the other. If at the end he could no longer make films of sustained brilliance, he could yet produce passages of remarkable beauty, and he had earned the right to speak simply and directly with his viewers. He sustained his artistry across an entire lifespan, past the point at which other filmmakers give up. If the film as a whole is not, the end of *Madadayo* is a fitting capstone to a monumental career, providing closure and release upon the life and its work. In his last years, Kurosawa's determined and sustained commitment to his beloved medium of cinema left its own testament. The dwelling endures.

9 The Legacy

When Akira Kurosawa died at age eighty-eight on September 6, 1998, the cinema lost one of its giant figures. Kurosawa belonged to a very rare and select group, and his death diminished the medium even as his works have enriched it. Without Kurosawa, Steven Spielberg, George Lucas, and Martin Scorsese would have been without the most intense cinema experiences of their early years, experiences that showed them what the medium could accomplish. Lucas, for example, said that seeing his first Kurosawa film, *Seven Samurai*, had been "a powerful experience for me. I'd never seen films like that before in my life, and it was a profound experience."[2] Scorsese said that *Ikiru* provided him with "one of the most intense emotional experiences of my teenage years."[3] Without Kurosawa, there would have been no John Woo or Sergio Leone, at least as we presently know their work. Without Kurosawa, the samurai film would have remained a stale and pompous form. His bedraggled, flea-bitten warriors humanized not just the sword-fight film but the historical past as represented through film. Instead of the pious, declamatory figures of standard chambara, Kurosawa offered the rude and hungry Sanjurō as well as the god-like but humanly vulnerable Kambei. And his action ballets transformed that genre. Kihachi Okamoto (*Sword of Doom* [1966]) and Masakai Kobayashi (*Samurai Rebellion* [1967], *Hara Kiri* [1962]) would not have choreographed their splendid action sequences as they did had not Kurosawa already shown them how to do it, as he showed a generation of American filmmakers how to tell gripping stories and stylize physical conflict in flamboyantly hypnotic terms. And without Kurosawa there would have been, for the West, no Japanese cinema, at least not when the West finally looked and saw it. *Rashōmon*, the film that augured this sudden attention, seemed mystically in synch with the existentialism of European culture, and it added a new proof to the epistemological and moral relativism of that era. Without Kurosawa and his work, so much of world cinema would be other than we know it today.

Appropriately, given his legendary stature, his passing triggered an outpouring of appreciation from world politicians and filmmakers. French President Jacques Chirac acknowledged his stature. Steven Spielberg called Kurosawa "the pictorial Shakespeare of our time," and Martin Scorsese remarked, "His influence on filmmakers throughout the entire world is so profound as to be almost incomparable. His passing is a unique loss—there is no one else like him."[4] After 1965, Kurosawa had found it difficult to sustain his career, but he was, typically, irrepressible. He turned to painting and drawing when the hiatuses between productions became too long, a practice he began with *Kagemusha* (1980). By doing this, Kurosawa returned to his origins. "I intended to be a painter before I became involved in film," he said. "When I changed careers, I burnt all the pictures that I had painted up until then. I intended to forget painting once and for all."[5] But he returned to it in late life, fulfilling his original career ambition. Furthermore, by drawing the images he planned to photograph, he provided potential investors with exciting visual descriptions of the films he proposed to make. And he fulfilled an old dream. "When I was young and still an art student, I used to dream of publishing a collection of my paintings or having an exhibition in Paris."[6] By the mid-nineties, he had amassed a considerable collection of artwork in connection with the pre-visualizations of *Kagemusha*, *Ran*, *Dreams*, *Rhapsody in August*, and *Madadayo*. Many of these images were published in book form and, like the career painter he wished to be, he enjoyed a 1994 solo exhibition of his art in Manhattan, one of the art capitals of the world. Sponsored by the Ise Art Foundation as part of a Japan-U.S. cultural exchange, the exhibit presented more than 100 drawings based on his films. Supplementing the exhibit and presented on high-definition television, a series of films directed by Masayuki Yiu examined how Kurosawa used his drawings to previsualize films.[7] When Kurosawa could no longer rely on having a series of ongoing film productions, his painting permitted him to continue functioning as an artist.

His legendary temperament, imperious and commanding, had been an indelible accompaniment to his art, and it remained with him into advanced age. In 1992, Kurosawa sued Toho, the studio for which he had made many of his pictures. Japanese copyright law excluded filmmakers from receiving royalties based on the screening of their films in

65. Kurosawa filming the "Village of the Watermills" segment of *Dreams*. His death triggered an outpouring of reaction throughout the world.

ancillary (nontheatrical) markets. Kurosawa took offense when Japanese Satellite Broadcasting spent $7.5 million to purchase the rights from Toho to show twenty-one of his films thirteen times each on satellite television.[8] Toho offered to compensate Kurosawa, but the amount was less than the half million dollars Kurosawa demanded. Kurosawa's suit struck a chord among Japanese filmmakers, who typically sign away their rights to a production once it commences, and it demonstrated that he remained a figure to reckon with in the Japanese film world.

Late in his life, the American cinema, to which he had given so much, recognized Kurosawa's achievement and its obligation to him. The Academy of Motion Picture Arts and Sciences honored him with a special Academy Award in 1990. Despite his stature and the enormity of his accomplishments, Kurosawa expressed great humility upon the occasion of this honor. Steven Spielberg and George Lucas presented him with the award at the 62nd Academy Award ceremony. They had been instrumental in helping him secure funding and distribution for *Kagemusha* and *Dreams*, and so it was fitting that they introduced him in this context. Accepting the award, Kurosawa said that, while he was honored, he was not sure he deserved the award since he felt that he did not yet understand cinema. "I really don't feel that I have yet grasped the essence of cinema. Cinema is a marvelous thing, but to grasp its true essence is very, very difficult. But what I promise you is that from now on I will work as hard as I can at making movies, and maybe by following this path I will achieve an understanding of the true essence of cinema and earn this award."[9] For Kurosawa, cinema was a path in life, a Way, a mystery to explore, with secrets so numerous one might never learn them all. And he kept his word. He continued making movies and finding new directions in the medium. In his last three films, he reinvented his work.

Kurosawa had not completed a film for six years prior to his death, but he had remained active and planned future films in spite of his increasing frailty and declining health. At the time of his death, his unfinished projects included a script based on a novel by Shugoro Yamamoto, whose other works Kurosawa used as the basis for *Red Beard* and *Sanjurō*. The projected film was to have been called The Ocean Was Watching and would have dealt with an unusual subject for Kurosawa—the lives of two Tokugawa-era prostitutes. Kurosawa's films are resolutely male-centered and typically place female characters on the periphery of the action, so this new one would have represented a considerable departure for him both in style and subject matter. But it was not to be. Kurosawa completed the script in 1993, but it languished due to a distressingly familiar problem. He could not secure funding for the project, which was budgeted at $15 million. As a result, this giant filmmaker spent his last years in another period of enforced idleness like those that had bedeviled his career since the completion of *Red Beard* in 1965.

Kurosawa's death followed by nine months the death of Toshirō Mifune, the actor so closely linked to his films and whose passing emblematized the closure of Kurosawa's heroic cinema and the impassioned filmmaking that had marked the springtime of each man's career. Mifune's extraordinary screen persona, of course, had been in significant ways Kurosawa's creation, and in turn it helped make Kurosawa's filmmaking remarkably popular. Audiences loved Mifune's charisma in ways they had not taken to Susumu Fujita and Takashi Shimura, who incarnated earlier Kurosawa heroes before Mifune came on the scene. The end of Kurosawa's ongoing collaboration with Mifune proved to have major repercussions for the subsequent films. The films after *Red Beard* notably lack the strong, striving protagonists that Mifune played and the engagement with social transformation that these characters and their quests symbolized. How different *Ran* would have been with Mifune! Absent Mifune, Kurosawa found a different kind of filmmaking to practice, but it was never again a populist or popular cinema, and it became increasingly didactic and remote in tone. To an extent, these changes are attributable to Kurosawa's own remarkable ability to grow old with the medium. But Kurosawa had also risen to the intensive spirit of his collaborations with Mifune. Each man brought out something of the warrior artist in the other, and Mifune's departure after *Red Beard* marked the end of that most fruitful period in Kurosawa's career and of the kind of cinema they had practiced together. Thus, Mifune's death was a melancholy reminder of what once was in Kurosawa's cinema, when the filmmaker had dared big dreams for his country and for world society, and of how far he had come from those dreams in the style and sensibility of his last works. And with Kurosawa then an invalid and confined to bed, Mifune's death inevitably presaged The Emperor's own end.

Kurosawa's passing marked the end of an era in world cinema. Few of the international art film directors (e.g., Federico Fellini, Satyajit Ray, Ingmar Bergman) who gained world attention in the postwar years remain alive or active as filmmakers. Kurosawa's death signaled the terminus of the postwar art cinema, but it is more significant than that. He left a tremendous legacy to world cinema. In this closing chapter, I should like to assess the nature of his legacy and influence. This will provide some closure on his career, and it will enable us to ask about the ways in which Kurosawa's filmmaking remains important and vital for contemporary cinema. A convenient place to begin is to ask a question that, at first, might hardly seem to need asking at all. Why do so many filmmakers feel indebted to Kurosawa and regard him as a formative influence on their work? This question, in turn, generates three other queries. What components of Kurosawa's work have exerted the greatest influence, and on which filmmakers? To what extent do these components typify the totality of Kurosawa's work, and what is their place within the overall design of that work?

Upon Kurosawa's death, Donald Richie called the director a "prophet without honor in his own country."[10] Richie's comment refered to Kurosawa's difficulties in securing Japanese backing for his films and also to the relative disrespect in which succeeding generations of Japanese filmmakers held this old master. Kurosawa's stature was burdensome for younger directors struggling to make their mark and their names. His shadow loomed too large on the cinematic landscape, making it more difficult for them to emerge into their own spotlights. Many seemed to resent the accolades that Kurosawa had earned. In contrast to this sad situation, a generation of American filmmakers readily adopted Kurosawa as a mentor figure so that, late in his career, he found more acclaim overseas than in his own country. These were filmmakers who came of artistic age in the late 1960s and early 1970s, precisely during the period that Kurosawa's career in Japan began to founder. Enamored of the movies, cineastes all, this cohort of filmmakers included George Lucas, Steven Spielberg, Martin Scorsese, and Brian De Palma. Each of these filmmakers practiced an aggressive style of filmmaking that emphasized elaborate visual design, montage editing, and fluid camera movements. In Kurosawa, they found a filmmaker who was a master of montage and sinuous camera moves and who put this style in the service of crisp storytelling. *Seven Samurai*, in particular, is a peerless example of fast-paced narrative action that fashions a complex storyline, featuring a large number of characters and composed of scenes that are brief, that climax quickly, and that are extremely focused as units of narrative. The premise of the film—samurai defending a farming village from bandits—is simple and elegant yet produces enormous riches, as Kurosawa turns this three-hour adventure epic into a philosophical examination of class heritage, history, and group allegiances during the Sengoku Jidai. At every moment in the film, style serves story, even as the sensuousness of that style—the frenzied montages of battle, the fluid pans and tracks that follow running warriors—affords considerable pleasure in its own right.

For filmmakers like Spielberg, Lucas, and De Palma, intent on making *popular* movies rooted in the basic genres, Kurosawa's achievement in *Seven Samurai*—his demonstration of how to make one of the ultimate, exciting narrative films—was resonant and became a kind of template for their own work. Furthermore, these are directors whose films have typically stressed physical action and who found the kinetic properties of cinema to be very appealing. Lucas's *Star Wars* films, Spielberg's Indiana Jones pictures as well as *Jaws* (1975) and *Close Encounters* (1977), and De Palma's gallery of films, including *The Fury* (1978) and *Dressed to Kill* (1980), all represent an essentially physical approach to cinema. This approach stresses action-based storytelling using audiovisual designs that provide continuous visual stimulation. The adrenaline-fueled rush that *Jaws*, *Dressed to Kill*, and *Star Wars* (1977) give audiences is based in this aesthetic. It is achieved through the rapid

66. Kurosawa's work left an indelible impact upon world cinema, especially American directors and stars. Actor Richard Gere embraced the opportunity to work with Kurosawa on *Rhapsody in August.*

editing of dynamically changing shots that feature an unceasing chore-ography of character and camera movements. Scorsese has been less enamored of narrative than the others in this cohort, less interested in subordinating style to story. His work, though, is just as sensuous in its formal design and typically features extremely elaborate camera moves and percussive editing.[11] Speaking in terms that apply to his genera-tional cohorts, De Palma stressed his belief that kinesis is essential to cinema, is, in fact, one of its most appealing and enduring properties:

> Motion pictures are a kinetic art form; you're dealing with motion and sometimes that can be violent motion. There are very few art forms that let you deal with things in motion and that's why West-erns and chases and shoot-outs crop up in film. They require one of the elements intrinsic to film: motion.[12]

Kurosawa thus stands behind the blockbuster turn in American cin-ema that began in the 1970s. This cohort of filmmakers helped redefine cinema as an intensely physical experience, and their kinesthetic designs were essential to the appeal of this new style of filmmaking. The two filmmakers most identified with blockbuster filmmaking—Lucas and Spielberg—regarded him as a mentor figure and his work as a guide in fashioning the kind of emotionally powerful cinema experiences that they had encountered in his films. The sensuousness of Kurosawa's style and his storytelling skill were essential guides to their efforts to take American cinema toward the provision of more kinesthetic narrative pleasures. This was a new direction for cinema in the 1970s. Hollywood had always excelled at storytelling, but until the advent of Spielberg and Lucas, its narratives had never been as aggressive or insistent. In this regard, Kurosawa's influence was paradoxical; the sensuousness of his style was persuasive even as the ethical goals of his filmmaking were not. Kurosawa never regarded box-office success as the *sin qua non* of good filmmaking. During the postwar years, though, Kurosawa did aim to make a popular cinema, one that would reach "all the people," and one, moreover, that was populist in its outlook. His films were to "benefit all mankind" and the only way he might do this was to make films accessible and pleasurable for a large audience. The ways he found to do this—his techniques for creating kinesthetic narratives—proved enormously persuasive to the American filmmakers intent on creating their own popular cinema, even as they replaced Kurosawa's sociopolitical goals with their own commercial ends.

Kurosawa's narrative methods exerted other influences upon contemporary cinema. These, though, did not derive from the kinesthetic qualities of his work, and I will turn to them in a moment. More yet needs to be said about the sensuousness of Kurosawa's style. As De Palma pointed out, the kinetic experiences that cinema offers viewers are often of a violent nature, and for the last thirty years the cinema has trafficked heavily in graphic violence. Unfortunately, Kurosawa's work has been of seminal influence here as well. Kurosawa's flamboyant images of violence—the dog trotting with a human hand in its mouth and the severed arm in *Yōjimbō*, the geyser of blood from a slashed chest in *Sanjurō*, the audible breaking of bones during the fight in *Red Beard*— showed subsequent filmmakers how to design violence that would be both memorable and intensely cinematic. The American critic Richard Corliss pointed to this when assessing Kurosawa's impact upon American filmmakers:

> He was one of the first to aestheticize violence, to make it sexy, make it hurt. Every face-off in pouring rain can be traced to the

drenched battles in a half-dozen Kurosawa classics. Yet he did not find combat romantic; to him it revealed the brutality of man, of life. To see the random carnage in *Saving Private Ryan*'s Omaha Beach scenes is to be reminded of Spielberg's debt to the muddy, bloody climax of *Seven Samurai*, the poetic overkill of Mifune's death in *Throne of Blood*.[13]

Kurosawa aestheticized violence in startling and unforgettable ways that, unlike the efforts of lesser filmmakers for whom effect is all, managed to convey the humanity of those involved. These include the desperate, mortal fight in *Drunken Angel* between Mifune's dying gangster and his crime boss, when they upend a can of paint and wear the whitewash like clowns, the frenzied clash between cop and killer in *Stray Dog* that is punctuated by the distant song of happy children, the splendid final duel in *Yōjimbō* when the hero faces impossible odds and smiles amid swirling clouds of dust, the human porcupine at the end of *Throne of Blood*, the geyser of blood in *Sanjurō* followed by a terrible silence as Mifune gazes at his fallen foe. Despite his prowess in composing these outré images, Kurosawa seemed to sense where graphic violence would go in cinema, the artistic and ethical dead end in which it would trap filmmakers drawn to it. He grasped that the emotional gratifications provided by these remarkable moments were suspect, and as his vision of life darkened, he backed away from these suspect pleasures. The deaths in *Kagemusha* and *Ran* hold no triumph, little glory, and much pain. This is why his work encapsulates the evolution of violence in modern cinema. He showed filmmakers how to do it, and then he showed them why it should not be done. He intuited where it would take us and realized that it was not a journey worth making. His work thus has a breadth and moral integrity that transcends its sometimes flamboyant violence.

With this important caveat in mind, it is nevertheless important to see how the influence operated. It was not just the startling flamboyance of Kurosawa's violence that had such a profound effect on world cinema. It was the method of stylization that he bequeathed future filmmakers. His use of slow motion, multicamera filming, and montage editing to stylize violence decisively changed modern cinema. Although he employed slow motion in a scene of violence in his very first film, *Sanshirō Sugata*, he there simply dropped a slow motion shot into the body of a normally paced scene. The effect was surprising and memorable but not enough to change the medium. By contrast, in *Seven Sam-*

urai, in the scene where Kambei kills the thief who has kidnapped a child, Kurosawa *intercuts* slow motion and normal-speed shots to produce dynamic, dialectical space-time tensions. Kurosawa intercuts three slow motion shots of the dying thief crashing through a door, rising up on tiptoes, and collapsing upon the ground with three normal-speed shots of horrified onlookers. Because motion is also occurring in these shots, Kurosawa builds a sustained contrast and conflict between these different temporal modes and extends this across the series of six shots. He had found a device as well as its application and design. So many of the essential discoveries about how to use slow motion in scenes of violence have been made here. The slow motion shots must be brief, of very short duration, and here they are. Slow motion, by itself, tends toward inertia, an impeding of the flow of action, and thus a loss of dynamism. This tendency must be overcome by skillful editing in which it is essential to reference slow motion with normal-speed action. Thus, Kurosawa appreciates the paradox implicit in the scene's construction: the surrounding normal-tempo action energizes the slow motion insert, provided it is brief. Because the slow motion interludes are brief, Kurosawa maximizes the temporal oppositions, which in turn gives the slow motion material a kinetic charge. For the viewer, he creates a perceptual shock that stems from the misalignment of time within the montage, and by keeping the shots brief, he can slip easily into and out of the decelerated moments. This small scene in *Seven Samurai* is the textbook on slow motion and violence for modern filmmakers.[14]

As his career developed, Kurosawa showed only an occasional interest in slow motion. It did not figure as an ongoing part of his style. Despite this, the impact of his demonstration in *Seven Samurai* has been enormous. It taught succeeding generations of filmmakers how to incorporate slow motion into scenes of violent action and, aside from the use of squibs to represent bullet strikes, no device in the arsenal of modern movie violence has been used as frequently or extensively. Two filmmakers, in particular, brought ultraviolence into the mainstream of commercial cinema by popularizing this device: Arthur Penn in *Bonnie and Clyde* (1967) and Sam Peckinpah in *The Wild Bunch* (1969). For the concluding gunbattle in *Bonnie and Clyde*, Penn used Kurosawa's method of multicamera filming and extended it by employing different film speeds to capture a range of varying slow motions. Then, like Kurosawa, he intercut the footage so as to slip dynamically in and out of differing temporal modes. Penn has said that he knew instantly how this last scene would be shot and edited and that Kurosawa's films provided the model. "Having seen enough Kurosawa by that point, I knew how to do it."[15]

Peckinpah extended Kurosawa's style even further, incorporating his multiple camera method, telephoto lenses, and slow motion in the violent epic *The Wild Bunch*, a film whose all-male band of adventurers, martial values, and setting in a period of historical crisis have direct antecedents in *Seven Samurai*. In making this film, Peckinpah was intent on surpassing the violence Penn had shown in *Bonnie and Clyde*. Thus, Kurosawa's stylistic template extends through Penn to Peckinpah. Although he denied that Penn's film had any influence on him, Peckinpah's archived papers contain a letter from Warner Bros. to the production manager of *The Wild Bunch* confirming shipment of a print of *Bonnie and Clyde* to Peckinpah's Mexico location the weekend of March 23–24, 1968. This was immediately prior to the start of principle cinematography on *The Wild Bunch* on March 25. Peckinpah evidently wished to study Penn's design in order to surpass it.

That Peckinpah felt the force of the Kurosawa lineage upon his own work is evident in his remark to *Film Quarterly*'s Ernest Callenbach that he wanted to make Westerns like Kurosawa made Westerns.[16] When a colleague told Peckinpah that the editing in *The Wild Bunch* was comparable to Kurosawa's achievement in *Seven Samurai*, Peckinpah proudly replied, "Better."[17] The Kurosawa lineage attained a degree of explicitness even among Peckinpah's crew members. During production of *Cross of Iron* (1977), production designer Ted Haworth told Peckinpah that a particular action effect would be "Kurosawa Peckinpah at his best."[18] Interestingly, in light of this lineage, Peckinpah's archived papers contain an exchange of correspondence with Toshirō Mifune. As *The Wild Bunch*, so indebted to *Seven Samurai*, went into production, Mifune wrote to Peckinpah to wish him the best of luck with the new picture.[19] Just before the film went into national release in June 1969, Peckinpah wrote to Mifune to express his wish that the Japanese actor would find the picture enjoyable.[20] Years later, when Kurosawa had finished *Kagemusha* and was arranging for its promotion and release, he personally invited Peckinpah to attend the picture's Tokyo premiere as part of a select group of personal guests. Peckinpah wrote back to formally accept this invitation.[21] Upon meeting Kurosawa, Peckinpah thanked him for having done the work that made *The Wild Bunch* possible.

The kinetic attributes of Kurosawa's style, then, entered deeply into international cinema. In terms of the representation of violence, they influenced Arthur Penn and Sam Peckinpah and, from there, Hong Kong director John Woo, as well as virtually everybody since. Every filmmaker who uses slow motion, montage, and multiple cameras to stylize violence in the ways that Kurosawa had demonstrated in *Seven Samurai* owes him a great debt. Furthermore, Kurosawa's narrative economy, tied to his fluid camerawork and dynamic montages, showed the emerging 1970s cohort of American filmmakers how to tell a story with cohesion, momentum, and grace. Kurosawa swiftly set up the narrative premises of his films, often in their opening acts, and what fascinating premises these were: a cop pursuing a thief who has stolen his gun, a threatened village deciding to hire samurai for its defense, a samurai manipulating rival gangs into destroying each other, a kidnapper snatching the wrong child from his intended victim, and witnesses recalling fundamentally different versions of a crime. Even when Kurosawa included long scenes of exposition at the outset of a film, their design was often masterfully cinematic, as at the beginning of *Yōjimbō* when the innkeeper introduces Sanjurō to all the major players in the drama by opening and closing a series of wooden blinds.[22] Brilliantly conceived and plotted, Kurosawa's narratives formed an enduring example and ideal for filmmakers of all variety and genres: John Sturges (*The Magnificent Seven* [1960]), Martin Ritt (*The Outrage* [1964]), Sergio Leone (*A Fistful of Dollars* [1964]), Walter Hill (*Last Man Standing* [1996]), Ron Howard (*Ransom* [1996]), George Lucas (*Star Wars* [1977]), Brian De Palma (*Snake Eyes* [1998]). Even if they are not transposing a Kurosawa narrative, many filmmakers have felt obligated to reference his work in their own: Walter Hill (*48 Hrs.* [1982]), Clint Eastwood (*Pale Rider* [1985]), Philip Kaufman (*Rising Sun* [1993]), and John Sayles (*Lone Star* [1996]).

Perhaps the most famous of these films, inspired wholly or in part by Kurosawa's work is *Star Wars*, George Lucas's science fiction adventure, which he freely modeled on a variety of cinematic sources and cultural archetypes. Most people know, in general terms, that Kurosawa's *The Hidden Fortress* [1958] was a major influence on Lucas's design of this film. The obvious similarities between the films are clear. These include characters (Lucas's robots R2D2 and C3P0 as transpositions of the feuding peasants Tahei and Matakishi) and narrative situations (in both films a princess and her loyal band, dethroned, are fleeing through enemy territory). But, for Lucas, the real structural significance of *The Hidden Fortress*, and of Kurosawa's work in general, is not as widely known. Lucas was deeply impressed by Kurosawa's ability, in his period films especially, to rapidly establish an extraordinarily detailed historical context without explaining much to the viewer. Lucas felt that this conjunction of rich period detail, the absence of overt historical contextualization, and the presence of archetypal character dramas took the films in the direction of myth. Many of Kurosawa's period dramas take place during the sixteenth-century civil wars, and Kurosawa evoked this period with keen attention to detail. Kikichiyo, for example, the farmer who becomes a warrior in *Seven Samurai*, is symptomatic of the fluid class boundaries of that period, a fluidity that fascinated Kurosawa. Kikuchiyo, though, is also a character without a biography. The narrative delineates no past for him, no family, not even a reliable age. He is defined, instead, through his appetite for adventure. He is, therefore, simultaneously mythic and historic. In a similar way, the ronin hero of *Yōjimbō* expresses both the tumult of the age (in this film, the late Tokugawa period) and the grandly expressed material of myth. Sanjurō has no past, no name even, and he enters and leaves the film a figure of inherent mystery. Yet he confronts the rising capitalist class of late Tokugawa times, and with a neo-Confucian righteousness he sweeps it away. Sanjurō's ronin status emblematizes the plight of the samurai class in mid-nineteenth-century Japan *and* the character's mythic grandeur. In *Throne of Blood* and *Ran*, Kurosawa uses the Sengoku Jidai to make poetic statements about the timelessness of human evil and self-destruction.

Kurosawa evokes the regional wars and clan rivalries of the Sengoku period in a very general and abstract way throughout *The Hidden Fortress*. The reasons for the strife between Princess Yukie, her general, and their regional enemies remain unexplained in the narrative. It is sufficient, simply, that they exist and that the territory has been blockaded to impede the flight of the princess. Along the way, Kurosawa offers epic historical vignettes showing forced labor, conscript armies, and those made homeless and displaced by the ongoing strife. Furthermore, as in many of his other films, Kurosawa begins the narrative *in medias res*. Tahei and Matakichi are wandering a desolate plain, wearied by long years of war, when they are abruptly surrounded by a band of samurai on horseback intent on executing an enemy soldier. Kurosawa plunges his viewer into a fully developed historical world and into action already unfolding, whose inception predates the start of the film.

Lucas appreciated these narrative stratagems. He, too, began *Star*

Wars in the thick of things, with the princess and her band battling the forces of Darth Vader. More significantly, *Star Wars* was the middle installment of a projected group of nine films. As such, it places the viewer in the midst of a huge narrative cycle with its elaborately detailed fantasy universe, one filled with a multitude of characters and subplots but with minimal explanation of the shape and stakes of the struggle. As in Kurosawa's period works, this universe is already fully animated when the film begins. By reaching for the general through the specific, by going deeply into history to find myth, Kurosawa furnished Lucas with a singularly powerful narrative method and template. The younger filmmaker reciprocated by elaborating a filmic universe whose fame and popularity led curious viewers, who otherwise would never have known Kurosawa, to *The Hidden Fortress* and to the filmmaker who stands, distantly, behind *Star Wars*. Such is the web of inspiration and obligation that forms a stylistic lineage.

It is a statement of the obvious to point out that, with the impact of *Jaws* and *Star Wars* in the mid-seventies, this style of fluid storytelling and kinetic filmmaking has become the normative pattern for international commercial cinema. Through this cohort of filmmakers, then, Kurosawa's extraordinarily kinetic designs passed into general significance for contemporary narrative cinema. To the extent that a kinesthetic style has come to dominate the design of contemporary narrative film (at least in those pictures budgeted for the greatest box-office impact), the legacy of Kurosawa has been tremendous. He showed everyone how to make movies *move*. But it is a curiously skewed legacy that comes to terms with only a subsection of his style. His work is broader and richer than its most evident influences would indicate. In some ways, *Seven Samurai* is an anomaly among his films. He never again made a picture with the sheer narrative drive which that picture possesses. *Yōjimbō* is a very plot-driven film, heavy on action choreography, and the narrative in *High and Low* is tautly constructed, but these films also have long, deliberative sequences in which little overt action occurs. Kurosawa was *not* a director of fast-paced movies. For the most part, he favored a leisurely pace, and many of his films—*Drunken Angel, Record of a Living Being, Ikiru, Throne of Blood, The Lower Depths, Red Beard*—are slowly paced. Kurosawa's normative pattern was a singular one. He alternated between two stylistic designs that rarely are conjoined by filmmakers within a single film or series of films. *Stray Dog, High and Low, Throne of Blood*—in these and other films, Kurosawa mixes scenes of furious action with long sequences of slow duration in which very little activity occurs. So many Kurosawa films have long, deliberative dialogue scenes in which the visual center of attention is the frozen formality of the participants, often a more important attribute than what the characters are saying. Kurosawa's style is intriguingly dualistic in this regard. It is both fast and slowly paced, and it fluctuates continuously between these two modalities. The powerful, racing narrative engine of *Seven Samurai* is quite atypical of Kurosawa.

This conjunction of design approaches is one of the most distinguishing features of his work. Kurosawa used rapid, montage cutting, abundant camera movement, and crisp action choreography *as well as* a contrary design featuring lengthy shots, fixed and unmoving camera positions, and scenes with minimal to no physical action. His work continually switches between these dynamic and static designs, often within the same film (e.g., *Throne of Blood, High and Low, Ran*). While the overall emphasis upon these design approaches shifts somewhat during his career, with stasis assuming greater prominence in the later works, Kurosawa was always drawn to both designs and showed great affinity for each. At the time he made his pictures, his use of multiple cameras as standard procedure for all scenes (not just those of violence), long takes, and his disjunctive manner of editing were quite unlike the norms of popular cinema, as they derived from Hollywood production. The American style of decoupage quickly became the accepted style for world cinema, and it was not built around long takes. Kurosawa preferred to cover a scene with multiple cameras and few takes because it extended the playing time for his actors and thereby elicited better performances. By contrast, Hollywood production built a film out of many short shots. As David Bordwell points out,

> Sustained takes required lengthy rehearsal, and if someone made a mistake during filming, the entire cast and crew would have to start all over again. From the standpoint of industrial organization, it is reasonable to break the scene into shorter, simpler shots that can be taken separately, many of which need occupy only a single player and a few staff.[23]

While Bordwell points out that Hollywood-style editing and long takes "often functioned as flexible, nonexclusive options" in the work of some filmmakers, it is not a common conjunction, certainly not to the extent that Kurosawa has stressed these designs. More commonly, filmmakers will incline toward either kinesis or stasis and will build designs around those objectives that incarnate those qualities. Kurosawa, though, used both, with approximately equal emphasis and did so throughout his career. Furious violence punctuates the prolonged and rigid tableaus in *Throne of Blood*, *Kagemusha*, and *Ran*. *Ikiru* gives way to stasis in its second and concluding narrative section, as *High and Low* did throughout its first half.

Thus, while the kinetic aspects of Kurosawa's filmmaking have perhaps exerted the greatest influence upon subsequent filmmakers, this influence tends to skew appreciation of the actual balance of these elements in his work. And it indicates that other essential aspects of Kurosawa's formal designs—primarily, his fondness for stasis and tableau compositions—have proven much less influential. Furthermore, how Kurosawa's work has influenced subsequent filmmakers, while important, does not enable us to address a more fundamental and comprehensive question, namely, that of Kurosawa's place in cinema history. If he were merely a director whose work formed a tradition and lineage for other filmmakers to follow, he would have a place in film history, but it would say nothing about the quality of the work itself. The lasting significance of Kurosawa's work is to be found not in technique or formal design, as accomplished as these are in his films, but rather in connection with the uses to which he put film.

For Kurosawa, cinema was a means of investigating the world around him and his fellow human beings and of approaching closer to truth. In this regard, his work transcends the realist-formalist split that has dominated so much of film history and the theory that has come of it. As previous chapters have shown, Kurosawa's is a deeply formalist cinema, with many unique visual patterns that are elaborated across the body of work. But Kurosawa's dialectical style, composed of opposite and contending elements and designs, derived from reality as he understood it. History is cataclysmic; life is a trial. The individual is thrust into a hostile universe and to survive must struggle, and the struggle is unceasing. The contending and tense elements of Kurosawa's style—its formalism—derives from this fundamental reality. Kurosawa was an artist who believed in truth and who believed that the artist had an awesome responsibility, that of showing the essential conditions and dilemmas of human existence. He had a credo and philosophy as an artist: "Being an artist means never averting one's eyes." The artist of integrity must have the courage to confront the most awful and perplexing aspects of human cruelty and duplicity, to show these directly and without flinching, and thereby to invite the viewer to contemplate them. He derived this philosophy from a lifetime of experience that taught him to associate trauma with personal growth and acquired wisdom (a process that he translated into the narratives of his great films). This credo was at the base of Kurosawa's appreciation for Dostoevsky, and especially of the moral challenge that he felt Dostoevsky's literature posed to his own work, a challenge Kurosawa felt his work must be worthy to meet. In *Red Beard*, one feels Kurosawa working with passion and intensity in an effort to draw closer to the mysteries of human existence, and the spirit of Dostoevsky has never been stronger in his work than here.

For Kurosawa, the cinema was more than a medium of telling stories or making money. That he excelled at telling stories is certainly one attribute of his genius, just as his disdain for the business aspects of the industry is one attribute of his ambitions for the medium. For Kurosawa, cinema was a means of embodying his solidarity with other human beings and his warrior's sense that this life requires courage from each of us if we are to survive its pains and trials. The profound reason for his popularity with audiences lies here. In his films, viewers feel their own humanity acknowledged and feel the artist reaching out to them with compassion and regard. The sense of humanity, and the regard for it, is immense in his work. As Stanley Kauffmann has noted, "As with all great artists in every art, there is a sense of hugeness in Kurosawa. Whether he is creating the saga of seven sixteenth-century samurai on the cusp of a different Japan or accompanying a mortally ill civil servant in modern Tokyo, the inner dimensions are immense. This is the world's great egalitarianism: the secrets in every human being, perceived by true art, are immense, spatial."[24]

There are few filmmakers whose works communicate these qualities, and their intense significance for Kurosawa is evident in the way he used cinema as a popular medium, telling stories within enduring genres as a means of reaching people and reaching out to them. His staggering success in this regard can be measured by the singular nature of his achievement. He always insisted that he made movies for the Japanese audience, but he counted himself as a global citizen, a citizen of the world. His audience indeed became an international one and, though this caused him considerable trouble at home among envious younger filmmakers, Kurosawa knew that by making his films for Japanese viewers he would also be reaching viewers throughout the world. In this way, he remained true to his life's project, the project of his Meiji-era cohorts, of integrating Japan with the West and with inter-

67. In *Seven Samurai,* Kambei's eyes fill with tears when he realizes that the proud samurai Kikuchiyo was really born a lowly farmer. The extraordinary humanity and compassion of Kurosawa's filmmaking touched audiences worldwide.

national culture. Kurosawa's cinematic project was to synthesize culture at an international level, making it, both historically and socially, specific and universal.

Here is where his lasting place in cinema history lies. Amid the splinter groups and tribalisms of our postmodern period, Kurosawa's modernism points toward the unifying characteristics of human beings. He believed in them, just as the history of his generation and of his country showed that internationalism was a reality that could be sought and achieved. Kurosawa was a filmmaker who used the medium to respond to extraordinary historical and cultural challenges and who understood that films are of life, not above or separate from it. Kurosawa could not have used the medium in his grandly ambitious way without basing his work around a core set of values. At times, this made the films preachy. But those values—of heroism, justice, and tenacity in the face of misfortune—are what audiences responded to as much as the bravura technique. Director John Sayles perceived and acknowledged this aspect of Kurosawa's work:

> There's also something that I like, that a lot of people may feel is very sentimental, and that's the fact that Kurosawa's movies have values in them. . . . I think Kurosawa really understands that, and he understands what it's like when people go under, when they're not strong enough. But he's also fascinated by the people who could walk away from trouble, or who could become one of the powerful, but who decide to risk [themselves] for the helpless.[25]

To be sure, this is an old-fashioned stance. "Humanism" is today a suspect term, as seen in the withering glare of our postmodern period, as are the notions of truth and the artist's commitment to the pursuit of truth. But these were the ideals that drove Kurosawa's commitment to cinema and his belief in the transforming power of art. And when measured against the self-conscious filmmaking produced by more stylistically radical or intellectually inclined filmmakers, the international popularity of Kurosawa's work is an irrefutable proof of his achievement. Director Frank Capra wrote that only the morally courageous are worthy of speaking to their fellow human beings for two hours in the dark.[26] Kurosawa possessed this courage. His cinema is deeply formalistic, yet those forms are simply his means to an end that he regarded as paramount. That end is the recognition of common humanity and of common suffering. Few filmmakers have had the drive, the overpowering sense of responsibility, and the gifts necessary to take viewers on this journey. Kurosawa did and, doing so, he showed what cinema might yet accomplish.

Notes

Introduction

1. David Desser, *The Samurai Films of Akira Kurosawa* (Ann Arbor, MI: UMI Research Press, 1983), p. 144.
2. See, for example, David Bordwell, *Ozu and the Poetics of Cinema* (Princeton, NJ: Princeton University Press, 1988); Bordwell, "On Our Dream Cinema: Western Historiography and the Japanese Film," *Film Reader* 4 (1979): 45–62; Edward Branigan, "The Space of Equinox Flower," *Screen* 17 (Summer 1976): 74–105; Noël Burch, *To the Distant Observer: Form and Meaning in the Japanese Cinema* (Berkeley and Los Angeles: University of California Press, 1979), pp. 217–246 for discussion of Mizoguchi; David Desser, *Eros plus Massacre* (Bloomington: Indiana University Press, 1988) for a study of cinematic modernism in Japan; Stephen Heath, "The Question Ōshima," *Wide Angle* 2, no. 1 (1977): 48–57; Kristin Thompson and David Bordwell, "Space and Narrative in the Films of Ozu," *Screen* 17 (Summer 1976): 41–73. Peter Lehman discusses tensions among the interpretive positions of Western critics of Japanese film in "The Mysterious Orient, the Crystal Clear Orient, the Non-Existent Orient: Dilemmas of Western Scholars of Japanese Film," *Journal of Film and Video* 39 (Winter 1987): 5–15.
3. The crowning work resulting from this research is David Bordwell, Janet Staiger, and Kristin Thompson, *The Classical Hollywood Cinema: Film Style and Mode of Production to 1960* (New York: Columbia University Press, 1985).
4. See Burch, *To the Distant Observer*, pp. 291–321, and Burch's entry on Kurosawa in *Cinema: A Critical Dictionary*, ed. Richard Roud (Norwich, Great Britain: Fletcher and Son, 1980), pp. 571–582.

5. Desser, *Samurai Films of Akira Kurosawa*, p. vii.
6. Ibid., p. 6.
7. Ibid., p. 146.
8. See, for example, Tony Rayns, "Tokyo Stories," *Sight and Sound* 50 (Summer 1981): 174.
9. Desser, *Samurai Films of Akira Kurosawa*, pp. 14–55.
10. See the essays on *Dodeskaden* and *Dersu Uzala* in Donald Richie, *The Films of Akira Kurosawa*, rev. ed. with additional material by Joan Mellen (Berkeley and Los Angeles: University of California Press, 1984), pp. 184–203.

Chapter 1: Viewing Kurosawa

1. Quoted in Yasunari Kawabata, *The Existence and Discovery of Beauty*, trans. V. H. Viglielmo ([Japan]: Mainichi, 1969), p. 44.
2. An explicitly political film, *Those Who Make Tomorrow* was planned to dramatize the importance of unions and worker solidarity and was produced as part of the new postwar context of labor union activism. Kyōko Hirano discusses these aspects of the film in "Japanese Cinema Under the American Occupation: 1945–1952" (Ph.D. dissertation, New York University, 1988), forthcoming from the Smithsonian Institution Press. Donald Richie discusses the background of the making of the film in *The Films of Akira Kurosawa*, p. 28. Kurosawa has pointed out that his section of the film was shot in just one week. See Michel Mesnil, *Kurosawa*, (Paris: Seghers, 1973), p. 118. Kurosawa omits the film from discussion in his autobiography.
3. See Fred Hiatt, "Making the Film of His Dreams," *Philadelphia Inquirer*, January 1, 1989, p. 2H.
4. Joseph L. Anderson and Donald Richie, *The Japanese Film: Art and Industry*, expanded ed. (Princeton, NJ: Princeton University Press, 1982), p. 254. This is the standard English-language history on the Japanese cinema, first published in 1959 and recently updated to cover developments since the 1960s.
5. Ibid., p. 451.
6. Ibid., p. 456.
7. Tadao Satō, *Currents in Japanese Cinema*, trans. Gregory Barrett (New York: Kodansha International, 1982), pp. 236–237.
8. Anderson and Richie, *The Japanese Film*, pp. 452, 453.

9. Akira Kurosawa, *Something Like an Autobiography*, trans. Audie Bock (New York: Alfred A. Knopf, 1982), p. vi.

10. Quoted in Audie Bock, "Kurosawa on his Innovative Cinema," *New York Times*, October 4, 1981, sec. 2, p. 21.

11. Greg Mitchell, "Kurosawa in Winter," *American Film* 7 (April 1982): 51.

12. David Desser offers a detailed study of the Japanese New Wave in *Eros plus Massacre*.

13. Desser discusses the shifts within the Japanese film industry that helped foreground the work of these directors. Ibid., pp. 8–10.

14. Quoted in Joan Mellen, *Voices from the Japanese Cinema* (New York: Liveright, 1975), pp. 252, 253.

15. Ibid., p. 288.

16. Rayns, "Tokyo Stories," p. 176.

17. Ibid.

18. Quoted in Derek Elley, "Kurosawa at the NFT," *Films and Filming*, no. 380 (May 1986): 18.

19. Quoted in Mesnil, *Kurosawa*, p. 107.

20. Ibid., p. 105.

21. The art cinema has recently been discussed as a distinct narrative mode, employing its own codes and formal structures. See David Bordwell, *Narration in the Fiction Film* (Madison: University of Wisconsin Press, 1985), pp. 205–233.

22. Anderson and Richie, *The Japanese Film*, p. 380.

23. Charles Higham, "Kurosawa's Humanism," *Kenyon Review* 27 (Autumn 1965): 742.

24. Jay Leyda, "The Films of Kurosawa," *Sight and Sound* 24 (October–December 1954): 78. This is an interesting essay for historical reasons: it was written shortly after the international discovery of Kurosawa and Japanese film, and it conveys the excitement of the period.

25. Vernon Young, "The Hidden Fortress: Kurosawa's Comic Mode," *The Hudson Review* 14 (Summer 1961): 275.

26. Norman Silverstein, "Kurosawa's Detective-Story Parables," *Japan Quarterly* 12, no. 3 (July–September 1965): 354.

27. David Robinson, "Dodeskaden," *Monthly Film Bulletin* 42 (May 1975): 103.

28. Akira Iwasaki, "Kurosawa and His Work," in *Focus on Rashōmon*, ed. Donald Richie (Englewood Cliffs, NJ: Prentice-Hall, 1972), p. 25.

29. Audie Bock, *Japanese Film Directors* (New York: Kodansha International, 1978), p. 138.
30. Keiko McDonald, *Cinema East* (East Brunswick, NJ: Associated University Presses, 1983), p. 71.
31. Richie, *The Films of Akira Kurosawa*, p. 183.
32. Irving Babbitt, "Humanism: An Essay at Definition," in *Humanism and America*, ed. Norman Foerster (New York: Farrar and Rinehart, 1930), p. 26.
33. Ibid., p. 30.
34. Norman Foerster, "Preface," *Humanism and America*, p. xiv.
35. Burch, "Akira Kurosawa," p. 582.
36. Richie, *The Films of Akira Kurosawa*, p. 18.
37. Iwasaki, "Kurosawa and His Work," p. 29.
38. Ibid.
39. Donald Richie, "Kurosawa on Kurosawa," *Sight and Sound* 33 (Summer 1964): 111.
40. Satō has also made this point in reference to Kurosawa's work. *Currents in Japanese Cinema*, p. 50.
41. Desser, *Samurai Films of Akira Kurosawa*, p. 7.
42. See, for example, ibid., p. 58.
43. Kurosawa, *Something Like an Autobiography*, p. xii.
44. Higham, "Kurosawa's Humanism," p. 739. In addition to the comparison with Ford, Higham also suggests influences from George Stevens and William Wyler. Regarding the general issue of American influence, Kurosawa has made an interesting reply. In an interview in 1965, he was asked about "the American influence which some critics thought they discerned in *Seven Samurai*." In reply, Kurosawa related the following anecdote: "The critics must have seen the shortened version for export. M. Langlois, after having seen the complete version, has recently written to me to say that he made a mistake in talking about this American influence." Quoted in Mesnil, *Kurosawa*, pp. 110–111.
45. Tom Milne, "Dersu Uzala," *Monthly Film Bulletin* 45 (January 1978): 5.
46. John Pym, "Kagemusha," *Monthly Film Bulletin* 47 (December 1980): 237.
47. John Gillett, "Kurosawa's Army," *Sight and Sound* 49 (Spring 1980): 73.
48. Anderson and Richie, *The Japanese Film*, p. 409.
49. Richie, *The Films of Akira Kurosawa*, p. 223.

50. Ibid., p. 147.

51. Dan Yakir, "The Warrior Returns," *Film Comment* 16 (November–December 1980): 57.

52. Kenneth S. Nolley, "The Western as Jidai-Geki," *Western American Literature* 11 (November 1976): 232.

53. Ralph Croizier, "Beyond East and West: The American Western and Rise of the Chinese Swordplay Movie," *Journal of Popular Film* 1 (Summer 1972): 230.

54. Alain Silver, *The Samurai Film* (South Brunswick, NJ, and New York: A. S. Barnes and Co., 1977), p. 36.

55. Nigel Andrews, "Sanjurō," *Monthly Film Bulletin* 38 (January 1971): 14.

56. Desser, *Samurai Films of Akira Kurosawa*, pp. 110–116.

57. Milne, "Dersu Uzala," p. 5.

58. Richard Combs, "A Shaggy Ghost Story," *Sight and Sound* 50 (Winter 1980–81): 62.

59. Richie, *The Films of Akira Kurosawa*, p. 147.

60. Joseph L. Anderson, "When the Twain Meet: Hollywood's Remake of *The Seven Samurai*," *Film Quarterly* 15 (Spring 1962): 58.

61. Ibid.

62. Desser, *Samurai Films of Akira Kurosawa*, pp. 9, 13.

63. Ibid., pp. 23–25. Joseph Anderson also notes important differences in the presentation of landscape in the Western and in samurai films. "Japanese Swordfighters and American Gunfighters," *Cinema Journal* 12 (Spring 1973): 9.

64. Stuart Kaminsky, *American Film Genres* (New York: Dell Publishing Co., Laurel Edition, 1977), p. 49.

65. Satō, *Currents in Japanese Cinema*, p. 51. Anderson notes that the racial conflicts that are often central to the Western (i.e., between Indians and whites) have no counterpart in the samurai film. "Japanese Swordfighters and American Gunfighters," p. 10.

66. See, for example, Richie's discussion in *The Films of Akira Kurosawa*, pp. 156–157.

67. Desser, *Samurai Films of Akira Kurosawa*, pp. 31–51.

68. Ibid., p. 39.

69. Paul Seydor, *Peckinpah: The Western Films* (Chicago: University of Illinois Press, 1980), pp. 137–139.

70. Desser does point out, however, that some samurai films celebrate the hero who acts with impunity and is able to transcend social codes. See his discussion of "Zen Fighter" films in *Samurai Films of*

Akira Kurosawa, pp. 39–43. Anderson notes that the samurai heroes often sense the possibility of alternative courses of action, even though they are constrained from choosing them. "Japanese Swordfighters and American Gunfighters," p. 5.

71. Richie, *The Films of Akira Kurosawa*, p. 147.
72. See, for example, Donald Keene, ed., *20 Plays of the Nō Theatre* (New York: Columbia University Press, 1970), p. 9; and Makoto Ueda, *Literary and Art Theories in Japan* (Cleveland, OH: Western Reserve University Press, 1967), p. 155.
73. Quoted in Yakir, "The Warrior Returns," p. 57.
74. Desser notes the influence on Lucas's *Star Wars* and discusses the debts Sturges and Peckinpah owe to Kurosawa. *Samurai Films of Akira Kurosawa*, pp. 140–144.
75. Christopher Frayling discusses the impact of spaghetti Westerns on the American cinema in *Spaghetti Westerns* (Boston: Routledge and Kegan Paul, 1981), pp. 280–286.
76. Quoted in Yakir, "The Warrior Returns," p. 57.
77. Quoted in Richie, "Kurosawa on Kurosawa," p. 112.
78. Burch, *Cinema: A Critical Dictionary*, p. 573.
79. Satō notes that the influence of foreign films upon Japanese filmmakers has been "considerable"; *Currents in Japanese Cinema*, p. 32. In Kurosawa's case, if direct influence is difficult to establish, his familiarity with the works of foreign directors has been considerable.
80. Quoted in Elley, "Kurosawa at the NFT," p. 18.
81. Quoted in Yakir, "The Warrior Returns," p. 57.
82. Eugene Soviak, "On the Nature of Western Progress: The Journal of the Iwakura Embassy," in *Tradition and Modernization in Japanese Culture*, ed. Donald H. Shively (Princeton, NJ: Princeton University Press, 1971), pp. 32–33.
83. John Whitney Hall, "Changing Conceptions of the Modernization of Japan," in *Changing Japanese Attitudes Toward Modernization*, ed. Marius B. Jansen (Princeton, NJ: Princeton University Press, 1965, reprint 1972), p. 12.
84. See, for example, Robert N. Bellah, "Ienaga Saburō and the Search for Meaning in Modern Japan," in *Changing Japanese Attitudes*, p. 369.
85. Donald H. Shively, "The Japanization of the Middle Meiji," in *Tradition and Modernization*, p. 118; Carol Gluck, *Japan's Modern Myths* (Princeton, NJ: Princeton University Press, 1985), p. 20.
86. Gluck, *Japan's Modern Myths*, p. 113.

87. Akira Iwasaki has defined Kurosawa and his work in explicit generational terms: "Kurosawa belongs to a more recent generation which must look to the West for help in defining Japan, which verifies and analyzes the one by constant reference to the other." "Kurosawa and His Work," p. 22.

88. Henry DeWitt Smith, II, *Japan's First Student Radicals* (Cambridge, MA: Harvard University Press, 1972), passim.

89. Bellah, "Ienaga Saburō," p. 422.

90. Robert Ward and [Yoshikazu Sakamoto], eds., *Democratizing Japan: The Allied Occupation* (Honolulu: University of Hawaii Press, 1987), p. 423.

91. Ibid.

92. See, for example, Marius B. Jansen, "Tokugawa and Modern Japan," p. 319, and John Whitney Hall, "The Castle Town and Japan's Modern Urbanization," pp. 169–188, in *Studies in the Institutional History of Early Modern Japan*, ed. John W. Hall and Marius B. Jansen (Princeton, NJ: Princeton University Press, 1968).

93. Jansen, "Tokugawa and Modern Japan," p. 329.

94. McDonald, *Cinema East*, p. 71.

95. Hall, "Changing Conceptions of the Modernization of Japan," p. 12.

96. Herbert Passin, "Modernization and the Japanese Intellectual: Some Comparative Observations," in *Changing Japanese Attitudes*, p. 476.

97. Shūichi Katō, *A History of Japanese Literature*, vol. 3, trans. Don Sanderson (New York: Kodansha International, 1983), pp. 113–114.

98. Donald Keene, *Dawn to the West* (Fiction) (New York: Holt, Rinehart and Winston, 1984), pp. 305–354, 386–440.

99. Bordwell, *Ozu and the Poetics of Cinema*, p. 41.

100. Jansen, "Tokugawa and Modern Japan," p. 330.

101. Shūichi Katō, *Form, Style, Tradition: Reflections on Japanese Art and Society* (New York: Kodansha International, 1986), p. 57.

102. Satō, *Currents in Japanese Cinema*, p. 9.

103. For the Taishō period, see Bernard S. Silberman and H. D. Harootunian, eds., *Japan in Crisis* (Princeton, NJ: Princeton University Press, 1974). Silberman ("Taishō Japan and the Crisis of Secularism," pp. 437–453) discusses Taishō Japan in terms of a crisis over needs for social order and the frightening potential for complete freedom inhering in a "secular, voluntarist" conception of society, which, he suggests, typified Taishō society.

104. Gluck, *Japan's Modern Myths*, p. 39.

105. George M. Wilson, "Restoration History and Shōwa Politics," in *Crisis Politics in Prewar Japan*, ed. George M. Wilson (Tokyo: Sophia University, 1970), p. 78.

106. See, for example, Curtis's argument that the Liberal Democratic Party has evolved from a party of conservative interests to a flexible, broad-based party responsive to divergent social interests, and McKean's discussion of the outcome of the Big Four pollution suits. Gerald L. Curtis, *The Japanese Way of Politics* (New York: Columbia University Press, 1988), pp. 236–249; Margaret A. McKean, *Environmental Protest and Citizen Politics in Japan* (Berkeley and Los Angeles: University of California Press, 1981), p. 34.

107. Jansen, "Tokugawa and Modern Japan," p. 329.

108. For characterizations of the relation of big business to citizens' grievances, see McKean, *Environmental Protest*, p. 42, and William W. Lockwood, *The Economic Development of Japan* (Princeton, NJ: Princeton University Press, 1954, expanded ed. 1968), pp. 565–566.

109. Desser, *Samurai Films of Akira Kurosawa*, p. 78.

110. See, for example, Ivan Morris, *Nationalism and the Right Wing in Japan* (Westport, CT: Greenwood Press, 1974; orig. pub. Oxford University Press, 1960), pp. 384–388; Chie Nakane, *Japanese Society* (Berkeley and Los Angeles: University of California Press, 1970; reprint 1972), passim.

111. [Takeo Yazaki], "The Samurai Family and Feudal Ideology," in *Imperial Japan, 1800–1945*, ed. Jon Livingston, Joe Moore, and Felicia Oldfather (New York: Pantheon Books, 1973), p. 60.

112. Robert J. Smith, *Japanese Society: Tradition, Self, and the Social Order* (New York: Cambridge University Press, 1983), p. 87.

113. Kazuo Kawai, *Japan's American Interlude* (Chicago, IL: University of Chicago Press, 1960, reprint 1969), pp. 48–49.

114. H. D. Harootunian, "A Sense of an Ending and the Problem of Taishō," in *Japan in Crisis*, p. 19.

115. Scholars disagree about whether Japan's wartime government was fascist. Masao Maruyama describes the contours of Japanese fascism, but others have pointed out that the wartime regime was not a totalitarian state, that its coercive power, the degree of conformity exacted from the populace, was far less than what prevailed in Nazi Germany. See Maruyama, *Thought and Behavior in Modern Japanese Politics*, ed. Ivan Morris (New York: Oxford University Press, 1963, expanded ed. 1969), pp. 25–83. For a contrary view, see Ben-

Ami Shillony, *Politics and Culture in Wartime Japan* (Oxford: Clarendon Press, 1981), pp. 15–16.

116. Kurosawa, *Something Like an Autobiography*, p. 146.

117. *Eiga Junkan* (Special issue, 1956), cited in Bock, *Japanese Film Directors*, p. 167.

118. Kurosawa, *Something Like an Autobiography*, p. 146.

119. Smith, *Japanese Society*, p. 49.

120. Kiefer, "The danchi zoku and the evolution of modern mind," quoted in Smith, *Japanese Society*, p. 70.

121. A later generation of Japanese directors, those collectively referred to as the New Wave, emphasized the individual in their studies of youthful rebellion and criminality. Despite their vociferous denial of any influence from Kurosawa, the variant concept of the self found in Kurosawa's films, embodying a social critique, may be seen as an important link to the New Wave.

122. Richie notes the loneliness of the hero in *The Films of Akira Kurosawa*, p. 61.

123. Quoted in Mesnil, *Kurosawa*, p. 103.

124. Even in private, however, Kurosawa is reported as rarely discussing or offering opinions on political issues. Audie Bock, personal conversation, February 9, 1989.

125. Richie, *The Films of Akira Kurosawa*, p. 113.

126. Quoted in Mesnil, *Kurosawa*, pp. 102–103.

Chapter 2: The Dialectics of Style

1. Robert Treat Paine and Alexander Soper, *The Art and Architecture of Japan* (New York: Penguin Books, 1955, reprint 1985), p. 21.

2. Kurosawa, *Something Like an Autobiography*, p. 71.

3. Ibid., p. 182.

4. Ibid., p. 95.

5. Ibid., p. 93.

6. See Ryūsaku Tsunoda, Wm. Theodore de Bary, and Donald Keene, eds., *Sources of Japanese Tradition*, vol. 1 (New York: Columbia University Press, 1958, reprint 1964), p. 114.

7. Kurosawa, *Something Like an Autobiography*, p. 147.

8. [Motokiyo Zeami] *On the Art of the Nō Drama: The Major Treatises of Zeami*, trans. J. Thomas Rimer and [Masakazu Yamazaki] (Princeton, NJ: Princeton University Press, 1984), p. 88.

9. Ibid., p. 98.

10. Ibid., p. 105.

11. Smith, *Japanese Society*, pp. 98–99.

12. Ibid., p. 99.

13. Richie, *The Films of Akira Kurosawa*, p. 214.

14. Quoted in William Wolf, "Wisdom from Kurosawa," *New York Magazine* 13 (October 20, 1980): 91.

15. Quoted in Kyōko Hirano, "Making Films for All the People: An Interview with Akira Kurosawa," *Cineaste* 14, no. 4 (1986): 24.

16. Alan W. Watts, *The Way of Zen* (New York: Vintage Books, 1957), p. 77.

17. Heinrich Dumoulin, *A History of Zen Buddhism*, trans. Paul Peachey (New York: Pantheon Books, 1963; Beacon reprint 1969), p. 50.

18. Ibid., p. 161.

19. D. T. Suzuki, *Zen and Japanese Culture* (Princeton, NJ: Princeton University Press, 1959, reprint 1973), p. 13.

20. Quoted in Hirano, "Making Films for All the People," p. 24.

21. Wolf, "Wisdom from Kurosawa," p. 91.

22. Quoted in Richie, "Kurosawa on Kurosawa," p. 110.

23. Similarities between the artistic projects of Kurosawa and Brecht have also been noted by Burch, *To the Distant Observer*, pp. 307–308, and by Joan Mellen, "The Epic Cinema of Kurosawa," *Take One* 3 (June 1972): 16.

24. For a discussion of the importance of pleasure in Brecht's work, and a critique of modernist critical and aesthetic practices that dismiss a sense of play from the artwork, see Sylvia Harvey, *May '68 and Film Culture* (London: BFI Publishing, 1980), pp. 69–82.

25. Bertolt Brecht, *Brecht on Theatre*, trans. John Willett (New York: Hill and Wang, 1957, reprint 1979), p. 71.

26. Hirano, "Making Films for All the People," p. 25.

27. Ibid.

28. Rayns, "Tokyo Stories," p. 171.

29. Yakir, "The Warrior Returns," p. 55.

30. Kurosawa discusses this research in Rayns, "Tokyo Stories," pp. 171–172.

31. Quoted in Yakir, "The Warrior Returns," p. 56.

32. Richie, *The Films of Akira Kurosawa*, p. 97.

33. Production and signifying practices of the Hollywood cinema are explored in detail in Bordwell et al., *Classical Hollywood Cinema*.

34. In *To the Distant Observer* Burch discusses the visual codes of early Japanese cinema and hypothesizes their gradual displacement in the 1940s by a more Westernized approach modeled on the Hollywood cinema.

35. Kurosawa discusses the cutting of this sequence, with the assistance of his teacher Kajirō Yamamoto, in *Something Like an Autobiography*, pp. 105–106.

36. Richie, *The Films of Akira Kurosawa*, p. 23.

37. Mellen, *Voices from the Japanese Cinema*, p. 56.

38. As Richie points out, Kurosawa's narratives tend to center around the education of a hero. *The Films of Akira Kurosawa*, p. 18.

39. Bordwell et al., *Classical Hollywood Cinema*, p. 25.

40. The code of eyeline matching, generally based on shot-reverse-shot editing, has been much discussed in the literature. For additional discussion, see Bordwell et al., *Classical Hollywood Cinema*, pp. 56–57, and Bordwell, *Narration*, pp. 110–113. For a classic reading of shot-reverse-shot "suturing" of screen space, see Jean-Pierre Oudart, "Cinema and Suture," *Screen* 18 (Winter 1977–78): 35–47, and for its ideological implications, see Daniel Dayan, "The Tutor-Code of Classical Cinema," in *Movies and Methods*, vol. 1, ed. Bill Nichols (Berkeley and Los Angeles: University of California Press, 1976), pp. 438–451. Dayan's position is analyzed by William Rothman, "Against 'The System of the Suture,' " in *Movies and Methods*, pp. 451–459, and by Bordwell in *Narration*, pp. 110–111.

41. Noël Burch has also noted this quality of Kurosawa's cinema and considered its relation to Japanese culture. See his discussions of Kurosawa in *To the Distant Observer*, pp. 291–321, and in *Cinema: A Critical Dictionary*, pp. 571–582.

42. Ana Laura Zambrano, "Throne of Blood: Kurosawa's Macbeth," *Literature/Film Quarterly* 2 (Summer 1974): 262–274.

43. Ueda, *Literary and Art Theories in Japan*, p. 155.

44. [Zeami] *On the Art of the Nō Drama*, p. 52.

45. Ibid., p. 58.

46. Ibid., p. 191.

47. Ibid., p. 97.

48. Keene, *20 Plays of the Nō Theatre*, p. 117.

49. This sequence where Sanshiro and Yano glimpse Sayo in prayer before the shrine was the first sequence Kurosawa shot as a director. He discusses the mixture of trepidation and excitement he felt in *Something Like an Autobiography*, p. 124.

50. Robert Ellwood and Richard Pilgrim, *Japanese Religion: A Cultural Perspective* (Englewood Cliffs, NJ: Prentice-Hall, 1985), p. 105.

51. Richard N. Tucker, *Japan: Film Image* (London: Studio Vista, 1973), p. 84.

52. Desser, *Samurai Films of Akira Kurosawa*, pp. 135–136.

53. Ibid., p. 136.
54. Joseph Strayer, "The Tokugawa Period and Japanese Feudalism," in *Studies in the Institutional History*, p. 8.
55. Ibid., p. 9.
56. John Whitney Hall, "Feudalism in Japan: A Reassessment," in *Studies in the Institutional History*, p. 47.
57. Ibid., pp. 19, 26–27.
58. Kurosawa, *Something Like an Autobiography*, pp. 132–133.
59. Kurosawa's discussion of this concept can be found in *Something Like an Autobiography*, pp. 107–108, and in Richie, *The Films of Akira Kurosawa*, pp. 225–226.
60. Kurosawa, *Something Like an Autobiography*, p. 135; Richie, *The Films of Akira Kurosawa*, p. 24.
61. Richie, *The Films of Akira Kurosawa*, p. 24.
62. Richie also notes the triangular compositions in *Rashōmon*. Ibid., pp. 77–88.
63. George Sansom discusses the incident in *A History of Japan*, 3 vols. (Stanford, CA: Stanford University Press, 1958–1963, reprint 1987), 1: 289–334.
64. Ibid., p. 326.
65. Richie is especially good on the meaning of Kurosawa's staging of this final dance. *The Films of Akira Kurosawa*, p. 35.
66. Ibid., p. 34.
67. Kurosawa discusses this in *Something Like an Autobiography*, pp. 142–144.
68. David Desser, for example, identifies Kurosawa with a mode of filmmaking that "is in all important respects modeled on the classical Hollywood style." *Eros plus Massacre*, pp. 20, 21.
69. The culmination of this work is Bordwell et al., *Classical Hollywood Cinema*.
70. Ibid., p. 50.
71. Ibid., p. 63.
72. Bordwell notes that Kurosawa's disjunctive cutting requires an effort at perceptual reorientation by the viewer. Ibid., pp. 362–363.
73. Kurosawa's fondness for geometric design has often been remarked upon by his commentators. Excepting Burch, and Bordwell (see note 72), however, it is not generally seen as evidence of a distinct mode of film practice, alternative to that of Hollywood. For discussions of Kurosawa's visual geometry, see J. Blumenthal, "Macbeth into *Throne of Blood*," *Sight and Sound* 34 (Autumn 1965): 192; Burch, *To the Distant Observer*, p. 319; Anthony Davies, *Filming Shake-*

speare's Plays: The Adaptations of Laurence Olivier, Orson Welles, Peter Brook, and Akira Kurosawa (New York: Cambridge University Press, 1988), pp. 161–164; Higham, "Kurosawa's Humanism," p. 741; Marsha Kinder, "Throne of Blood: A Morality Dance," Literature/Film Quarterly 5 (Fall 1977): 341; Keiko McDonald, "Swordsmanship and Gamesmanship: Historical Milieu in Yōjimbō," Literature/Film Quarterly 8 (Summer 1980): 193.

74. Burch, To the Distant Observer, pp. 291–321.

Chapter 3: Willpower Can Cure All Human Ailments

1. Jerome B. Cohen, Japan's Economy in War and Reconstruction (Minneapolis: University of Minnesota Press, 1949; Greenwood reprint 1973), p. 406.
2. Shillony, Politics and Culture in Wartime Japan, p. 81.
3. Cohen, Japan's Economy in War and Reconstruction, p. 386.
4. [Hyōe Murakami], Japan: The Years of Trial, 1919–52 (Tokyo: Japan Culture Institute, 1982), p. 200.
5. Cohen, Japan's Economy in War and Reconstruction, pp. 387–388.
6. Kase Toshikazu, Eclipse of the Rising Sun, quoted in Peter Calvocoressi and Guy Wint, Total War: Causes and Consequences of the Second World War (New York: Penguin Books, 1972, reprint 1979), p. 877.
7. Shillony, Politics and Culture in Wartime Japan, p. 11.
8. William Miles Fletcher, III, The Search for a New Order: Intellectuals and Fascism in Prewar Japan (Chapel Hill: University of North Carolina Press, 1982), p. 10; Henry DeWitt Smith, II, Japan's First Student Radicals, pp. 190–191.
9. Gluck, Japan's Modern Myths, p. 32.
10. Ibid., p. 283.
11. See Shillony's discussion of efforts to overcome modernity and negate select Western values during the war in Politics and Culture in Wartime Japan, pp. 141–151.
12. See Tsunoda et al., Sources of Japanese Tradition, pp. 785–795.
13. Ibid., p. 789.
14. Ibid.
15. Ibid., p. 788.
16. Ibid., p. 790.
17. [Daikichi Irokawa], The Culture of the Meiji Period, trans. Marius B. Jansen (Princeton, NJ: Princeton University Press, 1985), pp. 245–246.

18. Kawai, *Japan's American Interlude*, p. 40.
19. Shillony, *Politics and Culture in Wartime Japan*, p. 16.
20. See the discussions in Theodore H. McNelly, "Induced Revolution: The Policy and Process of Constitutional Reform in Occupied Japan," in *Democratizing Japan*, pp. 76–106. Kazuo Kawai discusses the cultural implications of the shift from Imperial to popular sovereignty in *Japan's American Interlude*, pp. 56–58.
21. Kozo Yamamura discusses these suspicions in *Economic Policy in Postwar Japan* (Berkeley and Los Angeles: University of California Press, 1967), p. 2. Lockwood and Kawai point out, however, that the zaibatsu were not coterminous with either the state or the militarists in prewar and wartime Japan. Lockwood, *The Economic Development of Japan*, p. 564; Kawai, *Japan's American Interlude*, pp. 153–155.
22. For a discussion of the Supreme Commander for Allied Powers' (SCAP) economic reforms and their reception in postwar Japan, see Yamamura, *Economic Policy in Postwar Japan*.
23. McNelly makes the point that democracy had "roots" in Japan prior to the Occupation reforms in "Induced Revolution," pp. 101–102.
24. Bellah, "Ienaga Saburō," p. 402.
25. Morris, *Nationalism and the Right Wing in Japan*, p. 383.
26. Shūichi Katō, "Japanese Writers and Modernization," in *Changing Japanese Attitudes*, p. 441.
27. Satō, *Currents in Japanese Cinema*, p. 116.
28. Mesnil, *Kurosawa*, p. 104.
29. Shillony discusses the general lack of resistance in wartime Japan by artists and intellectuals and how many used their work and media in support of the war or politics of national expansion. *Politics and Culture in Wartime Japan*, pp. 110–133.
30. Kurosawa, *Something Like an Autobiography*, pp. 145, 146.
31. Hirano, "Japanese Cinema Under the American Occupation," pp. 13–14.
32. Ibid., p. 45.
33. Hirano provides a list of topics encouraged and prohibited by CIE's film policy. Ibid., pp. 50–51, 60. She also provides numerous case studies of films that were altered or censored, sometimes suppressed, by Allied authority. See also Anderson and Richie, *The Japanese Film*, pp. 160–161.
34. Hirano, "Japanese Cinema Under the American Occupation," p. 239.
35. Ibid., p. 20. Kurosawa has remarked that "most Japanese in those

post-war years simply swallowed the concepts of freedom and de-mocracy whole, waving slogans around without really knowing what they meant." *Something Like an Autobiography*, p. 145.

36. Kurosawa says that the Japanese censors treated filmmakers like "criminals" and describes their rout under the Occupation as a "delight beyond measure." *Something Like an Autobiography*, p. 144. By contrast, he speaks respectfully of the American censors (p. 144). An enlightening remark about how oppressive he found the wartime atmosphere is the following: "Being young in those times consisted of suppressing the sound of one's own breathing in the jail cell that was called the 'home front' " (p. 150).

37. Morris, *Nationalism and the Right Wing in Japan*, p. 384.

38. Desser, *Samurai Films of Akira Kurosawa*, p. 5.

39. Kurosawa, *Something Like an Autobiography*, p. 145.

40. Satō, *Currents in Japanese Cinema*, p. 123.

41. [Zeami] *On the Art of the Nō Drama*, pp. 34–35.

42. Kurosawa, *Something Like an Autobiography*, p. 185.

43. In his new film, *Dreams*, Kurosawa returns to what has been an obsessive idea in his work, the seductive power and charm of the imagination. Whereas in all earlier films, the dreamworld was pitted against the cruelties and harshness of the real one, the new work is devoted entirely to a series of dreams he has experienced since youth.

44. Kurosawa, *Something Like an Autobiography*, p. 177.

45. Richie, *The Films of Akira Kurosawa*, p. 69.

46. Kurosawa, *Something Like an Autobiography*, p. 178.

47. Richie, *The Films of Akira Kurosawa*, p. 62.

48. Kurosawa, *Something Like an Autobiography*, p. 146.

49. Kurosawa discusses these strikes in *Something Like an Autobiography*, pp. 164–168. As always, ambivalent in relation to political activity, Kurosawa is critical of both the leftist union leading the strike and of Toho's president, whose intransigence helped worsen the crisis.

50. Hirano refers to the film's "ideological vacuousness" in "Japanese Cinema Under the American Occupation," p. 300. She also quotes (p. 302) from an analysis by Nagisa Ōshima on the postwar cinema in which he criticizes the film's vague politics as an attempt to absolve the filmmakers and all Japanese from the responsibilities of wartime collaboration.

51. Ibid., pp. 281–283.

52. Ibid., pp. 283–284.

53. From a feminist perspective, Joan Mellen discusses the restricted place women hold in Kurosawa's cinema. *The Waves at Genji's Door* (New York: Pantheon books, 1976), pp. 41–56.

54. Ibid., pp. 45–46.

55. Ibid., p. 45.

56. For details, see Kurosawa, *Something Like an Autobiography*, pp. 148–149, and Richie, *The Films of Akira Kurosawa*, p. 37.

57. Richie, *The Films of Akira Kurosawa*, p. 47.

58. Kurosawa's emphasis on individual struggle and heroic dedication as a remedy for postwar collapse may be seen as consistent with the mandate of Occupation censors that "filmmakers propagate the notion that such conditions would be alleviated through 'patience and work' "; Hirano, "Japanese Cinema Under the American Occupation," p. 85. Nevertheless, Kurosawa's portrayal of black market criminality in *Drunken Angel* drew complaints from CIE as being excessive. Hirano notes various endings that were proposed for the film. She also speculates that the critical, less empathetic treatment of the criminal in *Stray Dog* was probably more palatable to the CIE censors. Ibid., pp. 123, 125.

59. See the essays on neorealism in André Bazin, *What is Cinema?*, vol. 2, trans. Hugh Gray (Berkeley and Los Angeles: University of California Press, 1972), and the discussion of neorealism in Robert Phillip Kolker, *The Altering Eye* (New York: Oxford University Press, 1983), pp. 44–55.

60. Richie, *The Films of Akira Kurosawa*, p. 47.

61. Ibid., p. 50.

62. For a good discussion of this, see Barbara Wolff, "Detectives and Doctors," *Japan Quarterly* 19 (January–March 1972): 83–87. Tadao Satō also notes this in *Currents in Japanese Cinema*, p. 121.

63. Kurosawa, *Something Like an Autobiography*, p. 54.

64. Kawai, *Japan's American Interlude*, pp. 228–231.

65. Kurosawa, *Something Like an Autobiography*, p. 156.

66. Joseph M. Kitagawa, *Religion in Japanese History* (New York: Columbia University Press, 1966), p. 280.

67. Kurosawa, *Something Like an Autobiography*, p. 162.

68. Ibid., p. 173.

69. Richie, *The Films of Akira Kurosawa*, p. 59.

70. Audie Bock suggests that a "push-and-release" rhythm is characteristic of all Kurosawa's best films. *Japanese Film Directors*, p. 176.

71. Noël Burch remarks that excess—both visual and dramatic—is a constant in Kurosawa's work. *To the Distant Observer*, pp. 294–296.

72. Hirano notes that the rice planting scenes in *No Regrets* also employ a silent film-style montage. ("Japanese Cinema Under the American Occupation," p. 298.) The length of the *Stray Dog* sequence, however, makes it far more audacious.

73. Richie, *The Films of Akira Kurosawa*, pp. 59, 61.

74. Kurosawa, *Something Like an Autobiography*, p. 130.

75. Ibid., p. 158.

76. Richie has also remarked on the eerie beauty of this scene. *The Films of Akira Kurosawa*, pp. 60–61.

77. The differences between dialogic and monologic perspectives are defined and discussed by Mikhail Bakhtin in *Problems of Dostoevsky's Poetics*, ed. and trans. Caryl Emerson (Minneapolis: University of Minnesota Press, 1984), pp. 52–75.

78. See, for example, the discussion of *Mother Courage* in Frederick Ewen, *Bertolt Brecht: His Life, His Art, and His Times* (New York: Citadel, 1969), pp. 353–361.

79. Kurosawa remarked, "For this film [*Drunken Angel*], I had originally wanted to use the Dreigroschenoper music, but we could not get the rights, so we used cheap guitar music as a substitute." *Interviews with Film Directors*, ed. Andrew Sarris (New York: Discus Books, 1967, reprint 1969), p. 293. Michael Jeck brought this reference to my attention.

80. Brecht, *Brecht on Theatre*, p. 15.

81. Ibid., p. 44.

82. Kurosawa discusses his affection for "unformed" characters in *Something Like an Autobiography*, pp. 129–130. Richie also points to the importance for Kurosawa's films of the "unformed" hero, in *The Films of Akira Kurosawa*, p. 18.

83. Brecht, *Brecht on Theatre*, p. 247.

84. Richie, *The Films of Akira Kurosawa*, p. 89.

85. Richie briefly discusses this dissolve in ibid., p. 90.

86. Ibid., p. 93.

87. Burch finds this gap to motivate the formal design of the flashbacks, themselves a series of gaps, during the funeral sequence. *To the Distant Observer*, pp. 303–304.

88. Ibid., p. 303.

89. Takie Sugiyama Lebra, "Nonconfrontational Strategies for Management of Interpersonal Conflicts," in *Conflict in Japan*, ed. Ellis S.

Krauss, Thomas P. Rohlen, and Patricia G. Steinhoff (Honolulu: University of Hawaii Press, 1984), p. 56.

Chapter 4: Experiments and Adaptations

1. Hirano, "Making Films for All the People," p. 25.
2. Kurosawa, *Something Like an Autobiography*, p. 28.
3. Ibid., p. 17.
4. Ibid., p. 22.
5. Ibid.
6. Ibid.
7. Tsunoda et al., *Sources of Japanese Tradition*, p. 330.
8. Kurosawa, *Something Like an Autobiography*, p. 156.
9. McDonald, *Cinema East*, p. 72.
10. Hajime Nakamura, *Ways of Thinking of Eastern Peoples*, rev. trans. ed. Philip Wiener (Honolulu: East-West Center Press, 1964, reprint 1968), p. 414.
11. Sōseki described individualism this way in a lecture on the topic, according to Howard S. Hibbett, "Natsume Sōseki and the Psychological Novel," in *Tradition and Modernization*, p. 309. Hibbett writes (p. 346) that "For Sōseki . . . individualism and alienation were the inescapable conditions of a modern consciousness." The observation also applies to Kurosawa's cinema, where, in a typical example, the birth pangs of Watanabe's enlightenment accompany the trauma of the alienated self.
12. Bakhtin, *Problems of Dostoevsky's Poetics*, p. 104.
13. Ibid., p. 105.
14. Richie, *The Films of Akira Kurosawa*, p. 228. Richie suggests that Kurosawa's own life and personality are lived in accordance with bushidō.
15. For discussions of bushidō, see Tsunoda et al., *Sources of Japanese Tradition*, pp. 389–391, and Kenneth Dean Butler, "The Heike Monogatari and the Japanese Warrior Ethic," *Harvard Journal of Asiatic Studies* 29 (1969): 93–108. Daisetz T. Suzuki discusses the codes of samurai behavior as related to Zen and the cult of swordsmanship in *Zen and Japanese Culture*, pp. 89–214.
16. Satō, *Currents in Japanese Cinema*, p. 28.
17. H. Paul Varley cautions against overestimating the scope of this attraction. He maintains that it was the samurai elite who were drawn to Zen, while much of the class looked instead to the salvationist

sects of Buddhism. *Japanese Culture*, 3rd ed. (Honolulu: University of Hawaii Press, 1973, reprint 1984), p. 94.

18. Donald Keene, *Landscapes and Portraits: Appreciations of Japanese Culture* (Tokyo and Palo Alto, CA: Kodansha International, 1971), p. 15.
19. Kitagawa, *Religion in Japanese History*, p. 111.
20. Neil McMullin, *Buddhism and the State in Sixteenth-Century Japan* (Princeton, NJ: Princeton University Press, 1984), pp. 280–282.
21. Ibid., pp. 280–281.
22. Dumoulin, *A History of Zen Buddhism*, p. 167.
23. Ellwood and Pilgrim, *Japanese Religion*, p. 119.
24. Dumoulin, *A History of Zen Buddhism*, p. 50.
25. Suzuki, *Zen and Japanese Culture*, p. 10.
26. Dumoulin, *A History of Zen Buddhism*, pp. 161–164.
27. Satō feels the recurrent master–pupil relations in Kurosawa's films are evidence of an anxiety over generational ruptures in postwar Japan (i.e., parent–child estrangement). *Currents in Japanese Cinema*, pp. 124–131.
28. E. Steinilber-Oberlin, *The Buddhist Sects of Japan*, trans. Marc Loge (orig. pub. 1938; Westport, CT: Greenwood Press, 1970), p. 139.
29. Kurosawa, *Something Like an Autobiography*, p. 53.
30. Ibid., p. 5.
31. Ibid., pp. 10–12.
32. This point was suggested to me by Michael Jeck, whose company, R5/S8 Presents, distributes many of Kurosawa's early films in the United States.
33. Akira Iwasaki also notes the wordless quality of the masters' instruction in Kurosawa's films in "Kurosawa and His Work," in *Focus on Rashōmon*, ed. Donald Richie (Englewood Cliffs, NJ: Prentice-Hall, 1972), p. 24.
34. Suzuki, *Zen and Japanese Culture*, pp. 16–17.
35. Dumoulin, *A History of Zen Buddhism*, pp. 172–173.
36. Ibid, p. 173.
37. McMullin, *Buddhism and the State*, pp. 275–276.
38. Peter Pardue, *Buddhism: A Historical Introduction to Buddhist Values and the Social and Political Forms They Have Assumed in Asia*, quoted in McMullin, *Buddhism and the State*, p. 280. Ivan Morris offers a negative view of the stress of Heian Buddhism upon evanescence and impermanence in *The World of the Shining Prince* (New York: Penguin Books, 1964, reprint 1986), pp. 121–135. He finds

(p. 130) the social consequence of this emphasis to be "a sense of helplessness and resignation, a reluctance to take things into one's own hands or improve the conditions of one's existence."

39. Quoted in Morris, *The World of the Shining Prince*, p. 126.

40. Quoted in Keene, *20 Plays of the Nō Theatre*, p. 125.

41. Sansom, *A History of Japan*, 1: 436.

42. Hiroshi Kitagawa and Bruce T. Tsuchida, trans., *The Tale of the Heike* (Tokyo: University of Tokyo Press, 1975), p. 781.

43. Dumoulin, *A History of Zen Buddhism*, p. 14.

44. Ibid., p. 25.

45. In his discussion of Saburō Ienaga's work, Robert Bellah points to the "complex dialectic" acknowledged by Buddhism between a sinful world and religious ideals. "Salvation comes not through fleeing from the world but through 'facing it head on' and recognizing its sinful and suffering nature. . . . For Ienaga religion does not dissolve the tension between the real and the ideal—it offers no resolution at all on this level—but insists on remaining acutely conscious of it." "Ienaga Saburō," p. 398. This passage serves quite well as a description of how Kurosawa's moral vision is working in *Ran*. Kurosawa has likened the film's view to that of a "Buddha in tears." He confronts what he regards as the world's essentially sinful nature, issues a lament that is the film, and finds a kind of salvation in this recognition.

46. McMullin examines this campaign and its effects on Buddhism throughout *Buddhism and the State*.

47. Nakamura, *Ways of Thinking of Eastern Peoples*, p. 367.

48. See McMullin, *Buddhism and the State*, p. 282.

49. Ibid., p. 5.

50. Kurosawa, *Something Like an Autobiography*, p. 72.

51. Hirano, "Making Films for All the People," p. 25.

52. Ibid.

53. Kurosawa, *Something Like an Autobiography*, p. 193.

54. Bock, *Japanese Film Directors*, p. 170.

55. Kurosawa, *Something Like an Autobiography*, p. 61.

56. Wolf, "Wisdom from Kurosawa," pp. 92–93.

57. Rayns, "Tokyo Stories," p. 174.

58. Elley, "Kurosawa at the NFT," p. 18.

59. See, for example, Blumenthal, "Macbeth into *Throne of Blood*," pp. 190–195.

60. Rayns, "Tokyo Stories," p. 173.

61. See Kurosawa's account in *Something Like an Autobiography*, pp. 187–188; also Richie, *The Films of Akira Kurosawa*, p. 80.

62. Leyda, "The Films of Kurosawa," p. 74.

63. Bosley Crowther, "Gem from Japan," *New York Times*, January 6, 1952, sec. 2, p. 1.

64. Jesse Zunser, review of *Rashōmon*, in Richie, *Focus on Rashōmon*, p. 37.

65. John Beaufort, review of *Rashōmon*, in ibid., p. 39.

66. See Richie, *Focus on Rashōmon* and *Rashōmon*, ed. Donald Richie (New Brunswick, NJ: Rutgers University Press, 1987).

67. Parker Tyler, "*Rashōmon* as Modern Art," in *Focus on Rashōmon*, pp. 129–139.

68. Kurosawa, *Something Like an Autobiography*, p. 139.

69. Ibid., p. 183.

70. Ibid., p. 182.

71. Richie, "Kurosawa on Kurosawa," p. 112.

72. Kurosawa, *Something Like an Autobiography*, p. 182.

73. Ibid.

74. Harvey Thompson brought this reading of the sequence to my attention.

75. Anderson, "When the Twain Meet," p. 57.

76. See Victor Erlich, *Russian Formalism* (New Haven, CT: Yale University Press, 1955, reprint 1981), pp. 176–178.

77. Joseph L. Anderson, "Spoken Silents in the Japanese Cinema," *Journal of Film and Video* 40, no. 1 (Winter 1988): 13.

78. In light of Kurosawa's intent to recapture the silent film aesthetic in *Rashōmon*, Joseph Anderson's remarks about the function of the katsuben, the narrator of a silent film for Japanese audiences, are provocative, in that they suggest that *Rashōmon* has internalized the voice(s) of the katsuben as the competing discourses of narrative, image, and character: "The dominance and apparent reality of the images on the screen were readily deconstructed by the katsuben's words and demeanor. Indeed, the katsuben attacked the ontological status of the film. Was truth in the photographic images or in what the katsuben said? Which was unreliable?" "Spoken Silents," p. 25.

79. Sergei Eisenstein, *Film Form*, ed. and trans. Jay Leyda (New York: Harvest Books, 1949), p. 65.

80. See James Monaco, *The New Wave* (New York: Oxford University Press, 1977), pp. 187–212.

81. For Dostoevsky and Kurosawa, narrative is charged with psychic and emotional dislocations. Is their shared epilepsy a basis for this prizing of discontinuity, for their apocalyptic sensibilities? Kurosawa alludes to his epilepsy in *Something Like an Autobiography*, pp. 119–120.

82. See Konstantin Mochulsky, *Dostoevsky: His Life and Work*, trans. Michael A. Minihan (Princeton, NJ: Princeton University Press, 1967, reprint 1973), pp. 353, 368, 404.

83. Michael Jeck called my attention to Kurosawa's avoidance of portrayals of a timeless Japan. Joan Mellen suggests that Kurosawa's narratives tend to take place during moments of historical transition, as the old order crumbles and the new has not yet appeared. *Voices from the Japanese Cinema*, p. 56.

84. Michael Holquist, *Dostoevsky and the Novel* (Evanston, IL: Northwestern University Press, 1977), p. 30.

85. Mellen, *Voices from the Japanese Cinema*, pp. 44, 45. In his autobiography, Kurosawa reflected upon his youthful commitment and upon his inability to feel at home with Marxism. "I had tried reading *Das Kapital* and theories of dialectic materialism, but there had been much that I couldn't understand. For me to try to analyze and explain Japanese society from that point of view was therefore impossible. I simply felt the vague dissatisfactions and dislikes that Japanese society encouraged, and in order to contend with these feelings, I had joined the most radical movement I could find. Looking back on it now, my behavior seems terribly frivolous and reckless." *Something Like an Autobiography*, p. 78.

86. Bakhtin, *Problems of Dostoevsky's Poetics*, p. 151.

87. Mochulsky, *Dostoevsky: His Life and Work*, pp. 234–235.

88. Bakhtin, *Problems of Dostoevsky's Poetics*, p. 149.

89. N. M. Lary, *Dostoevsky and Soviet Film: Visions of Demonic Realism* (Ithaca, NY: Cornell University Press, 1986), p. 91.

90. Bakhtin, *Problems of Dostoevsky's Poetics*, p. 52.

91. Ibid., p. 59.

92. Ibid., p. 69.

93. Donald Richie, "Dostoevsky with a Japanese Camera," Horizon 4 (July 1962): 45.

94. Richie, *The Films of Akira Kurosawa*, p. 229.

95. Kurosawa, *Something Like an Autobiography*, pp. 83–84.

96. Richie lists the original running time as 265 minutes in *The Films of Akira Kurosawa*, p. 234. The studio's suggestion that the film be cut

occasioned Kurosawa's famous retort that it be cut lengthwise, from beginning to end (ibid., p. 85).

97. This aspect of Dostoevsky is discussed extensively by George Steiner, *Tolstoy or Dostoevsky* (Chicago, IL: University of Chicago Press, 1959, reprint 1985).

98. Richie, *The Films of Akira Kurosawa*, p. 82.

99. Ibid., p. 85.

100. Mochulsky, *Dostoevsky: His Life and Work*, pp. 367–368.

101. See Mochulsky for a good reading of the novel's social critique. Ibid., pp. 334–381.

102. Richie, *The Films of Akira Kurosawa*, p. 85.

103. See Blumenthal, "Macbeth into *Throne of Blood*," pp. 190–195.

104. McMullin, *Buddhism and the State*, p. 63.

105. Interview with Kurosawa by Tadao Satō, quoted in Roger Manvell, *Shakespeare and the Film* (New York: Praeger, 1971), p. 102.

106. Blumenthal, "Macbeth into *Throne of Blood*," p. 195.

107. Ibid., p. 194.

108. Keene, *20 Plays of the Nō Theatre*, p. 74.

109. Richie, *The Films of Akira Kurosawa*, p. 115.

110. Ibid., p. 117. Richie suggests that many of Kurosawa's films are circular in structure (p. 217).

111. These metaphors are discussed by Blumenthal, "Macbeth into *Throne of Blood*," pp. 191–195; by Davies, *Filming Shakespeare's Plays*, pp. 152–166; and by Richie, *The Films of Akira Kurosawa*, pp. 120–122.

112. Keiko McDonald discusses Noh motifs in the film in *Cinema East*, pp. 154–167, and in "Noh into Film: Kurosawa's *Throne of Blood*," *Journal of Film and Video* 39, no. 1 (Winter 1987): 36–41.

113. [Zeami] *On the Art of the Nō Drama*, pp. 34–35.

114. Keene discusses this in *20 Plays of the Nō Theatre*, p. 11.

115. Satō interview, in Manvell, *Shakespeare and the Film*, p. 103.

116. [Zeami] *On the Art of the Nō Drama*, p. 75.

117. Satō interview, in Manvell, *Shakespeare and the Film*, p. 104.

118. Burch, *To the Distant Observer*, p. 310. Davies also discusses this in *Filming Shakespeare's Plays*, pp. 159–161.

119. Desser, *Samurai Films of Akira Kurosawa*, p. 73.

120. See, for example, Tsunoda et al., *Sources of Japanese Tradition*, pp. 255–260; and Suzuki, *Zen and Japanese Culture*, pp. 217–267.

121. Suzuki, *Zen and Japanese Culture*, pp. 271–289.

122. Paine and Soper, *The Art and Architecture of Japan*, pp. 159–160.

123. Satō interview, in Manvell, *Shakespeare and the Film*, p. 104.

124. Paine and Soper, *The Art and Architecture of Japan*, p. 167.

125. Kurosawa, *Something Like an Autobiography*, p. 81.

126. Ibid., p. 82.

127. Quoted in Edward Braun's introduction to Maxim Gorky, *The Lower Depths*, trans. Kitty Hunter-Blair and Jeremy Brooks (London: Eyre Methuen, 1973), p. xii.

128. Mochulsky, *Dostoevsky: His Life and Work*, pp. 244–249.

129. Richie also cites this scene as an example of compositional asymmetry. *The Films of Akira Kurosawa*, p. 132.

Chapter 5: Form and the Modern World

1. Brecht, *Brecht on Theatre*, p. 30.

2. Harvey distinguishes between instrumentalist and transformative views of art and discusses them in more detail in *May '68 and Film Culture*, pp. 45–86.

3. For a discussion of historical and contemporary currents in political cinema see Kolker, *The Altering Eye*.

4. Eisenstein, *Film Form*, p. 234.

5. Bertolt Brecht, "Against Georg Lukács," trans. Stuart Hood, *New Left Review*, no. 84 (March–April 1974): 50.

6. Dana Polan, *The Political Language of Film and the Avant-Garde* (Ann Arbor, MI: UMI Research Press, 1981), p. 29.

7. Fredric Jameson, *Marxism and Form* (Princeton, NJ: Princeton University Press, 1971, reprint 1974), p. 408.

8. Walter Benjamin, "The Author as Producer," in *The Essential Frankfurt School Reader*, ed. Andrew Arato and Eike Gebhardt (New York: Urizen Books, 1978), pp. 254–269.

9. Richie, "Kurosawa on Kurosawa," pp. 200–201.

10. Ibid, p. 201.

11. Tadao Satō notes that Kurosawa deals with the bomb as "a psychological force devastating human life from within, rather than simply as an outer force of destruction." *Currents in Japanese Cinema*, p. 199.

12. Mellen, *The Waves at Genji's Door*, p. 203.

13. Robert A. Scalapino and Junnosuke Masumi, *Parties and Politics in Contemporary Japan* (Berkeley and Los Angeles: University of California Press, 1962, reprint 1967), pp. 125–153.

14. Richie, *The Films of Akira Kurosawa*, p. 111.

15. Mellen, *The Waves at Genji's Door*, p. 205.

16. Richard Tucker has provided some preliminary discussion of the stylistic effects of these lenses in *Japan: Film Image*, pp. 78–79.

17. Richie, *The Films of Akira Kurosawa*, p. 104.

18. Paine and Soper, *The Art and Architecture of Japan*, pp. 179–180.

19. Kurosawa, *Something Like an Autobiography*, p. 196.

20. Herschel B. Chipp, ed., *Theories of Modern Art* (Berkeley and Los Angeles: University of California Press, 1968), p. 216.

21. Audie Bock finds this to be a negative quality of Kurosawa's mature style: "Kurosawa's scope films take on a static, staged air, as if he had to strain to fill the broad space with interesting blocking of the actors." *Japanese Film Directors*, p. 174. But see my discussion for an alternative view.

22. See, for example, Lockwood, *The Economic Development of Japan*, pp. 234, 565–566.

23. Kawai, *Japan's American Interlude*, p. 134.

24. Yamamura, *Economic Policy in Postwar Japan*, p. 53.

25. See Scalapino and Masumi, *Parties and Politics in Contemporary Japan*; David E. Apter and Nagayo Sawa, *Against the State* (Cambridge, MA: Harvard University Press, 1984); and McKean, *Environmental Protest and Citizen Politics in Japan*.

26. Curtis, *The Japanese Way of Politics*, p. 249.

27. Richie, *The Films of Akira Kurosawa*, p. 183.

28. Ibid., p. 143.

29. Satō notes that when an individual tries to fight social evils alone, "he inevitably invites self-annihilation." *Currents in Japanese Cinema*, p. 123. As we shall see, *The Bad Sleep Well* is a formal study of that process of self-annihilation.

30. Yamamura, *Economic Policy in Postwar Japan*, pp. 110–128.

31. Richie, *The Films of Akira Kurosawa*, p. 141.

32. Richie and Mellen both note this weakness. Richie, *The Films of Akira Kurosawa*, p. 143; Mellen, *The Waves at Genji's Door*, p. 406.

33. Richie discusses this aspect of *The Bad Sleep Well* in *The Films of Akira Kurosawa*, pp. 140–141.

34. Richie, too, finds it a "brilliant" sequence. Ibid., p. 144.

35. Ibid., p. 150.

36. Kurosawa indicates that "the audience must have deduced that it must be the then Premiere Kishi who is the ultimate source of corruption and who is talking at the other end of the telephone. . . . The company would not have distributed [the film] if this unidentified character had been identified." Hirano, "Making Films for All the People," p. 24.

37. Richie, *The Films of Akira Kurosawa*, p. 149.

38. Ibid., p. 167.

39. Burch, "Akira Kurosawa," p. 576.

40. Richie, *The Films of Akira Kurosawa*, pp. 163–164. The Japanese title of the film is "Heaven and Hell."

41. Gondō's inability to understand how the display of his wealth could be resented by those who are impoverished is especially ironic, given that the narrative establishes him as a self-made man, who rose from humble beginnings to his present position through hard work.

42. Richie, *The Films of Akira Kurosawa*, p. 167.

43. Ibid., p. 168.

44. Although Kurosawa adapted the story from a novel by Ed McBain, the implications of the novel's story are ones he could clearly make his own.

45. Richie reads this exchange as a humanistic statement by Kurosawa that the characters, as suffering human beings, are "equal." *The Films of Akira Kurosawa*, p. 170.

46. Richie also notes the haunted quality of Gondō's lingering presence in the final image but reads it in terms of character psychology rather than as a blockage in the forms of the film itself and its inquiry. Ibid.

Chapter 6: History and the Period Film

1. Jean-Paul Sartre, *Critique of Dialectical Reason*, vol. 1, ed. Jonathan Rée, trans. Alan Sheridan-Smith (London: Verso, 1982), p. 148.

2. Bordwell, *Ozu and the Poetics of Cinema*, pp. 43–44; Satō, *Currents in Japanese Cinema*, pp. 131–139.

3. See Donald Richie, *Ozu* (Berkeley and Los Angeles: University of California Press, 1974).

4. Bordwell, *Ozu and the Poetics of Cinema*, p. 42.

5. Bock, *Japanese Film Directors*; she discusses Mizoguchi and feminism on pp. 40–51.

6. Ibid., p. 48.

7. This is by no means an orthodox view of Mizoguchi. His work is also interpreted as trenchant social criticism. See, for example, Mellen, *The Waves at Genji's Door*, pp. 252–269.

8. Richie, *The Films of Akira Kurosawa*, p. 97.

9. Kurosawa, *Something Like an Autobiography*, p. 28.

10. Ibid., pp. 29–30.

11. Ibid., pp. 64–68.

12. Ibid., p. 81.
13. Ibid., p. 114.
14. Will Wright discusses the "professional" Westerns, those dealing with competing groups of gunmen, in *Sixguns and Society* (Berkeley and Los Angeles: University of California Press, 1977), pp. 85–123, 164–184.
15. Anderson, "When the Twain Meet," pp. 55–58.
16. Richie, *The Films of Akira Kurosawa*, p. 103.
17. McMullin, *Buddhism and the State*, p. 63.
18. Hall, "The Castle Town and Japan's Modern Urbanization," p. 172.
19. George Elison, "The Cross and the Sword," in *Warlords, Artists, and Commoners*, ed. George Elison and Bardwell L. Smith (Honolulu: University Press of Hawaii, 1981), p. 56.
20. See, for example, John Whitney Hall, "Japan's Sixteenth-Century Revolution," in *Warlords, Artists, and Commoners*, pp. 7–21.
21. The term "Great Unifiers" is used by Hall in ibid., p. 7.
22. This systematization is discussed in Tsunoda et al., *Sources of Japanese Tradition*, pp. 385–391.
23. Ibid., p. 386.
24. Yakir, "The Warrior Returns," p. 56.
25. Ibid.
26. Not all the bandits are portrayed as killed. One runs off, and the fellow who is with the chief when Kikuchiyo is shot inadvertently vanishes. We do not see him being killed. I thank Michael Jeck for pointing this out to me.
27. For a reading of this sort, see Frederick Kaplan, "A Second Look: Akira Kurosawa's *Seven Samurai*," *Cineaste* 10 (Winter 1979–80): 42–43, 47.
28. Desser, *Samurai Films of Akira Kurosawa*, p. 83. The anecdote is contained in Suzuki, *Zen and Japanese Culture*, pp. 128–129.
29. This was pointed out to me by Michael Jeck.
30. Zeami discusses this distinction in *On the Art of the Nō Drama*, p. 71.
31. Mellen, *The Waves at Genji's Door*, p. 92.
32. Desser interprets this image as embodying Kurosawa's ambivalence toward the peasantry, portraying their misery yet also poking fun at them. *Samurai Films of Akira Kurosawa*, p. 81. One might, instead, regard this composition in purely formal terms, as yet another example of Kurosawa's Eisensteinian fascination for pure visual abstraction.

33. Silver has discussed this shot in the general context of Kurosawa's construction of visual metaphors. *The Samurai Film*, p. 48.

34. Nakane, *Japanese Society*, p. 83.

35. Mellen, *Voices from the Japanese Cinema*, p. 56.

36. Mellen, *The Waves at Genji's Door*, p. 97.

37. Carmen Blacker, "Millenarian Aspects of the New Religions in Japan," in *Tradition and Modernization*, p. 563.

38. Mitsuru Hashimoto discusses the socio-economic framework of peasant uprisings in late Tokugawa times. "The Social Background of Peasant Uprisings in Tokugawa Japan," in *Conflict in Modern Japanese History*, ed. Tetsuo Najita and J. Victor Koschmann (Princeton, NJ: Princeton University Press, 1982), pp. 145–163.

39. Irokawa, *The Culture of the Meiji Period*, p. 265.

40. Desser, *Samurai Films of Akira Kurosawa*, pp. 87–88.

41. Desser makes a similar point in his discussion of these characters. Ibid.

42. Sartre, *Critique of Dialectical Reason*, pp. 125–139.

43. Sansom, *A History of Japan*, 1: 6.

44. Northrop Frye, *Anatomy of Criticism* (Princeton, NJ: Princeton University Press, 1957, reprint 1973), p. 207.

45. Desser suggests that Kurosawa's samurai films "take place at a frontier, a frontier where boundaries are not so much physical as moral." *Samurai Films of Akira Kurosawa*, p. 77.

46. Anderson, "When the Twain Meet," p. 56.

47. Noel Perrin, *Giving Up the Gun* (Boulder, CO: Shambhala, 1979), p. 25.

48. Alain Silver notes the significance of this final shot, as does Joan Mellen, who also discusses the film's symbolic treatment of the relation of the seven samurai to the Sengoku era. See *The Samurai Film*, pp. 48–49; and *The Waves at Genji's Door*, pp. 98–99.

49. Frye, *Anatomy of Criticism*, p. 208.

50. David Desser suggests that the failure of the seven samurai is emblematic of the failure of postwar humanism as an aesthetic and political strategy. *Eros plus Massacre*, p. 22.

51. Richie, *The Films of Akira Kurosawa*, pp. 135, 137.

52. Alain Silver compares Sanjurō to other Kurosawa heroes and notes that Sanjurō uses his wit and sword to cut through "the complex fabric of personal and social exchange." *The Samurai Film*, p. 53.

53. Thomas C. Smith discusses social and economic developments in the Tokugawa period in *The Agrarian Origins of Modern Japan* (Stanford, CA: Stanford University Press, 1959, reprint 1965).

54. W. G. Beasley, "The Samurai Tradition," in *Imperial Japan 1800–1945*, ed. Jon Livingston, Joe Moore, and Felicia Oldfather (New York: Pantheon Books, 1973), p. 18.

55. Tsunoda et al., *Sources of Japanese Tradition*, p. 429.

56. Ibid., pp. 431, 432.

57. Richie, *The Films of Akira Kurosawa*, p. 151.

58. Mellen's discussion of the film can be found in *The Waves at Genji's Door*, pp. 22–26.

59. McDonald discusses some of the film's self-referential qualities in "Swordsmanship and Gamesmanship," p. 195. Others, too, have noted these qualities, but what should be stressed is their motivating context (i.e., the unanswered problems posed by *Seven Samurai*).

60. Mellen, *Voices from the Japanese Cinema*, p. 57.

61. Joseph Anderson ("Japanese Swordfighters and American Gunfighters," p. 13) notes that Sanjurō arranges action and events as if he were a director. Desser (*Samurai Films of Akira Kurosawa*, p. 104) notes the tension within the film between "performance and observation," between Sanjurō's tendency to trigger an event and then sit back to watch it. Richie (*The Films of Akira Kurosawa*, pp. 153–154) writes that the film uses performance, movement, and music in a theatrical or presentational manner. This theatricality, this tension between performance and observation, should be seen as a formal structure cast by the collision of Kurosawa's ethical desires and a recalcitrant world and as a precursor of the reification of style and movement found in his films of the 1970s and 1980s.

62. This angularity has fascinated commentators. See, for example, McDonald, "Swordsmanship and Gamesmanship," p. 193; and Richie, *The Films of Akira Kurosawa*, pp. 152–153. Richie attributes it to the cameraman Kazuo Miyagawa, but, as we have seen, Kurosawa's work has always delighted in such qualities.

63. Suzuki, *Zen and Japanese Culture*, pp. 89–95.

64. Mellen, *The Waves at Genji's Door*, p. 25.

65. Silver, *The Samurai Film*, p. 53.

66. Sigmund Freud, *Totem and Taboo. The Basic Writings of Sigmund Freud*, ed. A. A. Brill (New York: The Modern Library, 1938, reprint 1966), p. 873.

67. For discussion of this see Richie, *The Films of Akira Kurosawa*, p. 160.

68. Yakir, "The Warrior Returns," pp. 56–57.

69. Paul Schrader, *Transcendental Style in Film* (Berkeley and Los Angeles: University of California Press, 1972).

70. Richie, *The Films of Akira Kurosawa*, p. 171.

71. Ibid.

72. McDonald, *Cinema East*, pp. 71–87.

73. Joan Mellen has called it "amorphous." *The Waves at Genji's Door*, p. 99.

74. Japan's New Wave is covered in detail by Desser, *Eros plus Massacre*.

75. David Wilson and Donald Richie have both invoked Dickens when discussing *Red Beard*. See Wilson, "Red Beard," *Monthly Film Bulletin* 36 (January 1969): 3; Richie, *The Films of Akira Kurosawa*, pp. 175, 177.

76. Richie attempts a defense against the charge of melodrama in *The Films of Akira Kurosawa*, p. 175.

77. Ibid., p. 171.

78. Mochulsky, *Dostoevsky: His Life and Work*, p. 34.

79. Taking his cue from Siegfried Kracauer, George Wilson points to the "difficulty of creating an appropriate unitary narrative form to capture the nuances" of periods of rapid social transformation. "Pursuing the Millennium in the Meiji Restoration," in *Conflict in Modern Japanese History*, p. 194n.

80. Blacker, "Millennarian Aspects of the New Religions," p. 587.

81. Ernst Cassirer, *The Philosophy of Symbolic Forms*, vol. 2, trans. Ralph Manheim (New Haven, CT: Yale University Press, 1955, reprint 1977), p. 85.

82. Mircea Eliade, *The Myth of the Eternal Return*, trans. Willard R. Trask (Princeton, NJ: Princeton University Press, 1954, reprint 1974), pp. 89, 90.

83. Richie, *The Films of Akira Kurosawa*, p. 175.

84. Wolff, "Detectives and Doctors," pp. 86–87.

85. Sansom, *A History of Japan*, 1: 435.

86. Ibid.

87. Mesnil, *Kurosawa*, p. 105.

88. Ibid.

89. Bock, *Japanese Film Directors*, p. 180.

90. Mellen notes Kurosawa's apparent loss of faith in the ability to create a better world in her essays in the expanded edition of Richie's *Films of Akira Kurosawa*, p. 189.

91. See Apter and Sawa, *Against the State*; McKean, *Environmental Protest and Citizen Politics in Japan*; and Scalapino and Masumi, *Parties and Politics in Contemporary Japan*. Tadao Satō perceptively

suggests that Kurosawa's anarchistic visions were incompatible with a Japan that had recovered from the war. *Currents in Japanese Cinema*, p. 121.

92. Robert E. Ward, "Conclusion," in *Democratizing Japan*, p. 429.
93. Interview with Masahiro Shinoda by Nobuyuki Asai in *Japan New York* 10 (January–February 1980), quoted by Kyōko Hirano in an unpublished manuscript.
94. Desser, *Eros plus Massacre*, p. 31.

Chapter 7: The Late Films

1. Kitagawa and Tsuchida, trans., *The Tale of the Heike*, p. 780.
2. Richie, *The Films of Akira Kurosawa*, p. 184.
3. Wolf, "Wisdom From Kurosawa," p. 91.
4. Rayns, "Tokyo Stories," p. 174.
5. Bock, "Kurosawa on His Innovative Cinema."
6. Ibid.
7. Michael Jeck called my attention to a conversation he had in 1978 with Daisaku Kimura, a camera operator on *Dodeskaden* and later a director of photography. Kimura told him that on *Dodeskaden* the set-ups generally employed only two cameras, set at right angles to each other.
8. Mellen, *Voices from the Japanese Cinema*, p. 44.
9. Yakir, "The Warrior Returns," p. 57.
10. David Desser sees Kurosawa's use of the linear narrative as evidence of the influence of Hollywood filmmaking. While admitting that such narratives are suited to foregrounding the actions of the individual, Desser distinguishes the "bourgeois individual" of Kurosawa's films from the nature of the self explored by directors like Ōshima working in the modernist tradition: "The radical individualism of the New Wave filmmakers was not a bourgeois individualism which posited a transcendental subject outside culture; rather it was the assertion of a will already formed by culture struggling with that culture." *Eros plus Massacre*, p. 77. As these chapters have tried to show, however, Kurosawa's work until the 1970s was deeply committed to exploring precisely this intersection of self and culture and the ensuing struggle.
11. Robinson, "Dodeskaden," p. 103.
12. Mochulsky, *Dostoevsky: His Life and Work*, p. 72.
13. Mellen in Richie, *The Films of Akira Kurosawa*, p. 189.

14. Takafusa Nakamura, *The Postwar Japanese Economy*, trans. Jacqueline Kaminski (Tokyo: University of Tokyo Press, 1981), p. 210.

15. McKean, *Environmental Protest and Citizen Politics in Japan*, pp. 17–34.

16. Mellen, *The Waves at Genji's Door*, p. 56.

17. In her essays on *Dodeskaden* and *Dersu Uzala* in the expanded edition of Richie's book, Mellen discusses Kurosawa's loss of faith in social justice and the substitution in its place of an ethic grounded in fantasy and the purity of unspoiled nature. *The Films of Akira Kurosawa*, pp. 184–203.

18. Quoted in Greg Mitchell, "Kurosawa in Winter," p. 48.

19. Bock, "Kurosawa on His Innovative Cinema," p. 21.

20. In this context, H. D. Harootunian's discussion of the Meiji-era writer-critic Tōkoku Kitamura is of interest. Harootunian describes how, for Kitamura, an aesthetic and ethical stance valorizing pure inwardness and the imagination was a response to, and a substitute for, failed political aspirations. The essay is cautionary in pointing out how an aesthetic relying upon the exclusive claims of the inner life may result in a loss of the public, political realm. Harootunian's conclusion describes the dilemma faced by Kurosawa's late works in their melancholy and bitterness: "If the relationship between private and public was in fact [assessed to be] one of distance, if separation was the condition of their common existence, then it was virtually impossible for the self to reach out sympathetically to move others and to change the outer world." H. D. Harootunian, "Between Politics and Culture: Authority and the Ambiguities of Intellectual Choice in Imperial Japan," in *Japan in Crisis*, p. 136.

21. Bock, "Kurosawa on His Innovative Cinema," p. 21.

22. Kurosawa, *Something Like an Autobiography*, p. 33.

23. Ibid., p. 46.

24. Mellen in Richie, *The Films of Akira Kurosawa*, p. 199.

25. Mellen also notes the design of this shot. Ibid., p. 201.

26. Bellah, "Ienaga Saburō," p. 392.

27. Yakir, "The Warrior Returns," p. 56.

28. Mellen in Richie, *The Films of Akira Kurosawa*, p. 197.

29. For a good discussion of Kurosawa's treatment of the urban environment see Wolff, "Detectives and Doctors," pp. 83–87.

30. Richie discusses these circumstances and the film's difficult production history in *The Films of Akira Kurosawa*, pp. 205–207.

31. Rayns, "Tokyo Stories," p. 172.

32. Sansom, *A History of Japan*, pp. 70–71.
33. Rayns, "Tokyo Stories," p. 172.
34. Audie Bock called this to my attention.
35. For an alternative cinematic treatment of the same phenomenon— use of a shadow warrior by clan officials—see The *Third Shadow Samurai* (1963), directed by Umetsugu Inoue.
36. Rayns, "Tokyo Stories," p. 172.
37. Working from a semiotic perspective, Marsha Kinder deals with the film as an analysis of signs and signification. *"Kagemusha," Film Quarterly* 34 (Winter 1980–81): 44–48. Taking his cue from Kinder, David Desser extends this reading in *Samurai Films of Akira Kurosawa*, pp. 116–128.
38. Audie Bock briefly assesses the autobiographical implications of Kurosawa's recent films. See "Kurosawa: His Life and Art," in *Rashōmon,* ed. Donald Richie (New Brunswick, NJ: Rutgers University Press, 1987), pp. 23–28.
39. Desser rightly points out that this montage owes a lot to Eisenstein's methods of using images to triangulate an event or concept without showing it directly. *Samurai Films of Akira Kurosawa*, p. 127. Kurosawa points out that the sequence reverses a convention of Westerns wherein one "invariably fires to hit the rider" rather than the horse. Quoted in Yakir, "The Warrior Returns," p. 56.
40. Steinilber-Oberlin, *The Buddhist Sects of Japan,* p. 29.
41. Apter and Sawa, *Against the State,* pp. 226, 227.
42. Quoted in Yakir, "The Warrior Returns," p. 57.
43. Quoted in Bock, "Kurosawa on His Innovative Cinema," p. 21.
44. Hirano, "Making Films For All the People," p. 23.
45. Paine and Soper discuss the relations between compositional and narrative principles in the scrolls in *The Art and Architecture of Japan,* pp. 133–157.
46. Akira Kurosawa, *Ran*, trans. Tadashi Shishido (Boston: Shambhala, 1986), p. 46.
47. Hirano, "Making Films For All the People," p. 23.
48. Ibid.

Chapter 8: The Final Period

1. Kamo no Chōmei, *Hōjōki*, trans. Donald Keene in Donald Keene, ed., *Anthology of Japanese Literature* (New York: Grove Press, 1960), p. 211.

2. Joseph McBride, ed., *Filmmakers on Filmmaking*, vol. 1 (Los Angeles: J.P. Tarcher, Inc., 1983), p. 194.

3. My thanks to Peter Lehman for calling my attention to Meyer's discussion.

4. Leonard B. Meyer, *Music, the Arts and Ideas* (Chicago: University of Chicago Press, 1967), p. 192.

5. Ibid., p. 199.

6. Noting this quality, Linda Ehrlich writes, "it is as if the director has lost faith in his audience's ability to understand all but the most blatantly presented message." Linda C. Ehrlich, "The Extremes of Innocence: Kurosawa's Dreams and Rhapsodies" in Mick Broderick, ed., *Hibakusha Cinema: Hiroshima, Nagasaki and the Nuclear Image in Japanese Film* (New York: Kegan Paul International, 1996), p. 161.

7. Tadao Sato, "Kurosawa's *Rhapsody in August*: The Spirit of Compassion," trans. Linda Ehrlich, *Cineaste* 19, no. 1 (1992): 48.

8. Ibid., pp. 48, 49.

9. Ehrlich, "The Extremes of Innocence," pp. 160–177.

10. Mick Broderick suggests that the silence of the characters manifests a characteristic trait of those who survived the bombing, namely, an inability or unwillingness to verbalize or otherwise describe the experience. Broderick, "Introduction" in Broderick, *Hibakusha Cinema*, p. 12. Kurosawa's presentation does indeed keep the viewer outside the exchange between the characters, preserving its privacy and mystery.

11. "The Hard Sell: Japanese Cinema in a Slump," *The Economist*, April 20, 1991, p. 92.

12. Konstantin Mochulsky, *Dostoevsky: His Life and Work*, trans. Michael A. Minihan (Princeton, NJ: Princeton University Press, 1973), p. 72.

13. Ibid.

14. Quoted in Warner Bros.' production and publicity package for *Dreams*.

15. Elisabeth Bumiller, "Akira Kurosawa, Dreaming Up a Film," *The Washington Post*, September 14, 1990, p. C1.

16. Quoted in Warner Bros.' production and publicity package for *Dreams*.

17. Akira Kurosawa, *Something Like an Autobiography*, trans. Audie Bock (New York: Knopf, 1982), p. 150.

18. Mikhail Bakhtin, *Problems of Dostoevsky's Poetics*, ed. and trans.

Caryl Emerson (Minneapolis: University of Minnesota Press, 1984), pp. 52, 59.

19. Donald Richie, *The Films of Akira Kurosawa*, 3rd ed. (Berkeley and Los Angeles: University of California Press, 1996), p. 228.

20. Quoted in Warner Bros.' production and publicity package for *Dreams*.

21. "The Conversation: Kurosawa and Garcia Marquez," *Los Angeles Times Calendar*, June 23, 1991, p. 28.

22. Ibid., p. 29.

23. Tadao Sato, "Kurosawa's *Rhapsody in August*: The Spirit of Compassion," trans. Linda Ehrlich, *Cineaste* 19, no. 1 (1992): 48.

24. Ibid., p. 49.

25. Ibid.

26. Donald Richie, "'Mono no aware': Hiroshima in Film" in Broderick, *Hibakusha Cinema*, pp. 20–37.

27. Matthew Bernstein and Mark Ravina, "*Rhapsody in August*," *American Historical Review* 98, no. 4 (October 1993): 1163.

28. Yomota Inuhiko, "Transformation and Stagnation: Japanese Cinema in the 1990s," *Art and Text*, no. 40 (1991): 77.

29. Ibid., p. 1162.

30. Quoted in James Goodwin, "Akira Kurosawa and the Atomic Age," in James Goodwin, ed., *Perspectives on Akira Kurosawa* (New York: G.K. Hall, 1994), p. 138.

31. Ibid., p. 137.

32. Kurosawa, *Something Like an Autobiography*, pp. 32–33, 35.

33. Kurosawa, *Something Like an Autobiography*, p. 140. He describes his marriage ceremony as a chaotic affair "with the air raid sirens howling throughout" (p. 137).

34. Kamo no Chōmei, *Hōjōki*, in Keene, *Anthology of Japanese Literature*, p. 197.

35. Ibid., p. 204.

36. Ibid.

37. Donald Keene, *Seeds in the Heart: Japanese Literature from the Earliest Times to the Late Sixteenth Century* (New York: Henry Holt and Co., 1993), p. 761.

38. Dennis C. Washburn, *The Dilemma of the Modern in Japanese Fiction* (New Haven: Yale University Press, 1995), pp. 37–52.

39. Kurosawa, *Something Like an Autobiography*, p. 13.

40. Alain Riou, "*Madadayo*," *World Press Review* 43, no. 5 (May 1996): 44.

41. Ibid.
42. Kamo no Chōmei, *Hōjōki*, in Keene, *Anthology of Japanese Literature*, p. 198.
43. Ibid., p. 210.
44. Herschel Chipp, ed., *Theories of Modern Art* (Berkeley: University of California Press, 1968), p. 35.

Chapter 9: The Legacy

1. Kurosawa, *Something Like an Autobiography*, p. 90.
2. George Lucas, "Kurosawa and *Ran*," in James Goodwin, ed., *Perspectives on Akira Kurosawa* (New York: G.K. Hall, 1994), p. 39.
3. Martin Scorsese, "Eulogy," *Time*, September 21, 1998, p. 29.
4. Elizabeth Snead, "Cinema Loses Its Shakespeare," *USA Today*, September 8, 1998, p. 2D.
5. Akira Kurosawa, "Drawing and Directing," trans. Margaret Benton in Akira Kurosawa, *Ran*, trans. Tadashi Shishido (Boston: Shambhala, 1986).
6. Ibid.
7. Barbara MacAdam, "Samurai Artist," *ArtNews* 93, no. 5 (May 1994): 33.
8. Garth Alexander, "Japanaese Helmers Direct Rights Effort," *Variety*, May 11, 1992, pp. 79–80.
9. Quoted in Goodwin, p. 41.
10. *USA Today*.
11. I should also note that, in regards to lens preferences, whereas Kurosawa is a telephoto man, Scorsese follows Orson Welles in favoring wide angle lenses.
12. Marcia Pally, "'Double' Trouble," *Film Comment* 20 (Sept.-Oct. 1984): 14.
13. Richard Corliss, "Long Live the Emperor!" *Time International*, September 21, 1998, p. 58.
14. In this regard, David Weddle errs when he claims that Kurosawa does not dynamically incorporate slow motion into the editing of *Seven Samurai*. Weddle might have noted, more accurately, that Kurosawa only does it in this one scene rather than at multiple points throughout the film. See David Weddle, *If They Move... Kill 'Em: The Life and Times of Sam Peckinpah* (New York: Grove Press, 1994), p. 271.
15. Gary Crowdus and Richard Porton, "The Importance of a Singular,

Guiding Vision: An Interview with Arthur Penn," *Cineaste* 20, no. 2 (Spring 1993): 29.

16. Ernest Callenbach, "A Conversation with Sam Peckinpah," *Film Quarterly* 17, no. 2 (Winter 1963–64): 10.

17. Sam Peckinpah Collection, *The Wild Bunch*—Correspondence, letter of April 4, 1968, folder no. 35.

18. Sam Peckinpah Collection, *Cross of Iron*—script notes, letter of February 5, 1976, folder no. 26.

19. Sam Peckinpah Collection, General-miscellaneous, letter of December 30, 1968, folder no. 127.

20. Sam Peckinpah Collection, General-miscellaneous, letter of June 23, 1969, folder no. 127.

21. Sam Peckinpah Collection, General-miscellaneous, letters of February 28, 1980, and March 25, 1980, folder no. 175.

22. Director John Sayles pointed to the cinematic beauty of this scene: "One thing that interests me is that he gets away with something that is almost impossible now: he includes a very long exposition sequence. And he does it in a beautiful, very architectural way, using this old, traditional Japanese house which has these sliding doors." Leslie Felperin, "John Sayles Walking Alone," *Sight and Sound* 6, no. 9 (Sept. 1996): 23.

23. David Bordwell, *On the History of Film Style* (Cambridge: Harvard University Press, 1997), p. 198.

24. Stanley Kauffmann, "On Films, Afterlives," *The New Republic*, October 26, 1998, p. 24.

25. Felperin, "John Sayles," p. 24.

26. Frank Capra, *The Name above the Title* (New York: Macmillan, 1971), p. 486.

Films Directed by Akira Kurosawa

Sanshirō Sugata (1943)

The Most Beautiful (1944)

Sanshirō Sugata, Part II (1945)

They Who Tread on the Tiger's Tail (1945)

No Regrets for Our Youth (1946)

One Wonderful Sunday (1947)

Drunken Angel (1948)

The Quiet Duel (1949)

Stray Dog (1949)

Scandal (1950)

Rashōmon (1950)

The Idiot (1951)

Ikiru (1952)

Seven Samurai (1954)

Record of a Living Being (1955)

Throne of Blood (1957)

The Lower Depths (1957)

The Hidden Fortress (1958)

The Bad Sleep Well (1960)

Yōjimbō (1961)

Sanjurō (1962)

High and Low (1963)

Red Beard (1965)

Dodeskaden (1970)

Dersu Uzala (1975)

Kagemusha (1980)

Ran (1985)

Dreams (1990)

Rhapsody in August (1991)

Madadayo (1993)

Bibliography

Anderson, Joseph L. "Japanese Swordfighters and American Gunfighters." *Cinema Journal* 12 (Spring 1973): 1–21.

———. "Spoken Silents in the Japanese (Cinema." *Journal of Film and Video* 40, no. 1 (Winter 1988): 13–33.

———. "When the Twain Meet: Hollywood's Remake of *The Seven Samurai*." *Film Quarterly* 15 (Spring 1962): 55–58.

———, and Donald Richie. *The Japanese Film: Art and Industry*. Expanded ed. Princeton, NJ: Princeton University Press, 1982.

Andrews, Nigel. "Sanjurō." *Monthly Film Bulletin* 38 (January 1971): 14.

Apter, David E., and Nagayo Sawa. *Against the State*. Cambridge, MA: Harvard University Press, 1984.

Bakhtin, Mikhail. *Problems of Dostoevsky's Poetics*. Ed. and trans. Caryl Emerson. Minneapolis: University of Minnesota Press, 1984.

Beasley, W. G. "The Samurai Tradition." In *Imperial Japan, 1800–1945*, ed. Jon Livingston, Joe Moore, and Fclicia Oldfather. New York: Pantheon Books, 1973.

Bellah, Robert N. "Ienaga Saburō and the Search for Meaning in Modern Japan." In *Changing Japanese Attitudes Toward Modernization*, ed. Marius B. Jansen. Princeton, NJ: Princeton University Press, 1965, reprint 1972.

Benjamin, Walter. "The Author as Producer." In *The Essential Frankfurt School Reader*, ed. Andrew Arato and Eike Gebhardt. New York: Urizen Books. 1978.

Bernstein, Matthew and Mark Ravina. "*Rhapsody in August*." *American Historical Review* 98, no. 4 (October 1993): 1161–1163.

Blacker, Carmen. "Millenarian Aspects of the New Religions in Japan." In *Tradition and Modernization in Japanese Culture*, ed. Donald H. Shively. Princeton, NJ: Princeton University Press, 1971.

Blumenthal, J. "Macbeth into *Throne of Blood*." *Sight and Sound* 34 (Autumn 1965): 191–195.

Bock, Audie. *Japanese Film Directors*. New York: Kodansha International, 1978.

———. "Kurosawa: His Life and Art." In *Rashōmon*, ed. Donald Richie. New Brunswick, NJ: Rutgers University Press, 1987.

———. "Kurosawa on His Innovative Cinema." *New York Times*, October 4,1981, sec. 2, p. 21.

Bordwell, David. *On the History of Film Style*. Cambridge: Harvard University Press, 1997.

———. *Narration in the Fiction Film*. Madison: University of Wisconsin Press, 1985.

———. "On Our Dream Cinema: Western Historiography and the Japanese Film." *Film Reader* 4 (1979): 45–62.

———. *Ozu and the Poetics of Cinema*. Princeton, NJ: Princeton University Press, 1988.

———. Janet Staiger, and Kristin Thompson. *The Classical Hollywood Cinema: Film Style and Mode of Production to 1960*. New York: Columbia University Press, 1985.

Branigan, Edward. "The Space of Equinox Flower." *Screen* 17 (Summer 1976): 74–105.

Brecht, Bertolt. "Against Georg Lukács." Trans. Stuart Hood. *New Left Review*, no. 84 (March–April 1974): 39–53.

———. *Brecht on Theatre*. Trans. John Willett. New York: Hill and Wang, 1957, reprint 1979.

Burch, Noël. "Akira Kurosawa." In *Cinema: A Critical Dictionary*, ed. Richard Roud. Norwich, Great Britain: Fletcher and Son, Ltd., 1980.

———. *To the Distant Observer: Form and Meaning in the Japanese Cinema*. Berkeley and Los Angeles: University of California Press, 1979.

Calvocoressi, Peter, and Guy Wint. *Total War: Causes and Consequences of The Second World War*. New York: Penguin Books, 1972, reprint 1979.

Cassirer, Ernst. *The Philosophy of Symbolic Forms*. Vol. 2. Trans. Ralph Manheim. New Haven, CT: Yale University Press, 1955, reprint 1977.

Chipp, Herschel B., ed. *Theories of Modern Art*. Berkeley and Los Angeles: University of California Press, 1968.

Cohen, Jerome B. *Japan's Economy in War and Reconstruction*. Minneapolis: University of Minnesota Press, 1949; Greenwood reprint 1973.

Combs, Richard. "A Shaggy Ghost Story." *Sight and Sound* 50 (Winter 1980–81): 61–62.

Croizier, Ralph. "Beyond East and West: The American Western and Rise of the Chinese Swordplay Movie." *Journal of Popular Film* 1 (Summer 1972): 229–243.

Crowdus, Gary and Richard Porton. "The Importance of a Singular, Guiding Vision: An Interview with Arthur Penn." *Cineaste* 20, no. 2 (Spring 1993): 4–16.

Crowther, Bosley. "Gem From Japan." *New York Times*, January 6, 1952, p. lx.

Curtis, Gerald L. *The Japanese Way of Politics*. New York: Columbia University Press, 1988.

Davies, Anthony. *Filming Shakespeare's Plays: The Adaptations of Laurence Olivier, Orson Welles, Peter Brook, and Akira Kurosawa*. New York: Cambridge University Press, 1988.

Desser, David. *Eros plus Massacre*. Bloomington: Indiana University Press, 1988.

———. *The Samurai Films of Akira Kurosawa*. Ann Arbor, MI: UMI Research Press, 1983.

Dumoulin, Heinrich. *A History of Zen Buddhism*. Trans. Paul Peachey. New York: Pantheon Books, 1963; Beacon reprint, 1969.

Eisenstein, Sergei. *Film Form*. Ed. and trans. Jay Leyda. New York: Harvest Books, 1949.

Eliade, Mircea. *The Myth of the Eternal Return*. Trans. Willard R. Trask. Princeton, NJ: Princeton University Press, 1954, reprint 1974.

Elison, George. "The Cross and the Sword." In *Warlords, Artists, and Commoners*, ed. George Elison and Bardwell L. Smith. Honolulu: University Press of Hawaii, 1981.

Elley, Derek. "Kurosawa at the NFT." *Films and Filming* 380 (May 1986): 18.

Ellwood, Robert, and Richard Pilgrim. *Japanese Religion: A Cultural Perspective*. Englewood Cliffs, NJ: Prentice-Hall, 1985.

Ehrlich, Linda C. "The Extremes of Innocence." In *Hibakusha Cinema: Hiroshima, Nagasaki and the Nuclear Image in Japanese Film*, ed. Mick Broderick. New York: Kegan Paul International, 1996.

Erlich, Victor. *Russian Formalism*. New Haven, CT: Yale University Press, 1955, reprint 1981.

Ewen, Frederick. *Bertolt Brecht: His Life, His Art, and His Times*. New York: Citadel, 1969.

Felperin, Leslie. "John Sayles: Walking Alone." *Sight and Sound* 6, no. 9 (September 1996): 22–24.

Fletcher, III, William Miles. *The Search for a New Order: Intellectuals and Fascism in Prewar Japan*. Chapel Hill: University of North Carolina Press, 1982.

Foerster, Norman, ed. *Humanism and America*. New York: Farrar and Rinehart, 1930.

Frayling, Christopher. *Spaghetti Westerns*. Boston: Routledge and Kegan Paul, 1981.

Freud, Sigmund. *Totem and Taboo. The Basic Writings of Sigmund Freud.* Ed. A. A. Brill. New York: The Modern Library, 1938, reprint 1966.

Frye, Northrop. *Anatomy of Criticism*. Princeton, NJ: Princeton University Press, 1957, reprint 1973.

Gillett, John. "Kurosawa's Army." *Sight and Sound* 49 (Spring 1980): 71–73.

Gluck, Carol. *Japan's Modern Myths*. Princeton, NJ: Princeton University Press, 1985.

Goodwin, James. *Perspectives on Akira Kurosawa*. New York: G.K. Hall, 1994.

————. "Akira Kurosawa and the Atomic Age." In *Perspectives on Akira Kurosawa*, ed. James Goodwin. New York: G.K. Hall, 1994.

Gorky, Maxim. *The Lower Depths*. Trans. Kitty Hunter-Blair and Jeremy Brooks. London: Eyre Methuen, 1973.

Hall, John Whitney. "The Castle Town and Japan's Modern Urbanization." In *Studies in the Institutional History of Early Modern Japan*, ed. John W. Hall and Marius B. Jansen. Princeton, NJ: Princeton University Press, 1968.

————. "Changing Conceptions of the Modernization of Japan." In *Changing Japanese Attitudes Toward Modernization*, ed. Marius B. Jansen. Princeton, NJ: Princeton University Press, 1965, reprint 1972.

————. "Feudalism in Japan: A Reassessment." In *Studies in the Institutional History of Early Modern Japan*, ed. John W. Hall and Marius B. Jansen. Princeton, NJ: Princeton University Press, 1968.

————. "Japan's Sixteenth-Century Revolution." In *Warlords, Artists, and Commoners*, ed. George Elison and Bardwell L. Smith. Honolulu: University Press of Hawaii, 1981.

Harootunian, H. D. "Between Politics and Culture: Authority and the Ambiguities of Intellectual Choice in Imperial Japan." In *Japan in Crisis*, ed. Bernard S. Silberman and H. D. Harootunian. Princeton, NJ: Princeton University Press, 1974.

————. "A Sense of an Ending and the Problem of Taishō." In *Japan in Crisis*, ed. Bernard S. Silberman and H. D. Harootunian. Princeton, NJ: Princeton University Press, 1974.

Harvey, Sylvia. *May '68 and Film Culture*. London: BFI Publishing, 1980.

Hashimoto, Mitsuru. "The Social Background of Peasant Uprisings in To-kugawa Japan." In *Conflict in Modern Japanese History*, ed. Tetsuo Na-jita and J. Victor Koschmann. Princeton, NJ: Princeton University Press, 1982.

Heath, Stephen. "The Question Ōshima." *Wide Angle* 2, no. 1 (1977): 48–57.

Hibbett, Howard S. "Natsume Sōseki and the Psychological Novel." In *Tradition and Modernization in Japanese Culture*, ed. Donald H. Shively. Princeton, NJ: Princeton University Press, 1971.

Higham, Charles. "Kurosawa's Humanism." *Kenyon Review* 27 (Autumn 1965): 737–742.

Hirano, Kyōko. "Japanese Cinema Under the American Occupation: 1945–1952." Ph.D. dissertation, New York University, 1988.

———. "Making Films for All the People: An Interview with Akira Kuro-sawa." *Cineaste* 14, no. 4 (1986): 23–25.

Holquist, Michael. *Dostoevsky and the Novel*. Evanston, IL: Northwestern University Press, 1977.

Irokawa Daikichi. *The Culture of the Meiji Period*. Trans. Marius B. Jansen. Princeton, NJ: Princeton University Press, 1985.

Iwasaki, Akira. "Kurosawa and His Work." In *Focus on Rashōmon*, ed. Donald Richie. Englewood Cliffs, NJ: Prentice-Hall, 1972.

Jameson, Fredric. *Marxism and Form*. Princeton, NJ: Princeton University Press, 1971, reprint 1974.

Jansen, Marius B. "Tokugawa and Modern Japan." In *Studies in the Institutional History of Early Modern Japan*, ed. John W. Hall and Marius B. Jansen. Princeton, NJ: Princeton University Press, 1968.

Kaminsky, Stuart. American *Film Genres*. New York: Dell Publishing Co., Laurel Edition, 1977.

Kamo no Chōmei, *Hōjōki*. In *Anthology of Japanese Literature*, trans. Donald Keene. New York: Grove Press, 1960.

Kaplan, Frederick. "A Second Look: Akira Kurosawa's *Seven Samurai*." *Cineaste* 10 (Winter 1979–80): 42–43, 47.

Katō, Shūichi. *Form, Style, Tradition: Reflections on Japanese Art and Society*. New York: Kodansha International, 1986.

———. *A History of Japanese Literature*. Vol. 3. Trans. Don Sanderson. New York: Kodansha International, 1983.

———. "Japanese Writers and Modernization." In *Changing Japanese Attitudes Toward Modernization*, ed. Marius B. Jansen. Princeton, NJ: Princeton University Press, 1965, reprint 1972.

Kauffmann, Stanley, "On Films, Afterlives." *The New Republic* (October 26, 1998): 24.

Kawai, Kazuo. *Japan's American Interlude*. Chicago, IL: University of Chicago Press, 1960, reprint 1969.

Keene, Donald. *Seeds in the Heart: Japanese Literature from the Earliest Times to the Late Sixteenth Century*. New York: Henry Holt and Co., 1993.

———. *Dawn to the West* (Fiction). New York: Holt, Rinehart and Winston, 1984.

———. *Landscapes and Portraits: Appreciations of Japanese Culture*. Tokyo and Palo Alto, CA: Kodansha International, 1971.

———, ed. 20 *Plays of the Nō Theatre*. New York: Columbia University Press, 1970.

Kinder, Marsha. "*Kagemusha.*" *Film Quarterly* 34 (Winter 1980–81): 44–48.

———. "*Throne of Blood*: A Morality Dance." Literature/Film Quarterly 5 (Fall 1977): 339–345.

Kitagawa, Hiroshi, and Bruce T. Tsuchida, trans. *The Tale of the Heike*. Tokyo: University of Tokyo Press, 1975.

Kitagawa, Joseph. *Religion in Japanese History*. New York: Columbia University Press, 1966.

Kolker, Robert Phillip. *The Altering Eye*. New York: Oxford University Press, 1983.

Kurosawa, Akira. *Ran*. trans. Tadashi Shishido. Boston: Shambhala, 1986.

———. *Something Like an Autobiography*. Trans. Audie Bock. New York: Alfred A. Knopf, 1982.

Lary, N. M. *Dostoevsky and Soviet Film: Visions of Demonic Realism*. Ithaca, NY: Cornell University Press, 1986.

Lebra, Takie Sugiyama. "Nonconfrontational Strategies for Management of Interpersonal Conflicts." In *Conflict in Japan*, ed. Ellis S. Krauss, Thomas P. Rohlen, and Patricia G. Steinhoff. Honolulu: University of Hawaii Press, 1984.

Lehman, Peter. "The Mysterious Orient, the Crystal Clear Orient, the Non-Existent Orient: Dilemmas of Western Scholars of Japanese Film." *Journal of Film and Video* 39 (Winter 1987): 5–15.

Leyda, Jay. "The Films of Kurosawa," *Sight and Sound* 24 (October-December 1954): 74–78, 112.

Lockwood, William W. *The Economic Development of Japan*. Princeton, NJ: Princeton University Press, 1954, expanded ed. 1968.

MacAdam, Barbara. "Samurai Artist." *ArtNews* 93, no. 5 (May 1994): 33.

Manvell, Roger. *Shakespeare and the Film*. New York: Praeger, 1971.

Maruyama, Masao. *Thought and Behavior in Modern Japanese Politics*. Ed. Ivan Morris. New York: Oxford University Press, 1963, expanded ed. 1969.

McDonald, Keiko. *Cinema East*. East Brunswick, NJ: Associated University Presses, 1983.

———. "Noh into Film: Kurosawa's *Throne of Blood*." *Journal of Film and Video* 39, no. 1 (Winter 1987): 36–41.

———. "Swordsmanship and Gamesmanship: Historical Milieu in *Yōjimbō*." *Literature/Film Quarterly* 8 (Summer 1980): 188–196.

McKean, Margaret A. *Environmental Protest and Citizen Politics in Japan*. Berkeley and Los Angeles: University of California Press, 1981.

McMullin, Neil. *Buddhism and the State in Sixteenth-Century Japan*. Princeton, NJ: Princeton University Press, 1984.

McNelly, Theodore H. "Induced Revolution: The Policy and Process of Constitutional Reform in Occupied Japan." In *Democratizing Japan*, ed. Robert Ward and [Yoshikazu Sakamoto]. Honolulu: University of Hawaii Press, 1987.

Mellen, Joan. "The Epic Cinema of Kurosawa." *Take One* 3 (June 1972): 16–19.

———. *Voices from the Japanese Cinema*. New York: Liveright, 1975.

———. *The Waves at Genji's Door*. New York: Pantheon Books, 1976.

Mesnil, Michel. *Kurosawa*. Paris: Seghers, 1973.

Meyer, Leonard B. *Music, the Arts and Ideas*. Chicago: University of Chicago Press, 1967.

Milne, Tom. "Dersu Uzala." *Monthly Film Bulletin* 45 (January 1978): 5.

Mitchell, Greg. "Kurosawa in Winter." *American Film* 7 (April 1982): 46–51.

Mochulsky, Konstantin. *Dostoevsky: His Life and Work*. Trans. Michael A. Minihan. Princeton, NJ: Princeton University Press, 1967, reprint 1973.

Monaco, James. *The New Wave*. New York: Oxford University Press, 1977.

Morris, Ivan. *Nationalism and the Right Wing in Japan*. Westport, CT: Greenwood Press, 1974 reprint; orig. pub. Oxford University Press, 1960.

———. *The World of the Shining Prince*. New York: Penguin Books. 1964, reprint 1986.

Murakami Hyōe. *Japan: The Years of Trial, 1919–52*. Tokyo: Japan Culture Institute, 1982.

Nakamura, Hajime. *Ways of Thinking of Eastern Peoples*. Rev. trans. ed. Philip Wiener. Honolulu: East-West Center Press, 1964, reprint 1968.

Nakamura. Takafusa. *The Postwar Japanese Economy*. Trans. Jacqueline Kaminski. Tokyo: University of Tokyo Press, 1981.

Nakane, Chie. *Japanese Society*. Berkeley and Los Angeles: University of California Press, 1970, reprint 1972.

Nolley, Kenneth S. "The Western as Jidai-Geki." *Western American Literature* 11 (November 1976): 231–238.

Paine, Robert Treat, and Alexander Soper. *The Art and Architecture of Japan*. New York: Penguin Books, 1955, reprint 1985.

Passin, Herbert. "Modernization and the Japanese Intellectual: Some Comparative Observations." In *Changing Japanese Attitudes Toward Modernization*, ed. Marius B. Jansen. Princeton, NJ: Princeton University Press, 1965, reprint 1972.

Perrin, Noel. *Giving Up the Gun*. Boulder, CO: Shambhala, 1979.

Polan, Dana. *The Political Language of Film and the Avant-Garde*. Ann Arbor, MI: UMI Research Press, 1981.

Pym, John. "Kagemusha." *Monthly Film Bulletin* 47 (December 1980): 237–238.

Rayns, Tony. "Tokyo Stories." *Sight and Sound* 50 (Summer 1981): 170–176.

Richie, Donald. "Dostoevsky with a Japanese Camera." *Horizon* 4 (July 1962): 42–47.

———. "Mono no aware: Hiroshima in Film." In *Hibakusha Cinema: Hiroshima, Nagasaki and the Nuclear Image in Japanese Film*, ed. Mick Broderick. New York: Kegan Paul International, 1996.

———. *The Films of Akira Kuusawa*. Rev. ed. with additional material by Joan Mellen. Berkeley and Los Angeles: University of California Press, 1984.

———. "Kurosawa on Kurosawa." *Sight and Sound* 33 (Summer 1964): 108–113.

———. *Ozu*. Berkeley and Los Angeles: University of California Press, 1974.

———, ed. *Focus on Rashōmon*. Englewood Cliffs, NJ: Prentice-Hall, 1972.

Robinson, David. "Dodeskaden." *Monthly Film Bulletin* 42 (May 1975): 103.

Sansom, George. *A History of Japan*. 3 vols. Stanford. CA: Stanford University Press, 1958–1963, reprint 1987.

Sarris, Andrew, ed. *Interviews with Film Directors*. New York: Discus Books, 1967, reprint 1969.

Sartre, Jean-Paul. *Critique of Dialectical Reason*. Vol. 1. Ed. Jonathan Ree. Trans. Alan Sheridan-Smith. London: Verso, 1982.

Satō, Tadao. *Currents in Japanese Cinema*. Trans. Gregory Barrett. New York: Kodansha International, 1982.

Satō Tadao. "Kurosawa's *Rhapsody in August*: The Spirit of Compassion." Trans. Linda Ehrlich. *Cineaste* 19, no. 1 (1992): 48–49.

Scalapino, Robert A., and Junnosuke Masumi. *Parties and Politics in Contemporary Japan*. Berkeley and Los Angeles: University of California Press, 1962, reprint 1967.

Schrader, Paul. *Tanscendental Style in Film*. Berkeley and Los Angeles: University of California Press, 1972.

Seydor, Paul. *Peckinpah: The Western Films*. Chicago: University of Illinois Press, 1980.

Shillony, Ben-Ami. *Politics and Culture in Wartime Japan*. Oxford: Clarendon Press, 1981.

Shively, Donald H. "The Japanization of the Middle Meiji." In *Tradition and Modernization in Japanese Culture*, ed. Donald H. Shively. Princeton, NJ: Princeton University Press, 1971.

Silberman, Bernard S. "Taishō Japan and the Crisis of Secularism." In *Japan in Crisis*, ed. Bernard S. Silberman and H. D. Harootunian. Princeton, NJ: Princeton University Press, 1974.

Silver, Alain. *The Samurai Film*. South Brunswick, NJ, and New York: A. S. Barnes and Co., 1977.

Silverstein, Norman. "Kurosawa's Detective-Story Parables." *Japan Quarterly* 12, no. 3 (1965): 351–354.

Smith, II, Henry DeWitt. *Japan's First Student Radicals*. Cambridge, MA: Harvard University Press, 1972.

Smith, Robert J. *Japanese Society: Tradition, Self, and the Social Order*. New York: Cambridge University Press, 1983.

Smith, Thomas C. *The Agrarian Origins of Modern Japan*. Stanford, CA: Stanford University Press, 1959, reprint 1965.

Soviak, Eugene. "On the Nature of Western Progress: The Journal of the Iwakura Embassy." In *Tradition and Modernization in Japanese Culture*, ed. Donald H. Shively. Princeton, NJ: Princeton University Press, 1971.

Steiner, George. *Tolstoy or Dostoevsky*. Chicago, IL: University of Chicago Press, 1959, reprint 1985.

Steinilber-Oberlin, E. *The Buddhist Sects of Japan*. Trans. Marc Loge. Westport, CT: Greenwood Press, 1970 reprint; orig. pub. 1938.

Strayer, Joseph. "The Tokugawa Period and Japanese Feudalism." In *Studies in the Institutional History of Early Modern Japan*, ed. John W. Hall and Marius B. Jansen. Princeton, NJ: Princeton University Press, 1968.

Suzuki, D. T. *Zen and Japanese Culture*. Princeton, NJ: Princeton University Press, 1959, reprint 1973.

Thompson, Kristin, and David Bordwell. "Space and Narrative in the Films of Ozu." *Screen* 17 (Summer 1976): 41–73.

Tsunoda, Ryūsaku, Wm. Theodore de Bary, and Donald Keene, eds. *Sources of Japanese Tradition*. New York: Columbia University Press, 1958, reprint 1964.

Tucker, Richard N. *Japan: Film Image*. London: Studio Vista, 1973.

Tyler, Parker. "*Rashōmon* as Modern Art." In *Focus on Rashōmon*, ed. Donald Richie. Englewood Cliffs, NJ: Prentice-Hall, 1972.

Ueda, Makoto. *Literary and Art Theories in Japan*. Cleveland, OH: Western Reserve University Press, 1967.

Varley, H. Paul. *Japanese Culture*. 3rd ed. Honolulu: University of Hawaii Press, 1973, reprint 1984.

Ward, Robert E., and [Yoshikazu Sakamoto], eds. *Democratizing Japan: The Allied Occupation*. Honolulu: University of Hawaii Press, 1987.

Washburn, Dennis C. *The Dilemma of the Modern in Japanese Fiction*. New Haven: Yale University Press, 1995.

Watts, Alan W. *The Way of Zen*. New York: Vintage Books, 1957.

Wilson, David. "Red Beard." *Monthly Film Bulletin* 36 (January 1969): 3.

Wilson, George. "Pursuing the Millennium in the Meiji Restoration." In *Conflict in Modern Japanese History*, ed. Tetsuo Najita and J. Victor Koschmann. Princeton, NJ: Princeton University Press, 1982.

————. "Restoration History and Shōwa Politics." In *Crisis Politics in Prewar Japan*, ed. George M. Wilson. Tokyo: Sophia University, 1970.

Wolf, William. "Wisdom from Kurosawa." *New York Magazine*, October 20, 1980, 91–94.

Wolff, Barbara. "Detectives and Doctors." *Japan Quarterly* 19 (January–March 1972): 83–87.

Wright, Will. *Sixguns and Society*. Berkeley and Los Angeles: University of California Press, 1977.

Yakir, Dan. "The Warrior Returns," *Film Comment* 16 (November–December 1980): 54–57.

Yamamura, Kozo. *Economic Policy in Postwar Japan*. Berkeley and Los Angeles: University of California Press, 1967.

Yazaki Takeo. "The Samurai Family and Feudal Ideology." In *Imperial Japan, 1800–1945*, ed. Jon Livingston, Joe Moore, and Felicia Oldfather. New York: Pantheon Books, 1973.

Yomota Inuhiko. "Transformation and Stagnation: Japanese Cinema in the 1990s." Trans. Chiaki Ajioka. *Art and Text* 40 (1991): 74–77.

Young, Vernon. "The Hidden Fortress: Kurosawa's Comic Mode." *The Hudson Review* 14 (Summer 1961): 270–275.

Zambrano, Ana Laura. "*Throne of Blood*: Kurosawa's Macbeth." *Literature/Film Quarterly* 2 (Summer 1974): 262–274.

[Zeami Motokiyo.] *On the Art of the Nō Drama: The Major Treatises of Zeami*. Trans. and ed. J. Thomas Rimer and [Masakazu Yamazaki]. Princeton, NJ: Princeton University Press, 1984.

Index